LAST OF THE
COLD WAR SPIES

ALSO BY ROLAND PERRY

Non-Fiction
The Fifth Man
Hidden Power: The Programming of the President
Monash: The Outsider Who Won a War
The Exile: Wilfred Burchett, Reporter of Conflict
Mel Gibson: Actor, Director, Producer
Lethal Hero
Elections Sur Ordinateur
Miller's Luck: The Life and Loves of Cricket's Cavalier
Bradman's Best
Bradman's Best Ashes Teams
The Don
Captain Australia: A History of the Celebrated Captains of Test Cricket
Bold Warnie
Waugh's Way
Shane Warne: Master Spinner

Fiction
Program for a Puppet
Blood Is a Stranger
Faces in the Rain

LAST OF THE COLD WAR SPIES

THE LIFE OF MICHAEL STRAIGHT

THE ONLY AMERICAN IN BRITAIN'S CAMBRIDGE SPY RING

ROLAND PERRY

DA CAPO PRESS

A Member of the Perseus Books Group

Designed by Trish Wilkinson
Set in 11.5-point Adobe Garamond

Library of Congress Cataloging-in-Publication Data
Perry, Roland
Last of the Cold War spies : the life of Michael Straight—the only American in Britain's
Cambridge spy ring / Roland Perry.— 1st Da Capo Press ed.
p. cm.
Includes bibliographical references (p.) and index.
ISBN-13 978-0-306-81428-0 (alk. paper)
ISBN 0-306-81428-5 (alk. paper)
1. Straight, Michael Whitney. 2. Espionage, Soviet—Great Britain—History.
3. Spies—United States—Biography. 4. Spies—Great Britain—Biography. I. Title.
UB271.R92S76   2005
327.1247073'092—dc22
                                                    2005004790

First Da Capo Press edition 2005

Published by Da Capo Press
A Member of the Perseus Books Group
http://www.dacapopress.com

Da Capo Press books are available at special discounts for bulk purchases in the
U.S. by corporations, institutions, and other organizations. For more information,
please contact the Special Markets Department at the Perseus Books Group,
11 Cambridge Center, Cambridge, MA 02142, or call (800) 255-1514 or
(617) 252-5298, or e-mail special.markets@perseusbooks.com.

1   2   3   4   5   6   7   8   9—08   07   06   05

TO THE MEMORY OF
DOROTHY WHITNEY ELMHIRST

CONTENTS

Contents

PREFACE

Despite Michael Straight's 1963 "confession" to the FBI that his covert KGB activity ceased in 1942, there is much material to establish otherwise, and FBI files (based mainly on the agency's interrogation of him), the MI5 and CIA files, and testimony from others, as well as his own actions, tell a different story. Straight's own *Apologia* demonstrates his thirty-year effort to cover up first his secret recruitment by the KGB and then his continuing secret activity. It also explains some of the forces that directed this intellectually gifted, fiercely ambitious American.

Friends, enemies, and close family members and their diaries provided far more revealing details of how others saw this important figure in their lives. Further information and observations came from interviews with people who knew Straight while they were employed by the KGB, CIA, FBI, MI6, and MI5. They confirmed his activities and his character. Many other sources were helpful, including the NSA (Venona), FBI, CIA, United States State Department, and British intelligence files. Transcripts from the House Un-American Activities Committee, the U.S. Senate, and other hearings were more than useful, as was the Dartington Hall archival material.

The recent release of Straight-related KGB files, generally submitted as summaries, was carefully orchestrated to be in line with what was already known about Straight's work as a KGB agent. But *Last of the Cold War Spies* reveals how Michael Straight was present at many of the important events and places at the heart of the Cold War. On every occasion and in every place he was on a KGB assignment. This distinguishes *Last of the Cold War Spies* from the plethora of books that were published on both sides of the Atlantic after the collapse of Communism. Many espionage writers rushed for Moscow gold and collaborated with KGB agents to create works that were dependent on what was supplied by Russian intelligence. These writers produced millions of words, yet next to nothing that was memorable or revealing. The KGB and its successor were always in control of what came out of their archives. No significant information was made public that Western intelligence didn't already know. The mass of disinformation generated was a gigantic KGB con. *Last of the Cold War Spies* was not written in collaboration with a former KGB operative. Although the book references KGB archive material, it keeps it in proper perspective as representing the view of Russian intelligence, which continues to deceive the West fifteen years after the collapse of Communism.

Roland Perry
Australia 2005

LAST OF THE
COLD WAR SPIES

INTRODUCTION

Michael Whitney Straight was always going to be different from the rest of the Cambridge University ring of spies recruited by Russian intelligence in the 1930s. First, he was the only American among a group otherwise boasting British backgrounds. Second, he was the wealthiest. And third, he was the most ambitious. He wanted to succeed at something *other* than being a thief and errand boy for Joseph Stalin. Most of the others in the ring were dedicated wholly to a life of espionage work. To say the others were motivated by ideology is not enough. Once the Stalinist brand of Marxism was exposed as a fraud, many were disillusioned but still carried on.

Kim Philby suggested he only ever wanted to be a spy, which indicated a mind excited by the thrill of deception. His thrill turned sour when he defected to Russia, where his bosses shunned him. The rejection turned him suicidal and exacerbated his alcoholism.

Guy Burgess's KGB-admired capacity for imaginative lying and scheming was cut short by his own whimsical decision to defect with Donald Maclean in 1951. Burgess hated his life in Russia and died in miserable conditions in 1963.

Donald Maclean, like Kim Philby, took his Soviet agency seriously all his life. He carried on his work in Russia long after defecting. Although

1

he was motivated by ideology, from all accounts he had a sad life in Russia despite never regretting his spying.

John Cairncross, the brilliant, impoverished Scotsman, became an expert on the French writer Molière. While more proud of his profound undercover work for the KGB, especially with the Battle of the Kursk, which helped change the course of World War II, Cairncross was happy to be acknowledged for his academic success. He was blown as a spy in 1951.

Victor Rothschild spread his tentacles everywhere on behalf of British, Israeli, and Soviet intelligence and put his prodigious intellectual capacities across several disciplines. At the beginning his support for the Soviet Union was rooted in self-preservation and the practical realities of prewar Europe. The Rothschild family had been a target for Hitler and the Nazis in every country they occupied. Postwar, his reasons were more murky. Like his forebears who had considerable influence in Europe in the nineteenth century, Rothschild thrived on secrecy, subterfuge, and behind-the-scenes machinations. He was happy in the back rooms of power manipulating events to achieve success for his nefarious projects.

Anthony Blunt's espionage work was marginalized after the defection of Burgess and Maclean, although he still on occasion met with his Soviet control, Yuri Modin. He had another, more visible career as the royal art curator and competent lecturer and writer of turgid art books. Like Rothschild, he thrived out of the limelight, in the hidden world of the palace and the esoteric world of art academia.

Michael Straight, in contrast to all of them, saw himself at twenty-one years of age as being able to combine his clandestine work for the Russians with a very public life as a politician. Like Rothschild, his forebears from the nineteenth century set the pattern for his ambitions. Before he was recruited, Straight harbored aspirations of running for Parliament in the United Kingdom. When he arrived in New York in 1937, he canvassed by knocking on doors for a local politician. After the war in late 1945, he approached the Democrats about running for Congress. When that bid was thwarted because of his student-days communist affiliation at Cambridge, he became a key strategist in the early campaign of Soviet supporter Henry Wallace's bid for the presidency in 1948. After he failed as a politician, he fell back on the editorship of the family magazine, *The New Republic*. From this position, Straight had a lesser platform than mainstream politics, yet it was still a more public role than anyone else in the ring had cultivated. From the mid-1950s to the end of the 1960s he used the pretense of being a novelist and playwright to carry out KGB-directed espionage missions. Straight's role as a federal arts administrator in the late 1960s meant even more public exposure and perhaps fulfilled a secondary ambition—a cover for his Russian intelligence work and propaganda.

Michael Straight, more than anyone else in the Cambridge ring, was predisposed to the secret life he chose in Russian intelligence. The influences of his wealthy background, his socially conscious mother, and the siren call of Stalinism that he followed with such passion determined his career path and life. His belief that Stalin himself arranged for his placement in the United States, as well as the emotional blackmail inflicted on him by Burgess, propelled the ambiguous Straight into a secret world. Rebecca West, in her book *The Meaning of Treason*, wrote of the peculiar attraction of the espionage demimonde that, although not the whole reason, was still appropriate for Straight:

> Sweet it is to be not what the next man thinks one, but far more powerful, to know what he wrote in a letter he was so careful to seal; to charm the confidence of the unsuspecting stranger; to put one's finger whimsically through the darkness and touch the fabric of the state, and feel the unstable structure rock, and know it's one's doing and not a soul suspecting it, and to do all this for nobility's sake.

The objective for Straight and his fellow spies in the Cambridge ring was to topple the structure of the capitalist state and to see it everywhere emerge as communism. The dream of revolution in the 1930s gave way to the reality of World War II, and aspirations for change were put on hold. The postwar divide between East and West caused even the most fanatical communists to realize that democracies and capitalism would be hard to topple.

Yet, for some, the expectations remained. In March 1950 when Straight appeared before the notorious House Un-American Activities Committee (HUAC), he gave an indication of this when discussing the fate of the American Communist Party:

> We believe if it (the Communist Party) becomes a clear and present danger, then by that time communism will have triumphed in the rest of the

world before it becomes a threat in this country. We think the critical front is in Berlin, Southeast Asia, India and Rome.

Change, it seemed, would take time, and the rest of the world had to fall before the United States was ripe for change. As the 1950s progressed, the resolve of the United States to fight communism everywhere remained firm. Straight's expectation changed to just hope. By the late 1950s, Cold War realities set in, and hope for revolution evaporated. By 1963, Straight went to the FBI and made a misleading confession of sorts about his past. He at first appeared to expose others in the Cambridge spy ring. But he gave away nothing. He, Blunt, and others continued on with a long-term disinformation campaign.

By the end of the 1960s, Straight was in the Nixon administration channeling U.S. taxpayer funds for the arts into dramatizing revolution on stage. Although this was hardly the real thing, for a cultured sophisticate like Straight it provided enough revolutionary oxygen for him to enjoy the job. After all, he was still doing useful work for the cause, and he remained an agent of considerable influence.

PART ONE

TO THE MANOR BORN

1

DESTINY DICTATOR

Michael Whitney Straight's potentially rich destiny was prepared long before he was born on September 1, 1916. His maternal great-grandfather, Henry B. Payne, a lawyer from Ohio, set a pattern early in the nineteenth century by making a fortune from railroads and becoming a state senator. He yearned to be president and sought that high office for two decades before giving up at age 77. This penchant for, and circumstance of, money, political power, and ambition carried to the next generation when Payne's vivacious daughter Flora married another lawyer, Yale-educated William Collins Whitney. With Flora's money and eventually his own, the cool and charming Whitney was touted as a presidential candidate, and he remained a pivotal force in the Democratic Party. Although he refused endorsement himself, no one could be elected as party candidate without his support.

Whitney divided his time between New York and Washington and decided there was more challenge in business and joining the robber baron class. This would ensure power for his lifetime and succeeding generations far beyond one person's short reign of Oval Office influence.

With this power came inevitable corruption, especially in dealing with the New York-based Metropolitan Street Railway Company. He used his legal knowledge to create an intricate corporate monster. It allowed him to act like a businessman who responds to bankruptcy on the horizon by transferring property to his wife. This was done on a grand scale after Whitney and his partners watered down the company's stock by recapitalizing, speculating in it, cornering, and dumping it. When the Metropolitan did collapse in 1908, Whitney and partners had long since milked it dry. Many American investors were left with nothing.

Whitney died in 1904 and so missed the opprobrium heaped on his partners. Yet, judging on his own power and influence, had he lived he would have been hardly touched. There were pious hearings at which Whitney's partners mumbled admissions about "considerable stock-jobbing and stock-watering." There were no prosecutions or convictions. Lawsuits were threatened but from small investors without the legal clout to have effect. In the end not even a scapegoat was found.

Whitney's daughter Dorothy (Michael Straight's mother) was born in Washington in 1887. She was twenty-one years old when the scandal of the Metropolitan became public in 1908. It was on the front page of *The New York Times* for months, and she was very much aware of it. Dorothy was too bright, sensitive, and religious not to be touched by the ramifications of the way the family fortune had been acquired. She took on the guilt of her father's fiscal follies. Apart from her moral nature she grew into her teens aware of social issues at a time of reform in the United States. The first great trustbuster, Republican Theodore Roosevelt, was elected president in 1904. Across the Atlantic, England produced a liberal reform government two years later. Roosevelt became a good friend. Dorothy was drawn into campaigns to end corruption in city government.

A handsome woman, she could not avoid the perils of being an heiress. American as much as European society was awash with predators who would have settled for a woman worth a mere $100,000, let alone Dorothy's $7 million. The suitors came in droves. If they failed to notice her concern for poverty or her aid to immigrants during the great wave of the time, these eligible empty shells were shown the door. Her mental checklist of compatibility was longer than any other rich woman's in the United States. Even if he appeared to pass every test, there was another hurdle that would test a man's mettle. Dorothy was six when her mother died, which made her an orphan in her mid-teens. Her closest relationship had been formed with a worldly English governess, Beatrice Bend. She was Dorothy's adviser, educator, elder sister equivalent, friend, and replacement parent. The man that was able to lure her away from such an emotional bond as Miss Bend would have to have radiant qualities.

That man was Willard Dickerman Straight, seven years Dorothy's senior and like her an orphan. Willard's father, Henry, a state school natural sciences teacher, died of tuberculosis when Willard was five. His mother, Emma, also a teacher, contracted the ubiquitous disease after a year in Tokyo. She died in 1890, leaving Willard without parents at age ten.

He was fortunate to be adopted by Dr. Elvire Ranier, one of the few women physicians in the United States. But the comfort and security was not enough to counter the anxiety felt by a sensitive, intelligent child. His two major constants in life had been taken from him. Young Willard developed a temper and was willful and incorrigible at school. Ranier countered with discipline. This only exacerbated the boy's personality problem. He was expelled from school. His foster mother sent him off as a high school junior to Bordentown Military Academy in New Jersey. The school made him.

He reveled in the soldierly regimens, which took his mind off his personal tragedy and tempered his temperament. His self-confidence built and stabilized enough to give his keen intellect a freer run. He averaged more than ninety in his grades and considered a military career via West Point. Willard's love of drawing and design—he had been a sketcher ever since he could hold a crayon—overrode his desire to lead. He entered Cornell University to study architecture. The more liberated atmosphere drew out other traits in the former problem child. He proved an exceptional student, capable leader, and inspired writer of humor and literature, while never putting down the sketching easel. Willard played the guitar and had a fair tenor voice.

He graduated in 1901, and his ambition and adventurous spirit helped him accept a job in China in the Imperial Maritime Customs Service on a respectable $750 a year. The organization was an arrogant colonial set-up that collected China's customs revenues and remained independent of Chinese control. The position served Willard by allowing him to demonstrate his linguistic gifts, learning Mandarin. The Customs Service also showed him bureaucracy of any kind was not for him. He jumped at an opportunity in 1904 to become a Reuters and Associated Press correspondent in the Russo-Japanese War. Five years after leaving Bordentown Academy, he was back on a militaristic track.

He was sent first to Tokyo. His diary claimed a torment of choice between admitted selfish ambition and artistic idealism. Willard desired to make his name in high places and money along the way. He could not see himself as the penniless bohemian. Willard knew that there was "too much ambition in my cosmos to let the schemer be driven out by my better nature, hence much tribulation and many an unhappy hour, and uneasy time, for I am not true to myself."[1]

This mild agony and self-effacement did not cloud his move up the ladder to the choking altitude he aspired to reach. He was, usefully, pro-Japanese as they strove to take Manchuria and Korea. In Tokyo Willard found himself socializing with Edwin V. Morgan, 40, scion of the wealthy upstate New York family. Describing the handsome correspondent, sixteen years his junior, Morgan noted that Willard was "tall, slim, with reddish-brown hair, of unusual frankness and charm of manner, perfectly at ease."

At the end of the Russo-Japanese War, Morgan hired him as his private secretary with the rank of vice-consul at Seoul. Young Willard was now on an escalator rather than a ladder. This led him for the first time into the company of a social circle that excited him; the visiting Alice Roosevelt (daughter of Theodore) and the diminutive E. H. Harriman and his family were among them. Harriman may or may not have been in the robber baron class, but he certainly played with the new toys and inventions of their kind of business, especially trains. His $70 million fortune came from controlling the Union Pacific Railroad and the Pacific Mail steamship line spanning the Pacific. He dazzled Willard by airing his ambition to create a round-the-world transportation system. Harriman wanted to hook up the Trans-Siberian Railway (from which he would lease rights) with a steamship line from the Baltic to New York.

Willard found Harriman's beautiful, bright, and pampered daughter Mary very much to his liking. Even the most guileless of young men could have seen the advantages of marrying into such a family. However, there was no rush; indeed, to have pushed would have been folly. He could hardly have kept her in the luxury to which she had become accustomed, at least not yet.

When Japan demonstrated it was running Korea rather than giving it independence, the place for a legation was Tokyo, not Seoul, which was closed. Willard, now 25, was offered a job with Morgan in Cuba. He took it, despite his love for Asia.

In the summer of 1906, he received a summons to Washington from President Roosevelt, who had heard good things of the young man from both his daughter Alice and especially Harriman. Known as the "Little Giant of Wall Street," Harriman needed someone in place in China to complete his dream of that global transport network. Who better than bright-eyed and brilliant Willard, who spoke Chinese and who made it clear that he wished to be fluent in the language of big business. He was posted as consul to Manchuria in the thriving industrial city of Mukden, the once-Tartar capital 500 miles northeast of Beijing. He made a success of it despite his tendency to fits of depression when his work became a matter of persistence and determination. He would often consider bailing out for a more lucrative position. Yet he stayed based in Mukden. Harriman even urged for his appointment as minister to China, but it was impractical. He was only 27 years old. Such a posting would have caused rebellion among the old guard at the U.S. State Department, who relied on seniority for advancement rather than ability.

While Harriman looked for a promotion for Willard in his work, he demoted him in his private life by preventing his marriage to Mary. The reasons boiled down to the fact that Willard didn't have the right pedigree or wealth. Coupled with that was Harriman's need for Willard to be in place in China and to concentrate on the job. Marriage into the family might have made the manipulation of Willard's talents in China more difficult.

Neither Mary nor Willard appeared shattered by the break. He was soon dancing attendance on Katherine Elkins in Washington, another daughter of immense wealth. Her father was coal and industrial mogul Stephen Benton Elkins, a Republican senator from West Virginia and a former secretary of war in the Harrison administration. Then there was one Dorothy Whitney with whom he dined and played tennis on Long Island at the banker Edwin Morgan's.

In 1909, the State Department decided on so-called dollar diplomacy in China by encouraging private American bankers to take part in a $25 million loan to China, which the British, French, and Germans were then negotiating for the construction of the Hukuang railways. The New York bankers chosen—known as the American group—were managed by J. P. Morgan & Company and included Kuhn, Loeb & Company; the First National Bank; and the National City Bank.

They needed a representative in China. Willard was approached. At 29, he resigned from the State Department. He saw the possibilities if he could succeed in negotiating with the Chinese to accept the loan. It would be tough: the Chinese wanted the easiest terms. The European partners in the loan would push for harsh penalties from the Americans for their late entry.

As he faced his greatest challenge, Willard's personality continued to impress everyone. He could be mixing with elderly bankers and diplomats one moment and then move to a group of young employees at the legation. He would pick up a guitar and entertain with improvised, amusing lines from literature.

It was this breadth of character and style that impressed Dorothy. If he had been all banker, she would have been uninterested. Coincidentally or otherwise, she arrived in Beijing on a world trip and was feted like a royal. One of those assigned to her was Willard. Their early delicate diary entries were noncommittal but agreeable about each other. For instance, Dorothy's November 5, 1909, entry read: "Such gorgeous days. Mr. Straight took us this morning to the drum tower, which we climbed for the beautiful view."[2]

On November 11, Willard sang and played guitar for her and wrote: "Record breaker. Beautiful day, lunch at Wan Chow Sze—ride along the Jade Canal afterwards. A little music then another fireside talk with DW." It was gentile code for falling in love.

By the last night after a fortnight in each other's company, November 13, Willard, who referred to her as "the Princess" in his diary, was out of code and transcribing his feelings: "It was hard not to ask her to stay on and live there (at the bankers' compound). . . . Quiet dinner and a little choking at the throat, I think."

A similarly smitten Dorothy noted: "Our last evening—it is so sad."

Willard's post-Dorothy entries showed him depressed and miserable without her. The romance blossomed in correspondence as he demonstrated his wit and literary skills. After six months, they met in Milan at the Hotel de Ville in May 1910. He proposed. She demurred and then rejected him. It created a dilemma for Willard, but he could not dwell on it, for he had to press forward with the Chinese loan. He took a train to Paris, where his task was to reach agreement with the Europeans, which he did. The letters between him and Dorothy continued despite the setback, and they began to cover the ground that had troubled her. He explained away Mary Harriman and fretted about Dorothy learning of his fleeting affection for Katherine Elkins. He didn't wish to be seen as a gold-digger. Yet his chasing of only heiresses set him up to be branded this way by the inevitable relationship breakers in the chattering class of New York and Washington.

They contrived to meet, and her attraction to him strengthened. By late 1910 their love epistles were again peppered with coded words known only to them. During this time, Willard felt the pressures over the loan. Although it was unsaid, his chances of marrying Dorothy were contingent on the Chinese signing. His standing would be immense for one so young—the elevation would overcome his outsider status in New York and lack of means.

Finally, on April 15, 1911, the Chinese signed the loan agreement. Willard's self-confidence and prestige were boosted as never before. His success gave him the platform for his acceptability. He and Dorothy became engaged on July 20 and married on September 7 in a morning civil ceremony in Geneva, followed at noon by an Episcopal service. They later traveled by train across Siberia to Manchuria and China, arriving in Beijing on October 11, the day that the Sun Yat-sen rebellion broke out. The Straights endured the fall of the Manchu dynasty over the next few dangerous months, in which they were trapped during looting riots and attempts to burn Beijing. They were forced to stay inside the U.S. legation compound protected by marines.

When peace was restored, they left Beijing via the Trans-Siberian railway in March 1912 to a send off by about eighty of the foreign elite in China.

The trip was arduous for Dorothy. She was pregnant.

2

BIRTH, DEATH, AND CIRCUMSTANCE

The Straights returned to the United States, and Willard, practically a stranger to New York society, took up a Wall Street position with J. P. Morgan on an increased salary of $20,000. They bought a Packard car, leased a five-story townhouse at 22 East 67th Street, and spent leisure time at the Whitney home in Old Westbury, Long Island. Willard could not keep up the lifestyle expected of the family on his respectable salary. He found himself in the position of William Whitney when expenses were subsidized by the $250,000 a year earned from the investment of Dorothy's fortune, which had increased to more than $10 million.

Their first child, Whitney Willard, was born in November 1912. After three months of Dorothy's attention, he was assigned to a governess for most of the day. It was similar to her own early days, except she made sure that her quality time with young Whitney was filled with attention and caressing, which she had lacked. The employment of an English nanny allowed the Straights to go as a couple to the theater and opera as before and to attend the usual rounds of tennis, polo, and golf.

While Willard worked, Dorothy took up her liberal enterprises with a vengeance. She stood up for women's suffrage, the State Charities Aid, and the YWCA. If she wasn't supporting a Democratic candidate somewhere, she was doing something for a committee to care for poor children and women of the district. At night, she might be at a book club reading, or listening to lectures at the Economics Club, which was taken up with novel ideas concerning socialism and the single tax. Then there were Women's Trade Union meetings about the unemployed, as well as Bible classes. Dorothy was quietly, determinedly spiritual.

She was going far beyond the public obligations of the New York social set and into the realms of self-sacrifice in paying for the sins of the father. Yet while William Whitney's failings may have been a subconscious motivation, she was of such a mind that even without them she would have taken the same path.

— • —

Two years after securing the loan for China, Willard saw his triumph collapse. The loan was delayed by the Chinese revolution, then thwarted by President Woodrow Wilson and the American Group of bankers itself. Wilson thought the loan "obnoxious" because it threatened China's independence. The bankers fretted over the turbulent country's capacity to repay loans. The blow caused Willard anguish, but, bursting with ideas, he moved on.

He was concerned with the United States' direction, and he longed for it to be inspired with a long-term plan, particularly his. His schemes were similar to those of his friend and hero Theodore Roosevelt and to ideas honed by writer Herbert Croly. His book *The Promise of American Life* had bemoaned the lack of a blueprint for an American renaissance. Croly wanted the United States to move away from disorganized individualism to develop a sense of national purpose and good. Known for his honesty and idealism, he didn't want the rampant big corporations broken up but rather made more accountable and beneficial to the whole population. Willard felt much the same way and was a patriot despite his liking for imperialist ways. He had enjoyed his elitist experience in China and wanted the United States to exploit it more benevolently than he thought the British had, or the Japanese or Russians would.

Willard was in accord with Croly's thinking, even if they were coming from different directions. The writer was urging stronger leadership and national reform at home. Willard thought this would make the United States stronger abroad. He yearned to own a daily paper of influence but would settle, for the moment, for a magazine.

Dorothy was busy having their second child, Beatrice, early in August 1914, but she still made time to consider the dreams of others. The Straights, Croly, Judge Learned Hand, and Felix Frankfurter met at Westbury to discuss the birth of *The New Republic*. Dorothy subsidized the magazine, which began after the fall elections of 1914. Croly was appointed to the staff, and Roosevelt became contributing editor. Soon journalists Walter Lippmann and Walter Weyl were on board having weekly editorial meetings with the Straights. Willard and Roosevelt saw it as a vehicle for their muscular view of U.S. foreign policy and international corporate adventures. Croly viewed it as a radical journal for espousing his developing ideas for change in the United States. They were all, despite their personal ambitions, constructive in their ideas about their nation. A common denominator was a better, more socially responsible United States.

Meanwhile, war broke out in Europe, with Imperial Germany declaring its intentions against Russia, then France. Straight could hear those distant drums. They had first beat for him at military college, then in the Russo-Japanese conflict, and more recently in the Chinese revolution. He was dissatisfied with his lot at the House of Morgan and bored with international banking. He had his club, polo, golf, tennis, politics, and the new magazine, which he was not supposed to attempt to influence, although he tried, particularly over policy concerning the United States' preparedness for war. The machinations of dealing with other people's money was no fun compared to the rest of his activities.

Dorothy, who kept control of the purse strings, would not indulge his craving for a newspaper. She urged him to stick with the Morgan job. She liked its security, and she knew her man to be impatient and lacking in perseverance.

The last straw at Morgan for Willard came when he spent much time speaking to business groups about the trade opportunities presented by the war. He and Dorothy had entertained the heads of the Anglo-French commission at Westbury when they visited the United States. Willard had created the market by working hard at inspiring both the sellers and buyers to deal. Then he found himself left out of the bank's plans to furnish the Allies with money to continue their purchases from the groups he had encouraged.

Willard resigned September 18, 1915, soon after the Straights had moved into their newly built Georgian red brick at Fifth Avenue and 94th Street. He announced he would study international law at Columbia. Inside three months of beginning law, he again proved his incapacity to stay the course and accepted the position of third vice-president to the new American International Corporation, beginning early in 1916.

Willard was still at AIC on September 1, 1916, when Dorothy gave birth to their third child, Michael Whitney, the biggest arrival at nearly 10 pounds. The new arrival inspired his father to paint a serene seascape the next day during a contented period in the short life of the Straight family.

Six months later Willard changed course yet again. After failing to land a State Department job in Washington, he was commissioned into the army as a major in the adjutant general's reserve corps and assigned to Governor's Island, just fifteen minutes by boat from lower Manhattan. The lure of the military had snared Willard after several flirtations. He left the AIC while keeping a few financial projects going and attempted to pull strings for a position on the General Staff. When sent to Europe, he again failed to get himself frontline duty in command of a battalion or on the staff of a division. In France he had the unglamorous post in charge of the War Risk Insurance Bureau for the U.S. Army. Yet it carried responsibility. He arranged for countless U.S. servicemen to insure their lives in an operation that would have rivaled the biggest insurance company.

Dorothy was uneasy about his rush to the military and the subsequent distance between them. Typically in times of stress, she increased her activity by joining the Mayor's Committee on National Defense and the Red Cross. She worked in a YMCA canteen, continued to push for the suffragettes, and made time for the New School for Social Research. She made herself far busier than Willard. When the Insurance Bureau work was completed, he wandered around the U.S. military in Paris as a sort of itinerant staff officer. It left him low. He summoned the spirit to write to Dorothy, whom he delighted in calling "Miss Chairman of all things," telling her to inform each of their boys:

Always to get his foundations solid—before he started to climb—and to—
by constant practice and the most consistent effort—train himself to have
his bowels move each morning as soon as he is dressed. You've no idea
what these things mean. . . . From the latter I am suffering constantly—
and it's only a question of training. As to the former—that has been my
great handicap in life. I've always been finding myself in places more important than I was really competent to hold. I've never had the foundation
for the jobs I've had—except perhaps the political foundation for the
Chinese loans business—and for my job in the State Department.[1]

After the war, Willard, still in Paris, supported President Wilson in his
push for a League of Nations and managed to get on the staff of the president's chief assistant—Colonel House—at the Peace Conference.
Willard was involved in final negotiations when he contracted influenza.
It developed into pneumonia. He died on December 1, 1918, at age 38,
leaving Dorothy a widow at 31.

She had been planning to come to Paris to be part of the Conference
at the president's request, but instead she stood at Willard's grave in the
war cemetery at Suresne. Later she went to Langres Cathedral seeking
some communication with her dead husband. They had once had a tele-
pathic experience when he was there and she was in the United States.
On returning home, she turned more to Christian Science and her own
spirituality, even going to séances held by a Maryland medium. Her
notes show that she believed that she made contact with Willard
through the medium. He told her he had been "there" with her on several occasions.

Dorothy asked him for guidance on raising and educating the children. His responses, via the medium, appeared reassuring.[2]

Whitney, he told Dorothy, would stand out as a good character and
businessman, who would work and play tirelessly; so, he should be encouraged along those paths. Beatrice, on the other hand, would be more
challenging for her parents and would develop later in life, probably in
some creative area because she had "artistic talent." Michael would be
more intellectual and would need instruction on overcoming hurdles. He
would have a literary bent; so, he should be guided into social and economic education and work.

The response from Willard through the medium proved to be pre-
scient for the three children, then only six, four, and two years.

One of Michael Straight's earliest memories was of being taken by a nanny to his mother in Willard's study where she had shut herself on learning that he had died. The two-year-old was meant to bring comfort but was struck by terror when he saw her at a desk, head in her hands. Michael was removed from the scene, kicking and screaming. It was one black spot in an otherwise good memory of his early life.

Later in life Straight hinted that Dorothy buried herself in her work after her husband died rather than finding solace in her children. Trendy child-rearing experts at the time suggested mothers should not be overly affectionate to their children. Michael had a British governess, May Gardner, but maintained that he and his siblings where shown love only in their limited quality time with Dorothy. Nevertheless, Straight's upbringing seemed happy, healthy, and normal, allowing for the privileges he experienced. He was sent to Lincoln, a progressive school near Harlem, which had a mix of social backgrounds.

Another childhood memory was being chauffeured to school in a Packard limousine. The chauffeur would open the car door; Straight recalled then being set upon by his less privileged classmates. Yet Straight, a talker rather than a fighter, coped well enough. There were many pleasant memories from home and at Old Westbury on the weekends.

May Gardner reinforced the young Straight's sense of superiority over the staff on the estate. Yet their proximity and the fact that there were few little boys of his own age nearby on Long Island meant he could not remain remote from the chauffeur's son, Harry, or Jimmy Lee, the second son of the head gardener at Old Westbury. These working-class sons were Straight's age, and both became playmates. They knew their place and were reminded of it in a milieu more akin to upper-class England than the mythological egalitarianism of early twentieth-century America.

Miss Gardner remained the constant in Straight's early formative years to age nine. She was the victim of his earliest recorded deception. The diligent nanny gave him daily doses of cod-liver oil to correct a vitamin D deficiency. He pretended that it made him sick. Miss Gardner was sympathetic. This resulted in her reading aloud to him and bringing him supper in bed.

A few years after Willard's death the occasional suitor would come to Old Westbury seeking Dorothy, who although in her 30s was still one of the most attractive prospects in the United States. If anything, her checklist for a suitable partner had increased after Willard. She found most of the hopefuls pale imitations of him. She would discourage them by always having other guests in their company.

In 1920, Leonard Knight Elmhirst, a Cambridge history graduate, came, not seeking her hand but a donation to save the Cosmopolitan Club at Cornell University, of which Leonard was president. Leonard wanted $80,000 to keep the club—which included students from twelve nations—afloat. Dorothy went to Cornell the following year and had a look. She was impressed.

"Of course I'm going to help," she told the cheerful Englishman, seven years her junior. She found herself curiously attracted to this tall, smiling idealist whose polite charm was engaging. He had a few characteristics similar to Willard, such as a good tenor voice, the ability to quote verse at appropriate times, and an interest in Asia. And he was not rich. Yet that was where the similarities ended. Willard had a grand design to get rich in China. Leonard wanted to help the starving masses in India by increasing their agricultural productivity.

Leonard was the second of eight sons of a modest Yorkshire parson-landowner whose forebears had cultivated the same land in West Riding since 1320. He had been expected to follow his father into the pulpit, but the war and the loss of two brothers in it had shaken his faith.

Leonard had gone to the United States to study the advanced methods of farming at Cornell. He liked Dorothy's looks and charm, grace and bearing. Unlike the others, who saw an easier life through marriage to her money, he was more intimidated by it than attracted. It made him conscious of his impoverished state as he washed dishes to pay his way through university and struggled to find something other than a frayed shirt for visits to Old Westbury. Dorothy was aware of his circumstances and encouraged his friendship.

When Leonard graduated from Cornell, he took off for India to join the spiritual leader, Rabindranath Tagore, in rural reconstruction work in Bengal. Tagore commissioned Leonard to train students at the leader's International University and carry out research. Inside two years, in a remarkable pioneering achievement, he was able to leave his project in the hands of an all-Indian staff. Leonard's confidence grew through this period as he reported his progress to Dorothy in a steady stream of letters, to which she responded with money for the project. He returned to Cornell as a man with missions in life, and he advised Dorothy on the design of a union building at the university, which would be her memorial to Willard. It was opened in 1924.

Leonard's experiences with Tagore had determined his own career ambitions, which would include agriculture in England. He was bursting with radical ideas for rural development and education—in fact, a utopian community. This dedication and his selfless efforts in India on behalf of the poor attracted Dorothy and paralleled her own self-imposed destiny of social responsibility. She became even more impressed when he assured her his brave new world would include experiments in her passion—the arts. Leonard had matured. He seemed more at ease, so much so that he proposed marriage.

She rejected him, but he persisted. Leonard needed her for his dreams to materialize. She finally accepted. They were married in the garden of Old Westbury in April 1925.

<hr />

Leonard Elmhirst had certain parameters in mind in April 1925 when he began his search for an English base for his utopian dream. Some were provided by Rabindranath Tagore, who urged him to look for a spiritual place because "the practical work of craftsmen must always be carried out in partnership with the divine spirit of madness, of beauty, with the inspiration of the same ideal of perfection."

This was in accord with Dorothy's desires. She too wished to experience a center with soul, even a mystical past. It shored up Leonard's own shaken faith. He saw a London real estate agent.

"It must be beautiful, we're starting a school," Leonard told the man at Knight, Frank & Rutley. "We expect to make farming pay, it must have a reasonably productive soil and climate, and as much variety as possible, woods, forest, orchards et cetera."

Leonard had the agent's attention.

"See if you can give me all those," he added, "and historical associations thrown in. Yes, and in Devon, Dorset, or Somerset."

Unsaid was the fact that Tagore had suggested Devon first. It had deep, rich soil, rolling plains, and narrow valleys. Winding, tight lanes gave it a sense of seclusion, which evoked a timeless separateness from busy, over-crowded London or England's industrial heartlands. The region could attract "some budding poets," Tagore suggested, "some scapegoats who no one else dares to acknowledge."

The agent gave Leonard a list of forty-eight estates in the West Country. He looked at and rejected a "dull" Georgian Manor in Exeter, and then turned his attention to the second location on the list. It was South Devon's Dartington Hall, a Tudor manor of the late fourteenth century. He inquired about the area prior to the 1390s when John Holand built it into a fine country house laid out as a double quadrangle on an acre.

Dartington, or Homestead of the Meadow by the River Dart, was first mentioned in the registers of Shaftesbury Abbey of 833. Leonard learned of its acquisition after 1066 by William de Falaise, one of the companions-in-arms of William the Conqueror. In 1113 it belonged to the Fitzmartin family, who added the property to their possessions in Wales and the southwest, leasing it as small manors and homesteads. They erected the first stone church and buildings above the archway of the north end courtyard. In 1290, a banqueting hall was added.

The Fitzmartins sold Dartington to the Audeleys in 1348. Because the Audeleys had no heirs, the property reverted to the Crown. In 1384, Richard II granted it to John Holand, his half-brother, whom he later created Earl of Huntingdon and Duke of Exeter. The Holands lost Dartington in the mid–fifteenth century during the War of the Roses. For the next one hundred years it was tossed back and forth between a disinterested Crown and several ambivalent owners.

In 1559, Sir Arthur Champernowne purchased Dartington, and his family remained its owner for the next 366 years—until Leonard arrived from London in a newly bought Talbot car. The Champernownes had Dartington on the market for some time. Its sad state of disrepair, which featured broken arches and buildings—minus the odd roof—as well as its placement in a small sea of mud, left a long line of unprepossessed potential buyers. But not Leonard.

He felt a nervous tingle bumping along a narrow road of the estate beside the river Dart until a path upward brought him to the Hall. Instead of an ugly skeleton ready for a bulldozer he imagined the beauty of its construction when the Holands set up the first rectangular court—the north wing with its archway, the barn, and extended Fitzmartin buildings; the east and west wings containing the lodgings of the private battalions of armed retainers; and the south wing including the banqueting hall, the tower, the kitchens, the serving quarters, and the private apartments.

Leonard had done his homework. He appreciated the civilizing development that the Champernownes had achieved when the feudal system ended and there was no longer need for the rural aristocracy to keep armies and maintain a grand, fortified residence. The private apartments had been converted into a gabled mansion and the solar story had been reconstructed. The sunken garden for jousting tournaments enjoyed by John Holand had been turned in part into an Italian garden. The Champernownes had also put in a bowling green in about 1675, when it was fashionable.

Leonard was enchanted with the estate. He told Dorothy he worshipped the beauty of the property. It combined a natural setting with the work of "generations of men" who attended to its appearance. He saw it as a suitable home for the family and for her, "a squire's wife."[3]

Whether Dorothy, the heiress and fighter for women's rights, saw herself quite this way is not recorded, but she was captivated by her husband's optimistic vision. She came to Dartington and loved hearing what he would do to the courtyard and banqueting hall to make it suitable for her ideas. They encompassed singing, music, lectures, ballet, theater, and art.

Herbert Croly was one of several advisers who did not want Dorothy to migrate to England. He thought it would be a retrograde step for the three children. But Leonard won her over by informing her that the community they would create would include a progressive school.[4]

With their first child on the way, Dorothy returned to Westbury to prepare Whitney, Beatrice ("Biddy"), her friend Nina, Michael, and May Gardner for their big move. The boy Straight said his good-byes to his friends with the mixed feelings of a nine-year-old. Fate would draw one of them, Jimmy Lee, the gardener's second son, into his life at a pivotal time four decades later.

———— • ————

Young Straight awoke early in mid-June 1925 as the ocean liner *George Washington* scythed through the Channel's calm seas and approached Plymouth Harbor. Despite his misgivings, it was an exciting moment to be met by Dorothy, Leonard, and Whitney, now 14 years old, to commence a new life.

Straight claimed he was different from his 14-year-old brother and 12-year-old sister. They already knew what they wanted to do in life. Whitney, the gallant adventurer, wanted to race cars and fly, and he took advantage of Dartington's intention of a progressive, liberated education to do exactly what he wished. Beatrice wanted to be an actress. Even at 10 she was directing plays, with all the hired staff in the United States forced to watch her performances whether they wished to or not. But Michael, like most people his age, had little real idea of what he wanted to do with his life. He may have imagined it, but the governess seemed to him to be setting him apart from everyone else. She almost bossed him into keeping a diary, and it forced Straight into thinking he might actually develop as a creative author.[5]

Straight assessed all the children's relationships with Leonard, the alleged interloper in his eyes. He claimed that Whitney's removal from the United States put him at cross purposes to Leonard. But this was contradicted by Whitney's liberation at Dartington and his being able to do as he wanted—dash around in fast transport on the ground and in the air. Beatrice spent six years at Dartington getting useful training as an actress, leaving at 18 to become a successful thespian. But she did return to begin a theatrical school under Michael Chekhov. Straight reckoned he was too young at 10 to be hostile to Leonard.

In keeping with the intent at Dartington, Straight was given a small garden, which he had to upkeep himself. While he hoed it one day in that first Dartington summer, May Gardner came to say a tearful good-bye. Straight felt liberated. He would no longer have her stand over him while he said his prayers each night before bed. Straight was relieved to be free from the burden of religious obligations, especially when the governess demanded that he kneel by his bed each night where he had to say a prayer he found repugnant:

If I die before I wake
I pray the Lord my soul to take . . .

With Gardner's departure, he stopped praying altogether, leaving a belief vacuum. By his teenage years at the radical Dartington, he had supplanted the concept of a religious god with a Pantheon of political gods. Foremost among them were Marx, Lenin, and Stalin.

———— ◆ ————

Straight wished to give the impression of being a child adrift and therefore vulnerable to other influences that would fill the vacuum that he said he had when compared to his siblings. Straight and these influences were about to embrace each other.

3

MARX AND SPARKS

Despite their wealth and background, Leonard and Dorothy did not plan to ride to the hounds or open up the great banqueting hall to the local gentry, who would have seemed at home in a Jane Austen novel. Instead they strove to integrate the impoverished surrounding villages in their grand experiment in education and the arts. Their aim was the union of the best elements of town and country and the development of agriculture and industry.

They made themselves unpopular with the gentry by shutting off Dartington's 800 acres to the foxhunters. Much to the chagrin of the local rector, The Reverend J. S. Martin, the Elmhirsts did not plan to patronize the local church on the main road. They preferred the privacy of their own home. Martin, Leonard noted, seemed to think from then on that the devil had moved his headquarters from Moscow to Dartington Hall. Perhaps most of all, the locals resented Dorothy, a wealthy American. She didn't quite conform to the protocol of socializing with wives of the surrounding estates and the local aristocracy. She had her own workload and was as busy with her plans to create a suitable household and to develop the arts as Leonard was in putting up structures to house them.

In the first couple of years, the Elmhirsts and their strange goings-on alienated the local community leaders. Dartington became the focal point of gossip over such trivialities as the children bathing nude in the river or mixed-sex showers in the school dormitory.

Outside reaction led the newcomers to turn inward. Leonard brought his three brothers, Pom (who became Dartington's legal adviser), Vic, and Richard, from Yorkshire to cut down trees, clear the undergrowth, remove the Victorian shrubberies and weeds, and strip away the formal flower beds from the sunken garden, or tiltyard. A dramatic landscape of terraces emerged from beneath a worn out surface and blended into a wider river valley. The great trees planted by the Champernownes stood tall and grand. Sweeping views materialized. The gardens were shaped to blend with surrounding countryside. The industrious Elmhirsts and experts from England and the United States helped in the rebuilding. Roofs went on, walls were fortified, new structures erected. The combined effect of Leonard's vision and Dorothy's garden creations was to establish an estate that had more grandeur than at any time in its thousand-year-plus history.

In 1927, the Elmhirsts put on their first major play at Dartington, *The Unknown Warrior*, which had achieved success in London. It was performed in the solar, the restored meeting room near the equally restored great hall.

In between inviting actors, musicians, artists, dance troupes, philosophers, and writers to visit and "perform" at Dartington, Dorothy managed to have two children with Leonard, Ruth in March 1927 and Bill in February 1929. She also worked with Leonard on education plans, which were set out in a rather lofty, philosophical prospectus, where learning was to be associated with practical experience. For instance, a teenager could learn about the business of poultry farming in a poultry project. It was called learning by doing. The "school" was to be self-governing. There was to be no discipline—a reaction to the rectitude that both Dorothy and Leonard experienced at school. The curriculum was to flow from the children's own interests, which turned out to be haphazard and less rewarding than supposed.

Whitney, at age 15 in 1927, found he had to learn Latin to enter Cambridge. Beatrice never learned to spell, and Michael Straight complained in old age that his grammar was poor. In fact, none of the original students, who along with the three Straights included fourteen local and other kids from poor backgrounds, could spell or do algebra or geometry.

By contrast they attended lectures by speakers such as Bertrand Russell, Aldous Huxley, and A. S. Neill and had visits from T. E. Lawrence and George Bernard Shaw. A teacher, Wyatt Trevelyan Rawson, taught Freudian psychoanalysis and interpreted dreams for the children in class. Michael Chekhov taught drama. H. N. Brailsford, the socialist writer, stayed at Dartington for six weeks during the autumn term of 1928. Consequently, the more intellectual students in the early teens, such as Straight, were semiliterate and innumerate but capable of grasping the big, persuasive ideas of the time. They comprehended a bit of Freud and the broad principles of Marxism-Leninism despite being unable to articulate them on paper with grammatical clarity. In September 1929, Michael Young (later, Lord Young of Dartington), a "pauper" as he called himself, began at the Hall when stars of the ideological firmament were frequenting there more than ever. He was Straight's age, and they were thrown together, according to Young, because of Dorothy's propensity to find permanent playmates for her children.

Young loved the freedom after a succession of preparatory and state schools in London and Australia, where straps and canes were used on hands, knuckles, legs, and buttocks. He was amused by the mixed-sex showers, which Leonard had suggested would take the curiosity out of the youngsters and reduce sexual tensions. "I had found it had the opposite effect," Young noted in interviews.

As for the unisex dormitories, a worry in his five years at the Hall was the prospect of pregnancies. "There were surprisingly few compared to other schools," he observed, "but it wasn't for want of trying."

Young had not long been at Dartington when he became fascinated by the new panacea that was Marxism. It was fashionable among thinkers at the leading universities. Both boys were inspired by a desire to change the world through revolution. Their isolation in the Dartington educational milieu assisted their precocious development. They were at least aware that their inspirations were radical and a threat to the establishment, even the liberal, democratic views of Dorothy and Leonard. It forced them into a bond, an early adolescent cabal, which, despite their intellectual equality, Straight appeared to dominate.

"He was arrogant and could be cruel," Michael Young recalled.[1] "He was extrovert and I, introvert." He remembered them being "more rivals than friends," although they remained friends through that original bond into their 80s.

Teachers at Dartington noted that Straight was difficult, uncooperative, and rude. Wyatt Rawson, trying out his newly discovered Freudian analysis, found Straight to be "tremendously under the influence of an English governess [the redoubtable May Gardner], who kept his emotions arrested at an age of about five."

Straight used to repeat this amateur observation over the decades in an attempt to show that he was in need of being attached to somebody or something—that he was vulnerable to his later recruitment to a secret cause. On a 1929 trip with his parents to Bengal to see Tagore, he found his stepfather (here in a diary entry dropping the affectionate nickname "Gerry" for Leonard) remote and Dorothy naive. Straight seemed to be painting her as not the best mother a sensitive lad could have. This added to the image of a poor little rich boy who needed that sense of belonging once more. Thus he was later open to being fostered in the communist cause. Added to this was his professed alienation in the United Kingdom since leaving the United States, which was again to propose that he had no true motherland. He was implying that when another was later offered, he was attracted.

An alleged example of parental guidance, or lack of it, concerned a play that his mother put on at Dartington when he was 13, *Le Tombeau Sous l'Arc de Triomphe* by Paul Regnal. Its central character was a French soldier who volunteered for a suicide mission. He was given twenty-four hours to be with his father and his betrothed. Straight claimed to Dorothy that he did not understand the soldier's mentality. If he was the top fighter, why did he have to sacrifice himself? Dorothy cut him off by implying he was ignorant. Then she pointed out that the soldier's status caused him to be obligated to make the sacrifice.

Straight claimed, unconvincingly, that this all related back to his agony over his father's desire to abandon his family and go off to war. Dorothy never went beyond the explanation that the top man should lead the way in sacrifice. Straight said this befuddled him. The impression he wished to convey was that he had developed a deep sense of noblesse oblige, after the example set by his father and upheld by his mother.

Just like his father, he would put his hand up if he were ever asked to serve for a cause in which he believed. Again, this temperament, when coupled with his emotional statelessness, implied that Straight would be vulnerable to any later overtures to become a KGB agent.

The self-portrait of Straight as an emotionally defenseless neo-orphan waif did not sit with those who knew him intimately. Young found him a dominant personality obsessed with extreme left-wing ideology and driven to fulfilling political ambitions through it. "He was extremely good-looking," Young recalled, "an Adonis with intellectual gifts to match."

Straight was very competitive. He hated losing even on the tennis court, which was one of the few areas Young managed to conquer him.[2]

Even as a young teenager, Straight could summon an excess of charm and apply it at will. His self-styled emotional retardation seemed even more implausible when he encountered the curvaceous dancer, Margaret Barr, an Australian communist of 24 who came to teach dance at Dartington in 1930.

Straight thought that she was dark, dramatic, bold, and strong. He likened her to a statue by Gaston Lachaise.

Margaret took class twice a week, and Straight, just 14, set out to impress her with his knowledge of communist ideals and by his working hard at exercise routines started by her mentor, Martha Graham. These exertions won Margaret's attention. He proved to be a fair dancer, and she cast him in leading roles she had created. Margaret's epic was a clichéd heroic-workers-versus-the-fat-capitalist-boss saga—typical of that produced in Moscow and Leningrad by order of the state—performed to the Second Symphony of Jean Sibelius. Straight led a large chorus of workers out of poverty and oppression and into a painless new order. The show received a mixed reaction. Left-wing critics invited down from London for the opening night liked it. Admiral Sir Barry Domville, who had two children at Dartington, thought it was evidence that the school was a potential hotbed of Soviet propaganda and influence, and said so. Pom Elmhirst, as left wing as anybody at the Hall, threatened him with a libel suit.

Straight continued for more than a year in his pursuit of Margaret until she relented, and they began a furtive love affair in her cottage. Straight insisted on outlining this in detail to a salivating Michael Young.[3] Margaret and Straight stole away to Dorothy's weekend cottage in Cornwall and read *Lady Chatterly's Lover* aloud. Straight was Mellors, the working class gardener, who had the affair with Connie (Margaret's role), the upper-class wife.

By 1932, the school—under the leadership of W. B. (Bill) Curry—had shed its unstructured attitude to the basics of education. Now any student could move on to higher formal qualification. English had to be taken every year. The fundamentals in arithmetic, languages, history, geography, and science were taught. The principle of enticing VIPs to visit Dartington continued. By now leaders in all walks of life were being invited or were coming on their own volition to examine the experiment. The contrast in visitors was notable. Rabindranath Tagore, always willing to lend his wisdom to his good friend Leonard, was there for some time in 1930. Tagore pleased Dorothy by declaring that the estate grounds had spiritual roots. He claimed that they went back to Christ's time and that the natural springs and water beds had healing properties.

At the other end of the belief spectrum, the Comintern—the international arm of Russia's espionage operations, which ran communists and parties in other countries—was interested in the key British educational institutions for propaganda and recruitment. They had infiltrated Oxford and Cambridge, from where the nation's leaders in every field had come and would come. The Comintern, which had been set up and directed by Leon Trotsky, had a patient long-term view about recruitment. If they could nurture the right kind of idealist—one with the potential to climb into high ranks of politics, intelligence, or the military—from early undergraduate days, it fitted their plans. Even if the recruit was a sleeper (mole)—quietly working in a chosen field for even twenty years before being directed to spy—that was in accord with communist strategy. Marx wrote about it, Lenin articulated it, and Trotsky, then later Stalin (to a telling degree), implemented the long-term plan. It applied as much to industry as it did to espionage. But in the seventy years of communist domination of Russia it was more successful in the latter.

Dartington's radical approach to education even attracted the Soviet ambassador, Ivan Maisky, who was invited to visit the Hall in mid-May 1933. Pom Elmhirst, Straight, Young, and the other students warmly greeted him and his wife.[4] Maisky gave his usual glowing chat about the Soviet Union, stayed two days and nights, and dined with the Elmhirsts. No doubt Straight, then 16, impressed the ambassador with his keen mind. Over dinner on May 14, the estate patriarch, Leonard—a liberal and open-minded humanist—spoke about his visit to Russia in 1930 and how he admired its scientific developments in artificial insemination and in cattle. Leonard told the ambassador how he had tried to introduce such techniques in England, a point that would have raised the ambassador's eyebrows. Ever since Trotsky's instructions soon after the revolution for communists to steal everything they could from the capitalist nations, Soviet representatives abroad had been desperate to "gather" as much data of any kind, including scientific information, for the advancement of "the great Soviet experiment." Leonard's effort on behalf of his more modest experiments at Dartington was a case of plagiarism. It was no worse than what the Soviets were doing.

Dorothy too was open to the superficial Soviet line of propaganda. She espoused "internationalism"—international peace, the breaking down of national barriers, goodwill to all men and women. All Russia's key representatives preached internationalism while planning the undermining of the British system and all other Western democracies, in their various states of decay and fragility in the 1930s.

———— •————

The school itself, at least, became international and fashionable in an eclectic circle of, as Aldous Huxley remarked, the "'odd, the odious, the famous and the fatuous, the accomplished and the artistic." He sent his son Matthew there but was not pleased that he chose carpentry as his main subject. It wasn't sufficient for Matthew to plead that it had been good enough for Christ, so why not him? Bertrand Russell took a liking to the school too and sent along his two children, Kate and John, by his second wife, Dora. Sigmund Freud's architect son, Ernst—a refugee from Nazi Germany—enrolled his three sons. The eldest, Stefan, complained that it lacked games and competition in work. He missed racing to finish his algebra sums.

Among the other talented creatives to put in cameo appearances were the painter Ben Nicholson and his later wife, the sculptor Barbara Hepworth. Victor Gollancz, the publisher and life-long Stalin enthusiast, turned up, as did the controversial Jacob Epstein, another notable sculptor.

Dartington started as "alternative" and took a huge left turn as it developed and departed radically from traditional schooling. Leonard had disliked his own establishment schooling and wanted something different. Dorothy veered away from the norm too as a follower of John Dewey, an American educator and philosopher. He was also one of the founders of the philosophical school of pragmatism, a pioneer in functional psychology, and a representative of the progressive movement in U.S. education, which was only too willing to embrace the far left. Dartington was also a coeducational boarding school, something unheard of in the establishment system. British institutions and conventions were not studied or lauded at Dartington. In other words, this new radical facility was looking for a utopia that would overthrow tradition where learning was a preparation for a vocation. Dartington wanted education to relate to the here and now. For instance, the students would be shown how to tend pigs and clean out their pens, the latter being a solitary lesson for most in what they would never do for the rest of their lives.

Dartington was a state within a state—self-enclosed and self-governing. There was little to relate to in outside communities in rural Devonshire, which was isolated enough as it was. The headmaster, W. B. Curry, was a pacifist whose guru was Bertrand Russell. Curry was cut off from the British establishment and essentially a radical, although he would not have seen his politics in this light. (When World War II broke out, Curry couldn't cope and committed suicide, which in a perverse way meant that he stuck to his anti-war principles.)

The school also had a heady atmosphere of sexual freedom and liberal thought. It absorbed the "in" ideology of Marxism. It looked to a false and idealized vision of the mysterious Soviet Union as a trendsetter for life, society, and political development. Not surprisingly, seven of Straight's final-year class of ten went on to join the Communist Party. Dartington was a wonderful breeding ground for communism despite the fact that only Straight's "lover," Margaret Barr, was the one raw and knowing Communist, although she never taught it. (Barr moved to Australia, where she joined the communist movement there.) She limited her Dartington teaching to dancing and to "hands-on" sex education, with Straight chosen as the only one-on-one student. Straight absorbed the naive communist indoctrination while making the banal claim that he was naturally the creative type, particularly in writing and art, although Dartington offered nothing in these fields.

———•———

In this rarefied atmosphere of alleged political and creative enlightenment and inspiration, in the summer of 1933 Straight, then 16, took the school certificate exam. He failed mathematics, which meant he would have to sit out a year before going on to Cambridge. He thought of himself as a poet/writer but was made to realize that to attain his vague, unshaped dreams of saving the world through revolution, he should comprehend economics, especially at Cambridge. It was reputed to be the most radical university in the country next to the London School of Economics (LSE). In the 1930s, especially the early part of the decade, economics was viewed by the leading left-wing intellectuals as the key to understanding Marxism.

This was made clear to Straight when he used family contacts to meet liberal American jurist Felix Frankfurter, who was living in Oxford in 1933, on sabbatical from his job as professor at the Harvard Law School. The New Dealer and close friend of Franklin Roosevelt suggested he see the leading academic Marxist, Harold Laski, professor of political science at LSE, even though Straight's mediocre exam performances didn't warrant entry there. Laski, who was a regular contributor to *The New Republic*, was impressed enough by Straight to use his influence as chair of its admissions committee in order to get him in.[5]

Straight moved to London and joined his brother Whitney, who had left Cambridge. They rented an "elegant" house in Mayfair from the writer P. G. Wodehouse, who gave a dinner in their honor. He spoke in support of Adolf Hitler and Benito Mussolini.

Whitney showed his eccentric side by having the dining room redone in a luminescent paint, purchasing six big paintings by Ben Nicholson, and buying a monkey, which had its home on the top floor. Soon Whitney, a racing car driver, took off for the European circuit, with his team of mechanics and Maseratis, leaving Straight with a footman to look after him and the monkey. It was a bizarre start for the budding revolutionary, but despite these upper-class trappings, Straight tackled his new life at the LSE with zeal. He become a member of the Communist-controlled Socialist Club, joined in debates, attended radical rallies, and used his wealth to get noticed. He became a card-carrying member of the Communist Party of Great Britain, associating rarely with anyone at the university except like-minded Soviet-supporting Communists, such as Geoffrey Marmont, editor of the radical magazine *The Student Vanguard*, who late in 1934 committed suicide; American Frank Meyer (expelled and deported to the United States in 1934 for his radical activities); Oxford graduate Peter Floud, who became a leading communist intellectual;

Krishna Menon (later the foreign minister of India); Leo Silberman, a German refugee, later murdered in an intelligence operation involving South Africa; Michael Young, who studied law; and many others.

Frank Meyer ran a fund for refugees from Nazi Germany, and Straight donated twenty pounds, which was ten times that raised in seven weeks. It allowed him to ingratiate himself with Meyer, LSE's most militant Communist. Straight got on the LSE hockey team by using his Ford convertible to chauffeur other players to games. These were undergraduate lessons in how he could buy access to what he desired, a practice he would call on as a matter of course to far greater effect for decades to come.

4

CAMBRIDGE CONSOLIDATION

The London School of Economics had given Straight experience at communism beyond Dartington. Cambridge, he hoped, would provide the opportunity to embrace it further, although he was not aware of how that would occur and what form it would take. He began, age 18, at Trinity College, in the autumn of 1934. Its style and atmosphere attracted him from day one.

His digs were in a lodging house on Trumpington Road, and he still had a "gentleman's gentleman"—bequeathed by Whitney—to prepare his daily wash basin and once-a-week bath and to lay out his clothes. Well-scrubbed and nicely attired in shirt, tie, and student's gown, the young freshman set about organizing the best tutor for his purposes in economics. First there was Maurice Dobb, a leading member of the British Communist Party and a "spotter" for the Comintern. Straight moved from him on to a classical economist, Denis Robertson, but he was angling for tuition under Joan Robertson, reputed to be the most brilliant of John Maynard Keynes's disciples. Straight was a big supporter of Keynes. His economics represented a break from the noninterventionist classicists, who thought government interference should be kept at a minimum and who were shocked by Keynes's articles and lectures on the General Theory of Employment, Interest, and Money, which would later (1936) be published in book form. This theory embraced big spending and expansion of government, especially during recession, to escape a slump and to reduce unemployment.

This theory sat well with socialist thinking despite Keynes's not advocating full socialism, which meant government "control of the means of production and exchange." Yet it was acceptable to Marxists, for the time being, given the West's history. It meant an economy following Keynes would be conditioned to big government spending. This was a step toward total government control that could be implemented by a change from something like a New Deal administration in the United States or Labour in the United Kingdom to something more radical.

Keynes's main concepts emerged during the Great Depression when the Western world was looking for solutions to mass unemployment as economies declined and big corporations slugged it out with powerful unions. He was the foremost economic thinker of the era, and Straight wanted to be as close to him as possible. Straight showed his prowess by studying hard and coming top out of two hundred students in the first examination in the Economic Tripos. He was one of only four to gain a first. It was proof on paper of what everyone who encountered him on an intellectual level thought. Here was an articulate youth with an exceptional brain and ambition to match. The door was open to Robertson and Keynes. Straight's diligence ensured he was on the way to matching wits with the most formidable minds on the campus.

His examination success marked him as an academic high-flyer, with money and social position. He was a perfect target for Soviet recruitment, for the odds were that Straight would reach the highest echelons of the profession he chose. What made him even more interesting was the fact that his background meant he could, if willing, be pushed to the top in either the British or U.S. establishment.[1] Yet to be assessed were his temperament and commitment: in KGB terms the extent to which he would be willing to go and how far he could be directed.[2] Arnold Deutsch, the Jewish Austrian Comintern agent, was already aware of him. Yet Straight was still a raw 18-year-old and could not be simply signed up like a football recruit. He had to be tested, indoctrinated, and inspired before being approached by a Comintern representative—a process that took years in peacetime. Once a new agent was in place, Stalin and the Moscow Center would not accept anything short of a lifetime's commitment to their cause, unless he or she were found to be incompetent. A burnt out agent who was of no further use would be pensioned off at a rate commensurate with performance. Rebellion or defection would see the agent marked for assassination.

Straight's initial steps toward a consolidation of his communist links came when two gowned, second-year Trinity students—the bird-like and clever James Klugman and the dark, brooding, and intense John Cornford—came unannounced to his modest lodgings one chilly evening in November 1934. Klugman was from a wealthy Jewish family and had been educated at Gresham's, an old and unconventional public school, as had his friend Donald Maclean, a member of the Cambridge ring of Soviet spies then being formed. Klugman had "spotted" and helped recruit John Cairncross, a brilliant scholarship winner from a poor Glasgow background, to the ring. Cornford was the son of Charles Darwin's granddaughter and a Trinity classics don. He had been a Marxist at Stowe School before he won an open scholarship to Trinity at age 17 in 1932.

The two visitors—the leaders of the Cambridge Communist movement—wanted Straight to become a member of the communist-controlled Cambridge University Socialist Society. The controllers were directed by the British Communist Party, headquartered in King Street, London, which in turn took its orders from Moscow. His name, he was told, had been mentioned to them by comrades at the LSE. Straight had no hesitation in joining; he regarded it as a major turning point in his life.[3] He went to society meetings and discussed issues with Klugman and Cornford, who set about ironing out what they believed to be his naïveté concerning the class struggle. Straight was an eager, willing, and quick student. He was passed from "A" to "B" then "C" contacts—each successive person more important in the secret system—until March 18, 1935, four months after meeting them. Then he moved from being one of fifty avowed communists in the society to one of twelve students in the Trinity College "cell" or communist group. It was his introduction to the clandestine world; the cells kept quiet about their membership.

Cells were split into three groups. The first included those interested in communist ideology. The second worked openly for the party and carried green membership cards. The third group of "moles" was more sinister. They prepared themselves for influential posts in British life and later infiltrated the professions and government. Not even close friends or family were aware of their communist affiliations.

Straight enjoyed the intrigue. It gave him a special thrill to add a hidden layer to his busy, more public applications on campus. The experience drew him closer to unsmiling and dedicated Cornford, whom he admired. Cornford introduced him to Harry Pollitt, the working-class leader of the British Communist Party and a Soviet agent. The two men got on well. Straight began "giving as much money (in cash) as I could without feeling the pinch" to the party.[4] The contributions had the dual effect of linking him more strongly with the British Communist Party's hierarchy and of pleasing Cornford, whom Straight wished to impress.

———— • ————

Several communists, including those at the Soviet Embassy in Kensington Gardens, the British party's headquarters in King Street, and many on the Cambridge campus, were now aware of Straight's potential. Reports filtered back to key recruiter Deutsch, who was orchestrating a trip to Russia for a group of young communists.[5] He made sure Straight was to be included. The three-week trip was meant to give them a sanitized, controlled look at the "workers' paradise." The holiday was also a chance for Russian intelligence to assess each student's suitability for future recruitment. A list was passed on to Trinity's Charles Rycroft (later a distinguished psychiatrist) and John Madge, who organized the students to pay £15 each for the Intourist round-trip by steamer to Leningrad. Also on board the ship in August 1935 were Straight's Dartington chum, Michael Young; Brian Simon (another member of the Trinity cell and a future member of the British Communist Party); Charles Fletcher-Cooke, also at Trinity (then a Union radical, later a Tory member of Parliament); Christopher Mayhew (a future Labor minister and lord) and his friend, Derek Nenk, both of Oxford University; art academic and French tutor at Cambridge Anthony Blunt (a member of the university's growing ring); and his brother Wilfrid, an art teacher. The trip would build Straight's relationship with the tall, lean Anthony Blunt with the cutaway mouth and aloof demeanor.

The two had a link from 1935, the first year they met. They didn't fraternize much after hours. Blunt was a predatory homosexual, and Straight had hopes of being a hunter in the opposite camp. Blunt was a KGB recruiter, and Straight was intrigued by the secret communist milieu at the university, thus making himself available. Straight tried to make out that their backgrounds and circumstances were similar, but he was clutching at straws to explain away the ease of their relationship.

Straight told journalists and family members that Blunt and his brothers were brought up strictly and in an atmosphere of missionary zeal. His father, an Anglican priest, was never close to his sons. He loved sports and was devoted to John Ruskin, the nineteenth-century English writer, critic, and artist who championed the gothic revival movement in architecture and the decorative arts. He had a big influence upon public taste in art in Victorian England. Ruskin inspired opposition to laissez-faire philosophy. By age 13, Blunt hated all sports and loathed Ruskin. By contrast, his mother coddled him. She was linked to aristocracy and in marrying a priest had moved down the social scale.[6]

Straight tried hard to put a fanciful spin on Blunt's communism, blaming it on his family relationships. He supposed that Blunt's mother really loved his father because Blunt Sr. answered to God, a higher calling. Therefore, Straight postulated, Blunt Jr., in yearning for his mother's attention, himself sought a better calling, communism. This intellectual fairyland avoided certain contradictory points. First, Blunt only accepted certain Marxist doctrine, particularly his Stalinist, ridiculous view of art (and even this died away after he left Cambridge). However, when it came to political power linked with international Marxism, he had limited views and left that to the articulation of others, such as Guy Burgess.

Still, Straight connected Blunt's family relationship complexities to his own, especially the lack of a warm connection to his mother and a fatherless past. Straight, too, wanted everyone to believe he was drawn to a bigger ideal that would usurp the father-figure role. Then there was the broader claim of the influence, or lack of influence, of a national identity. Blunt, it was pointed out, spent important years (from ages 5 to 14) in France. This upbringing allegedly led to his having no allegiance to England. This idea may have had some credence if Blunt had been brought up in Germany or Russia, who had opposing ideals to England. But France in ideological terms (let alone geographical) was not that far from the island across the Channel.

Perhaps Straight's biggest stretch in discussions with Blunt's biographer Miranda Carter was an attempt to fill in the dots between negative feelings for England and homosexuality, which in turn found an outlet in underground communism. One problem with this thinking was that homosexuality at the time was an even bigger crime in the Soviet Union than it was in England. Straight liked also Blunt's citing of the dictum of homosexual English novelist E. M. Forster that if he had to choose between betraying his friends and his country, he hoped that he would have the guts to betray his country. Yet this argument went nowhere either, unless that friend was a communist agent. Betraying a fellow spy would see the betrayer on a KGB death list, a more telling test of courage.

Once more, Straight tried to foster parallels with his own background and lack of patriotism, which was again implausible. The United States and the United Kingdom, his two homes, were bound by a democratic ideal that he could not fail to recognize. To suggest that he would drift stateless and find himself in a slipstream toward Russian communism was improbable, even absurd.

Third, Straight suggested that Blunt was bored with religion at home, and with his father in church, not to mention the twice-daily compulsory chapel services at his school, Marlborough. The argument was that once he entered Cambridge, he was open to other religions, primarily art, and presumably then communism, which was an even more unbelievable point than that of the lack-of-a-father-figure. Yet Straight saw more similarities with Blunt to his own case by forever laboring the idea that he had given away religion early in life.

A fourth alleged similarity was their experience and attitude to education. But Dartington had led Straight directly to communism, whereas Blunt had been at an elite school, for which he had contempt. Yet he never lost his support for what it represented—elitism—which he supported, believing that the masses had to be led. It was hardly a position that would have driven him to communism with its alleged ideals of equality. (Although in this respect, he found he had a quaint kinship with the true impact of communism, which developed its own elite and divided from the masses.) This attitude was also unlikely to have driven Blunt to spy and betray his country.

———

The ten tourists bound for Russia were told to pack suitably shabby clothes—no smart cravats, ties, jackets, shirts, trousers, and shoes. It was a novel experience for most of them, who had been used to semiformal wear at least on campus and sometimes smart attire at night. The organizers did not wish the group to stand out for fear of reaction from the proletariat. Better to conform to the impoverished, from whom they would be shielded as much as possible.

The group sailed from London Bridge at the beginning of August. Madge organized ship-board seminars to prepare and lift their expectations. These would distract them from the disturbing start for most concerning the ship's filthy toilets and cramped two-berth cabins where eight of them slept. "Even for some of us who liked close male company," Wilfrid Blunt remarked dryly, "this was a bit much."[7]

Wilfrid slept on deck, where he was further irritated by a Chinese deck-hand who wanted to show him dirty postcards. "What made it worse," he remarked, "was that they were pictures of women."

During the seminars, the lugubrious Blunt sat to one side and listened in silence. He seemed to be weighing the reactions to Madge's comments. One member raised the matter of the toilets. Madge dismissed it as irrelevant and only something that would be brought up by someone from a privileged bourgeois background. The ship's crew, the gullible group were reminded, were performing to a higher ideal. They could hardly be expected to concern themselves with such a triviality.

Straight shared neither Wilfrid's disdain for the ship's conditions nor his reticence. He was excited. He treated the trip as a true pilgrimage. He was overawed by the sight of a large female deckhand, which he took as symbolic of female emancipation and equality in a more advanced society. It was free of class barriers, both social and sexual. Straight took photos of her with his expensive Leica camera, of which she was wary. He was aglow with the thrill of a voyage to utopia, the new society of the Soviet Union.

Blunt and Fletcher-Cooke left the ship for one day to visit a German medieval town on the Baltic coast. Straight snapped them being lowered over the side in a boat.

When they arrived at Leningrad, a member of the party cried: "Freedom at last," then stumbled on a sign ordering them not to walk on the grass verge. Brian Simon enjoyed himself. "They [the Russians] seemed to be pushing ahead all the time," he noted through rose-tinted spectacles. "There was no unemployment. A planned economy seemed to be working."[8]

Charles Fletcher-Cooke was more circumspect. He had been given a grant to study libel law under communism and plenty of contacts. But on arrival he found they had disappeared. He learned later of Stalin's purges.

From the first day in Leningrad they were given the usual tours of monuments to the October Revolution in 1917 and were kept well away from locals. Christopher Mayhew tried to engage them but was shunned. He wondered if it were his bad Russian, but none of the tourists understood that there was real fear in the country. Engagements with foreigners were forbidden. Any breach of this would run the risk of a heavy reprisal.

"They provided a bus [in Leningrad] for us," Lord Young recalled, "and treated us royally." Unlike Rycroft, Mayhew, and Wilfrid Blunt, he found the whole trip "great fun" and kept an enthusiastic diary.[9]

Blunt avoided the dreary factory tours. He took his brother with him to the Hermitage, which took days to view. They both later wrote about it. The Blunts met Lady Muriel Paget, who was working on behalf of the British born "marooned" for one reason or another in Russia. Her flat, Wilfrid noted, had an air of conspiracy, with figures half-glimpsed coming and going.[10]

The tour party took the night train to Moscow and stayed at the Moscow Nova at the corner of Red Square. There seemed to be much going on in the Russian capital. The seventh, and last, International Congress of the Comintern was passing resolutions on forming "popular fronts." These Soviet-controlled organizations aimed at forming links with socialist parties in all Western European countries. The legitimate cover was an effort to defeat fascism. The second, more clandestine objective was to infiltrate non-Communist groups in order to gain control of public opinion throughout Europe.

The group was shown the Metro. Blunt wrote excitedly: "The Metro . . . is perfect in comfort and efficiency, but it has a Parisian chic and one almost expects a top hat to emerge from its doors."

It resembled the neo-Baroque music halls of Europe, but it was limited in size—a fraction of the Paris Metro or the London Underground—and was more of a showpiece for visitors with a limited function for the average Muscovite. The gullible visitors were happily sucked into its apparent opulence. Blunt went further in his appreciation by suggesting that buildings in Moscow and Leningrad were superior to the best in London's Regent Street and London University.

The tourists were very open to accepting the propaganda being thrown at them on their carefully managed tour, especially about increases in production of all industries. If any of the tour noticed anything that indicated backwardness in the economy, or poverty and squalor, they were reminded that the Soviet Union was in the middle of a five-year plan. All would be sorted out in the medium-term.

There was not a whisper of the forced "collectivization"—the brutal takeover of farms throughout Russia and the Ukraine—that led to the deaths of between 15 and 20 million peasants. Not a word was mentioned of the burgeoning state concentration camps—the gulags that in August 1935 controlled five percent of the population for forced labor (and by 1939 would control ten percent).

Despite their gullibility, none failed to notice the restrictions on foreigners. Mayhew was keen to take photos of the Kremlin surrounded by its high walls. "We weren't allowed to take shots," he recalled, "we could do nothing. I got Anthony Blunt to hold my legs while I leant out of the hotel window so that I could take a picture."[11]

Restrictions did not subdue Straight's enthusiasm. At the hotel, he put on some drab clothes and asked Charles Rycroft if he looked like a proletarian. "No," Rycroft replied, "you look like a millionaire pretending to be a proletarian."

Undaunted, Straight later was observed caressing a mantelpiece in the hotel dining room and mumbling: "This is made from Soviet timber, Soviet marble. . . . "

A highlight in Moscow that excited some of the group was a visit to the Home for the Rehabilitation of Prostitutes. The visitors were led to believe that the women at the home had been taken off the street, given psychiatric counseling, and directed toward retraining in factory work. The Intourist guide (a KGB agent), with the help of the home's "manager," babbled on about how the women were guided into seeing the error of their ways by "instruction in the moral values engendered in the State by the teachings of Marx and Lenin."

"It was run by the KGB," Young remembered with a smile sixty-one years after the visit. "We were far more interested in the women themselves than how they were being rehabilitated. They were of all ages, and stunning, very beautiful."

In actuality the KGB controllers of the home were the women's pimps. It was the practice of Russian intelligence since the czars to use prostitutes to gain information. Stalin's era had seen the increased development of the "honey-trap," where women were forced at home and abroad to seduce diplomats, foreign agents, and businessmen into relationships in order to blackmail them. Not every woman at the rehabilitation center was used this way. But by controlling them, the KGB could pick, choose, and direct whom they liked.

Some of the party wanted to take pictures of the women. They pretended to be interested in the home and its inhabitants. But shots were forbidden. Once a photograph was taken, the women pictured could never be used in operations against Westerners.

Again Blunt was able to leave the tourists with his brother and spend time at the Pushkin Museum, but they did attend a shoe factory. They were also entertained by Noel Charles, the acting counselor at the British Embassy. The dinner they attended at the Embassy, without dinner suits, verged on farce.

Over predinner drinks, Wilfrid was asked if he intended to publish any more diaries. "I have not published my diaries," Wilfrid replied tartly.

"Oh," the host replied with a frown.

"Perhaps more poetry?" the hostess inquired, expecting to restore the moment.

"I'm not a poet," Wilfrid responded. "I think you are confusing me with Wilfrid Scawen Blunt, our cousin."

"Oh, yes, of course," the host said, ushering them into dinner.

At the table, while other guests chatted, Charles remarked to Blunt: "I thought your brother appeared somewhat young to be the Blunt we were expecting."

A miffed Wilfrid, aged about 30, overheard the comment and butted in: "Yes, Scawen Blunt would be more than ninety."

"Oh, and how is he?"

"Dead, actually."

"I am sorry."

"I shouldn't be," Wilfrid said. "He has been gone since 1922."[12]

The evening at the embassy seemed even more bizarre in retrospect to Wilfrid when he learned that the butler at the embassy was a Soviet agent.

For a short time in Moscow, Blunt moved more easily with other members of the party, including Straight and Young. There were conversations, but Straight and Young claimed they could remember nothing of substance. Blunt was keen to engage Straight. He liked to cultivate the wealthy for his own purposes and those of his true masters. He had already ingratiated himself at Trinity with Victor Rothschild, the rich scion of the banking family, whose generosity was appreciated for both causes.

Blunt had benefited from the future lord's largess in loaning him money for paintings and his willingness to be involved, for the time being, on the fringes of the Comintern's plans for the United Kingdom. In turn, Blunt had been most supportive when Rothschild was on manslaughter charges (which were later dropped) in 1932 when he killed a cyclist outside Cambridge while speeding in his Bugati.

In Straight's case, the trip was designed to ease Blunt into a relationship with the teenager, which he did to perfection. Straight was impressed by his cultivated air.

He suggested Blunt was remote and mysterious for most of the tour, which was not Wilfrid's perspective, for he was with him almost all the time. Nevertheless, according to Yuri Modin, Blunt slipped away alone one night in Moscow to meet Nikolai Bukharin, the Bolshevik and Marxist theoretician and economist. Guy Burgess, a member of the Cambridge Soviet ring of agents, had met him in Moscow a year earlier.[13] Bukharin, 46, was then editor of *Izvestia*, the official government newspaper, and was busy writing the new Soviet constitution, but his star was in decline following Stalin's purges. He was a prominent member of the Comintern, and as such advised Burgess and Blunt on tactics. Their discussions covered methods in selecting and managing likely new agents. Burgess had been advised to change his image and pretend to be a fascist supporter in order to infiltrate right-wing circles in England. Blunt, who had not been as militant and vocal as his lover Burgess, was told to continue his work as an art historian and stay at Cambridge as long as possible.

Straight would have loved to have met such a romanticized figure as Bukharin, but no one at the Moscow Center was ready to allow it. Nor was he then a fully fledged Soviet agent. Yet he and Young did manage to break away from the rest of the party, albeit for a less exciting assignment—an attempt to arrange an exchange of theater companies. The Jooss Ballet Company, which was at Dartington, wished to come to Russia. Straight and Young went to see if the Vakhtangov Theatre Company, named after its director, would like to visit England. They saw the director's widow and a deal, in French, was struck.

Straight tried to impress Vakhtangov's widow that his stepfather ran an experimental enterprise, with special socialist significance, which was a bit like a Greek city-state. Straight only made Madame Vakhtangov understand that Leonard was a farmer—a Kulak. She was disdainful. Farmers were class enemies of the workers. She inquired about Straight's mother. "He tried again in French to portray Dorothy in her full artistic milieu at Dartington, but could only make her comprehend that she was a farmer's wife," Michael Young recalled. Madame Vakhtagnov frothed about the iniquity of a woman's lot as a Kulak slave. It was the fate to which women were condemned in capitalist societies.[14]

After visiting Moscow, the tiny party went on an arduous two-day train trip to Kharkov and Kiev, while the Blunts stayed behind. Wilfrid continued his art pilgrimage. Anthony met his KGB masters from headquarters at Dzerzhinsky Square for further inspiration and instruction.

Straight, Young, and the others were forced to suffer the airless discomfort of a primitive train. The depressing atmosphere caused them to dwell again on the scatological. The lavatory had a poster for those who could not read. It showed the difference between a peasant, whose aim and method was inadequate for reasonable hygiene, whereas an enlightened worker demonstrated how it should be done. Most of the tourist's fellow passengers were apparently not enlightened, Young recalled.[15]

It was a case of welcome to the real world of the workers' paradise, yet most of these youthful communists were kept ignorant of more pertinent realities, such as the mass arrests going on across the country, the torture, and the general development of the then-worst police state in the world, fascist Germany included.

The Russians encountered on board the train seemed a little primitive and xenophobic as they drank vodka, smoked, and boiled tea. They gave no clues to the blinkered bunch of foreigners of the nation's plight. No communication meant no hints about the Stalinist malaise that had gripped Russia and turned it into a state of fear. An instance of harsh scare tactics and the nation's poverty came when the students were stunned at night to hear gunfire. The train shunted to a halt. The curious travelers hurried to the end of their carriage to see a small group of starving children cowering on the steps. They had stolen on board at a remote stop in the middle of the night. The guards were searching for them. The shots were meant to make them flee the train.

At Kiev such incidents became dim memories in between slumber as the tourists were taken by bus to a hotel, then a horse race meeting. "It was rather like the Melbourne Cup," Young remembered imaginatively. "All the jockeys wore brightly colored caps and there was a big, raucous crowd."

The tour was also taken to a camera factory in Kiev. "The plant was run by a big fat man who happened also to be the headmaster of a school," Young said, putting a benevolent spin on Russian intelligence operations once more. "The school was set up and controlled by the KGB. It was composed of homeless children from the Russian Civil War who had been brought together by the KGB. In the morning they would do their school work, have lunch, and then go to the factory to make cameras."

Without prompting, Young then began to speak of an incident at the factory involving Straight. "Michael Straight had a Leica camera, and the plant manager took a great interest in it," Young said. "He asked Straight if he could take it away and examine it. Straight agreed. It was taken to bits, photographed, put back together and returned."[16] It was a mild form of spontaneous industrial espionage that delighted the 19-year-old Straight.

The group returned to Leningrad and on September 12 joined the merchant vessel *Smolny* for the return trip to London. Also on board was Harry Pollitt, whom Mayhew recalled spent his time making notes and planning a new offensive against fascists. Pollitt's appearance made sure that MI5 scrutinized the names of all who sailed with him. Nancy Cunard, the millionaire London hostess, happened to be on board. She provided light relief for the other travelers by flirting with a black Russian dancer and with Wilfrid Blunt, when both would have preferred each other.

Once back in Cambridge, Blunt reported to Deutsch on the trip and then wrote an art report about it for *The Spectator*. His experience had only confirmed his dedication to communism. This was more than hinted at in his writing, where under Straight's precocious influence, he attempted to apply Marxist theory to aesthetics. Works of art, Straight suggested, could be judged by their historical impact instead of their intrinsic worth.

Blunt continued with this kind of analysis, which damaged his reputation as an art historian and critic. Marxism, rather than a fair aesthetic sense, dominated his judgment. This reached a point of absurdity when he later attacked Picasso, one of the most important artists of the twentieth century, for his painting, *Guernica*, which had been inspired by the horrors of the Spanish Civil War. Blunt, in a deluded critique, dismissed it as "disillusioning . . . it is not an act of public mourning but the expression of a private brain storm, which gives no evidence that Picasso has realized the political significance of Guernica."[17]

Blunt's assessment of the potential recruits on the Russian trip was more acute. His job—and to a lesser degree Burgess's—now was to seduce to a deeper cause those who showed the right temperament and dedication on the tour.

Top of the list was Michael Straight.

5

IN THE RING

Dorothy became worried as Straight entered his second year at Cambridge and took up residence in suite K5 at Trinity College with another communist, Hugh Gordon. His letters and utterances to her waxed between fanaticism and a callousness she had not before detected in her son.

He mentioned to her and others the death of the poet, A. E. Housman, who had lived in the suite above his. Straight and his friends had ignored him as he shuffled down the stairs and into the diminishing autumn sunshine for his daily constitutional walk. They laughed him off when he tapped his cane on the ceiling to noisy K5, where the students reveled below playing loud music on Straight's gramophone. One day the cane stopped tapping.

Straight demonstrated the indifference and arrogance that touched Michael Young at Dartington when he wrote that they did not pause to mourn Housman. The poets of his generation were the ones who moved them. Cambridge was not now a place for old men.[1]

No creative or intellectual writers motivated Straight, although he was inspired, in a limited way, by the ideas behind Keynes's book, *The General Theory of Employment, Interest, and Money*. This book was not published until 1936, but all economics students such as Straight were familiar with everything in it long before this. Keynes had been preaching his views in lectures and papers since he first appeared at King's College in 1909.

The Spanish Civil War, rather than thoughtful documentation, moved Straight's generation. If he and his contemporaries read anything it was supporting magazines such as *The News Chronicle, New Statesman,* and *Palme Dutt's Monthly.*

Straight began misleading his mother and the family, dolling out just enough careful information that would lead her to believe he was a socialist (not a dirty word in 1935) or a liberal working in communist cells, but not out of any conviction. He admitted he was recruiting others to the cause but alleged, disingenuously, that he didn't know what was driving him to do it.

Remarks to his mother and family members demonstrated that he was seeking Dorothy's approval by suggesting that his activities in the communist cells were not carried from a sense of conviction. He even wondered if he was damaging the lives of new people he was drawing into the movement. He claimed, plaintively, he didn't know why he was doing it.[2]

However, by late 1935, he had strong feelings of affection for Cornford, Klugman, and Dobb; they gave him an inexplicable sense of comradeship. But just in case his parents became concerned, he let them know that he had been all evening with Klugman, his brother Whitney's friend Guy Burgess, and an art historian named Anthony Blunt. This sugar-coated his closeness to the two leading Soviet spies and recruiters at the university. The family knew Whitney was a true-blue conservative, and Dorothy and Leonard would have assumed that Burgess was probably conservative and most likely harmless. Blunt's profession would have seemed also to be nonthreatening and on the surface, apolitical.[3]

By this stage Burgess was cultivating right-wing groups and was using Whitney for introductions to influential conservative figures. The views of Whitney, the playboy sports enthusiast, weren't in accord with the rest of the family. He had no time for radical politics. A fellow rich racing-car fanatic, Victor Rothschild, had first introduced Burgess to Whitney in 1934.

Still Dorothy was worried. Implanted in her mind was the 1919 message about Straight from her dead husband Willard via the Maryland medium: he will have a very deep mind and he will have to be taught to meet problems of all kinds. Furthermore, Tagore had spent May and June of 1935 at Dartington and had refreshed her strong spiritual feelings. It was time to dispatch someone like him to her son to assess the situation. She sent her close friend Gerald Heard, a philosopher with spiritual interests.

He wrote to Straight and said he was coming to Cambridge in November. He was invited to lunch. Straight knew his mother's concerns and was a step ahead of her. He invited Cornford to the lunch, having forewarned him of Dorothy's worries. There was small talk for an hour before dictatorship was discussed.[4] Heard tried to draw Cornford out on his Marxist views, but he was evasive. The philosopher asked him if he really believed that any individual was wise enough or good enough to hold unchallenged authority, even for an hour.

Cornford gave an irrelevant light answer to this allusion to Stalin by saying that the communist movement had put the fear of God into the bourgeoisie. Heard reported back to Dorothy, and her fears were lessened. Straight decided he would invite Burgess and Blunt to Dartington as soon as his second-year exams were over so they could allay any further concerns. He knew Burgess, with his capacity for charm and intellectual brilliance, had already become the Rothschild family's financial adviser. (Dorothy was not in need of financial advising, for she was in the process in the winter of 1935–1936 of giving up her American citizenship and creating a tax-free family trust, which incorporated all her American properties, including Westbury and *The New Republic*.) Blunt, too, could impress, not so much with his charm but more with his manners and erudition on art.

Meanwhile on campus, Straight coasted with his studies and threw himself into communist politics, working with Dobb planning demonstrations and parades and even some mornings selling *The Daily Worker*. He jumped on political platforms wherever he could and railed against fascism, one day in demanding sanctions against Italy in response to Mussolini's invasion of Abyssinia, the next in questioning actions of the Nazis in Germany, the following week in opposing Sir Oswald Mosley's British Union of Fascists.

A contemporary of Straight's characterized him at this time in the book *Anthony Blunt, His Lives* by Miranda Carter:

> So compelling was his personality that I was swept along in his wake. He was very left-wing. He was very wealthy. He was English and American.

He was handsome, gifted, versatile, precocious, virile. What on earth was he not? He played squash with one of the Sitwells . . . and he loved the masses. How could any of us resist this dynamic combination of playboy and Sir Galahad? The hunger marchers were made to march through Cambridge and we were to entertain them. I can see now the shuffling column taking a wrong turn in the direction of Midsummer Common . . . and being headed off by our hero, leaping along with all the agility with which he had once danced the part of the Dominant Male Principle in the choreography of Sibelius's second symphony.[5]

Straight's all-encompassing exuberance for matters communist even spilled into his creativity. He wrote and performed jazz songs that celebrated social issues.

Straight immersed himself further in Marxist theory at the newly formed Political Economy Club. He ran up against ridicule from Keynes, who called Marxism "complicated hocus-pocus, the only value of which was muddle-headedness. I read Marx like a detective story, trying to find some clue to an idea in it and not succeeding."

Straight brushed this surprising criticism aside. Keynes was well aware of the mood at Cambridge and that scores of dedicated undergraduates saw Marx as infallible. Perhaps it was an intellectual tease to stimulate minds that had been dulled by blind idolatry. By nature Keynes was an iconoclast whether in dealing with established laissez-faire economists or in his blistering sketches of President Woodrow Wilson, France's President Georges Clemenceau, and Prime Minister Lloyd George at the Versailles Peace Conference after WWI. They exacted excessive reparations from Germany, which Keynes correctly predicted could not be repaid.

Keynes's remarks about Marx did not affect his sympathy for communism in the 1930s. Despite being homosexual, he had married the talented and charming Russian ballerina Lydia Lopokova in 1925, which had given him strong links to certain Soviet citizens, as King's College archival letters, by and to him, testify. These included a brother in Leningrad with whom he corresponded at length and gave his expert analysis on Western economies and leaders—succinct intelligence, which a thousand agents would not have been able to steal or concoct.

When he wasn't at meetings and lectures being stimulated by Keynes, Straight was preparing for debates in the University Union Society where he and Cornford took up the communist cudgel against its conservative members. They ran together for the union committee and were elected. Straight proved a strong debater. It boosted his self-confidence. He saw himself as a future political leader. He discovered (he wrote several decades later) in the autumn of 1935 that he had the power to lead his generation and to take his place with the leaders of England in debates. He was "someone."

Straight knew his family history well and always thought that it was his birthright to lead. His great-grandfather, Henry B. Payne, sought the presidency until he was seventy-seven. His grandfather, William Whitney, was once touted as a candidate for the White House but instead was a force in Democratic Party politics. His father Willard, like Payne and Whitney, had the confidence of the presidents of his time. Straight felt political power and influence was in his blood.

His fever to go further and actually be a famous leader, perhaps prime minister, maybe president, was matched by the barely contained excitement of less public developments. Top of the list was his all-encompassing communist activity with the cells and the private chats with Blunt and Burgess. They had been directed by the Kremlin, and their "controls" Deutsch and Maly, to influence recruits with subtle talk about "old societies being replaced by new" and the historical need for revolution. There was no direct conversation about being recruited for Stalin's purposes. Straight was potentially a willing accessory to the Kremlin's operations, but the timing had to be right for full recruitment.

Blunt and Burgess spoke of the "The International"—the global communist movement, Stalin's tightly controlled subversive operation outside the Soviet Union. The utterances of Blunt and Burgess were sweetly digestible for gullible, and not so gullible, youths.

Straight was attracted to the idea of national boundaries being broken down because it lessened, he thought, the conflict between nations. He made out that he and his fellow communists/students fell for this utopian concept that would lead to some unspecified, ill-defined international government. The other factor was the leader of the Comintern, Bulgarian communist Georgi Dimitrov. Cambridge students were always searching for heroes, and this man seemed to be nearly perfect. He had defended against Nazi accusations during the German Reichstag (Parliament) fire trial of 1933. His position made the International movement even more alluring, although Straight was never under any illusion that the Comintern was anything other than an operation controlled by the Kremlin.

Straight took time off in December 1935 to indulge some passions reserved for those who could afford it: flying and racing cars. He joined Whitney, a superb if daring pilot, in a De Havilland Dragon for a flight to South Africa and its first Grand Prix. Whitney won in his Maserati, and Straight came in third in his sports car, built by Reid Railton around a Hudson engine.

Then it was back to Cambridge. Straight had a girlfriend at Dartington named Herta Thiele, a German dancer about his own age who had replaced the more mature Margaret Barr in his affections. But neither of them gripped his romantic interest like Teresa (Tess) Mayor, with whom he became acquainted in his second year. Tess was a stunning young firebrand, who in her first year—1935–1936—gained a reputation as a fanatical communist. Her Cambridge and literary pedigree was long. Her philosopher and educator father Robin had been a fellow of King's College and a member of the Apostles. Her mother was a playwright. The author F. M. Mayor was an aunt, as was writer Beatrice Webb.

Dark-haired Tess had a wide mouth, which gave her "a slight look of decadence, especially when she had been drinking."[6] Straight likened her to stunning Irish rebel Maude Gonne, the lover of poet and Irish nationalist politician William Butler Yeats. Straight thought Tess had Maude's gaunt nobility and some of her cold fire.

The Comintern became interested in her too. She slipped, like Straight, willingly into the web of Cambridge communists. Soon she was close friends with recruiters Blunt and Burgess. Rothschild was more than infatuated with her, as was Brian Simon, who was also struck by her looks and intellect.

Straight made a bid to seduce her, kicking his fellow lodger out of K5, playing Mozart, and pretending to read Yeats's poems as she arrived for afternoon tea. Perhaps his technique lacked something. He didn't succeed in his quest.[7] The KGB would later prove more dexterous in dealing with her.

Depressed and frustrated by his failure to woo Tess, Straight went to Blunt and told him the sorry story of unrequited love. The Trinity don listened and nodded understandingly. There was a time-honored solution to his problem, Blunt told him. Straight asked what that was.

"Have an affair with someone else."

Straight couldn't think of anyone who would match Tess or even take his mind off her. Blunt suggested there was one suitable woman.

"Who?" Straight wanted to know.

"Barbara Rothschild."[8]

It was well known that Victor and his vivacious, attractive wife Barbara (née Hutchinson, a member of the Bloomsbury literary circle) were not getting on. She was having plenty of affairs (as was he), and their hastily arranged marriage, now just short of two years, was on the rocks. Straight was reluctant. He seemed less than ambivalent toward Victor, whom he once called a "cold, repulsive figure." Straight wasn't sure Barbara was someone with whom he could have an affair, despite her spirited nature and sex appeal. Blunt suggested she was a passionate woman in need of a robust liaison.

Blunt then aroused Barbara's interest by telling her that Straight found her alluring. Barbara wanted a meeting. One night Blunt had a gathering of people for drinks in his elegant rooms in New Court, Trinity's most beautiful court. Not long into the evening, Barbara suggested that she and Straight go for a walk through darkened cloisters. Straight, still in two minds but caught in the daring and risk of the moment, went with her. Once out of sight, she embraced and kissed him. Barbara wanted an affair to begin immediately. Straight was uncertain, not knowing how Victor would react if he found out. Barbara was persistent. Blunt kept encouraging her and tried to push Straight. He was torn between at least some respect for (and fear of) Victor, his relationship with Herta at Dartington, his love for Tess, and the natural lust of a late teenager. At first he felt some debt to Blunt for attempting to help him out in his time of emotional need. But Blunt's motives were far more layered than an altruistic act for a young companion. Apart from wanting Straight obligated to him, Blunt was keen for Rothschild to be more dependent on him too. If Barbara were to have a significant affair, this adulterous relationship could be used to facilitate a divorce. This would put a presumably grateful Rothschild more in his debt.

There was a medium-term aim involved. The Comintern had not recruited the cautious Rothschild, although he was already a subagent, supplying information and help to the cause wherever he could. It wanted Rothschild further enmeshed in its espionage activity. He was the best-equipped and -connected communist supporter in the United Kingdom. As a prominent Cambridge scientist he knew the secret developments in everything from atom physics to biological weaponry. Victor would one day be the Third Lord Rothschild and useful as a member of parliament.

He already had connections through his family, one of the most prominent in the United Kingdom, with the country's great and good, from
Winston Churchill to Clement Atlee.

Blunt, with his feline capacities for tying people up emotionally, was
just the person to draw him in.[9] In Rothschild's case, Blunt was fond of
telling the story of how in 1933 he discovered a painting by Nicolas
Poussin—*Eliza and Rebecca at the Well*—and "borrowed" £300 from Victor to buy it.[10] The money was never repaid (despite the painting being
valued at half a million pounds at the time of Blunt's death in 1983).[11]

Although Blunt and Burgess were in part responsible for maneuvering
both Rothschild and Straight into the Soviet orbit, both their targets
knew what was being done to them. They were both attracted to the
thrill and danger of the secret world. Rothschild managed to create the
image of being outside the ring. He rarely dealt with the KGB directly
and mostly used the manipulative Blunt as the middleman or go-
between. Straight, on the other hand, was a different character altogether
and headed in another direction, albeit for the same cause. His ego and
public ambition were collectively far greater than that of Rothschild, who
preferred to remain behind the scenes in influencing events in the family
tradition. This stretched back to the financing of the British Army at the
Battle of Waterloo and the purchase of the Suez Canal for Prime Minister
Benjamin Disraeli.

At the time Straight told Cornford that he was disturbed by the intensity of his desire to excel in everything he did. In the main this applied to
his communist activities—they dominated his existence. When Straight
became a public figure in the 1980s over his espionage activity, he tried to
portray himself as the immature victim seduced by the wily Blunt. Yet it
was only one part of the equation. Straight was a willing, if unwitting,
player in suggestions that Blunt put to him, such as his handling of
Rothschild's disgruntled wife—an "assignment" that was to go on for
more than a year. Sexual and emotional weapons were part of the good
spy's large armory of deception. Blunt was fostering their development.

Early in 1936, Straight was nominated for the Apostles, the secret society
that had been hijacked by both Marxists and homosexuals in the 1930s.
It included Soviet ring spies Blunt and Burgess, Rothschild, and a long

list of fervent communists, including Alister Watson, Julian Bell, and Hugh Sykes Davies. Straight's nominator was David Champernowne, a member of the family that had sold Dartington to the Elmhirsts. Straight joined on March 8, 1936.

"I was deeply impressed," Straight said in a television interview with BBC's Ludovic Kennedy in 1983. "The Apostles were brilliant, cosmopolitan, and sophisticated." Being brought in as the only undergraduate was a huge honor for him. "I looked up to them. 130 years of intellectual leadership gave them a legendary status."

He was fascinated by the enigmatic Burgess:

> Burgess's comments were always a little hidden. He would never address himself to open questions. He would dodge and weave, and tell an anecdote rather than respond directly. Burgess was a sort of fallen angel. At first sight you saw his fair, curly hair, bright blue eyes and sensuous mouth. When you looked a little closer you noticed the fallen aspects: nicotine-stained fingers; black finger nails; an open fly; unbrushed teeth; a slovenly manner.

Straight was more impressed by Blunt: "Blunt on the contrary was elegant, knowledgeable, wise, kind and nonpolitical, certainly when we met in his rooms."

In the television interview Straight was asked about the homosexuality of Blunt and Burgess. He found Burgess very blatant; Blunt was more discreet. Straight, who was adamant about his heterosexuality, was never propositioned by them, presumably because they realized he was straight. Others, however, fell prey to Blunt's predatory ways, especially at parties in his rooms. In explaining his relationships with them and other homosexuals at Cambridge, Straight said that they were the "most sensitive and aesthetically knowledgeable people" at the university.

———————

In April 1936, Cornford, his girlfriend Margot Heinemann, and her brother Henry invited themselves to Dartington for a week of sun; sailing; golf; and, fittingly, Russian song and dance provided by members of the Chekhov Studio. They strolled arm-in-arm from the hall courtyard to the left of the Great Hall down a narrow path that led toward the ancient stone wall (the Sunny Border) and Tiltyard. Cornford in particular was interested in the latter's history of jousting knights. He was on his best behavior and for once put communist politics aside when in the company of Straight's parents. Straight had presented him at Dartington as a poet rather than a radical.

In mid-June, as planned, Blunt and Burgess were invited to Dartington. They were in full charm mode for Dorothy and Leonard. Burgess even played cricket in the garden with their seven-year-old son Bill. Burgess drank heavily and only when he was inebriated did he talk politics, which was kept general. He was handling well his double game of supporting the fascists while not sounding antiliberal. Instead of turning ugly when drunk, Burgess staggered off to his room to slumber.

Blunt discussed art for hours with Dorothy over tea and in the gardens, which were still a special sight in late spring. They walked and talked in the woodland where three great oaks met. She was impressed with his cultured manner and deep knowledge of all the major art works at Dartington. He touched on her love of Italian Renaissance paintings. He enthralled her with his comprehension of their religious significance and the influence of the Catholic Church over art and literature. Because of her own spirituality, she was left with an impression of a Christian aesthete. Blunt avoided politics and kept to himself his thoughts about Marxist doctrine being the key to great contemporary art.

The overall impact of these two on Dorothy was anodyne. Burgess, with his cherubic mien, seemed to her to have sensible, middle-of-the-road views. Blunt, whose mother was a second cousin to the Earl of Strathmore (his daughter was Lady Elizabeth Bowes-Lyon, the future queen), appeared to have no political hue at all, which befitted his pedigree. This lulled Dorothy into a false sense of calm following her concern over Straight's alarming letters about radical communism and unbridled love for his comrades. If people like these two were Michael's young mentors and friends, there seemed less to worry about.

Later, Straight continued his romance with Herta in Paris. They drove to Spain in July and were there just before a right-wing political figure,

Calvo Sotelo, was murdered with the connivance of the Spanish govern-ment security forces. It was the final outrage for the right and the army, who had been opposed to the "Popular Front" government, elected five months earlier in February. The Popular Front was a coalition of left-wing Republicans and socialists who had combined against Spain's strong fascist elements. All members of the front wanted the state to be a repub-lic, whereas the party's socialists wanted a purely socialist government. Just as socialists feared Spain's fascists, the right—the "Nationalists"—saw the Republican government as a prisoner of the revolutionary left. To a degree each side was correct in its judgment of the other.

Sotelo's assassination sparked an army uprising first in Morocco on July 17, which spread to the garrisons of metropolitan Spain in the fol-lowing days. General Francisco Franco emerged as the main Nationalist leader, and the fascist powers of Italy and Germany supported him. Britain and France opposed Franco and supported the tenuous yet legiti-mate Republican government but decided not to intervene. Stalin, how-ever, decided to get involved with substantial arms supplies to the Republicans. His price for support, as ever, was heavy. He wanted control of the government via the small Spanish Communist Party. Stalin sent his commissars to secure power. They ran into a range of communists—par-ticularly Trotskyites—and socialists who were not going to take orders from Stalin's henchmen. Stalin had a pathological hate and jealousy of Trotsky—Stalin's former comrade from the Russian revolution of 1917. His response was to send professional hit men, experienced assassins such as the notorious George Mink, to Spain to murder any communist who was not in total support of him and his commissars. This would ensure that Trotsky would have no influence in Spain.

Cornford was an early volunteer to fight the fascists. Although a hard-line Stalinist, he was for a short time in Catalonia in the Republican workers' militia fighting alongside mainly Trotskyites. This may have proved dan-gerous in view of Stalin's attitude, but he was struck with a stomach disor-der and forced to return to England for three weeks' recuperation. After this convalescence, he prepared to go back to Spain. Straight took the train with him to London to see Harry Pollitt and to recruit volunteers for a British contingent of communists. Straight saw off the assembled group, which included writers and poets, who were unused to knapsacks containing revolvers. He was touched by Cornford's commitment. This time he was headed not for the Republican-held Catalonia but rather for the Nationalist stronghold of food-producing regions and towns, such as Cordoba. It would be a more dangerous mission—Franco's forces had gained strength in the weeks Cornford had been away.

In September, Straight had his first taste of political campaigning with the Totnes Divisional Labor Party and thrived on the atmosphere. He befriended a working-class couple—the Ramsdens—and together they breathed life into party operations. Despite being just 20 years old, Straight yearned to run against the Conservative candidate but realized that would be impossible unless he renounced his U.S. citizenship, as Whitney had done. He was ambivalent about doing this. Also, there was always the chance that his communist activities at Cambridge would have been drawn to the attention of MI5. Straight was likely to have been considered a security risk. If so, he might be blocked from becoming a British subject.

Yet the urge within him was to test his intellect, oratorical skills, debating talent, and finesse in the public arena. He planned to put an acceptable face on communism, without referring to it as such, for broad voter consumption.

Straight's double life at Cambridge reached a peak at the beginning of his third year in the autumn of 1936. With Cornford in Spain and Klugman in Paris operating as a Soviet agent on assignment, the leadership of the communist movement at the university was his for the asking. But he avoided this important role. It entailed running the college cells, pulling in new recruits, and meeting with the U.K. party bosses in London. There was also the briefing of the sleepers or moles—former students who took jobs in their chosen professions and waited for instructions. He realized the value of all these functions and helped out where he could.

Yet it anchored him too much in the mire of bureaucracy, from which it would be difficult to extricate himself should he be called upon for a secret assignment for the cause. Straight observed his good friend Burgess at close quarters when he dropped all his left-wing links in 1934 after being briefed and instructed by Bukharin in Moscow. Straight was well aware of his work in infiltrating right-wing groups such as the Anglo-German Fellowship, which attracted the Prince of Wales, the future King Edward VIII, and his pro-fascist circle.

The Burgess switch in allegiance was Moscow-directed and supported by Rothschild and his family. The center also wanted intelligence on Nazi plans and fascist thinking in the United Kingdom, Germany, and France. Burgess was paid a £100-a-month retainer by the Rothschilds for this work under the cover of being a financial adviser, which on examination was an unlikely epithet for outrageous Guy. Straight was in regular contact with the flamboyant Apostle, who always came back to Cambridge for the society's meetings. Straight knew of Burgess's sudden change from rabid Marxist to keen fascist and that he was now working for Captain Jack Macnamara, a Nazi-supporting member of parliament. The deception intrigued Straight. Was he ready for a directive to carry out something as challenging? Burgess joked about his homosexual encounters with Macnamara and his Nazi friends. When drunk and high, he would hint to Straight that he had learned some useful intelligence from a Nazi diplomat. The impact of Straight's immersion in Marxist ideals and the romantic notion of the international communist movement made him aware of Burgess's true allegiance no matter what fascist facade he presented to anyone else.

Part of the strategy for Straight to develop a profile away from the university's communist bureaucracy was to intensify his work with the Apostles and the Cambridge Student Union. He ran for the presidency of the union in the autumn of 1936 and became a candidate in a well-defined struggle between communists and conservatives. In a close vote, Straight beat his opponent John Churchill and was made secretary of the union. He would later be vice-president before he took over the presidency, planned for the autumn of 1937.

Straight's infatuation with Tess Mayor did not decline, but he found someone to take his mind off her and his continuing flirtation with Barbara Rothschild. This was pretty Belinda (Bin) Crompton, the young daughter of an American, Catherine, and an English scientist. The family had recently moved to Cambridge to be near Binny's sister, also Catherine, who had married a young Cambridge graduate, Harry Walston. He would later be made a life-peer in Harold Wilson's government. (Catherine—the daughter—would eventually become the mistress of the writer Graham Greene, who had been a communist at Oxford and who would keep links with British and Soviet intelligence services throughout his life. Greene worked for Kim Philby at MI6 during WWII and kept in contact with him after he defected to Russia in 1963.)

The third Crompton sister was Bronte, who would soon marry a communist agent, Gustavo Duran. Duran, a general in the workers' militia during the Spanish Civil War, was brought to Dartington Hall by Michael Young in 1937. Duran met Bronte through Straight and Young. All three sisters became involved with communists, two of whom were agents. Straight and Duran were connected to the expanding Dartington Hall network of communists.

The Crompton family would provide a safe and comfortable environment for Straight, who was enchanted by Binny, just 16 and a student at the Perse School for Girls, should he consider marrying her. While she would be unaware of his secret life, he would be free to air his political views without inviting suspicion. If a partner was unsuitable (as in the case of Barbara Rothschild), even hostile to the cause, it could be disastrous. On the other hand, a sympathetic spouse could be discreet, understanding, and important in a crisis, as Melinda Maclean, wife of the Cambridge ring's Donald, would later prove to be.

6

GRADUATE IN THE ART
OF DECEPTION

John Cornford was shot dead on a rocky ridge while fighting above the Spanish village of Lopera on the Cordoba front on December 28, 1936. News of the just-turned 21-year-old's death took three weeks to reach communist party headquarters in England via the communist network. His close friend Straight had the difficult task of informing relatives and other companions. *The Cambridge Review* said his death was "a bitter loss to English thought as well as to the undergraduates and working-class of England." The literary publication *Granta* spoke of his heroism and noted his demise as "the deepest experience of our lives." A communist party member from London more prosaically referred to Cornford as "the finest type of middle-class comrade." The combined grief and adulation created Cornford as a martyr, which was most useful to the communist cause.

Straight found work for Cornford's wife at Dartington and a home for his son James with the Ramsdens, with whom he had worked on his first campaign a few months earlier at nearby Totnes.

Life went on at Cambridge. Straight still had his duties. He was secretary of the Apostles, whose active membership had shrunk. Apart from

Straight, the only other undergraduate member was Alan Hodgkin, a non-Marxist scientist, who was later awarded a Nobel prize for biophysics. Keynes called Straight for an urgent meeting. New undergraduates were needed. As the youngest Apostle, it was his duty to make recommendations. Straight used the chance to stack the society with communists. He put up John H. Humphrey, John Waterlow, and Gerald Croadsell, who would later be president of the student union. Keynes was aware that their politics were hardly going to diversify the society's discussion papers or create stimulating ideas. But he approved of their nomination. He thought they were all "amateur communists" who would grow out of their undergraduate rapture in revolution and, with guidance, become more mature thinkers, while not abandoning the communist ideal. Their proposed election to the Apostles on March 6, 1937, would now be a formality. A tougher case, however, would be Leo Long. (He was to be recruited by Blunt as a KGB agent at the beginning of WWII.) Blunt and Straight canvassed hard for him. Keynes saw him only as an active Trinity communist and did not object to a proposed election at a meeting on May 15. Straight's fifth success was later to be with Peter Astbury on June 5.

In his final year at Cambridge Straight had engineered an unprecedented hard-line communist control and influence over the university's most important intellectual society (a record of which Straight remained proud). In turn these five members influenced any new election of undergraduates. In the short term, Blunt had a new band of potential KGB agents from which to choose. Even if they rejected him, their experience in the Apostles and their oath of secrecy would mean that they would never betray him. Such maneuvering by Straight and Blunt ensured that until the beginning of WWII, Marxist thought was supreme at one of the two most influential educational institutions in the United Kingdom. The plans of the Comintern and the KGB could not have been more successful in laying a foundation for effective propaganda and influence for decades to come.

In early 1934 Guy Burgess, Kim Philby, and Donald Maclean had been recruited by a key KGB controller, Hungarian ex-priest Theodore Maly. Later that year Burgess recruited Blunt. Now it was time to step up the snaring of new agents. Straight, after the 1935 trip to Russia, was the prime target at Cambridge.

The KGB opened a file on Straight in January 1937 with a memorandum from Maly recommending his recruitment. It proposed that he be used either in England or the United States. Maly wanted more time to make up his mind on the important question of the location for work Straight would carry out.

Maly gave Burgess the mission of further assessing Straight. Burgess's assessment was another January 1937 entry in the Moscow KGB file:

> Michael, whom I have known for several years . . . is one of the leaders of the party at Cambridge. He is the party's spokesman and also a first-class economist. He is an extremely devoted member of the party. . . . Taking into account his family connections, future fortune and capabilities, one must suppose he had a great future, not in the field of politics but in the industrial and trading world. . . . One may reckon he could work on secret work. He is sufficiently devoted for it, though it will be extremely difficult for him to part with his friends and his current activities. . . . [1]

Straight had been so open in his support for communism in England—at the university and with the British party—making a clean break was perceived as difficult. Should, for instance, he be advised to stop giving the *Daily Worker* £1500 a year? Maly approached the party's leader, Harry Pollitt, for approval of the move from open to covert communist work. Pollitt agreed but didn't see why Straight couldn't continue to subsidize the newspaper. (He did continue the subsidy, increasing it to £2000 a year in quarterly installments of £500 clandestinely through KGB agents. His support for conspicuous communism, instead of being "open," would now be secret.)

Burgess's note for Maly added that Straight's "status in the party and his social connections are very significant. The question was whether to begin to act, when and how."

Burgess assigned Straight the code name "Nigel" (later he was called "Nomad"). Maly instructed Burgess to act. He in turn asked Blunt to lure Straight into the espionage net.

In early February 1937 Straight was summoned to Blunt's rooms. He expected him to bring up the continuing matter of the unhappy Barbara Rothschild, who was not satisfied by Straight's flirtations with her. Instead, Blunt rested his long frame languidly in an easy chair and without eyeballing the visitor asked what he planned to do after finishing at Cambridge.[2]

Straight wondered what was coming. Was this it? A proposal for the cause? He was aware of Burgess's fascist group infiltration and of Klugman's assignment in Paris. Cornford had just paid the ultimate sacrifice in Spain. Kim Philby (unbeknownst to Straight) was there now posing as a conservative journalist for *The Times* with Franco's forces and was just beginning to bombard the paper with unsolicited articles, all from the fascist side. Would Blunt and the Moscow Center have a mission for him?

Straight meandered over the possibilities, which were not pressing since he would never have to earn a living. Politics loomed large. He could become British. He spoke of running for parliament for the Plymouth Labour Party, although that constituency was a conservative stronghold. Straight thought he might wait for something more propitious. Blunt remained silent. His visitor stumbled on. He added that he could stay on at Cambridge and write a book about Thomas Malthus, the Cambridge mathematician who influenced Charles Darwin's "survival of the fittest" concept, or David Ricardo, an English economist on whom Marx had drawn.

Straight claimed he had been forced to join the underground network by depression, fascism, and the Spanish Civil War. But he made out he was adrift and vulnerable to being drawn further into the KGB web because he didn't need to work and had not given any deep thought to what he should do.

When he stopped considering the possibilities, Blunt informed him that some of their mutual connections had specific plans for him.[3] Straight was curious to know what. Blunt, at his most solicitous, worried about his chances of becoming naturalized. They discussed the warning by the home secretary Sir John Simon to Keynes that Straight would have to "curtail his political activities if he wished to become British." Simon meant business. In 1934 he had deported another American, Frank Meyer, for his disruptive communist politics at the London School of Economics. Straight in his electioneering at Totnes had already dwelt on the chance that MI5's file on him could be a problem.

It gave him pause. Blunt wondered if the United Kingdom was the best place for him. He painted a bleak picture of England as a declining nation, which had been a refrain of his and of Burgess's ever since they had first discussed international politics. Blunt suggested Straight's talent for politics, oratory, and public speaking as well as his economic training would be better put to use for the cause in the United States, which was destined to play a far larger role in world affairs.

At 20, Straight was too young for politics. However, Blunt was aware that the Moscow Center, and Stalin, considered Straight a possible long-term prospect as a politician in the United States. According to Yuri Modin, the most successful KGB control for the Cambridge ring, Straight was viewed as a potential top politico—a long-term "sleeper" candidate.[4] Stalin and the KGB would always be prepared to support and guide someone for however long it took to get an agent into high office, even the White House. In many ways, Straight was the near-perfect candidate. He was a dedicated communist, now moving into KGB agency, with all the right credentials for high office. Straight had the family background in Washington politics, not to mention Wall Street. He had independent wealth, a near-essential prerequisite, and his skills were outstanding. His height—6'3"—and good looks would win votes too, especially in the United States where Hollywood images were beginning to impinge on the political arena. The politics he espoused would have to be packaged to make them digestible to a majority vote. Yet he could always slip in under the guise of a liberal democrat, who had matured away from his wayward youth in faraway Cambridge, England.

Maly, the Comintern, and the Moscow planners were shrewd. Before Straight could even contemplate a political career, they had decided he should use his economics and family connections to establish something substantial while he was still too young for the hurly-burly of Washington and backroom wheeling and dealing. Why not in his father's old Wall Street firm, J. P. Morgan? Why not, Blunt suggested, become a banker?

This was not what Straight had expected. Blunt was urging him, or directing him, to go into international banking like Willard Straight. But the young Straight had no interest at all in such a profession. When he expressed this, Blunt became adamant. The mutual connections, which Straight was led to believe was the Comintern, and above it, Stalin himself, were giving him an order.[5]

Blunt implied that Moscow had decreed his assignment was to provide them with inside information about Wall Street's plans to dominate the global economy. Blunt had been ordered to help Straight prepare for this mission by breaking his political ties with communists. It was what Burgess, Philby, and others in the movement had done. Now it was his turn.

The pretext or excuse for such a sharp departure, Blunt explained, was his grief at Cornford's death, a plan devised by Burgess as verified in the KGB file on Straight. A note from Burgess to Maly said: "I would not have instructed A.B. (Anthony Blunt) to set to work without consulting you beforehand, if only [Straight's] departure from open work had not been so complicated and we had not had to use immediately a helpful circumstance, the death of John Cornford."

Straight saw the brilliance of this strategy but hated the timing. He was enjoying his life at Cambridge. To break off now would mean he would have to give up the presidency of the union that his recent appointment as secretary guaranteed. He would have to abandon his friends, family, and Dartington. Straight later claimed he felt violated by this directive, partly because it was emotional blackmail after the demise of Cornford. But he supposed the approach to him touched another nerve. He needed to show he could make a significant sacrifice for what he saw as a great cause—communism. He also believed he was strong enough to cope with whatever his recruitment meant, unlike his friend Leslie Humphrey, who fell unconscious with shock when Blunt approached him.

Yet the feeling of being used and abused was unlikely at the time and certainly not immediate. He was compliant, even helpful with a strategy. Straight suggested that to make such a break convincing—especially from open work as a committed, zealous communist—he would have to stage a nervous breakdown, some crisis of belief.

Blunt agreed. Straight thought he could carry off this grand deception, which would go beyond anything he had attempted before. This did not bother him. But he was troubled by the sacrifices required.

Blunt appeared compassionate and understanding. He pointed out that everyone had to give some things for the cause. Cornford was the classic example. He had died for it.

This argument swayed Straight, who remained uncertain about the immediate sacrifices. By the end of the meeting he had agreed to the plan.

Overnight and during the next day he thought about the proposition and returned to Blunt's rooms the next evening to ask him to reconsider. He reiterated that he did not want to become a banker and suggested that it would look phony to anyone who knew him.

Blunt, as ever, was sympathetic and promised to speak to their mutual friend, who was giving the instructions. Straight guessed that this mystery acquaintance was Burgess, who had the cunning to hatch such a bizarre but potentially effective scheme to go into international banking. Straight, though, wasn't stimulated by economics and finance, despite his exam results.

Straight's mentor and hero Keynes may have been obsessed with the machinations of capitalism, yet the student was less concerned. His lack of appreciation of the workings of free markets was due to his certitude, and that of those around him, that capitalism's days were numbered.

A week after being told he was still required to be a banker, Straight was again summoned to Blunt's rooms and was told that Moscow had rejected his appeal. Blunt kept his friendly but authoritative demeanor. He told Straight he would have to return to the United States. Straight again complained about the directive to become a banker. He could not see himself as a smart-suited businessman attending endless boardroom meetings in New York to decide how money was moved around. He seemed to find the concept of being a banker anathema, as did Rothschild at about Straight's age when he was employed in the family bank in 1931. Rothschild summed up banking as "consisting essentially of facilitating the movement of money from point A, where it is, to point B, where it is needed."[6]

Rothschild hated his six months at New Court in the City of London. "It was stuffy, anti-intellectual, moribund, boring, and rather painful," he told anyone else who would listen. The prospect of even a month in such an atmosphere mortified Straight. He told Blunt it ran contrary to everything he had achieved at Cambridge and to which he aspired. Blunt compromised by saying that he would have to go underground in the United States, even if he refused to become a banker. Straight still hoped to put off or stall a move at least until he had completed his studies and activities at Cambridge.

Blunt agreed to make another plea beyond the alleged mutual acquaintance.[7]

Blunt then implied that his appeal would reach Stalin himself.[8]

Yuri Modin, who later was personally assigned to send key information supplied by the Cambridge ring direct to Stalin, Lavrenty Pavlovich Beria, and Vyacheslav Mikhaylovich Molotov, supports this version of events. "The Moscow Center [of the KGB] would have considered the request," he confirmed, "and it would have been sent on to Stalin. He took a strong interest in the key agents we were recruiting in England. Straight was viewed as very important. Apart from the long term plans we had for him, his links right into the White House [via Straight's parents] even at that time assured Stalin's interest in him."[9]

Blunt, and therefore the KGB and Stalin, were aware that Dorothy was a friend of Eleanor Roosevelt, and that Leonard was in contact with President Roosevelt. The two couples often corresponded.[10]

Blunt remained firm that whatever the outcome of Stalin's decision about Straight becoming a banker, he would have to stage his "breakdown" right away and cut his ties with the communist movement. The moment to take advantage of the opportunity presented by Cornford's death was now. If he waited another week, it would be a month since he had heard the sad news from Spain. Blunt again reminded Straight that this was his chance to do great deeds for the cause. Cornford, he reiterated, had shown the way. If he were dedicated to the cause, he should follow that unselfish lead.

Straight made a firm commitment this time to take the assignment. It was February 11, 1937. His first act in his new role was to write family and friends that night. He informed them about the harrowing aftermath of Cornford's death when he told the family.

Straight then deepened his deception of the family by feigning a break with communism. His desire for the cause had, he alleged, been killed off with the death of Cornford.

Straight and Blunt devised the breakdown plan, which would entail demonstration of Straight's emotional crisis. He had regarded himself as an actor ever since his roles in Margaret Barr's dance theater productions at Dartington, and now he had a great challenge. He created quarrels with fellow communists and members of the Socialist Club, and did not turn up for meetings of the Trinity cell. He alienated his supporters in the union by advising them to vote for John Simonds (who had just recently joined the socialist society after starting out as a conservative) the following autumn—the time he himself was set to take over as president. Straight ridiculed the immaturity of union debates. Even photographs of him taken at the time of his fraud are different from those taken in the years before and after the fabricated crisis. They show him looking downcast and surly.[11]

Straight continued his act of depression.[12] The performances were daily, long-running, and multifaceted. His close communist friends came to K5 and tried to give him solace, but he remained listless, angry, and uncommunicative. Only one of his friends and a recruit to the Apostles, John H. Humphrey, guessed what was happening. He confided to Straight that Blunt had tried to set him a mission as well. Humphrey refused to go underground. He wasn't as dedicated as Straight. He finished by telling him he knew what was going on.[13] Straight responded by saying he didn't know what he was talking about.

In those initial staged weeks, he tried to have a real nervous breakdown, which would have taken method acting to new depths, but didn't succeed. Part of the strategy was to break some of his old friendships with communists and make new friends with people regardless of their political ties. One was John Simonds, by then middle of the road politically and heading hard-left. Another was left-winger Bernard Knox, who had been wounded fighting in Spain. A hint of his big lie came in his organized pursuit of Bin Crompton, which needed confidence and finesse. But as she was at school and not on the Cambridge campus, Straight could be himself while alone with her, without fear of being detected for his duplicity. (He also took time during this period of depression to flirt with 14-year-old Margot Fonteyn after a Royal Ballet performance in Cambridge.)

On March 18, 1937, Blunt, accompanied by a friend (Michael Eden), visited Dartington and had a long, private chat with Dorothy about Straight's condition. He reassured her that he was recovering well and would pull through. Dorothy spoke of her son's emptiness and grief. Blunt sympathized and promised to watch over him.[14]

By the end of the Easter term, Straight was talking about missing the finals because of his breakdown. He was so far behind in his work that there didn't seem much point in attending, he told his parents. He also announced that he wanted to return to the United States to live.

Dorothy and Leonard surprised him by agreeing with the latter. But they were unhappy with his decision not to take his finals and cited examples of relatives who had squandered opportunities.[15] Straight was taken aback by the vehemence of their response, but his parents were expressing normal concerns for a distracted son. If anything, Leonard and Dorothy were being both understanding and encouraging, given that they had been very concerned about his condition. Their response shook Straight, not because they were cold-hearted, but more because he may have thought that they had not been convinced by his histrionics. Yet he was not about to tell them the real reason behind his wish to leave Cambridge early. It left him cornered. He gave in and agreed to return to the university to take his final exams.

———— • ————

Burgess and Brian Simon (who was Blunt's lover, according to Straight) joined Blunt at Dartington for a drunken night a few days after he had arrived. Dorothy took Blunt aside and told him about her concern for her son. She wanted Blunt to look after him. Straight took the visitors to a rehearsal of the resident Jooss Ballet, which was too much for Burgess. On previous visits he had kept himself in check. The sight of the male dancers caused him to leer and make suggestive comments. Straight and Blunt were horrified should Dorothy get an inkling of his lascivious side. Burgess imbibed too much whisky and had to be removed from the rehearsal.[16]

When the three visitors had departed, Straight spoke more about his plans to live in the United States and to carve out a career in politics. Dorothy responded by saying that if that's what he wanted, why not start from the top and get some advice? Leonard suggested he would write to President Roosevelt and make an appointment to see him, while Dorothy wrote to his wife, Eleanor.

When the appointments were made, Straight accompanied Leonard on the trip to New York and Washington in late March 1937. Straight wanted to assess the home he had not seen for more than a decade and attempt to set up a job that would please his new, secret masters in Moscow. If Roosevelt, the most powerful man in the United States, could assist, all the better.

Leonard showed his humility in a March 31 letter to Dorothy:

I had terribly cold feet as the boat reached Quarantine—knew I couldn't measure up, felt no one would want me, that I was just a four flusher, putting one over, barging in on the White House just as an exercise for my sudden self conceit. . . . [17]

Leonard, in keeping with his unselfish nature, was putting himself out for his stepson as he always had done. He had been content to correspond over a range of subjects with Roosevelt, particularly agricultural matters. He and Dorothy had dined with the Roosevelts at the White House in 1933, but this was the first time he had taken advantage of this most important of contacts.

Dorothy's old retainers were waiting at the New York docks for them, and they were hurried through customs and chauffeured to Old Westbury. The staff lined up to greet them. Straight received a special wave from Jimmy Lee, the head gardener's second son, his old playmate. They were now men, but education, privilege, and money had separated them even further since those early days. Straight was like an English gentleman now to Jimmy, with a cultured accent and nearly a Cambridge degree behind him. And Jimmy? He was content to wear his overalls and work in the garden. But he had plans. He had been inspired by the news film about J. Edgar Hoover's "G-Men" at the FBI. Jimmy dreamt of one day working for that glamorized institution.

Leonard and Straight had tea at the White House with the Roosevelts. Leonard raised Straight's plans to live in the United States and to look for a job. Straight mentioned that he had studied under Keynes and that they were close friends. The president was impressed, for his New Deal programs had been influenced by the economist's theories. Keynes's name would open every door in government. Mindful of Leonard's interests, Eleanor Roosevelt suggested that Straight should have an agricultural post. Straight didn't respond to this. It was useless to him and his new KGB masters. Straight wondered if it were possible for him to have a job as one of the president's personal secretaries. Roosevelt, perhaps uncomfortable with this brash proposal, came up with something else—at a distance from the Oval Office. In his forthright, avuncular manner, he looked over his spectacles and told Straight that the National Resources Planning Board (NRPB)—a central planning group—was the place for him.

Straight found that not just Keynes's name helped around Washington. The president's recommendation went even further. The NRPB's director, Charles Merriam, was eager to employ him. Straight was thankful but wished to avoid departments that would not help his secret work. Blunt had told him to get a job at the State Department or even the White House. Innocuous planning boards had little access to information useful to the Kremlin.

Straight used the family magazine, *The New Republic,* to assist in his search. Its Washington correspondent, Jonathan Mitchell, took him on a tour of the New Deal agencies. Straight became imbued with a new sense of power. His family and contacts would give him a running start. The decision to work for the cause in the United States was taking on new dimensions.

On the trip home, Straight wrote a report for Blunt on his trip, which was sent on to Maly. This covered his meetings with the Roosevelts and all the other contacts, along with an assessment of his employment prospects. Straight was upbeat and always keen to impress his new masters. He thought he had a chance of employment at the treasury or the Federal Reserve Board, where "possibilities were great because of the influence of Roosevelt. . . . Treasury has great significance. Its head is Henry Morgenthau, who knows my parents well."[18]

Straight mentioned his proposal to be Roosevelt's personal secretary, a position which would have had his new masters salivating, but also told them that the president suggested the NRPB, putting a quaint spin on it: "Roosevelt himself picked out this job for me as the most important among those I could get and where I could be close to him." Apart from dropping Morgenthau's name, Straight also let Moscow know that he had access to Harry Hopkins, Roosevelt's closest aide, and Henry Wallace, the secretary of agriculture, which meant he "could easily find any job."

Maly's response through Blunt was to show concern that his American connections might think he was still a communist.

Straight responded that all his American relatives had treated him negatively because they were under the impression that he fought in Spain. The Moscow KGB archive shows that Straight wrote cynically:

Now I try to dispel this impression by the following means: a. I use brilliantine and keep my nails clean; b. by ardent speeches against the reds in some places; in other places I present myself as a radical.[19]

Straight, being sure to impress his foreign bosses, let them know his income was $50,000 annually. It would rise to $75,000 inside the next year.

Straight also informed Blunt that he had decided to return to Cambridge to take his exams. Blunt arranged with the Trinity bursar for rooms in New Court close to his, so he could keep an eye on his charge, not for Dorothy's sake, but rather for his own. Blunt wanted Straight to stick to his commitment concerning his U.S. plans. However, he saw the wisdom in letting him get through his finals, especially as the charade of mental illness had worked so well. A recovery from exams in June would not stretch credulity on or off campus.

When Straight returned, Blunt called him to his rooms for another private discussion, which was designed to keep the pressure on Straight, just in case he was considering reneging on his work for Moscow.

Blunt told him that Stalin had reviewed his case. Straight had to go ahead with the U.S. underground assignment. He had experienced the success of his deception and those heady times at the White House. He now had no choice but to go on with the plan.

———— • ————

Dorothy's concern for her son was still strong, despite his apparent recovery. She also asked Keynes to look after her son; Keynes obliged. He liked Straight's mind, looks, and politics. They had become good friends, despite their gap in experience and age (Keynes was 53). He invited Straight to his rooms for discussions about the Apostles. Straight continued to pretend he was depressed, using any reference to Spain, which was on the front page daily, or Cornford, as a stimulus for sudden melancholy. He did manage to discuss the last-minute details for the upcoming elections of Long and Astbury to the Apostles, which Keynes endorsed.

Straight kept the subtle, careful deception over his parents, telling them he was in a mess politically, emotionally, and academically. However, Keynes had taken him under his wing. They were going to the ballet and dining together afterward. Straight began chasing a 16-year-old American girl—Binny Crompton. Keeping the appearance of an honorable courtship, he told the family that he was uncomfortable when she began to respond.[20]

———— • ————

Despite his pulling away from Cambridge communist activity in 1937, Straight was still to have residual influence, which he and Tess Mayor regarded as of vital importance for the rest of their lives. Straight had a certain amount of control of the university's underground activity for a limited time. Tess was put up (knowingly) for membership of the cell in the Cambridge colleges for women: Newnham/Girton. Straight vetoed the proposal.[21]

This meant that Tess would be free for recruitment for the KGB via Blunt in 1938. Straight would have known about her recruitment, just as he did about all the agents. It was very much his business.[22]

Straight then unwittingly played a more than useful part in facilitating the very effective KGB spying team of Victor Rothschild and Tess Mayor (who married in 1946). First Straight's (Blunt-directed) dalliance with Barbara Rothschild (without Victor's connivance) helped cause the breakdown of that unsuccessful alliance with Victor. They divorced at the end of WWII. Tess and Victor became a fully fledged item—both as lovers and as double agents for the KGB—inside MI5 during the war, when she worked as his assistant. Had Tess joined the Cambridge communist movement in 1937, it is doubtful she would ever have been recruited by Soviet intelligence. Seven intelligence agencies (in the United Kingdom, France, the United States, and Russia) claimed that this couple, code named Rosa and Jack, were Soviet agents. They included MI5's Arthur Martin and Peter Wright (who refused to believe it at first, but later concluded it was correct), Soviet defector Anatoli Golitsyn, and the CIA's James Angleton. Tess's KGB agency explained the conundrum posed by Yuri Modin in my book *The Fifth Man*. How could five agents actually be six—"as with the three musketeers, who were four"? The answer is that Victor and Tess from 1939 until Victor's death in 1990 were considered as a team and therefore as "one." The fifth man, then, was Victor and Tess.

Straight claimed Simon and Blunt were lovers in 1937, and that Simon and Tess were lovers in 1939. He also gave nothing away by making the unsurprising admission to MI5 (during its interrogation of him in 1967) that Simon knew all about the KGB roles of Blunt and Burgess, despite telling Blunt's biographer Miranda Carter otherwise. Straight also gave nothing away by telling MI5 that Simon had happily taken on his job of assistant (KGB) talent spotter. He also gave a broad hint that Tess was under KGB control when acting as secretary to Lord Philip Noel-Baker, a Labor Government Minister, but when challenged by MI5 for a more direct statement, backed off as if he were just putting up a proposition. This was a direct contradiction to the ramifications of him telling MI5 that he vetoed Tess joining the Cambridge underground communist women's college cell. Straight couldn't resist attempts at misinformation.[23]

Straight staged enough of a recovery from his fake nervous breakdown in May 1937 to lobby left-wing support in the union for Haile Selassie, Ethiopia's emperor-in-exile, who had been pushed out of power by Mussolini's fascists. Selassie was invited to the Cambridge Union at the end of the month, causing a split in the union, for it signified communist ascendancy. Selassie's visit was marked by a student who climbed the tall spire of King's College and fixed an Ethiopian flag to it. Straight put aside his depression, stood at the oak dispatch box in the customary union officer's white tie and tails, scanned the rows of undergraduates jammed into the Victorian debating chamber's leather benches, and then delivered a speech of welcome. It had been translated into impeccable French by Blunt.

The diminutive, bearded Selassie, befitting his imperial status, deigned not to respond beyond a few words in his reedy voice. Instead, he presented the union with a gold-framed photograph of himself. Then with a regal grin, he signed the minute book and bowed. He straightened to see glowing red rockets' flickering light through the chamber's Gothic windows.

The fireworks came from Rothschild's home, Merton Hall, on the other side of the Cam River. Barbara was throwing a lavish party for Straight and his fellow union officers. Straight and others jumped in his sports car and roared over Magdalene bridge to the party. It was a warm spring night and a vodka and caviar supper was being served on the terrace. A Hungarian band was in the floodlit garden. Rothschild was there, cool as ever, smoking his favorite Balkan Soubranie cigarettes and playing duets with jazz pianist Cab Calloway. Straight was greeted with a sensual kiss from the radiant Barbara, who had been informed by Blunt that Straight was still infatuated with her.

They had had a few assignations during the past year. One had been by the Cam on a balmy spring night. They were passionate under a blanket after a dizzying champagne picnic. Barbara returned home, got into bed, and by candlelight started reading passionate poems by the sixteenth-century English poet John Donne, which Straight had given her. Rothschild came home and flew into a jealous rage. The scam had been set up by Blunt, who was still trying to help Rothschild facilitate a separation. Barbara later told Straight about her husband's behavior and Straight did his best to avoid both of them. However, he was curious to find that Rothschild's demeanor toward him remained the same. Blunt wondered why Straight had stopped seeing her and urged him to meet again because she may have been suicidal.[24]

Straight agreed to meet her again, but in London. He feared a confrontation with Rothschild.

Now, at her party for him, Barbara and Straight were near each other once more; it was unnerving for him. Barbara met Straight on a secluded garden seat. After an hour, Straight became concerned that her husband would stop his jazz playing and come looking for them. He departed before any speeches in his honor were made. Barbara was left to explain that Straight was exhausted after the union meeting and that he must study for his finals. Blunt was not so squeamish; he got drunk. During the evening he was discovered by Charles Fletcher-Cooke (who had been on the 1935 boat trip to Russia) in the garden in passionate embrace, first with a male undergraduate, then later with the wife of a don from Jesus College.[25]

Next morning, the hung over union members met for a photograph with Selassie, which Straight would treasure for the rest of his life. Many of the students in it were fellow communists, including Leo Long; Gerald Croasdell; Hugh Gordon; Leslie Humphrey; Peter Astbury; Jakes Ewer; Pieter Keuneman, who became leader of the opposition communist party of Ceylon; and S. M. Kumaramangalam, who was sent to prison as a communist in India. John Simonds and Maurice Dobb also featured, as did Abba Eban, later deputy prime minister but then foreign minister of Israel; Fletcher-Cooke; and Philip Noel-Baker, who would start the World Disarmament Campaign.

Blunt was conspicuous for his absence. He was stricken with a stinging hangover and, not surprisingly, fatigue. Yet he recovered in time to give Straight some final tips about how he might approach the cramming for his desperate bid to succeed in those final exams. Straight realized he could not squeeze a year into five weeks. He compiled a list of all the questions that had been given in the final examinations of the economic tripos (Honors) over the previous decade and then made a calculated guess as to which would be most likely to come up again. He studied responses to these and was confident enough to tell his family that his examiner was a political enemy of his. This, Straight figured, would work in his favor because the examiner would go out of his way to be fair. He did, giving Straight first-class honors in economics. His "miraculous" recovery from a nervous breakdown pleased his parents. They were now even more content to support his plan to find a career in the United States.[26]

<hr />

On June 9, Maly sent a memo to Moscow about his instruction to Straight to join the U.S. National Resources Board, without explaining that Straight himself had been recommended to it by Roosevelt. Maly considered Straight immature politically in the sense that he was not yet fully indoctrinated. He needed to be pumped with more ideology. The astute Maly also was unsure about the capacity of the U.S.-based KGB agent (with the anglicized pseudonym Michael Green) to handle Straight. Without saying it, Maly would have been thinking that only someone with his (Maly's) intellectual depth and background could meet Straight's high-minded expectations about a "new world order."

<hr />

Blunt and Straight met for the last time in Blunt's rooms in New Court in mid-June 1937. He had cleared his desks and was disgruntled. The university would not be reinstating Blunt as a don. It meant that both were prematurely leaving an environment they loved. The Moscow Center had wanted Blunt to stay on recruiting the best and brightest for the cause. But his stubbornness in repeating in almost all his art analysis the communist dictum that art had to be socially useful (and then attempting to reinforce it with nonsensical deductions) had upset too many of the established academic hierarchy.

Blunt, however, still had to carry on as a recruiter for Burgess and Maly and his ultimate employers in Moscow. It was time for Straight to be introduced to the 32-year-old KGB control Arnold Deutsch. Straight, it was hoped, was ready for his first step into the demimonde of espionage for the cause.

Straight was nervous at the prospect of meeting his first major KGB contact. Blunt added to the drama by explaining that strict methods had to be followed before they made a rendezvous with Deutsch. A few days later they went to London, Straight in his car and Blunt by train.

Straight was instructed to make his way to a location on Oxford Street mid-morning. On the way, he felt excited, but there was also a sense of foreboding.[27] What if he were followed and apprehended? Blunt had assured him that nothing would happen if they followed detailed procedures to avoid detection. Even if they were tailed, Blunt had explained, they were not giving the Russian anything, nor were they receiving written information. A meeting as such was not against the law; in any case, Blunt would have a cover story should anything happen. Despite his mentor's calm, Straight could not alleviate the fear of the unknown as he picked up Blunt near Oxford Circus.

It was crowded and a stiflingly hot day. Traffic was heavy, which was just what Blunt wanted. It would be more difficult to follow them. Straight was ordered on a circuitous route. Blunt monitored the side- and rearview mirrors, watching for "watchers"—the name for MI5 agents assigned to follow suspects. Blunt was aware that his art criticisms and communist sympathies may have been drawn to the attention of British intelligence. He could be tailed for a while just to see what his movements were now that his Cambridge days were over.

Straight was a more prominent target, especially with his recent support for Selassie. He had been marked down as a radical student to be watched since his LSE days. His postuniversity activities in England would most likely also be of interest to British intelligence. It was, in fact, a reason for Moscow's pushing Straight to the United States.

After an hour's drive around the roads of London's western outskirts, they stopped at a roadhouse on the Great West Road where Heathrow is now located. They parked the car and were met by the solidly built, dark-haired Deutsch. He had become the senior controller for the Cambridge ring after Theodore Maly had been ordered back to Moscow during Stalin's purges.

Deutsch was introduced to Straight as "George."[28] He suggested they go for a swim at a nearby public pool and have a drink and talk. Blunt and Straight sat in silence and watched as "George" went swimming in the crowded pool. After drying off his ample frame, he ordered beers and lit up a cigarette.

He looked Straight up and down. He did not seem interested as Blunt explained that Straight would be going to the United States. He would be working in Washington, D.C., George was informed. His disinterest may have been because the new recruit would not be under his control. George was not like the urbane, cultured Hungarian Maly. His manner was gruff, and he did not choose to reason with his agents. He gave orders and expected results.

The agent complained about the heat and jumped in the pool again while the others waited. Later George started explaining tradecraft—the way an agent should behave when making contact, phoning, keeping appointments, avoiding a tail, and so on. Blunt would later write a book on procedures for British intelligence, which would also be used by their Russian counterparts. He had already been through the basics with the new recruit. Straight's attitude had moved from awe to surprise and disappointment at being treated in such an offhand and patronizing manner.

He left the meeting with Blunt feeling let down. This agent had not been the expected urbane individual full of verve and ideals. Straight thought he seemed more like a small-time smuggling operator than a representative of a new international order.[29] Blunt sensed his disappointment at the time and explained that the meeting was an administrative detail—a formality to establish contact and to see that the new recruit was acceptable. A brief assessment would be recorded, passed back to Moscow, and placed in a Russian intelligence vault.

That assessment from Deutsch demonstrated that they had a mutual loathing for each other. The agent wrote:

[Straight] differs very much from people we have dealt with before. He is a typical American, a man of wide-ranging enterprise, who thinks he can do everything for himself. . . . He is full of enthusiasm, well-read, very intelligent, and a perfect student. He wants to do much for us, and, of course has all possibilities for this. . . . But he also gives the impression of being a dilettante, a young guy who has everything he wants, more money than he can spend, and therefore in part who has a restless conscience. . . . I think, under experienced guidance, he could achieve a lot. However, he needs to be educated and to have control over his personal life. It is precisely contact with people in his future profession which may turn out dangerous for him. So far, he has been an active member of the party and constantly surrounded by his friends.[30]

Straight gave Deutsch £500 for the *Daily Worker*, and for Deutsch this confirmed his needing "education" in order to be a fully fledged underground agent. Straight was still clinging to his former interests in open support for communism.

"In my opinion," Deutsch wrote in one of his two reports on Straight, "it is very important to take this money from him, since in his eyes, it speaks to his contract with the party which is very important to him."[31]

After their final meeting in August (the day before Straight left for the United States), there was a report from Deutsch that noted his lack of experience and his sometimes-exhibition of a childlike romanticism. "He thinks he is working for the Comintern [now on the way to being completely destroyed by Stalin] and he must be left in this delusion for a while."

Straight seemed to contradict Deutsch's assessment of his naïveté and beliefs. Before Straight's recruitment, Blunt had drawn him in with the use of the term "the internationale,"[32] but as explained earlier, Straight claimed to be aware that the Comintern was tightly controlled by Stalin.

For his part, Blunt kept on with the pretense that Straight was joining something grand and international. He reassured Straight that "George" was part of an elaborate, most important scheme in historical terms, which would gradually be revealed to him. Straight seemed to accept the explanation, even though he knew that the Comintern and its grandiose ideological aims were pipe dreams. The only explanation is that he would go along with the façade because he wanted communism to rule the world, no matter by what means. Deutsch was his first foreign clandestine contact after recruitment. Even if he was as disappointed in him as he claimed, he would carry on.

Blunt later briefed Straight about his return to the United States. A new Russian contact would be arranged there as soon as possible, but he would be on his own until then. Anything he discovered of interest to Moscow should be sent by mail (via a mutual friend) back to Blunt, who would have it transmitted to the Moscow Center.

Blunt asked him for something—a document—he could do without. Straight gave him a drawing done in blue ink by his girlfriend Bin. Blunt tore it in two, and handed one half back. The other half, he informed Straight, would be given to him by the New York KGB agent who contacted him.[33]

PART TWO

OUR MAN IN WASHINGTON

7

GREEN SPY

Straight arrived in the United States early in August 1937 when communist influence was peaking after nearly two decades of growth. The country was in the middle of industrial strife that Moscow hoped would lay the groundwork for the eventual rise and ascendancy of the Communist Party of the United States—CPUSA. The United States had embraced Roosevelt's New Deal, which had employed Keynesian economics to expand public works in an effort to decrease unemployment and stimulate growth after the Great Depression, which lingered long into the 1930s. The CPUSA had set up a series of revolutionary trade unions to contest the control of workers with the long-established American Federation of Labor (AFL). It was using people and money to increase its influence over the Congress of Industrial Organizations (CIO), which had been newly formed by John L. Lewis. The CIO was pushing to organize mass production industries such as automobiles, steel, and electrical machinery. One-quarter of the CIO's members were in unions led by communists.

Straight's return also coincided with communist infiltration of dozens of U.S. organizations dealing with every aspect of American life. Prominent writers, artists, and intellectuals flocked to communist-dominated groups such as the League of American Writers and the American League against War and Fascism. The American Youth Congress, a federation of the largest youth groups in the United States, was communist-led. The CPUSA was raising substantial money in Hollywood, capitalizing on its role in sending several thousand young men to fight for the Spanish Republicans in the Civil War.

Communists impressed some liberals in the United States with their support for Roosevelt and antifascism. So-called Popular Front alliances of liberals and communists were becoming political forces in elections. In New York, such a coalition took control of that state's American Labor Party, which held the balance of power between Republicans and Democrats. In Minnesota, a Popular Front faction took over the Farmer-Labor Party, which dominated Minnesota politics in the 1930s. Communists were also a force in Washington state, California, Wisconsin, and Michigan.

In 1937, nearly 100,000 Americans were CPUSA members. Straight felt inspired that he would be in the vanguard of revolution in the United States. Not yet 21, he could see himself prominent—a leader—in the rising support for the cause in his home country. He began to agree with Blunt's argument: the United States was a better place for him.

His first act was to visit Westbury. He had declared his love to Binny at the expense of his German dancer friend Herta Thiele. Straight hoped Binny would join him at his beautiful old home. He wanted to get on with his private life and establish a family, which would then allow him to follow his dreams, as well as instructions from Moscow.

John Simonds had come with him across the Atlantic and planned to spend two months in the United States traveling with Straight. Simonds, partly under Straight's considerable influence, had dumped his conservatism. After the U.S. tour, he would be ready to take the next step and embrace communism.

Straight bought a red convertible in New York, and he and Simonds drove north to the Adirondack Mountains for a fishing holiday before motoring on to Detroit, Michigan, to meet up with Roger Baldwin, the 53-year-old lawyer running the American Civil Liberties Union (ACLU). Straight's communist contacts had linked him up with Baldwin. Straight had offered to chauffeur him on a tour of the centers of unrest in the industrial Midwest and to "help while he makes speeches to local civil liberties groups," if he would let him and Simonds come with him. Baldwin agreed. His union would turn up wherever there was trouble to add comrade support to the communist-controlled unions of the CIO, which was fighting to unionize the big manufacturing plants in such industries as steel and automobiles. The communist aim was first to unionize, then to disrupt in order to weaken the United States' industrial might. The long-term aim (a decade or more) was to have the union and political base so powerful that a communist revolution would be possible.

This was Straight's first observance of communist agitation and disruption in the United States. Later, he would make an art form of latching on to a respectable "liberal" front such as the ACLU and presenting himself as a concerned libertarian.

The trip was a hands-on education for Straight in political conflict in the United States and gave him an idea of the possibilities for communist advance. It looked more than promising. He was inspired in Pittsburgh when Baldwin introduced him to Philip Murray, the president of the United Steel Workers, and the CIO's Lewis. Murray was a tough-talking, aggressive figure. He was willing to use violence to gain any form of union base in the big mills. This pleased the communists, although Murray was always uneasy with their support. In Chicago, steel workers had been killed in a fight with company security police.

In Terre Haute, martial law had been invoked for three months as the result of a labor dispute. Baldwin and Straight visited the local prison where 150 strikers were being held. Straight learned of bombings by unions to intimidate companies that had not unionized.

The final leg of the tour was through New York. Straight celebrated his 21st birthday on September 1, 1937, en route as Baldwin delivered militant speeches at meetings in several cities. He attacked corporations for violating their employees' civil rights; Straight was impressed and stimulated. At the end of the trip he saw the communist cause in the United States as different from that in the United Kingdom.

Straight thought that the tension encountered at strikes and civil rights meetings was far greater than anything that John Cornford could point to in his efforts to convince him that the class struggle was the central and enduring characteristic of English society.[1] Straight's communist vision—undiluted over sixty-six years—was that the strikes that he witnessed were part of an industrial struggle, not a class struggle.

While Straight was sorting out his Marxist terminology, Stalin was carrying on the great purge in Russia of those who adhered to Marxist/Leninist ideals. The leading figures of the 1917 Bolshevik revolution, such as Nikolai Bukharin, Lev Kamenev, Grigori Zinoviev, and A. I. Rykov, were charged with treason and espionage. Then they were put through the public "show trials," forced to confess to crimes, and then shot. Soon, apart from Stalin himself, only Trotsky was left alive from Lenin's original Politburo. He was in exile and top of Stalin's hit list. These eliminations were the most notable, but the dictator did not stop with his key opponents. He went on to liquidate more than half of the 1,961 delegates to the Seventeenth Communist Party Congress. Not satisfied, Stalin moved out from the center of power to destroy a further 400,000 of the Soviet Union's professional class, which included teachers, professors, scientists, and doctors. Then he turned on the elite of the military and exterminated 35,000 leaders, including 90 percent of the generals in the services.

While this butchering was in full swing at home, Stalin's assassins in Europe were culling those in the Comintern (such as Maly) who obeyed orders and returned to Moscow—unwittingly—for execution, and those who did not. One who decided to run was Ignaz Reiss, a Jewish Russian agent who worked for Nikolai Smirnov, the Paris head of the KGB. Smirnov had dutifully returned to Moscow in the summer to "make a report." He never returned to Paris and was shot along with thirty other key espionage chiefs and their wives.

Reiss, until then a loyal servant of Stalin, had had enough. He wrote a letter to him protesting the murders. Stalin responded by ordering that he be tracked down and eliminated. Reiss defected from his Paris post and headed for Switzerland. His mistake was to let a close German communist agent friend, Gertrude Schildbach, know his whereabouts. She told Moscow and was ordered to meet him for dinner in Chamblandes on September 4, 1937. After the meal, they went for a stroll. They ran into two assassins who bundled Reiss into a vehicle at gunpoint. Schildbach came along for the ride to a nearby forest. Reiss struggled as they dragged him from the car. Schildbach helped hold him down, then he was machine-gunned to death. His bullet-riddled body was dumped by the roadside between Chamblandes and Lausanne.

Reiss's good Jewish friend, Samuel Ginsberg—better known as Walter Krivitsky—who was in charge of KGB military operations in Western Europe, read about the killing of "Hans Eberhardt" in *Paris Matin* the following day. Krivitsky was stunned. Eberhardt was Reiss's false passport name. They had known each other since working in the communist underground during the Russo-Polish war. Krivitsky and his strikingly attractive blonde wife from St. Petersburg, Tanya, decided they would defect. Krivitsky turned to a contact, Paul Wohl, a Russian Jew who had taken American citizenship and was living at that time in Paris. They worked out a plan. Wohl rented a hide-out in the South of France, while Krivitsky proposed to the Moscow Center that he return home for consultation. On October 5, Krivitsky pretended to board the train for Le Havre where a Russian ship was waiting. He, Tanya, and their son Alex got off after a couple of stops and took another train to the hideout.

Krivitsky was given police protection over the next year while he went through a thorough debriefing by French intelligence. The debriefing filled eighty volumes. Krivitsky divulged the structure of Soviet intelligence across Western Europe. This included the broad setup of the network in the United Kingdom, for which Straight had become the most promising recent recruit.

The Moscow Center monitored Straight's movements into New York on September 1 via his correspondence with Blunt. Ten days later it sent the agent assigned to control Straight instructions to contact him. The new recruit was seen as someone who would lead the KGB to "sources of exceptional importance and value."[2]

After his Midwest tour, Straight set about securing a job that would give him access to material of use to his Soviet masters. Their preference was the White House or State Department.

He managed to gain another meeting with Roosevelt in October, meeting in the president's study. Straight told him that cutbacks had stopped his joining of the NRPB. Could he think of any other agencies that might take him on?

Roosevelt, appearing concerned, frowned and thought hard but couldn't think of one. He was not going to take on someone without a civil service rating and no work experience to speak of. There just would not be a spot for him in tight employment times, even with his impressive degree and training under Keynes. "Why not get some outside experience and then join the government?" Roosevelt finally suggested.

It was not what the driven young man wanted to hear. Forget the White House or the State Department. The president couldn't even come up with a single agency. Straight decided to pass the time while on the job search by gaining more electioneering experience. He had loved the cut and thrust of Plymouth and so went to Fiorello LaGuardia's headquarters in New York to volunteer in his mayoral reelection campaign. He worked Manhattan's East Side on Park Avenue where he was staying in his mother's apartment. It made his task easier. Straight pushed hard for votes for LaGuardia's deputy, Thomas E. Dewey.

He enjoyed the experience and was thinking ahead to the day he would fulfill his perceived destiny and run for high office. He felt he had been born to it. In the meantime he waited for that piece of paper with Binny's blue ink drawing to be presented to him. It was the reason he had returned to the United States. Blunt had taken the drawing from him on August 4, taking his phone number in New York as well. Straight would be there until contact was made.

It was late October. He was becoming apprehensive.

———— • ————

Straight was alone in his mother's apartment one night in late October 1937 when the phone rang. He answered it.[3] A man with a thick European accent said that he brought greetings from his friends at Cambridge. The caller told him the name of a restaurant he was in a few blocks away. Straight said he would meet him and hurried out, remembering to employ the tradecraft Blunt had taught him. An hour later, he entered the restaurant.

A chunky man in a tight-fitting business suit was sitting alone at a table for two and watching the entrance. Straight was a few inches taller than the man, who had a nose like a boxer's and thick lips.[4] Other descriptions of this man, whom Straight would know as Michael Green, added to his portrait. Russian agent Hede Massing, who defected to the FBI in 1947, regarded him as "one of the most pedestrian of my Russian co-workers." Green was "every inch the Soviet apparatchik or bureaucrat." This fitted Straight's appreciation of him over time as someone rather rigid in his approach, uninspiring and without flair.

David Dallin, the Soviet expert, was even less flattering. He spoke of his villainously low forehead "topped with straight, pale, reddish-blond hair." Dallin described his lips as "puffed" rather than thick, and for good measure added that they were "choked with saliva when in motion." Completing the sinister characterization, Dallin noted that "his eyes were slightly slanted up and inflamed. They were the small, unpretty eyes of the unimaginative, frightened little man."

Regardless of Green's appearance, Straight was in awe at that first encounter. The Russian stood up, smiled, shook hands, and uttered the "verbal parole" or passwords of prearranged greetings. This ensured he was not an imposter, on the very slim chance that the FBI had set up Straight.

The man shook his hand firmly, saying his name was Michael Green.[5] Green, alias William Greinke, Michael Ademic, and other names, had at least two code names for communications back to Moscow—MER and ALBERT.[6] His real name was Ishak Abdulovich Akhermov. Despite the efforts of defectors to vilify his appearance and manner, he was the most important and effective "illegal" (that is, not working via the Soviet Embassy and originally an illegal immigrant sent by Soviet Intelligence) KGB control in the United States during his two underground tours of duty from 1937 to 1946. Straight was one of the first agents he would run in the United States and was considered a very important recruit.

Despite his age and inexperience in espionage, Straight would not be farmed out to one of the local rings, such as that run by Nathan Gregory Silvermaster, the Russian-born Jewish underground leader. Straight was a deep-cover agent who would not be known as a spy to local rings. He would be run direct from Moscow via top Russian controls like Green. Straight would avoid involvement with local communist agents other than by chance or in the normal run of events where the interests of liberals and the extreme left merged publicly. Straight would continue to cultivate his image as an outspoken, concerned liberal that he had projected so well to his mother and the Roosevelts.

He had been informed by Blunt that he was being treated as someone special in the eyes of Stalin and the Moscow Center, and this made him edgy at the first meeting. He wanted to impress Green, who by contrast was at ease. Green apologized for not getting in touch earlier. He had the phone number but not the address, which he needed in order to make an initial meeting. He apologized for not having the other half of the drawing by Bin Crompton, which Blunt had taken from him. The control said he had mislaid it, which unnerved Straight, who kept asking for it. Green ordered a three-course meal; Straight had eaten earlier. He took in everything about the Russian: his English was good despite the accent. He had an affable manner. Straight began to relax. No FBI agents were likely to barge in and arrest him. He stopped asking for the piece of paper with his darling's drawing on it and began to like his first U.S. control.

Straight discussed his efforts to get work and his contacts, such as the president. Roosevelt had helped but not enough to get him a job. After his tour of the country, Straight floated the idea of working for General Motors in Detroit for a few months. He mentioned the possibilities in the State Department. Green seemed to like the General Motors idea.

The Russian finished his meal with coffee and a monologue on the developing aspects of the peace movement, which would become a regular refrain at other meetings.[7] It was part of the continuing preparation so well handled by Burgess and Blunt at Cambridge, who in turn had been earlier seduced by Maly and Deutsch. The lecture completed, Green asked his new agent if there were any questions on the topic. Straight said he had none, which showed unusual restraint. Green asked for his check. He told Straight to memorize the name and phone number of a "friend," Alexander Koral, in Brooklyn, whom he was to call in an emergency.[8]

Green said he would be in touch by phone and that the next rendezvous would be in Central Park.[9] Straight would follow the tradecraft of avoiding any possible American watchers so expertly taught by Blunt. This meant taking circuitous routes over hours to an appointment location.

———————

An early concern for Green was what he perceived as some circumspection, even caution on Straight's part concerning his attitude to Soviet foreign policy. The Moscow Center put this down to some Trotskyite friends of Straight, who were still imbued with the concept of the new world order as instigated by the (steadily dying) Comintern—that is, communism outside the Soviet Union.

Green was directed to keep working on his new charge. Moscow reminded its agent that Straight was his biggest assignment in the United

States. Green was directed to forget about General Motors in Detroit and to concentrate on getting his new American spy into the State Department.

Straight at last had a specific demand, rather than a general aim. The First Lady could be the conduit to the State Department. He could not approach her at the White House; it was too soon after seeing the president. He had to contrive a "chance" meeting with her, which he did at an unemployed miners' camp in West Virginia.[10]

He managed to raise the question of his job-hunting with the First Lady and how much he would like to work for the administration, particularly the State Department. They discussed this for some time. Much to his joy, Mrs. Roosevelt promised to write on his behalf to the undersecretary of state, Sumner Welles. A week later Straight had an appointment. He was briefed on the formidable Welles by the ever-faithful Jonathan Mitchell at *The New Republic*.

The novice's lack of experience was against him. Welles told him he had a hard road in front of him and appeared reluctant to help. He was told there were no openings at State.[11]

Straight waited for his next call from Green, and they met in Central Park. They walked together and discussed the problem of getting into State. Straight thought he should offer to work for nothing. His control appeared to be "appraising him and seemed to have prepared topics and lines of conversation to test his thoughts and points of view, and to shape his mind."[12] Straight found him exceptionally humorous and fond of plays on words.

They parted, planning another rendezvous at the New York Zoo.

———— • ————

Green told the Moscow Center that he and Straight had become friends and that the new young agent listened to his advice and followed it. But Green did not like him to keep the company of the editorial staff at *The New Republic*. The Soviet control worried that the free exchange of mainly liberal, pro-left views were a bad influence on Straight. How could he indoctrinate him with hard-line, Moscow-centrist Stalinist ideology when he was spending time with "a liberal like Roger Baldwin, outwardly a friend of the USSR but in his soul its enemy with great sympathy for Trotsky. [He] cannot help but exert a negative influence on [Straight]."[13]

Stalin's obsession with Trotsky had more than filtered through to his spies worldwide. They too had become paranoid about him and the way the West had romanticized him and his plight in exile.

The subject of Trotsky touched a raw nerve. At early meetings with Straight, Green felt some "ideological hesitation"—that is, uncertainty about Stalinism or Stalinist foreign policy. According to the edited files presented by the KGB, Moscow was alleged to have jumped to the conclusion that this was because he had Trotskyite contacts in the United States.

Straight made out that he was misleading the KGB by telling Green about his anticommunist links. The aim, he alleged, was to cause the KGB to think he was undependable and not to be relied on. He feigned limited interest in Russia and Trotsky. But was this a cover, with KGB connivance, for his attempts to infiltrate Trotskyite organizations, known to be connected to defector Walter Krivitsky?

Summaries of the KGB files again suggest that Straight did not quite comprehend what was expected of his new clandestine life when, according to Green:

[Straight] claimed that he has $10,000 to $20,000 in spare money and does not know what to do with it. He asked whether I need money; he could give it to me. This is his spare pocket money. I said that I do not need money personally; let him keep it or put it in a bank. As for his previous regular donations (to the *Daily Worker*), I will take them and pass them along accordingly. At another meeting, he gave me $2000 as his quarterly [sic] Party fee and claimed he would be giving me more in the future.[14]

The Moscow Center was not about to let this example of capitalist largesse slip by. It passed the money to a grateful Harry Pollitt in London and then directed Green to bring up the topic of the pocket money at their next meeting. The cryptic instruction was: "Receive this money [Straight's spare $10,000 to $20,000] and send it to us."

Presumably the extra dollars were absorbed into KGB consolidated revenue or shared out to other U.S. agents needing hard cash. One way or the other Straight continued his generous support for all things communist either with his formerly open outlets or in the espionage world.

Straight approached contacts at the State Department again and informed them his services were for free. He would take anything going, assist anyone. He was then taken on a temporary assignment in the department's Office of the Economic Adviser.

Straight was in. He could now become familiar with the old ornate, gray-stoned State Department with its high ceilings, circular staircases, and long corridors. The KGB expected he could also commence his work as a Soviet intelligence agent.

Straight moved to Washington to live and found a room in the redbrick house on 1718 H Street, which his father Willard and friends had shared as young bachelors. The sitting room was lined with Chinese wallpaper brought back from Beijing by Willard and photos of him and his friends. Also in residence were George Summerlin, the State Department's chief of protocol; journalist Joe Alsop; and a banker, Major Heath.

In December 1937, Straight met Green at the New York Zoo and informed him of his success at State. Green drew him out on his views about Germany's rearmament. From this discussion came Straight's first cover assignment—a report on Hitler's capacity to wage war, entitled Economic Impact of European Rearmament.

The project was to be Straight's excuse for accessing documents and views from Washington insiders that would be useful in the Kremlin. "Green was not there to act like a Cambridge don," Yuri Modin remarked with a hearty laugh when we discussed Straight's first project during our Moscow interviews in October 1996. "There was no point in him [Straight] handing in a nice analytical thesis for a mark out of ten. We wanted documentation about U.S. intelligence on a wide range of topics, in this case to do with the Nazis and their capacity for war."[15]

Straight threw himself into three months of work. He accessed all the documents he could, drew on published sources, and used the assignment to make Washington contacts. It got him around town and noticed.

In January 1938, Green let Moscow know of the success of Straight's getting into State: "Now he has been assigned to write a paper on international armaments."[16]

Straight relied on another KGB agent (possibly Alger Hiss, code named Eleven) within another department at State.

Green's report added: "he receives reports on this issue [armaments] by Ambassador. . . . [When] the paper is finished [Straight]) promises to give us a copy. Reading the Ambassadors' reports, he will remember the important items and pass them to me at our meetings. I send his first notes from the reports he read."[17]

Green also expressed his concern that Straight was making friendly contact with other Soviet agents in place at State, including Laurence Duggan and Alger Hiss. *The New Republic*'s Roger Baldwin had already introduced Straight to Duggan; Green reported that he ordered Straight to ignore Duggan. Each of the so-called progressives—including Hiss, Duggan, and Straight—recognized the views and positions of the others, but none realized that the others were agents. Consequently, there were discussions by all of them, including Straight, with their controls about the ideologically correct people with whom they came into contact.

Straight passed on his interest in Hiss to Green, who didn't react to the information that Hiss was ideologically progressive. Green was nervous that Hiss, who was run by the "Neighbors"—the GRU (Soviet military intelligence)—might try to recruit the younger man, especially as he was intelligent and articulate both orally and on paper. (Hiss was instructed by his GRU bosses not to build his relationship with Straight.)

In a December 1997 letter response to a review in the *New York Review of Books,* Straight tried to make it seem that he did not attempt to recruit Hiss. "[In a June 1938 dispatch to the KGB Moscow Center] Akhermov (Green) notes simply that I 'mentioned' Hiss as 'a very progressive man,'" Straight wrote. He went on to explain that saying (as a book reviewer did) he tried to recruit Hiss was a "distortion" and "laughable. Hiss was an important official in the State Department in June 1938. I was an unpaid volunteer aged 21."[18]

Straight's self-depiction was misleading. Like all key agents, he was on the lookout for possible new recruits to the KGB. His approach to his control about Hiss meant that Straight wanted Hiss considered for recruitment.

———

Straight continued to remain "uneducated." He couldn't contain his natural inclination to talk and talk about politics. Green expressed his concerns again. The Moscow Center acted by ordering Earl Browder, the

U.S. Communist Party's leader, to stop any party members making contact with Straight. Green in turn began to lecture Straight about not making any contact with communists. Straight had to make out he was a liberal who fitted nicely to the left of the Democratic Party. He would have been relieved that he was not asked to consort with fascists as his recruiter, Guy Burgess, did in England.

Straight kept up his image of broadening his links by socializing with prominent politicians. There was dinner with Dean Acheson, an international lawyer, later to be President Harry Truman's Cold War secretary of state. There was lunch with Bob La Follette (a liberal Republican senator from Wisconsin). He also met up with Maury Maverick, a liberal Texas congressman, whom Straight found uncouth. Yet he assessed him as the ablest of the progressives, who ranged from left-wing liberals to hard-line communists, both Stalinists and, like La Follette, Trotsky supporters.[19]

Maverick read aloud to him a speech that he was about to deliver in Congress. Straight was not impressed. He asked Maverick if he could rewrite it; Maverick agreed. *The New York Times* reported it, and Straight's credibility went up a fraction within the U.S. liberal community.

———————

Straight could not wait for the Crompton family's return to live in Rye, New York. Straight planned a meeting with Bin at Westbury. His priorities, however, centered around his secret work for Russian intelligence. Green kept in touch and began meeting Straight in Washington, where they both took precautions. The FBI, they both knew, was in the habit of tailing some Soviet embassy employees.

Security was not tight at State, which seemed to Straight like a gentleman's club. He had no trouble taking out documents. He and Green would meet at a restaurant, where papers would be handed over. Despite being wary, risks were taken. Straight recalled on one occasion dropping Green off near the Soviet embassy "so he could have copies made [microfilmed] of official State Department documents not for public consumption, and [which] may have borne the classification 'Confidential.'" Straight picked Green up later. The documents were handed back and replaced in State files.[20] Security, such as it was, never questioned the serious-looking, young "volunteer" in the smart suit, who often carried a bulging briefcase.

The first seeds of doubt about Straight's capacities as a secret agent began to form at the Moscow Center. It reiterated to Green that Straight had to be "educated" and "his brains rebuilt in our manner."[21] Clearly there was a problem in the center's understanding of their most important new recruit in the United States. He was a free thinker, not someone who could easily be brainwashed. He wanted to please his masters but couldn't compete with his own conscience—his own comprehension of events. The center thought it could dumb down the raw agent until he was more like an automaton.

He was viewed at this point as a sloppy undergraduate passing on stale data. The center instructed Green to get hold of only documents it was interested in. Short of that, he had to date his notes and specify the documents and their authors to gauge their import.

Green imparted the directive, and Straight labored on. He handed in his report on Hitler's rearmament to his superior at State, Herbert Feis, on the last Saturday in May, and another version to Green the same day. Then he rushed off to Westbury to see Bin. The romance was blossoming.

Moscow and Green continued to be let down. Green complained to the center that he talked long and hard with Straight every week but that he was making no headway. Straight seemed to Green and the center to be concerned about stealing classified documents. Straight maintained that he no longer received ambassadorial reports, and he continued to draw on published material for his claimed three or four economic reports passed to Green.[22]

Straight's claim covers up his capacity to access sensitive documents and take notes from them. There had to be more than three or four documents, given the number of meetings he had had with Green and other controls. But the key is not the actual documents but rather the information and analysis he passed on to his controls from them. Much like Burgess, he developed analytic and writing skills that allowed him to interpret secret data for Kremlin consumption. It was a Straight specialty.

In June 1938 Joe Alsop arranged a lunch meeting between Straight and Roosevelt's speechwriter, Tom Corcoran, who made a persuasive case for

Straight's contributing to congressman Maury Maverick's fight for reelection in San Antonio, Texas. He had won office in 1934 and was a true-blue New Deal liberal. Bankers and businessmen wanted Maverick out. He was one of many New Dealers they were going to destroy. Could Straight help?

Yes, he could, to the tune of $10,000—equivalent today to about $300,000—which was a sizable donation for a political campaign. In return Straight was to observe the campaign and be offered a job working for Corcoran, assisting him in political speeches for Roosevelt. Straight agreed. Once again, he had used his money to purchase a position for the cause. He had completed his main assignment at State, and because he had not pleased Green with his harvest from it, Moscow Center decided that there might be better pickings by being on the president's staff. He would have an office in the Department of Interior and easy access to the White House, which placed him at the hub of events politically. This appealed to Green and created a hope that he might still deliver useful documents.

Straight flew to San Antonio in mid-June, followed Maverick's campaign, and took shots with his trusty Leica of the old Mexican town within the city that the congressman had restored. People began to show Straight undue deference; he didn't know why. A reporter, whom Maverick was bribing to write favorable articles, later took Straight aside and asked him what it was like to work for the FBI. Maverick had spread the word that Straight was employed by J. Edgar Hoover and had been sent to make sure that the election was not stolen by Maverick's opponent, a local radio announcer backed by the top end of town.

Straight took the joke; he had no choice, but he was mortified. He certainly could do without the FBI paying him any attention, which it would do on the off chance it was mislead into believing he was an imposter. Maverick lost the election, but Straight's $10,000 investment was not a losing proposition. He had bought a few friends and a place near the top of the political table.

Straight became known in the bureaucracy as a liberal with communist sympathies. Despite directives from Moscow, he was sought out for assistance by communist agents from local rings, who were not aware that he was a deep-cover KGB spy. One was Zalmond David Franklin, a former member of the Abraham Lincoln Brigade that fought in Spain. Franklin gave him a list of written questions about Roosevelt's cabinet appointments and some political matters. Straight declined to cooperate without explaining why to the unsuspecting comrade:[23] he was servant to a deeper cause with a direct line to Moscow Center and the Kremlin.

Another seeker of help was the Czech-born agent Solomon Aaron Lichinsky—alias Solomon Adler—who according to Straight, looked like a ski instructor or storm trooper with "stiff blond hair."[24] Adler was a member of the local communist ring inside the Treasury Department, run by Silvermaster. He had no idea of Straight's secret work.

Adler saw him as a likely recruit. He told Straight to lay low and that he would be recontacted.[25]

Straight took a summer break from the State Department through August to spend time with Dorothy, who was staying in Woods Hole, Massachusetts, and Bin. He returned to his desk in September. His report on Hitler's rearmament was well received inside the department. Comments were attached to it from the secretary, Cordell Hull, who thought it "splendid," and Dean Acheson, who praised it. Alger Hiss worked on the floor below. Apparently defying Moscow directives, he called Straight down for a chat about the points he had raised. Unmindful of Green's worry about the closeness of Hiss, Straight found it pleasing that he was being encouraged by his Soviet masters and also patted on the back by those in his workplace. His boss, Feis, however, was not as impressed as Hiss. He offered no new assignments to reward his charge's initiative. A paid position did come up in the office, and Feis offered it to Straight with little enthusiasm.[26] It was turned down.

Straight gave Green documents in mid-September and waited for a firm offer from Corcoran for a role as an unpaid assistant speechwriter. It came a week later. At the passing of further intelligence at an October meeting, Straight told his control of his successful move to the Department of Interior and the White House, claiming in his autobiography that he deceived Green by saying he would be working for Harold Ickes, then interior secretary. The implication was that Ickes would be secretary of war and that Straight would then move with him.

Despite the lack of good espionage material coming from him, the center saw Straight as a long-term agent who had to be drawn in gradually and, it seemed from the correspondence between Green and the center, painstakingly. There was no thought of shutting him down, a point that became apparent in late 1938 when Blunt wrote to him asking for funds for refugees from the Spanish Civil War. Green was upset. He asked Moscow to order Blunt to cease this sort of contact. It once more brought Straight into the spotlight on both sides of the Atlantic as an open communist supporter.

8

THE INFORMANTS

Walter Krivitsky and his family were grateful for the police guard given by France's socialist minister for the interior, M. Dormoy, when they stayed next door to a police station at Paris's Hotel des Academies in the Rue St. Peres. Yet two attempts by Stalin's assassins to trap Krivitsky within thirteen months convinced him that he should defect to the United States. One attempt was at the Marseilles railway station at midnight when the family was returning to Paris. They spotted the hit squad waiting for them and managed to flee the scene. Later in Paris the family was lunching at a cafe off the Place de la Bastille when their police guard became suspicious of three men in a vehicle. The family was bundled out a rear exit.[1] Both times Krivitsky had noticed the broad, plump figure of Hans Bruesse, his former chauffeur while stationed in The Hague. The small-eyed, childish-looking Bruesse was a fearsome, cold-blooded operator whose talents ran from expert lock-picking to efficient killing. Bruesse was frequently at the Krivitsky's homes in The Hague and in Paris. Both men knew each other's foibles and habits. For this reason, Bruesse was able to track Krivitsky, and Krivitsky was able to elude him.

Constant police protection and the daily threat put enormous strains on the family, as did the fact that the KGB had increased its violent attacks in general against Soviet émigrés in France. The United States was inviting, but it did not prove so on the family's arrival in New York aboard the SS *Normandie* on November 10, 1938. Labor officials, who at that time controlled the immigration service, debated whether to deport them. The U.S. ambassador to France, William C. Bullitt, who was briefly back in Washington for talks with Roosevelt on the European crisis, intervened and secured a 120-day visitor's pass for Krivitsky. (Bullitt had been instrumental in attaining proper travel documents for him in France when he decided to leave.)[2]

New York was Krivitsky's base, and the family took several weeks orientating themselves to both the language and the concrete jungle. It was a culture shock, yet the city's strong Jewish influence was attractive. Krivitsky decided to write for a living. He would tell his story about working as a Soviet agent in Europe and the world dangers posed by Stalin and his henchmen. He saw book publishers and magazines but received only lukewarm responses. Very few in the media realized the true situation in Russia, nor the mayhem caused by Stalin's purges and hit squads. There was more concern in Jewish New York about the rise of fascism, with its direct attack on Judaism. Communist Russia had its pogroms, and anti-Jewish elements fostered by Stalin at his most paranoid were always dangerous, but the Nazis were public about their thuggish hate for Jews.

Krivitsky began writing a series of articles for the *Saturday Evening Post* with *Chicago Daily News* journalist Isaac Don Levine as his ghost writer. The only important individual in the U.S. government with any clout to sit up and take notice was a career State Department man, Loy Henderson. He had just returned (in October 1938) from a tour of duty in Moscow and was annoyed to find the indifference in Washington toward what was happening in Russia. Henderson had been monitoring communism since before the revolution and had sat in on the recent show trials. This long experience had made him a hard-liner when it came to Stalin. Henderson read Krivitsky's initial articles, then he contacted Don Levine, who tried to arrange a meeting with Krivitsky and Henderson. Krivitsky was reluctant. His own knowledge of Soviet espionage and information from fellow émigrés made him sure that Washington was riddled with Soviet agents. Anything he said would be reported back to Moscow.

Don Levine and Krivitsky's lawyer, Louis Waldman, reminded him that his visa expired in March. His cooperation with Henderson might help his citizenship application. Krivitsky then agreed to a meeting in room 385 on the State Department's eastern corridor on January 10, 1939.

Henderson and Edward Page, another hard-liner at State, listened in amazement to Krivitsky's revelations. They outlined the purges and even Hitler's desire to form a pact with Stalin.

Henderson was pleased. He suggested that further cooperation with the State Department's passport division—run by Shipley—would help secure Krivitsky's U.S. citizenship. Later, on January 10, Krivitsky met with Shipley, and he gave her a wealth of information on Soviet illegals—agents who had entered the country using false or forged passports.[3] The data were so valuable that Shipley asked him to return the next day.

Henderson encouraged Krivitsky to write more penetrating articles about Soviet Russia and Stalin, but Krivitsky was cautious. He knew he could still be a target for the KGB led by the murderous Nikolai Yezhov, who would be under pressure to eliminate all deserters from the Soviet cause. Confirmation of his fears came on March 7, 1939, when he was dining near Times Square with Lenin biographer David Schub, the editor of a New York Jewish daily.[4] They had just ordered their meals when three men came in and sat at the nearest table. Krivitsky recognized Sergei Basoff, an experienced Soviet agent, and got up to leave. Basoff followed him to the cashier's desk, where Krivitsky turned and confronted him.

"Are you here to assassinate me?" Krivitsky challenged him.

"No, no, I'm not. I'm here unofficially," Basoff replied.

"You just happen to turn up at this restaurant . . . ?"

"All I want is a friendly chat."

Krivitsky knew enough about that kind of approach. It was a pretext to murder. He hurried out with Schub and along to the nearby offices of *The New York Times*. Basoff and his companions followed, but Krivitsky managed to escape in busy Time Square.

This shock caused Krivitsky to follow up on Henderson's encouragement to expose Stalinism. In April, a series of articles—at the considerable sum of $5,000 a piece—commenced in the *Saturday Evening Post* in an attempt to alert the United States to the menace of "Stalin's Secret Service." They lacked specifics, but Krivitsky said he would "withhold total exposure" until the State Department granted him residential status.

Later, he bargained with the House Committee on Un-American Activities in order to stop his deportation.

The articles were a good introduction to Stalin's worldwide espionage net and did go as far as exposing the Soviet Trade Mission, Amtorg, as a front or cover for the KGB.

"Stalin's Secret Service has agents planted in all institutions, governmental and industrial," Krivitsky claimed. "The armed services have them too."

The exposé revealed communist assassinations in Spain and Stalin's desire for a pact with Hitler. The latter revelation was derided.

The British Foreign Office (with Guy Burgess putting out the press release) remarked: "On the whole we do not consider that these would-be hair-raising revelations of Stalin's alleged desire for rapprochement with Germany are worth taking seriously."[5]

The FBI's director, J. Edgar Hoover, was furious. Krivitsky had said that Soviet agents were slipping into the United States on forged passports. He had the affront to write that they were flouting American law by using rolls of counterfeit money. Even worse, from Hoover's viewpoint, Krivitsky alleged that right under the nose of the bureau, Russian communist hit men from the KGB were moving around in small squads murdering American communists in order to keep the local movement under Soviet control. It was too much for Hoover. He had spent the last decade cultivating the line that because of the patriotic work of the FBI, the United States was free of such atrocities and foreign influence.[6]

Hoover and others put pressure on the Labor Department to arrest and deport Krivitsky. However, some at State, such as Henderson, wanted to debrief him further. They supported him; Ruth Shipley extended his visa. Hoover saw the whole affair as a conspiracy led by the hated State Department, the FBI's arch rival, to undermine his power and the image of the FBI.

Yet even he was momentarily silenced a few months later, on August 23, 1939, when Joachim von Ribbentrop and Vyacheslav Mikhaylovich Molotov signed the Sino-Soviet Friendship Pact, which shook the world. The important factor in terms of the politico/military/intelligence worlds was that now the Nazis and the Soviets were united against all others, and their intelligence services would share secrets. Antifascist, left-wing sympathizers in the United Kingdom and the United States for the first time had to reassess their allegiances to Stalin. Everything now done for communism and mother Russia was also a direct service to Hitler.

Krivitsky, once viewed as a paranoid anticommunist troublemaker, was suddenly a prophet. His chances of becoming a U.S. citizen and making a life in his adopted country had increased. If he succeeded in settling in the West, he would disclose more of the deeper secrets he held. They would endanger key Western agents working for the KGB, including Straight and all those in the Cambridge ring.

———— • ————

Straight enjoyed his time with the Roosevelt speechwriting team of Corcoran and Ben Cohen (who was counsel for the National Power Policy Committee), which produced speeches for the president, the cabinet, and the liberal leaders of congress. Once more, Straight had access to a wide range of documents and people when preparing research for speeches. He passed on his analysis to Green when he came to Washington in June and September 1938.[7]

The Kremlin was being patient in dealing with a young spy for whom it had high regard and hopes, as they were with many agents, who were in place close to the center of power in Germany, the United Kingdom, France, and the United States. Stalin was obsessed with knowing in advance what his opposite numbers in the key world powers were thinking and planning. Over the period of his dictatorship, this intelligence was a key to his and the Soviet Union's survival. It gave him an edge in negotiation, strategy, and tactics in dealing with his "enemies" and "friends," depending on the state-of-play.

The Sino-Soviet alliance of August 1939 was an excellent cover for many communist agents to pretend to break from communism. French, British, and American agents entering intelligence areas in their countries as war broke out on September 1 would cite the pact as a reason for breaking their links. The major rings of Soviet agents, almost to a man, did not and could not break away. There was confusion, discussion, and then counseling from their controls, who had some explaining to do.

Stalin's move (for it was he rather than Hitler who sued for a peace, which he had wanted ever since the German dictator took power in 1933) was presented as a ploy. It was designed to feign the appearance of appeasement, which would in the end defeat fascism. How controls reconciled this with intelligence gathering being passed to Hitler's agents was tricky. But in a well-prepared plan, the Moscow Center managed to convince their agents they should maintain their belief in Stalin and that they were not forsaking their ideals. The pact was portrayed as temporary and expedient for the eventual dominance of world communism. The expert indoctrination of Stalin's most effective espionage network—the Cambridge ring—in the early 1930s by the urbane and intellectual Comintern representatives, such as Maly, had paid off.

Not one of them had a serious thought about stopping their work for Stalin, although Burgess blustered about it, and Blunt was at first distraught about projected consequences. Apart from these two, the ring's key agents included Donald Maclean, Kim Philby, and John Cairncross. Then there was Victor Rothschild—Lord Rothschild, as he had become in 1937. He was still not technically an agent reporting directly to a control, but he was vital for his access to key research institutes and for his connections. They allowed him to place others in key positions within the British scientific, diplomatic, and intelligence community when war broke out.

Rothschild was cautious about the pact but remained convinced that Hitler would turn on Stalin. Most of the main members of the Cambridge ring, including Tess Mayor (recruited in mid-1938 by her very close friends Blunt and Burgess), John Cairncross, and Alister Watson, also remained steadfast in their support for Stalin.[8]

In fact, the brainwashing about Stalinism had been carried on so impressively by Blunt and Burgess that later recruits into this premier group stiffened their resolve to continue spying. Even in the light of the horrific accounts of Stalinism as told by Krivitsky (which they had all read), these agents had been drilled into believing it was all part of the grand plan for the cause, which would dominate in the end.

On the off chance that agents wavered in their belief, they knew the consequences: they would be hunted down and killed. In the wake of Stalin's purge and murder of upward of a million "waverers," the threat was not just implied. It was a cold-blooded promise, an inevitability. Instead of the mass bludgeoning of 1935 to 1938 in Russia and worldwide, Stalin and his KGB heads were now selective, and they moved with the precision of surgeons. There was a brutal logic in their thinking. All who left the cause carried with them secrets that were a real danger. If they were interrogated willingly or otherwise by the FBI or British intelligence, they might be turned, or they might divulge whole networks. This would impede the vital flow of data to the Kremlin.

———— • ————

More than anyone in the Cambridge ring, Straight was upset by the pact. He refused to see Green for a month. He would not accept the argument that it was all part of Stalin's grand plan to defeat fascism. Green came to Washington in late October, two months after the pact, when the Red armies were advancing into Finland.[9] Straight and Green sat in a restaurant below Washington's Union Station. The control was gleeful about Soviet soldiers acting as liberators and triggering revolution, which would spread across Germany and France.

Then Straight gave Green a memorandum with his views on the Nazi-Soviet pact. It was not a note of protest as seen from the principled but foolhardy and courageous Ignaz Reiss, who signed his own death warrant by defying Stalin. Straight's memo, as explained by him, conceded that the pact had been a military necessity, given the refusal of the British and French governments to join in a common front against Hitler. (Read: Our Great Leader Stalin had no choice. He just had to have a pact with the devil.)[10] Straight went on to plead that the pact should not be extended from a military alliance to a political one. This was as unrealistic as it was unlikely. Stalin would never have contemplated a political linkup.[11] Yet it was Straight's way of making a protest without wanting to upset the Moscow Center or Stalin. Green assured him the memo would reach the Kremlin.

Straight now wondered about the fate of his control, who had been trained abroad before Stalin started his purges and who was at the end of 1939 about to return to Moscow.[12] (In fact, Green would return for a second tour of duty in 1942 and go on operating with his wife until 1946, when he received a tip-off that a former American Soviet agent, Elizabeth Bentley, was about to divulge his identity.)[13]

———— • ————

Straight found time apart from his dedicated Soviet secret work to keep his romance going throughout 1939 with Bin Crompton, which was often by correspondence. In early September, Corcoran gave him three days off from his White House research duties to marry her. They exchanged vows under an oak willow in Nantucket and went house-hunting in Washington.

The Straights rented a home in cobblestoned Prince Street, a former red-light district of Alexandria. He and Bin played host to a list of left-wing visitors over the new year and through the winter. In early 1940, Straight began doing some work with the Soviet-leaning American Youth Congress, which was supported by Mrs. Roosevelt. His efforts endeared him to the First Lady, and he and Bin were invited to the White House for dinner with her and the president.

This reinforced Straight's liberal façade. If he dined with Roosevelt, then he must surely be a liberal. The letters to the family all bolstered the image he wanted to present as a male incarnate of his mother: the selfless doer of good deeds concerning social issues, such as those that occupied the Youth Congress's forum. Dorothy controlled the family purse strings. Straight could not afford to let her think he was a dilettante communist, and definitely not the full-blown Soviet spy that he was. His share of the invested income from the trust she set up in 1936 was inviolate. It was in equal proportion for her other children: Whitney, Biddy, Ruth, and William. Even if she discovered he was a KGB agent, she could not change that. But she could decide to stop him becoming a trustee, if ever he wished to be one, and also stop his influence over how various trust monies were invested and spent. (For instance, trust money supported certain communist front organizations springing up regularly in the United States.)

———————

Krivitsky's 1939 articles in the *Saturday Evening Post* provoked a frightened American defector from communism, Whittaker Chambers, into meeting him. Chambers had started as an editor of the *Daily Worker*. His ring's leaders decided he should go underground as a clandestine agent shuttling between New York and Washington with top secret documents supplied by the networks operating inside the major government departments. Chambers took the perilous step of leaving Stalin's service in April 1938.

The meeting—arranged again by Don Levine—saw a brainstorming session between two of Stalin's key deserters. They found they could help each other with some of the puzzles of communist treachery over the past decade. Chambers gleaned most. He had been part of a ring that had been controlled by Moscow. He was intrigued to be told which branch of the Soviet intelligence service employed him and who his bosses were. As the two furtive, suspicious men began to trust each other, they went deeper into operations. Chambers would mention the case of a murdered colleague; Krivitsky would explain the hows and whys of a Soviet operation. At the end of it, Don Levine was inspired to alert the State Department. He organized a meeting for Chambers with an assistant secretary, Adolph Berle. Chambers, now with a far deeper comprehension of the scope of Soviet penetration of U.S. government, was able to furnish Berle with a detailed picture right down to the communist rings' chains of command and divisions of responsibility. He could even put names to top spies at State. He named six people, including Alger Hiss. Berle was stunned.[14]

Don Levine was not finished. He had learned from Krivitsky that the Soviets had penetrated the key government arms of the United Kingdom, the United States' most vital ally. Levine realized that any secrets passed by U.S. intelligence to the British would end up in Moscow and then Berlin. He thought the rot should be stopped. Krivitsky informed him that he had already outlined to the French the extent of infiltration and recruitment in the United Kingdom, but nothing had been done. Krivitsky feared that Soviet agents inside the French government may have sabotaged the information he had given them. There were even rumors, Krivitsky had heard from his contacts in Paris, that the eighty volumes of his debriefing had gone missing—sunk in a barge on the Seine where they were supposedly being stored for safekeeping.[15]

Don Levine acted again and went to the British embassy on Massachusetts Avenue to see the ambassador, Lord Lothian. Over tea in the elegant study of the ambassador's residence, Levine outlined the Krivitsky story. Lothian listened, his face frowning more as the revelations unfolded.

"The Kremlin has managed to plant two spies in the heart of Whitehall," Levine said.

"No, I can't believe that," Lothian replied. "You'd have to be more specific . . . "

"There's a Soviet agent working for the Foreign Office code-room as a cipher clerk."

"What?"

"He has been providing the Russians with cables."

"For how long?"

"A long time."

Lothian was skeptical. Like most in the British establishment, he could not bring himself to believe that one of them could possibly spy for the other side.

"Can you name him?" Lothian challenged.

"King," Levine replied.

"King?" Lothian said, still unconvinced. "King what? Something King? The King, perhaps?"

"That's his last name. That's all I know."

Lothian scribbled on a writing pad.

"There is another one," Levine added, making the most of his opportunity. Despite the resistance, he was not going to let the opportunity slip. "This spy has been described as a person of 'good family.' He has been assigned to the Imperial Defence Council."

"That's an office within the Cabinet," Lothian responded, his skepticism maintained. "Do you know his name?"

"No."[16]

Despite his incredulity, Lothian promised to inform the foreign office.

The reaction in England was unexpected. John Herbert King—the only cipher clerk of that name at the foreign office—was put under surveillance. He was found to be passing information about British foreign policy intentions to Moscow (via an "illegal" KGB contact in a clothing company in London's East End) as it was being sent to British missions abroad. King was arrested and given a ten-year prison sentence.

The shock at the foreign office was not so much that a Soviet agent had been active, but that the data received would go to the Germans. Hitler's intelligence service had used its pact with the Soviet Union to squeeze its agents for data damaging to the Allies. It was more productive to use Soviet agents than Nazis, who were under far greater surveillance. Messages coming in from U.S. embassies abroad began to support this by warning of a switch of espionage activity from Nazi to Soviet agents.

The U.S. embassy in Brussels noted in a secret cable to State: "Positive proof that the German and Soviet governments are working together in matters of espionage and sabotage. Soviet agents are being used for most important jobs as they are more likely not to be suspected."[17]

Once more, Krivitsky's credibility increased. He was called before a U.S. House committee, where he drummed home the consequences of the Nazi-Soviet Pact. "Stalin's pact with Hitler," he told an attentive group of congressmen, "is really like an alliance of the two armies operating in specific zones. I have no doubt that such exchanges of military secrets and information are indispensable to both Hitler and Stalin."[18]

At least some government representatives now had a rudimentary concept of the double threat from Nazi and Soviet spies. Some within the British foreign office also seemed shaken from their lethargy. They wanted Krivitsky in England for a thorough debriefing. He was reluctant to go, especially with his knowledge of Soviet penetration in the United Kingdom, which was as deep as in the United States. Yet he was still under political pressure from a range of individuals in U.S. government to leave. Some American liberals saw him as a threat to friendly relations with the Soviet Union. His extended visa would expire on December 31, 1939. Krivitsky's lawyer, Paul Waldman, thought he should use the trip to the United Kingdom as a break so he could return after six months (the minimum time), register as an alien, and recommence his quest for U.S. citizenship.

Krivitsky made arrangements for a boat to England, but White House officials became nervous. They thought that Stalin would find out about the debriefing plan and see it as an anti-Soviet move. The United States was still neutral and did not wish to antagonize Stalin.[19] Krivitsky, feeling unwanted and apprehensive, was told he would have to make his way to England via Canada. A few days before he was scheduled to go, two men were seen sitting in a car watching his apartment. The charade of sending him via Canada was unnecessary; Soviet intelligence was watching. They would be more than keen to stop his going to England.

Krivitsky and his family were given an escort to the border by the Radical Squad, a heavily armed New York police unit. They were then picked up by the Canadian Mounted Police and escorted to a hideout near Montreal. There were more threats within ten days of arriving. A KGB squad had located them, and the family was forced to change to a fresh safe house. The Mounties boosted their round-the-clock protection. After three weeks in Montreal, Krivitsky made a move without his family and boarded a Royal Navy submarine. The trip to England took twelve days.

TYLER KENT (exp sw)

Krivitsky arrived in London on January 19, 1940, and a few days later was ready to commence his interrogation by MI5, which had been briefed by the foreign office. It was to be directed by the deputy director of MI5's Division B, Guy Maynard Liddell, who controlled all counterespionage investigations. (He was himself later suspected of being a Soviet agent by many, including Maurice Oldfield, a postwar head of MI6. Much circumstantial evidence makes it a possibility.)

Krivitsky was very nervous in the initial discussions; he talked at length. Liddell listened and only prodded him now and again in order to see the broad dimensions of what he had to offer.[20] The defector calmed down with the softer approach of the British, although he would always have qualms. He knew of the penetration in the United Kingdom; it was a permanent psychological threat.

Liddell assigned the "tough-minded and rough-tongued" Jane Sissmore, a former barrister, to debrief him over three weeks.[21] She demonstrated skill, patience, and sensitivity in extracting information from Krivitsky, who was not an easy subject. He seemed hesitant over names and reluctant to divulge everything. He wanted something in reserve to ensure continued protection. He feared that if he told all he knew, he might be considered expendable. There was also the strong possibility that if he named names, particularly of Stalin's top agents in the Cambridge ring, or if he could give enough clues to expose them, he would invite certain death from the KGB hit squads. He more than once told his interrogator: "If you find that I have committed suicide, do not believe it."

Under guidance from Sissmore, who restrained herself and remained sympathetic, Krivitsky listed ninety-three agents working in the British Commonwealth, including the United Kingdom, Canada, Australia, and elsewhere. Sixty-one were named as operating in the United Kingdom or against British interests abroad. In total, six of these were "legal" spymasters either working at embassies or at Soviet trading organizations. Another twenty were named as "illegals." Krivitsky was able to detail their nationalities, including three Americans, three Germans, three Austrians, two Dutch, one Pole, and eight Russians. Nine had covers as businessmen and three as artists. Others varied in alleged occupations. There was a journalist, a secretary, a student, and even an ice-skater. The defector was vague about the work of the other four.

He divulged the names of leading illegals who had operated in London, including Arnold Deutsch, Max Petrovsky, and Theodore Maly and his subagent Gadar. Significantly, these had been senior Comintern figures who were now dead or departed from the United Kingdom. Krivitsky was playing it safe by naming them, as he had been in exposing King and Tyler Kent, an American cipher clerk in the U.S. embassy in London. These two agents were low-level, expendable, and replaceable.

He gave bigger clues on a more important agent when he told Sissmore about a White Russian called Vladimir von Petrov, who had been an important Soviet military intelligence (GRU) agent with valuable sources of secret data in Britain. One source had even supplied details about the British Secret Intelligence Services itself.

Some action seems to have been taken here by Sissmore, as the expanded file on von Petrov demonstrates, but it led nowhere, and no arrests were made. (Later, after Philby's defection in 1963, MI5 officer Peter Wright went through the file on von Petrov. He found that, according to a German intelligence officer interrogated after the Nazi defeat, the Paris-based von Petrov had also been a source about Britain for the Germans. A German naval officer went further and named von Petrov as a "Captain Charles Howard Ellis." Ellis was Australian and had a White Russian wife. When Kim Philby became head of Section 1X, the counterintelligence section of MI6, he reviewed the file and scribbled in the margin: "Who is this man Ellis? NFA," for "No Further Action." It would be one of many bits of intelligence supplied by Krivitsky that would haunt Philby for some time.)[22]

More pertinent to MI5's interests was Krivitsky's exposé of the thirty-five local agents run by the twenty-six legal and illegal spy-masters. There were sixteen British nationals. Eight were active in left-wing politics and the trade union movement; six were civil servants, and two were journalists.

Half of these names were new to MI5. Steps were taken to make sure their activities were not a threat to British interests, but none was prosecuted, nor were their identities revealed. Liddell argued that to expose them would dilute the effectiveness of Krivitsky's information.

"The Russians would only replace them with others," he told colleagues. "Better to 'neutralize' them."[23]

Sissmore tried to extract more about the two higher-ranking foreign office spies, whom the defector claimed he did not know by name. Sissmore showed him papers from the Imperial Defense Council's report of 1937, which he had read in Moscow before his defection. Krivitsky spoke about the agent involved as having a Scottish name and something Bohemian in his background. He was considered "artistic" and "sometimes wore a cape."

"He is of a good family and his father is prominent," Krivitsky recalled. "He [the agent] had been at Eton and Oxford."

"When was he recruited?" Sissmore asked.

"In the mid-1930s. He is an idealist working without payment."[24]

These clues were too broad, Liddell suggested. Some none-too-intensive inquiries were ordered to be carried out discreetly but led nowhere.[25] There were countless employees with Scottish names, and many had an Eton/Oxford background. All were found to be "clean." The Bohemian clue was ignored except that it fitted just one character, the bisexual, bagpipe playing ambassador, Lord Inverchapel. He had developed a deep admiration for the Soviet Union when posted to Stockholm in 1934. He was investigated, and nothing out of the ordinary was discovered, apart from his eccentricities and sexual proclivities.

The real spy to whom Krivitsky referred was the Cambridge network's Donald Maclean, who had not been at Eton or Oxford. Nearly a decade later, the defector's information would match that picked up by deciphering the cables sent from Washington to Moscow (known as the Venona decrypts), and Maclean would be forced to flee to Russia. But in February 1940 the data was sparse and not strong enough, unless a serious investigation was ordered. Liddell had neither the will nor the inclination to probe further.

A more potent clue pointing to another key spy in the Cambridge ring came when Krivitsky told Sissmore that "Soviet intelligence had sent a young English journalist to Spain during the Spanish civil war."[26] According to MI5 documents released late in 2001 by England's Public Record Office, Krivitsky said that Soviet intelligence directed another agent, Paul Hardt, to order the journalist to kill Franco.

Sissmore asked Krivitsky to put his memories on paper. The Russian wrote:

[Soviet intelligence] received orders from Stalin to arrange the murder of General Franco. Hardt was instructed by [intelligence] chief Yezhov to recruit an Englishman for the purpose. He did in fact contact and send to

Spain a young Englishman, a journalist of good family, an idealist and fanatical anti-Nazi. Before the plan matured, Hardt himself was recalled to
Moscow [during Stalin's purges] in 1937 and disappeared [i.e., was liqui-
dated].

Amazingly, one officer wrote in the margin of Krivitsky's report, "prob.
[probably] PHILBY."

Once more, Liddell did nothing to encourage investigation into such a
clue, citing the fact that there would be countless individuals with that
background. Furthermore, journalists, recruited or not, could do little
damage beyond propaganda. Although Krivitsky alluded to Philby, it is
unlikely he knew him by name. Krivitsky had heard about the journalist
in Spain while on his last trip to Moscow in 1937, which is shown in a
letter from the Moscow Center to the London KGB resident:

> Our source Johnson (the code name for Blunt) passed to us the testimony of
> Krivitsky. . . . (He) announced that Maly sent a British journalist from a
> good family that sympathized with the Soviet Union and who was recruited
> on ideological grounds to Spain to assassinate Franco. This example must be
> kept in mind when dealing with valuable agents. In his work Krivitsky had
> no connection to Stanley (code name for Philby), but apparently using the
> loose lips of our former staff at the residence in England, he received top
> secret information on Stanley. . . .[27]

Although not yet recruited to B Section of MI5, Blunt was already
close to Liddell, who would have mentioned Krivitsky's testimony to
him. The scare would play hard on Philby's mind over the next fifteen
years and for decades after that. He touched on it three times in his memoirs and elaborated further about the problems it caused him in his interviews with writers Phillip Knightley and Genrihk Borovik.[28] (When
British intelligence's Helenus "Buster" Milmo interrogated him after the
Burgess/Maclean defections in 1951, the Krivitsky comments led to a
question about the young journalist sent by the GRU to kill Franco.
Philby stuttered his way through this by pointing out that if he had been
the assassin, he had plenty of chances to murder Franco in six interviews
with him.)

At the time of Krivitsky's revelations, Philby had done excellent work
in Spain, but he had yet to penetrate British intelligence. He did so in

July 1940 when he joined the Special Operations Executive (SOE), which was to carry out sabotage in Europe, and a year later reached Special Intelligence Services (SIS), his long-term KGB assignment.

The worry for the Moscow Center with Krivitsky was the damage he could do if he disclosed something that led to even one member of the ring. If this were done, the whole network would be in danger of unraveling, and at a time when Stalin and the center had high hopes for its penetrating key areas of intelligence, the military, and weapons research. Not only would Cambridge ring agents such as Maclean, Cairncross, Burgess, and Straight be lost, the long preparation to groom Blunt, Philby, Victor Rothschild (who had joined MI5 in September 1939), Tess Mayor, Leo Long, Alister Watson, and several others for additional service in high places would be a failure.

In April 1940, a secret foreign office report on the Krivitsky case was circulated. It raised political issues generated by his visit to London and touched on some of the revelations, including hints about foreign office penetration. Maclean read the report and discussed it with his control, who had already been informed about it by Blunt, as had Burgess and Rothschild (who, with Tess Mayor, was also working for Liddell in Section B of MI5). The Cambridge ring was now fully alerted to the problems posed by this troublesome defector.

The dangers were underscored as Europe slipped deeper into war. Stalin would not trust the words of anyone, especially his newfound pact-partner, Hitler. He had to have accurate intelligence to make assessments of the intentions of all his key friends and foes.

Krivitsky had, in effect, been on Stalin's hit list since he defected in mid-1937. This was confirmed by Trotsky in April 1940 when he told contacts in Mexico that Stalin wanted two adversaries dead before all others: one was himself; the other was Walter Krivitsky, who knew too many secrets, particularly about the highly successful Cambridge ring.

Stalin was not about to let a great source of espionage dry up.

9

A DEFENSIVE MEASURE

Winston Churchill took over as prime minister of Great Britain in May 1940, and the changes that came with his ascension saw Guy Liddell elevated to chief of counterespionage in British intelligence. A month later his close friend Anthony Blunt was appointed as his assistant (at Victor Rothschild's recommendation) and Soviet intelligence had its strongest foothold yet inside its British counterpart. Guy Burgess soon after was to help Kim Philby into SOE and further strengthen the Soviet position. Then Burgess took off for Moscow via Washington and Japan with Oxford philosopher Isaiah Berlin, who wanted to become press attaché to the British embassy in Moscow now that the communist-supporting Stafford Cripps was installed there as ambassador. Burgess pulled strings at the foreign office to get himself a job as Berlin's assistant. But the mission for both was aborted in Washington when Cripps objected to the foreign office's appointing its choices to his staff.

Burgess arrived in Washington on July 8, 1940, and was invited to Straight's home for dinner.[1] The discussion was friendly, with Burgess regaling Straight with details of his cavorting in a Paris male brothel with the French government's chef du cabinet, Edouard Pfeiffer. Burgess seemed to have full confidence in his protégé. There was further chat that indicated to Straight that Leo Long had been recruited as a KGB agent by

Blunt. It was something Burgess would never have disclosed had he doubted Straight's "blood-brother" allegiances.

Straight described Long as the strong, silent type, a noble working-class scholar member of the Trinity cell, presumably like John Cairncross, another spy in the Cambridge ring. He was one of five successful recommendations for the Apostles when Straight stacked the society with hard-line communists in 1937.[2] One more of his appointees had been seduced into the next step and had followed him into KGB agency. According to FBI files, Burgess told Straight that at the annual Apostles dinner, held in London, Blunt had become "disillusioned when another [homosexual] Apostle made a play for Leo."

In the middle of the dinner, Burgess went further in his show of confidence in his protégé. "I've been out of touch with our friends for several months," he remarked, meaning KGB representatives. "Can you put me back in touch with them?" Straight denied in his autobiography (published in 1983) that he could or would. But when he was interrogated by the FBI (1963 to 1975), Straight said he "merely accepted this statement and made no comment and changed the subject."

Either way, apparently, he did not help Burgess link up with the KGB. Straight was adamant that this meeting was the first in which he realized that Burgess was a KGB agent. Until then, he said that he assumed that only he and Blunt were operatives. This was disingenuous and contradicts his other observations about Burgess, whom he knew or suspected was behind Blunt's overtures to him.

After this convivial meeting with his recruiter, Straight made a hasty, persistent attempt to pull every string he could to get back into State. Burgess and the KGB wanted him on assignment there once more. There was a rush for Straight to be in place to monitor Krivitsky's movements now that the defector was targeted for assassination.

According to FBI files, on July 9, 1940—the day after Straight's meeting with Burgess—he began moves to leave his speechwriting job at the White House to rejoin the State Department. A job on the British Empire desk had opened up, he informed family and friends. He said he was afraid of working for the State Department, particularly because he would be in intellectual exile after his stimulating work as a speechwriter for Roosevelt. He also worried about his wife's social life, which would not be as active as it had been while he was at the White House.[3]

Straight's lack of enthusiasm about joining State again was understandable if, as he claimed, he had left the department a year earlier to avoid Michael Green. If Straight needed assistance in getting the job, he had several avenues to follow. For instance, he could have called on his stepfather Leonard, who had cemented his friendship with the U.S. president. Leonard had dined at the White House with Roosevelt two months earlier in May 1940.[4] Then the president asked Leonard to ring him at the White House if there were anything vital England needed to withstand a then-expected Nazi invasion following the British retreat at Dunkirk in May. This resulted in Roosevelt giving fifty old destroyers to the Royal Navy in September.[5]

Yet Straight's connection to Ben Cohen and the president was probably enough without Leonard's intervention this time. Straight had progressed since his days as a callow youth in 1937 when he first visited the White House. He had done his own networking and had cultivated those useful to him.

The president sent a letter dated July 29 to State recommending Straight for a job, as did Ben Cohen.[6] Straight claimed that a job was offered at State by the assistant secretary in the department, James C. Dunn, because a desk had become vacant in the European Division. Verne Newton, the director of the Franklin D. Roosevelt Library, disputes this in his book, *The Cambridge Spies*: "The only thing the two had in common was immense unearned wealth," Newton commented. "Son of a Newark bricklayer and a high school dropout, Dunn escaped the tedium of minor State Department administrative posts when he married the heiress to the Armour meat-packing fortune."[7]

Furthermore, Dunn was an archconservative. He would not see eye-to-eye on anything with Straight whether he was acting as an archliberal or as a hard-line communist.

"Where Dunn became the son the Secretary of State Cordell Hull never had," Newton added, "Straight's ties were to the White House, which treated Hull like a leper."

James Dunn was the designated receiver of MI5 reports. British intelligence suspected that Straight had sought out and obtained a position of strategic importance to the KGB.[8] But it was unlikely to be the reason for joining State, even though the Cambridge ring—well placed within MI5—would have known of Dunn's role. There would be little point in the KGB receiving edited reports from MI5 through an agent with access to Dunn's files in the United States. It could have all the data it wanted from MI5 from its agents on the inside in London, such as Blunt, Rothschild, Tess Mayor, and possibly Liddell himself.

Rather than the desire to have Straight in the European Division, its assistant chief, Jack Hickerson, said that "we tried our damnedest to keep Straight out . . . we didn't want him. He wasn't our choice. He was not a professional. He had political pull and he used it."[9]

The president's power won the day, and Straight was in at State, again. He got through routine clearances, which did not delve back into his Cambridge past, and began work on August 27 as a Grade 4 full professional at $3,800 a year in the European Division. It was his first real paid government appointment.

Straight celebrated his twenty-fourth birthday in his underwhelming post. He had to sit and listen, Hickerson said, to the sad stories of the American expatriates who had returned from France when it was overrun by Hitler's armies. Expats feared the Nazis would take over their townhouses in Paris and their French country properties. Hickerson remembered Straight giving the expats solemn assurances that State officials would place rosters on their land saying "American Property." This cynical attitude added more to the apparent folly of Straight taking on such an innocuous position, unless he was there to monitor Krivitsky. He had nothing to gain from the position and much to lose. Had he been exposed at that time as one of Stalin's men in the United States, it would have been contentious, to say the least, and dangerous for Straight. So far none of the Cambridge ring had been exposed. Stalin; key members of the ring, such as Burgess, Blunt, and Philby; their controls; and the assassination squads at their disposal were combining to solve the Krivitsky problem.

———

Half of Trotsky's prophecy was fulfilled when one of Stalin's killers put an ice pick in his skull on August 20, 1940. Krivitsky heard the news while hiding out in Canada, where he had been since returning from England after his interrogations in January and February. He was shaken but determined to return to the United States to resume his drive for citizenship, which he did in late October. He felt certain that the information he gave

MI5 would not be acted on. He told friends that there did not seem the will in British intelligence to follow up on his leads. Liddell's reserve worried him.

However, Krivitsky was not aware that MI5's Jane Sissmore and others had been following up on his leads, such as those concerning one of his "serials" (agents) in Paris, von Petrov, who Krivitsky alleged had been an important agent for the GRU during the prewar period. This von Petrov (as explained earlier, really the Australian, Charles Ellis) had good sources in Britain as well as Germany, where he was operating as a double agent for the Germans and the Russians. MI5 now wanted to know more about him. It was also under pressure from the foreign office to obtain more intelligence on the alleged spies in its ranks. According to Peter Wright, MI5 had decided to send an officer to Washington to further debrief Krivitsky in late February or March 1941. Liddell favored Victor Rothschild, who was on good terms with the Americans following his commercial espionage in B Section when he recommended that all major German industrial organizations in the United Kingdom be sold off to U.S. companies. (Rothschild was later a key MI5 troubleshooter and interrogator, particularly of Nazi prisoners in Paris.)[10]

The Russians' worry would now be that Krivitsky might be prepared to divulge some of the "important" information he had so far withheld. This would have included new clues on the Cambridge ring, which in the months since his London debriefing and Liddell's promotion had entrenched itself further into the British intelligence services and other vital areas.

Stalin was receiving a whole raft of data that daily increased his strength in dealing with other governmental heads, and it was only the beginning. Even though by early 1941 the Russians were nervous about their pact with Hitler, the two nations were not yet at war. Stalin wished to remain well fed with intelligence. He insisted on seeing all the information coming in from the key spies, who were already becoming familiar to him and the Moscow Center by their code names . . . Johnson, Stanley, Madchen, Homer and others. Stalin demanded to see all messages as soon as they had been deciphered. It gave him great satisfaction to receive the truth from them about what his opposite numbers were actually thinking and doing, rather than what they were simply mouthing publicly or saying in communiqués to him.[11]

If one code name were uncovered, then the lot might be caught in a disaster for the Moscow Center. If Blunt were ever interrogated, his connections to recruits such as Straight might emerge, especially as their links at Cambridge only a few years earlier would be recalled.

Krivitsky, back in New York, was now a serious threat and would be in need of as much protection and help as possible. But he was at times doing little to help his cause. His prickly, difficult nature had seen him fall out with friends he needed, such as Isaac Don Levine. The journalist had wanted more details for their articles for the *Saturday Evening Post*. Krivitsky was torn between full disclosure and a desire to protect old comrades. He still believed in the 1917 Russian revolution and tried to make a distinction between its importance and Stalinism. Thus he held back "the most important" information.[12]

Krivitsky avoided anyone who might be connected to his past life in the KGB, such as Paul Wohl, who had worked for him as a Soviet agent in France and Switzerland. They had been friends on the first stay in New York. Krivitsky owed Wohl $200, and Wohl was trying to trace him for it.

There were still a few supporters. Whittaker Chambers was encouraging, as was Loy Henderson at State, whom he visited often at his office in November and December 1940. Henderson was helping with contacts and in pushing for the end of Krivitsky's immigration problems.

Just down the corridor from Henderson's office at State was the office of the European Division, where Straight was pretending to lend a sympathetic ear to expatriates from France. He could not have been better placed to observe Krivitsky's visits.

Krivitsky's main paranoia was that he was being watched, followed, eventually to be set up for a kill. He was trained in tradecraft and could slip away from the KGB watchers, as he had done on many occasions. But he feared most of all the friendly or anonymous face of someone such as Straight who could learn his movements on any given day and alert one of Stalin's three-man hit squads. They in turn would isolate and trap him.

He complained to friends about the constant feeling of being hunted. Yet he could live with this, just as long as he knew who the enemy was and where he was likely to be.

On one occasion he escaped in the New York subway when three people, one of whom he thought he recognized as George Mink, tried to corner him. Mink was a former head of the U.S. Communist Party's Seamen's Union, who traveled freely in and out of the country on a false passport. The "undereducated, arrogant, ruthless, and boastful" Mink was an experienced Russian assassin who had carried out many assignments during the Spanish Civil War. His hits included members of the British Independent Labour Party and the American Socialist Party. He was a close relative of Solomon Lozovsky, the chief of the Soviet Profintern—the communist-led international trade union organization. This connection in the mid-1930s saw Mink bounce from being a taxi driver in Philadelphia to the chairmanship of the Marine Workers' Industrial Union. He first came to the notice of authorities worldwide when he was arrested for raping a chambermaid in a Copenhagen hotel, where codes, addresses, and false passports were found in his possession. Mink spent eighteen months in jail and then returned to Washington, on another false passport.[13] He was well known to Krivitsky, who may have even directed him on occasions in Europe.

After spotting Mink, Krivitsky rang Henderson, who advised him to get in touch with the New York police. Krivitsky obeyed the directive, but the local precinct was not equipped or willing to give regular protection.

In January 1941, he had his second chilling reminder that his days could be numbered when he was passed a letter from Paul Wohl. It was addressed to the writer Suzanne La Follette, the sister of Bob La Follette, the Wisconsin senator, whom Straight had gotten to know while researching his thesis on Nazi rearmament early in 1938. Suzanne, a Trotskyite and member of the American committee for the defense of Leon Trotsky, had befriended and helped the Krivitskys. She had urged her brother to give support in congress for their attempts to gain citizenship. Suzanne was well known as a conduit for messages to the Krivitskys.

The KGB was aware of the La Follette-Krivitsky association for at least two reasons. Stalin had focused his secret police on any Trotskyites. Now the defector—its main assassination target—was associated with them. The La Follette link also provided a second avenue for Straight to explore if he had been ordered to help track Krivitsky. This may have been facilitated by his Trotskyite affiliations, which allegedly so worried his KGB masters when he first began operating in the United States.

The January 7, 1941, letter from Wohl to Suzanne said:

My dear Miss La Follette,

Will you please inform your honorable friend K. that an ominous person is in New York: Hans. This letter is addressed to you since K. hides from me. Obviously, to escape the serving of a summons for the remaining $200 which he owes me in virtue of a formal arbitration award to which I submitted at his request.

His devious practices hardly justify this warning. I hesitate to send it. It may be better to let the rats devour each other.

Yours Truly,
Paul Wohl[14]

Wohl's letter, however disgruntled, was a warning. "Hans" was Hans Bruesse, Krivitsky's former chauffeur in Europe. His arrival in New York (Wohl had spotted him at a Manhattan bus stop) meant one thing to Krivitsky. Bruesse, who had made two earlier attempts in France to eliminate him, would be teaming up with Mink and a third man for another attempt at his liquidation. Stalin had put a figure of $100,000 on Trotsky's head. Mink, who had failed to deliver in Mexico, would be ambitious to cash in on this new target.

Krivitsky now felt there was nowhere to turn in New York's glass canyons. He wanted to escape. He told friends he was thinking about moving to the country and planned to visit his new acquaintances Eitel and Marguerite Dobert, who ran a 90-acre chicken farm in rural Virginia near Charlottesville, about 100 miles from Washington, D.C. Eitel was an ex-Nazi stormtrooper who in the early 1930s gave up his fascist affiliations and fled to the United States. In recent years he had associated with communists, which led to his friendship with Krivitsky when they met at a writers' colony in upstate New York in November. Krivitsky rang Eitel and said he was coming to look at their chicken farm (although the Doberts later claimed they did not know when).

On Monday, February 3, Krivitsky went to see Chambers in New York. "We spent hours together, tramping the streets," Chambers recalled, "taking circuitous routes and watching, as in the underground old days, to see if we were followed."[15]

They talked about Krivitsky's problems and his fears about assassination. He reminded Chambers that if "they" decided to kill him, it would be made to look like a suicide. Stalin was happy to have Trotsky openly murdered in Mexico and Ignaz Reiss filled with bullets and left on a lonely road in Switzerland, but he was unlikely to be so brazen inside the United States. A suicide would be neater and less antagonistic to U.S.-Soviet relations. People like Bruesse and Mink were expert at setting up such a scene.

Chambers and Krivitsky also spoke about religion.

"Like me," Chambers wrote, "Krivitsky had become convinced that religious faith is a human necessity. . . . He asked me if I would arrange for his instruction so that he could be baptized and confirmed in the Episcopal Church."

According to Chambers, Krivitsky also told him that a few days before, he had stopped carrying a revolver and had placed it in a bureau drawer. His 7-year-old son Alex watched him. The boy asked why he had put the gun away. Krivitsky told him that "nobody carried a revolver in America."

"Papa," the child said, "carry the revolver."[16]

On Thursday, February 8, 1941, Krivitsky took the train alone south and once more visited the solicitous Henderson at State. (There, Straight was on good terms with those who could help him with his surveillance.) Krivitsky told Henderson of his plans for the weekend to visit his friends' chicken farm. He would stay there Friday and Saturday nights and return Sunday when he would catch the train back to New York, in time for testimony there about communist infiltration into education. He was thinking about buying his own farm.

Krivitsky told Henderson of his intention to purchase a gun in Virginia where, unlike New York and New Jersey, he did not need a permit.[17] He mentioned the news that the assassin Hans Bruesse was in New York, and gave this as the reason that he needed a weapon for protection.

After spending Thursday night in his Washington "safe house"—a hotel—he found his way to the Doberts' remote farm at Barboursville, Virginia, either by taxi or via a ride with an unidentified American.[18]

Barboursville, reached by taking Routes 66, 29, and 33 from Washington, D.C., even today is a small, isolated town. The area was not well marked. Finding the correct chicken farm was difficult.

The Doberts did not know how Krivitsky arrived on Friday, February 7, 1941. They did not see a vehicle, only the uninvited guest.

"There was a knock at the front door," Mrs. Dobert recalled. "I opened the door and there was Walter. I never thought to ask how he got there. Perhaps a taxi."[19]

The Doberts and Krivitsky talked in German into the night. He asked countless questions about chicken farming and seemed obsessed about becoming a farmer. But the attraction of the area's remoteness was uppermost in his mind.

"It's safe and peaceful here," he told them. Krivitsky, if armed and vigilant, gave himself some chance of surviving in such isolation. The Doberts were dubious about his desire to work on the land. Mrs. Dobert couldn't picture him doing it.[20]

"He was a total intellectual," she said. "Not the type!"

The Doberts were tired after a day's work, and they went to bed. Krivitsky woke them shortly afterward, complaining of a headache, which was keeping him awake. The genial Mrs. Dobert gave him some aspirin and writing paper.

Krivitsky remained restless through the night. He wrote letters and then early in the morning went for a long walk in the woods. The Doberts had found him highly strung previously. That weekend, they thought his manner in keeping with what they knew of his character. In other words, Krivitsky did or said nothing to indicate that he was abnormally on edge.

The next morning, Saturday, February 8, Mrs. Dobert drove him to a hardware store (the façade of which has been kept—it's now a restaurant) in Charlottesville. He bought a .38-caliber automatic pistol for fifteen dollars and two boxes of mushroom bullets, which were more lethal than those normally sold at the store. Krivitsky was chatty and upbeat, telling the clerk who sold him the gun and the store manager, Charles Henshaw, that he would soon be moving into the area. Back at the farm, Krivitsky spent the afternoon at target practice.

Late Sunday morning Mrs. Dobert drove Krivitsky to Washington. Along the way, they took a wrong turn, which saw them driving for some time on isolated back roads. Krivitsky was ever watchful, but no car followed them. They arrived at Union Station in the late afternoon.

Mrs. Dobert recalled the final matters discussed. "Do you want me to post those letters?" she asked him, referring to those he had written.

"I'll look after them myself," he replied.

"Have you got your 'artillery'?" she asked, referring to his pistol.

Krivitsky answered by patting his only luggage, a canvas bag.

"Do you think there is a place to have a bath here?" Krivitsky asked, glancing at the station entrance. "Most stations like this in Europe have one."

Mrs. Dobert didn't know. She felt conscious of the fact that there had not been running water at the farm, hence Krivitsky's concern about a bath. He had nearly an hour before the next New York train was due.

His last words to her were a sad refrain heard by several people who knew him at the time: "If anything should happen to me, look after Tonya and Alex."[21] Mrs. Dobert wished him a safe journey and left him walking toward the station.

Krivitsky's next known move was to walk at a 45-degree angle away from the front entrance across North Capitol Street NW to East Street, and then 50 meters down on the right-hand side of the street (as it would be entered from Union Station) to the small Bellevue Hotel. It would have taken him less than three minutes. One simple explanation for this was his need for a bath before his train at 6:30 P.M.: the Bellevue was the nearest decent hotel in the vicinity. Perhaps he was directed there by a station worker, or perhaps he found it himself. If he had spotted Bruesse or Mink, he would not have strolled to the nearest hotel and casually checked in.

The registry showed that he registered under the name of Walter Poref at 5:49 P.M. The staff did not notice anything unusual as he went up the elevator to the fifth floor, where he made two rights and found room 522 on the left of the corridor. The room (preserved until today by the management because of its "celebrity" status) he entered had an archway just beyond the door, a bathroom, and a bed. The room's window had a ledgeless sill looking out to a brick wall across a five-yard divide and a straight drop to the ground five levels below. The only possible exit or entry was the room's door.

———— • ————

Thelma Jackson, a 21-year-old maid, knocked several times on the door to 522 the next morning, Monday, February 10, at 9:30 A.M. When there was no answer, she used her passkey to open the door, although from the outside there was no way of telling if it was locked from the inside. In other words, if Jackson had simply turned the handle, it may have opened, although she assumed it was locked.[22]

She entered the room. She was shocked to see a man lying face down on the bed, his head toward the foot of the bed. A pistol was on the floor. Jackson noticed the blood, then a wound in the right temple. A .130-grain mushroom bullet had been fired into the temple. It had exploded out below the left ear, leaving a wound the size of a fist.

The Washington metropolitan police and the coroner were notified. Finding three notes, their quick, joint conclusion by 11:30 A.M., just two hours after Jackson found the body, was suicide. The room was ordered scrubbed clean, a job that was completed in an hour. Soon after that, room 522 was back on the hotel's inventory of available rooms.

The suicide finding was soon disputed by Krivitsky's lawyer, Paul Waldman, who arrived at 11:00 P.M. from New York. He viewed the body at the morgue and was suspicious about the head wounds. He noted that a self-inflicted wound would not have been made that way. The entry and exit holes of the mushroom bullet were consistent with a shot from the weapon held at least a yard from the head. To commit suicide this way would have meant Krivitsky's holding the gun at full stretch with his right hand and well above his head, which would be awkward and less likely to succeed. A more certain way to commit suicide would be to hold the gun close to the temple. The recoil of the gun would have pushed it further to the right, but it was found to the left of the body. The lawyer was told that the ejected cartridge case, but not the bullet itself, was found.

Waldman consulted police and held a press conference. He called for an FBI investigation. But J. Edgar Hoover made it plain that there would not be one. He resented Krivitsky for daring to suggest that the United States was riddled with Soviet agents. As director of the bureau, he was not about to support that statement by looking for a gang of Stalin's killers.[23]

Krivitsky was as unwanted in death as he was in life. The press furor that followed saw the coroner retract his suicide finding. Journalists converged on the Doberts's farm. Eitel was sure he had committed suicide because he had written notes on Friday night. Yet he had not seen them. Mrs. Dobert hesitated at first, then agreed with her husband about the thought that he must have been planning to kill himself. It was enough for the police and the vacillating coroner, who once more issued a suicide finding.

The original notes—on plain paper headed "Charlottesville, Virginia"—were never delivered to the three intended recipients: Tonya, Waldham, and writer and journalist Suzanne La Follette. Instead they received translations. Waldham challenged the translations and had them revised.

The longest letter was in Russian addressed to Tonya and Alex:

> It is very difficult. I want very badly to live but I must not live any longer. I love you, my only one. It is hard for me to write but think of me and then you will understand why I must go. Don't tell Alex yet where his father has gone. I believe that, in time, you should tell him, because that would be best for him. Forgive me. It is very difficult to write. Take care of him and be a good mother to him and be always calm and never get angry with him. . . . Good people will help you but no enemies of the Soviet People. My sins are very great.
>
> I see you, Tonya and Alex, I embrace you.[24]

These lines were typical of forced false confessions by countless Russians during the purges. The secret police branded them enemies of the Soviet people.

The letter to Waldman, in English, was briefer but added a strange postscript explanation for his actions:

> Dear Mr. Waldman,
>   My wife and boy will need your help. Please do for them what you can.

The postscript ran:

> I went to Virginia because I knew that there I can get a gun. If my friends get in trouble, please help them. They are good people and didn't know what I got the gun for.

The last letter, in German, to Suzanne La Follette read:

> Dear Suzanne,
>   I trust that you are well. I die in the hope that you will help Tonya and my poor boy. You were a good friend.[25]

All three recipients said that the syntax, postscripts, and general tone did not seem at all like Krivitsky's style.

———

In 1996, Yuri Modin suggested in our interviews what many had suspected since 1941: Krivitsky had been murdered. Modin's remarks to me were the first by a senior KGB operative admitting as much. He was supported by another ex-Russian spy who did not wish to be named. This is backed up by hints in secret Russian cables from Washington, which show that the death of Krivitsky was used as a warning to a defector, Viktor Kravchenko, from the Soviet Government Purchasing Commission. A message from the KGB in New York to Moscow remarks: "KOMAR [Kravchenko's code name] is well informed about KRIVITSKY case."[26]

Philby also gave some indication of foul play in his interviews with Genrihk Borovik. An exchange in his 1994 book, *The Philby Files,* is revealing: "We can assume that the OGPU [absorbed into the NVKD—the KGB's forerunner—in July 1934] finished him off," Borovik remarked when comparing Krivitsky to another defector, Orlov, who "was not harmed."

"Krivitsky, unlike Orlov, betrayed many people, including me," Philby responded with indignation. "It did not have tragic consequences for me, since he did not know my name or the paper where I worked. But if he had he would have betrayed me totally."[27]

A possible scenario of the events of the night of February 9 is this: Bruesse; Mink; and a third man, Jack Parilla, a known assassin with the nickname "the Hunchback," came to Washington on Friday, February 7, after a tip-off from Straight of Krivitsky's movements. They did not need to follow him to Barboursville. If they knew of his plans to catch the last train to New York at 6:30 P.M. on Sunday, they only needed to watch Union Station.

They tailed him to the Bellevue and entered his room in one of several possible ways. They could have used a passkey kept in a closet on each floor, or they could have forced their way in. Bruesse was an expert locksmith who could have picked the lock to room 522. The three killers, under orders to make an assassination look like suicide, forced Krivitsky to write suicide notes by saying that if he did not obey, Tonya and Alex would be murdered too. (That seemed to fit the tone of the note to them, especially the contradictory comment: "I want very badly to live, but I must not live any longer.")

No patrons or staff at the hotel heard a noise, but a weapon with a silencer could have been used. There was no solid proof (proper ballistics were not carried out, nor were fingerprints taken thoroughly) that the gun found by Krivitsky's side had been the one fired at him. Whichever way it happened, no sound of a shot is further evidence that it was not suicide.

Although there were no reported sightings of Bruesse in Washington, an FBI report said Mink was involved in stalking and killing Krivitsky. In addition, Parilla was reported there (by a witness to the senate subcommittee on security a few years later) from February 7 and through the weekend.[28]

Parilla was back in New York by February 13, drinking with merchant seamen at National Maritime Union headquarters.

"He loafed around for quite a while," the witness reported. "He got drunk, became very vicious, and dropped a hint of murder to several of the trusted seamen, who were comrades at the time."[29]

Despite all the questions about the death, and the many incoming reports to the FBI from agents suggesting foul play and evidence of it, Hoover refused to investigate. He used his autocratic power to shut down any attempts to portray it as other than suicide. It suited his political purposes at that time to brook no suggestion that the U.S. public was other than well protected against infiltration by foreign assassins. Meanwhile, three killers were free to roam the United States and the world, committing more mayhem.

———— • ————

The death meant that the biggest threat to Straight and the fellow members of his spy ring had been eliminated. Straight gave the impression that the event preyed on his mind to the extent that when an intruder tried to break into his house, he thought that the KGB was after him. But this was misleading. He was a member of the Cambridge ring and had helped in the assassination of Krivitsky. The KGB would have been pleased with his work.

Straight made out in his autobiography that he was fearful of the KGB because of what happened to Krivitsky.[30]

This was part of a cover for any Straight connection to the death. At no time had he made a serious attempt to leave the KGB. At this point he was deeply involved; he had nothing to fear from the KGB if he did his job. Once Krivitsky had been eliminated, the assignment was over. Straight wasted no time in leaving State; his job was done. Only three days after Krivitsky's body was found—on February 13—he landed this time at *The New Republic*, which was always going to be a safe haven. Not long after taking up his job as a journalist, a short article appeared in the February 24, 1941, edition of the magazine, two weeks after Krivitsky's demise:

Here was a man who had exposed the misdeeds of the worldwide Soviet organization. There is little doubt that Stalin would like to have seen him murdered. . . . At once his [Krivitsky's] friends, who naturally for this purpose included all of Stalin's enemies, declared he was a victim of a GPU [KGB] assassination. The press, always looking for anti-Russian items, gave great stress to this interpretation. The Washington Police, however concluded that Krivitsky died by his own hand. . . . To be sure, it is still possible to argue that, in a sense, Stalin killed him. He was so hounded and harried by the memory of what he had done and by fear of reprisals by his former comrades that he could hardly be called sane and responsible. . . .

To that point the item would have suited the sentiments of Stalinist agents. The irresponsible and insane traitor to the cause betrayed his comrades. The article could even have been construed as a warning to all those agents working for the KGB not to consider leaving Stalin's service. But the next paragraph was more definite. It warned not to become involved in the KGB's secret world: "We are beginning to learn that anybody who enters the secret service of a totalitarian ruler has already in a sense committed suicide. He is a dead man from the moment he takes the oath."

After his meeting with Guy Burgess on July 8, 1940, Straight informed his wife Bin of his secret work and his links to KGB agents Blunt and Burgess. Bin Straight said she was very disturbed by the news. She asked him to break off contact with Green by early the next year.[31] (Bin never had anything to do with his underground activities.) This disclosure was an added pressure. The Krivitsky affair drew Straight deeper into the KGB net.

Was it getting enough out of this very special agent? There was always a feeling, first allegedly expressed by Theodore Maly, that Green was not up to the task of nurturing this exceptional recruit. The thought gained currency at the Moscow Center.

Arguably the best controller of personalities as such, Yuri Modin, who handled the varying characters of the Cambridge ring with the natural aplomb of a man twice his age (he was 24 when he first met Cairncross and Blunt in England in 1947), would have dealt with Straight in a more lateral, sophisticated way.

His psychology in manipulating the childlike Cairncross, the cynical Blunt, the outrageous Burgess, and the tough-minded Philby was outstanding. Yet Straight was another individual altogether. In our interviews, Modin indicated that he would have done a better job than Green. "Straight was not handled well," he said. "It should have been done far, far better."[32]

All controls in the Comintern and after were encouraged to study the psychology of their charges and to know every detail about them. But following Maly and Deutsch, who had chosen Straight, there was a lapse in attitude of later Russian controls. Anatoli Gorsky, Ivan Milovzorov, and others had been too brusque with Burgess, Blunt, and Cairncross, even to the point of bullying them. While Straight never complained about Green this way, there seemed to be an emphasis on drilling rather than encouraging him. Green was efficient and friendly enough yet more concerned with his own point-scoring in Russia than playing psychological games. He had his own career to worry about, not to mention a score of other spies supplying data. These were low-key types who were more ideological than ambitious. They received enough stimulation from a stolen document here and piece of equipment to be photographed there. It was all for the cause and against fascism. That was incentive enough.

Yet even given a control like Modin, it is doubtful that Straight's political ambition would have been sated by any amount of praise, cajoling, encouragement, and ego-soothing. Straight had drives that had to be met. They went beyond being a small-time thief and research analyst for a foreign power. If he could, he would manage all his aspirations.

10

NEW REPUBLIC, OLD WAYS

Straight had to have a plausible reason for his sudden departure from State again, especially after using his connection to the president and the First Lady to get in the department both times. His thin explanation was Roosevelt's decision to replace Joe Kennedy as ambassador to Great Britain with John G. Winant, a former Republican governor of New Hampshire. The appointment was announced in the press on February 10, 1941, and shared the headlines with Krivitsky's death. Winant toured the State Department soon afterward, where he met Straight and talked about Great Britain for an hour.[1]

This hour, Straight claimed, inspired him so much that he wanted a job with the urbane, strong Winant. The haste with which he moved to have strings pulled for him had the same resonance as his original effort to enter government via the Roosevelts, along with his more recent bid to slip back into State. The first string to a possible new posting was Ben Cohen, who had joined Winant. Straight also phoned Felix Frankfurter (whom he had contacted in 1933 to help him get into the London School of Economics) at the Supreme Court and told him he wanted to be on Winant's staff in London.[2]

Winant was more successful than Jack Hickerson had been at State in blocking the precocious Straight, who again used his family (this time brother Whitney at a Royal Air Force base in the United Kingdom, which Winant visited) and connections to leap over career professionals. Yet if Straight were going to be thwarted, it had to be by the commander-in-chief, not a mere diplomat. Roosevelt, he claimed, had vetoed the request because he suspected Straight would resign from the embassy staff and join Whitney at the RAF.[3] The perspicacious president, it seems, was wise to Straight's apparently capricious nature. His basic drive, however, he explained, was that he wanted a challenge.

His mother must have been concerned that he was behaving similarly to his father, Willard. He didn't appear to have enough staying power for any one job. At the very least, his desire to leave government would have been a surprise. Weeks earlier Dorothy wrote from New York to Miss Hull-Brown, her secretary at Dartington, expressing her pride in Michael's progress. She noted that Michael had presided over a public event at which key politicians and the attorney general spoke. Dorothy was enchanted by a story of doing the rounds in Washington that said if you wanted something done, you saw President Roosevelt about it because he had "more influence with Michael Straight than anyone else!"[4]

Straight made sure to keep impressing his mother, and it enabled him to gain her approval for the move to *The New Republic*. The magazine's editor, Bruce Bliven, had no choice but to accept Straight's unabashed use of nepotism. Straight's view was that Bliven was not quite bright enough for his position. He was, Straight maintained, a working journalist rather than an editor of an intellectual journal.[5]

According to Straight, Leonard Elmhirst had told Bliven that *The New Republic*'s approach to the war was callous and timid. The magazine, which had survived for nearly thirty years, suddenly needed something more sensitive and courageous in its makeup. Bliven was in for a shock. The self-styled "loose cannon" Straight had already started work on a 30,000-word article, something new for the magazine. The topic? The U.S. defense program.[6] Bliven had no choice but to publish it as a special supplement, which took three weeks to produce.

There was a great deal of overlap while Straight finished his time at State, according to him, about April 24. (The FBI had his resignation from State as February 28, indicating he gave seven weeks' notice.)

After nearly thirty years of frugal budgets and advances, the magazine spent more—from week one of the brash young Straight's arrival—which was a sign of things to come. But he still had to justify increased expenditures at the battling, low-circulation magazine. Straight had found a little office for $50 a month in an old brownstone near Connecticut Avenue, coincidentally the place where his mother had been born. He hired writers Helen Fuller, Bill Salant, and Alfred Sherrard, along with two young economists from the Federal Reserve Board who had assisted him on the supplement.

The thirty-two-page report, "Democratic Defense," was published February 17, 1941. No doubt subscriptions to the magazine went up at the Kremlin and in Berlin. U.S. defense capability was an area of great interest to future enemies of the United States, particularly as it was expected sooner or later to enter the war. Now they could read about it in the Straight family organ.

The published report, for example, gave estimates of essential raw material production of steel and aluminum, which would easily have been extrapolated into defense industry production of, say, fighter aircraft. In one item titled, "Why We Are Falling Behind," the author noted: "Magnesium is a vital armament production. It is even lighter than aluminum and is equally strong. . . . I. G. Farbenindustrie raised German production in 1940 to 50,000 tons. Our production in 1940 was under 5,000."[7]

Another article, "Capacity and Defense," detailed everything from steel production to the military's copper requirements. And so it went.

Straight and his team were able to get in doors throughout the Washington defense industry on the basis that they were writing about the need to put the nation on a production footing in preparation for a war against fascism. It was a call not so much to arms but rather to massive central government control of essential industries. Fascism had presented an enemy that no liberal or anyone with the facts about its methods and intent could fail to hate. The only way to combat it, according to Straight and his crew, was with a full-blown socialist approach.

The report attacked Roosevelt's Office of Production Management and the businessmen he had called in to run it with such comments as "We have placed our defenses in the hands of men to whom the defense of democracy means the preservation of profits."[8]

The unions loved it. Straight's friend Felix Frankfurter rang and complained about the harsh judgment of businessmen. But Mrs. Roosevelt was interested enough to invite him to the White House for lunch. According to Straight, she was thrilled and had highlighted parts of the article for the president.[9] Roosevelt had never been quite as enthusiastic about Straight as his wife. She was not sure whether he bothered to read the highlighted pieces of the magazine. (On another occasion, when she insisted he read a Straight piece, he complained, "Do I have to?"[10])

——— ———

Straight's hefty lunge at big business was bold enough, but the supplement also stretched itself into a social treatise and touched on civil liberties. In this section was a full-blooded attack on the FBI. It noted the bureau's "compilation of a card index . . . listing thousands of individuals and groups, labor unions and labor leaders, writers, publishers, speakers and articulate liberals. . . ."[11]

There was a subtle attempt to protect Straight's own position:

Its preoccupation with political espionage may already have contributed to making the FBI less efficient in tracking down real spies and traitors. As early as 1938, at the trial of a German spy ring, the federal judge lamented the incompetence of the government's detectives in permitting the chief spies to slip out of their sight and out of the country . . .

Then, borrowing from Lenin, the writer of this section concluded with the phrase "What Must Be Done" (often used in print by Straight) and called for the firing of J. Edgar Hoover. He suggested that the FBI should be "deprived of authority to investigate the non-criminal activities of American citizens."

Hoover responded angrily by writing to the magazine and opening a file on Straight, Dorothy as the true "owner" of *The New Republic*, and some of its editors. Hoover had the magazine investigated, and this led to an FBI report to the criminal division of the Justice Department. It had to judge if prosecution were warranted against Editorial Publications Limited, *The New Republic*'s holding company, which was set up in Canada under the control of the family trust created in 1936 by Dorothy. Hoover wanted the magazine charged for failing to register "in compliance with the provisions of the Foreign Publications Act." The Justice Department investigated and decided that "prosecution was not warranted."[12] Yet this incident showed the extent of Hoover's thirst for revenge.

Undeterred, the magazine replied to Hoover's letter with an article in the April 28 edition. *The New Republic* defended its original attack, citing Hoover's remarks to a House hearing. It mentioned the FBI's fingerprinting of employees at industrial plants "to ascertain whether these individuals have been engaged either in criminal or subversive activities."[13]

A month later, in the May 26 edition, the magazine kept up the pressure on Hoover in an article, "The FBI and Its Money." This questioned the big boost in the bureau's budget and warned Hoover against the misuse of funds.

"We hope," the article began, "that J. Edgar Hoover uses his sixteen millions to detect any potential crime and not for any other purposes." It again went on to attack his card-indexing, wire-tapping, and "crack down" on minorities "holding unpopular beliefs."

It was just the sort of defiance from his enemies among "pinkos and liberals" which brought out the worst in Hoover. *The New Republic* building and Straight's Washington office were now under surveillance.

However, whether unaware or otherwise of the attention that he had drawn to himself, Straight was enjoying the change. *The New Republic* seemed to have given him a new lease on life. He wasn't a journalist at heart, but he was satisfied if he could become the voice of the young New Dealers working for a progressive defense policy. At least this was part of his cover.

He wrote several articles in 1941 and thought that they were the best commentary on the defense program. In his inimitable style he pulled together the far-left New Dealers who had lost favor with Roosevelt and focused them on a socialist approach to defense.

Straight reveled in pointing out a "conspiracy" that General Electric (GE) had with (German group) I. G. Farben "to obstruct the production of an element needed in the manufacture of armaments." GE dropped its advertising with the magazine. He attacked the War Department for opposing the creation of new defense plants. He penned another broadside at the Office of Production Management, listing its failures, industry by industry.[14]

Straight was getting the sort of public reaction at rallies and from irate recipients of criticism in reports, including one from Robert Patterson, the mild-mannered Secretary of the Army, that boosted his ego. It was the kind of nurturing he needed and had not had since his days in the Cambridge Union four years ago. His self-confidence was bubbling once more. Straight was starved of power aphrodisiacs, however minuscule in comparison to those in major corporations, or media outlets such as *The New York Times*, or in the White House. There, in the real fulcrum of world decision-making at a critical time, the president had majority opinion, that of countless minorities like the one Straight represented, and the vast international arena outside the United States to deal with in actuality. Yet it was the power of the presidency that really attracted him. There and only there he could appease the two demons of his secret affiliations and his public aspirations.

His political stirring at *The New Republic* was a beginning. He was already familiar with the workings of the president and the government. Straight worked assiduously on his contacts, usually within the hard-left and liberal spectrum. He considered they were enough—along with the sweep of world events—to allow him one day, in the not too distant future, to make a run for political office.

I'm not a journalist at heart, he told his family. He felt he could be a politician. Yet not just any politician.

The FBI file on Straight grew early in 1941 and included quotes from a February 15 article in the *Saturday Evening Post* called "Muddled Millions, Capitalist Angels of Left-Wing Propaganda." This named *The New Republic* and *The Nation* as the two journals that had "given most aid and prestige to the Communists in the country." The FBI estimated that the Straight family had subsidized *The New Republic* to the annual tune of $100,000.[15]

The report went on to add that "these communistically inclined publications [had] benefited from the Straight fortune to the extent of approximately $2,500,000." The agent filing the report had simply multiplied the number of years—around twenty-six—since the magazine's birth by $100,000 to arrive at the figure. This was the FBI at its feverish antiliberal best, but the report at the beginning of Straight's file did—for the wrong reasons—draw further attention to Straight and Dorothy, whose name also headed the file. Hoover, in his wild lashing out, had yet to distinguish between Dorothy's genuine liberalism and Straight's KGB links. By coincidence, and Straight's courage in letting anti-FBI attacks filter into *The New Republic,* Hoover had stumbled onto something far bigger than he would have dreamt. In effect, the opposing camps had underestimated each other. Each would discover this miscalculation in the next decade.

Despite the file, Straight was skipping away from Hoover's watchers with alacrity while drawing himself further into KGB networks. In March, French politician and secret KGB agent Pierre Cot (six times minister of air and twice minister of commerce between the wars), who was in exile in the United States, made contact with Straight via Green. (Cot would continue his secret work in a few months' time when taken over by Vasili Zarubin, the chief KGB resident in the United States. Zarubin reported to Moscow that he had signed on Cot as "agent DAEDALUS," who in the mid-1990s would be verified as a KGB man through the Venona decrypts.)

Soon after, Cot linked Straight with a "Louis Dolivet" who stayed at Straight's house in Alexandria for a night. Straight had first seen Dolivet, another Comintern/KGB man, in Paris in July 1937, on Straight's last vacation with his girlfriend Herta Thiele. Blunt had suggested Straight attend a rally for the World Committee for the Relief of Victims of German Fascism, where Dolivet spoke passionately against Hitler. The committee was a front run by the German communist Willi Muenzenberg, the KGB's pay-off man. Kim Philby had met him via the Cambridge network controls a few years earlier.

Straight claimed to be unaware that Dolivet was, like him, a KGB agent. He also made the spurious claim that had he known, he would "probably" have never introduced Dolivet to his sister Beatrice at an Overseas Press Club banquet in Washington. She was furthering her acting career but fell for Dolivet, who could see the advantages of marrying a rich, communist-leaning Straight. Apart from the money, he thought it would boost his chances of staying in the United States. They did marry a year later, although Dolivet—a Romanian whose real name was Ludovic Brecher—had trouble gaining citizenship. Dolivet had started a magazine in Europe, *Free World.* Thanks to Straight and his relationship with Beatrice, Dolivet received a big investment of $250,000 to start another front paper, *United Nations World,* designed to support—from a Soviet perspective—the idea of a United Nations.

Earlier Straight had managed to bluff the head of the federal government's visa division, Ruth Shipley, into giving a Spanish-born communist,

Gustavo Duran, a visa for the United States, where he and his wife Bronte (Bin Straight's sister) wished to live. Duran had been a general on the republican side during the Spanish Civil War.

Straight had let the conservative Shipley know that he was the son of Willard, whom she admired as a great U.S. consul.[16] When she examined Duran's papers, she noticed he fought in Spain. She asked which side he was on.

Straight replied deceptively that he had been on the "right" side. Shipley, believing he meant "right-wing," signed the papers. Straight also sponsored the entry of both Duran's friend and comrade-in-arms, communists Gustave Regler, whom Straight later described to the FBI as a Trotskyite, and Stephen Spender.

The Durans moved into Old Westbury for a time, as did the Dolivets, who would later introduce Straight to actors Orson Welles and Rita Hayworth. Over time Welles became "politically educated" by Dolivet.

"I was fascinated by him," Welles remarked, "and very fond of him."[17] Dolivet worked on Welles, hoping he would develop his political instincts, which were hard left, although Welles never admitted being a communist as such. Dolivet thought he might have a promising future in public life.

"Oh, he had great plans," Welles remarked. "He was going to organize it so that in fifteen years I would win the Nobel Prize (for peaceful political activism)."[18]

Dolivet soon had him making speeches at *Free World* dinners and functions and to politicians in Washington. Welles went on to address the Overseas Press Club and the Soviet-American Congress. The actor was willingly being used as a front for communist propaganda dressed up as liberal international thought.

Welles would later give serious consideration to a career as a senator, especially when his three other careers in film, radio, and theater faltered. In the meantime, he sharpened his ideas on paper in the *Free World* magazine, which was urging international cooperation through a UN organization.

This development came on the heels of Welles making *Citizen Kane*, which had caused Hoover to open a file on the actor at about the time the Straight dossier began in 1941. Kane had been loosely based on the life of right-wing newspaperman William Randolph Hearst. The film and the subsequent furor over its portrayal of the newspaper baron drew much comment in *The New Republic*, which supported it. The magazine included a piece on February 24 by a mysterious "Michael Sage" titled "Hearst over Hollywood." (Straight denied it was written by him.) The article attacked Hearst's efforts to stop distribution of the film. It was all grist for Hoover's burgeoning files on Straight and Welles, two new bureau enemies.

Hitler made his first major military error of World War II when his army crossed the Russian border and headed east on June 22, 1941. The impact buoyed rather than depressed Straight, who claimed to have been "besieged by new found friends" now that the center of communist power—Russia—was united against (rather than being officially partners with) the Nazis. He picked up the tempo of speeches at rallies in many federal agencies organized by the United Federal Workers Union and demanded with even greater fervor that the United States enter the war.

On December 7, 1941, the Japanese provided the stimulus needed by bombing Pearl Harbor. Roosevelt declared war on Japan and Germany. The United States—as the Russians and the British had long wanted— were in the fray. But Straight, the fierce advocate of fighting fascism, was not. Instead he decided to have a child, which would delay his entry into the services.

In December, Esmond Romilly, the radical nephew of Winston Churchill, was shot down by the Luftwaffe over the North Sea. Straight invited Romilly's wife Decca to Old Westbury for New Year's Eve. On New Year's Day they received a call from the White House. Churchill was there for secret talks with Roosevelt now that they were combining their fighting forces against the Germans, Italians, and Japanese. Churchill wanted to give his condolences to Decca in person. Straight and Bin drove her to see him. Mrs. Roosevelt met with Straight and told him she had been reading his articles in *The New Republic*. He found it an inspiring way to commence 1942.

Soon after Straight's visit to the White House, he had mixed feelings about the return of his control Michael Green to Washington, D.C., for his second tour of the United States. Straight's fears that he might be liquidated proved to be unfounded. Yet Green's return was confirmation that Straight was still considered by the KGB to be one of them.

When they met, Straight told him about his plans to write a book after completing the building of a new home in Weynoke, Virginia, and overseeing the design of the garden. The book, his first, titled *Let This Be the Last War*, was inspired by the governments of twenty-six nations signing the Declaration of the United Nations early in 1942. It was no more than a statement of intent, yet Straight saw it as a vehicle for portraying a world free of war, from a Soviet perspective. Green was not impressed, but his agent was persuasive and because of his financial independence had more maneuverability than the control's other spies. His privileged position meant he could put aside his work for *The New Republic* to indulge his intellectual aspirations. Green would have been frustrated by Straight's whims, but there was little he could do, short of strong-arm tactics, to make him accede to his directives. Straight's family trust money was being used to help many communist fronts in the United States. His connections and pull with, for instance, the visa and passport departments at State made him useful. Besides this, Green was aware that he came out of the Cambridge ring in England, which was regarded as "special" by the KGB Moscow Center.

Straight wrote during the summer after he and Bin had taken up residence at Weynoke. His book used the idea of a proposed United Nations to show how it should deal with the collapse of colonialism in a postwar world that would urgently need a worldwide policy of reconstruction. In effect, it was a communist blueprint for a postwar universe. In those secluded months of writing, Straight's mind drifted back to his not-so-distant Cambridge days in developing a Marxist treatise. There was much groveling to Stalin, the ultimate reader, with quotes from the ever-sage and avuncular leader.

Stalin was alleged to have told British newspaper proprietor Lord Beaverbrook in Moscow that it was not enough to turn out arms for factories. He, meaning the British government, had to keep up and create the spirit that enabled people to arm themselves. There were mandatory bashes at capitalism, especially Western companies that prospered from arms production when they were about to fail through inefficiency. Straight also provided prayers for a coming communist China. He saw the deepening divide in that nation between landlords and peasants and between the Kuomintang and liberal China. His writing provided many bland homilies about a world government of sorts. Only when such a utopian government was operating could any country progress to increased democratic freedoms.[19]

The book was also a restless summer escape. Straight was struggling with a regurgitation of his Marxist training in the hope of giving it some meaning beyond his espionage work. He had been in contact intermittently with Green now for a five-year period (from 1937 to 1942), yet Straight was dissatisfied and still not reconciled to those two internal drives. On the one hand, he was under pressure not to let his Cambridge friends down. They had a pact, an Apostles' creed that he felt compelled to adhere to. They believed they were on the correct path for proper Marxist historical development, and he was expected to assist them, or at the least not betray them. On the other hand, he wanted to fulfill his personal career ambitions. His burst into journalism had given him more than a taste for politics again. He thrived on the public rallies and the response from the crowd to rousing rhetoric. At Cambridge he had measured himself against the best minds in the union and felt he had stood taller than any of them in debate, argument, and management. In five years near the fulcrum of world power, Straight felt superior in ideas, intellect, ambition, drive, and vision to most of those he had met in the corridors of government. On top of this, he had learned how to use his money to get doors open and things done for himself.

Yet the timing was not quite right to make a move into congress. He had to put thoughts of a political career on hold while there was a war. He felt inclined to join the armed forces and achieve something that would add to his platform for politics. It could also be a chance to break from Green. When they had first met, just a few months after Straight had completed Cambridge, he was an arrogant yet raw 21-year-old, much in awe of the secret world he had been led into by Burgess and Blunt. Green had been part of his continuing indoctrination and influence. But five years later, at age 26, Straight had bought, cajoled, and pushed his way through a far broader education in Washington. Green had reduced in size as Straight grew experienced and made contact with the best and brightest in U.S. government. If Straight wanted to achieve for the cause, he wished to do it on his terms.

During the lazy summer months of 1942, Straight doubled up with the book by sending off related articles to *The New Republic*. When isolated within the journal, these excerpts seemed academic and misplaced, especially when the magazine was involved in a more real ideological war with the FBI. The attacks by it on Hoover continued and irritated him; Hoover was not used to such persistent criticism, even from the liberal press.

Green snapped Straight out of his campus reverie at Old Westbury with a phone call in August. He asked for a meeting, which had to be secret. FBI surveillance was tight, particularly in New York, where the main Soviet activity was going on. Straight took the Long Island Railroad from Westbury to Jamaica Station, where he was picked up by Green.[20]

They decided against a restaurant meeting, although once they had evaded any possible watchers, it would have been safe, especially in an area where Straight and Green were unknown. Instead they drove around the suburbs of Queens for more than an hour. Straight could not recall the specifics of the discussions, but he passed him information—a "memorandum." Straight claimed it was a summary of the arguments in his book. Green urged him to meet with KGB agent Earl Browder (code name RULEVOJ), the leader of the Communist Party of the USA, which in itself was a significant step. It meant drawing Straight into the broader secret world from which the Moscow Center had so far shielded him.[21]

While Straight was on call as a spy, he again could be also most useful to the KGB as a publisher hiring or gaining accreditation for journalists and as a financier. Green asked him to get accreditation papers from unsuspecting Ruth Shipley for U.S. entry of a female Swedish KGB agent, whose work cover was journalism, and another communist, Mark Julius Gayn, also a reporter. He had worked for the *Chicago Sun* and the *Washington Post* as its Shanghai correspondent. Gayn was a Chinese expert affiliated with the International Pacific Relations group, a communist front, which was receiving financial support from Straight through the Whitney Foundation.[22] Though obedient to Green's demands, Straight was irked by them, especially as he was near the end of a book, which needed his full concentration.

He finished it in November 1942 about the time of the birth of his first son, David, and then he joined the US Army Air Corps Reserve, starting as a private.

—————

In December 1942, Straight attended an Institute of Pacific Relations conference held at the Canadian resort of Mount Tremblant in Quebec. There he met two fellow communists from Cambridge who valued his financial support for the group. One was Canadian-born Egerton Herbert Norman, a rising diplomat in Canada's External Affairs Ministry attached to the staff of General Douglas MacArthur. The other was the "very egotistical, very self-indulgent" Michael Greenberg, a former Trinity-cell member from Manchester who, like Straight, had been recruited to the KGB.[23] Greenberg was helping to shape U.S. policy toward China and had diligently worked his way up the ranks in the Far East Division of the State Department.[24] After Cambridge, England, he went on to Cambridge, Massachusetts, in October 1939 on a Choate Scholarship to continue his studies of the development of British trade with China. It was a useful mask to hide his espionage agenda.

Apart from their indoctrination at Trinity, he and Straight had a connection with China. Straight was conscious of his father's fascination with the world's most populous nation and was keen to help it on the road to communism, which was Greenberg's role as a clandestine operator.

———•———

In late December 1942 Straight had another meeting with his control at a dimly lit restaurant, Longchamps, in New York. Green brought along his wife Helen Lowry, who was Earl Browder's niece. She went under the cover name ELIZA. Straight told the FBI that she was in early middle age and of "nice appearance." Her speech indicated she was American by birth. Helen, like her husband, was an "illegal." According to Straight, they "comported themselves like a happily married couple."[25]

The meeting demonstrated how valuable they thought Straight's work and services could be. Otherwise Green would not have introduced him to his wife, another important player in the Washington network. (She had been involved in running the rings associated with Elizabeth Bentley, the courier and later defector from the Soviet espionage setup, and Whittaker Chambers.) This would have been a waste of time and an unnecessary risk if Straight had not been regarded as a big asset, even if he were yet to reach his potential.

Straight handed over the accreditation papers for the KGB agents, the woman from Sweden and Mark Gayn. Helen Lowry urged Straight to see her uncle, which he again promised to do at the launch of his book in a few months time. Browder was then trying to set up a "back channel" link between the White House and the Kremlin. He wanted a contact close to Roosevelt who could carry messages to him from the Kremlin and get responses to them. Straight, a White House frequenter and friend of the Roosevelts, would have seemed a likely candidate for this role, but he would not like being used as a courier. It would also have exposed him to the Roosevelts as a communist, rather than the high-minded liberal that he purported to be. Someone else was chosen.[26]

Green asked Straight to recommend other people who were friendly and who could be of use to the KGB. He mentioned Greenberg, but Green showed no reaction. Straight realized that the KGB had already recruited him.

Straight assumed that Green was looking for a replacement for him in Washington, as he was soon due to join the Air Corps. This did not mean that they expected Straight to drift away from them while he was on reservist duty in other parts of the country. Green would have wanted a flow of data and/or assistance from all his agents for the hungry Moscow Center at a critical time as U.S. intervention in the European conflict increased. However, Straight intimated (to the FBI, when interrogated two decades later) that he took their restaurant conversation to mean he was free of Green's grip.

In a bizarre twist, Straight told the FBI that Green asked him to help find a place to live in Philadelphia "and in obtaining some small business that he could run." It was further evidence of the trust the KGB still had in their former star recruit and that he could not easily jettison his underground communist affiliations, even if he wished to. He met Browder as planned at the launch of *Let This Be the Last War*, in January 1943.

The book was met with mixed reviews. Friends were kind. Felix Frankfurter wrote Straight a "friendly" letter about it. John Maynard Keynes praised the effort in a letter to Dorothy. "But," he said, "I wish that Michael could regard politics more than he does as the art of the possible," which was a gentle way of marking down the tome's impracticality. The doyen of world economists was kinder to Straight than he had been to Marx, for he appeared to have succeeded in finding clues to ideas in Straight's treatise.

The most provocative review came from John Chamberlain in *The New York Times* of January 5, 1943. In his memoirs, Straight said Chamberlain found "my overwrought style repulsive." But the reviewer actually said he was "attracted and repulsed in equal measure" with the book itself. He was concerned more with the content and ideology than the style, which was used as a pretext for the reviewer's disagreement and irritation.

Chamberlain agreed with the proposition for a federalized Europe and a postwar UN keeping the peace and increasing standards of living everywhere. But he objected to the tone of the book, which "kept getting in the way of the sense. Mr. Straight . . . is so humorless in his style that I kept thinking of all the earnest reformers who have tried to drive fallible men beyond their powers of adaptation."

Acutely aware of where Straight was coming from, Chamberlain commented that he was even more of a perfectionist than "Lenin or Robespierre. He is long on denunciations of industrialists, politicians and soldiers, and he is short on the type of charitable realism that expects ten per cent of bungling for every 90 per cent of effective effort."

Chamberlain chided Straight for saying, "We are losing the war," and "Between the glorious defense of Stalingrad and our own ignominious inaction stands the greatest contrast of our entire war."

The reviewer commented: "But even as Mr. Straight was busy writing, the 'ignominious' and 'inactive' staff officers of General Eisenhower were planning a cross-water invasion, which clicked even more efficiently than the Nazi General von Falkenhorst's seizure of Norway."

Perhaps Chamberlain was aware of Straight's own inactivity and exhortations to others to fight. In a burst of perspicacity, given the writer's secret allegiances, the reviewer asked: "Does Mr. Straight doubt that Americans would fight with a fury comparable to that of the Russians if the Nazis were thundering at the gates of Akron, Ohio, or Manitowoc, Wis.?"

"Mr. Straight," he noted, "has an intellectual's fear and distrust of the incorrigible give-and-take of the American people." He went on to dissect the proposition that the Russians had superior war organization capabilities. Chamberlain pointed out that Americans had given them the plans and designs for power stations and factories making tractors, tanks, and machine tools.

"He can't see," Chamberlain admonished, "that our industrial effectiveness and our fighting spirit stem from the same beliefs which also led to 1929 [the Wall Street Crash] and its aftermath [of severe depression]. He can't see that faults and virtues are sometimes inseparable."

The reviewer had stumbled onto Straight's lack of experience of recent U.S. history. He had been in England from 1925 to 1937, particularly formative years in his country of origin. He had also never had much exposure to more pragmatic thought away from Marxist economic theory and philosophy, which left him without instincts for the masses, whom he felt born to lead. His wealth and privilege further removed him from the mainstream political themes, moods, fears, aspirations, and ideas that motivated Americans.

In an unfashionable yet insightful dig at the Soviet Union's totalitarianism, the reviewer remarked: "We are intolerant of people who would impose form and goals from above. And so we run into terrible troubles. But if we weren't that sort of people, we would never have invented the submarine and the airplane and the mass production line for the Russians to use. . . . " "I'm beginning to dislike people who insist," Chamberlain concluded, "that the only proper clothes for an American are sackcloth sprinkled with ashes."

Straight claimed in his memoirs to have been devastated by this review because at the time he was in a highly sensitized state. He made no reference later to whether or not, on reflection, he saw any value in Chamberlain's assessment of his first literary effort.

It began as an easy, safe war for Straight, who in mid-February 1943 arrived by troop train at Miami Beach. While he was in Florida, an American agent for the KGB—code named HARDY—was there preparing a succinct report on U.S. aircraft strength and movements for his Washington control, which was transmitted to Moscow on May 5, 1943.[27] HARDY's report "from personal observation and conversations with officers" noted the organization of "airplane runs on the southern route." It also detailed the activity at all the bases, including the type of aircraft dispatched. It was typical of reports relayed to the Moscow Center at this time when the Soviet high command was tracking U.S. military maneuvers as the war in Europe intensified. HARDY was probably Straight;

agents were often known by two or three names, and it's unlikely that two KGB agents would be sent to Miami.

He finished his training course in Miami and later Marietta College, Ohio, and ended up at Gunter Field, Montgomery, Alabama. He was taught to fly, but where his companions went on to see action (many of them died) in bomber command in Europe, Straight's knowledge of French was enough to miss the dangers of combat. Instead, from March 1944 he used this knowledge of the language to teach French cadets how to fly.

A few months later, U.S. vice-president Henry Wallace, with whom Straight was soon destined to become bound politically, embarked on a "fact-finding" tour of China. He was accompanied by communist Owen Lattimore, who was on the executive committee running *Pacific Affairs*, the official magazine of the Institute of Pacific Relations (IPR), which had developed a long way from its 1926 charter "to promote cooperation among the peoples and governments of the Pacific." IPR had been hijacked in the best tradition of creeping communism by Lattimore. It had developed into an organ for the promotion of Chinese communism. Lattimore was leading a faction of so-called China Hands (including Greenberg) in Washington, D.C., opposed to the then-main political power on the Chinese mainland, the Nationalists, under the command of General Chiang Kai-shek. The Nationalists were after an ambitious $1 billion loan, and the request had split the U.S. State Department into two factions. Veterans of the Far Eastern Division, led by Stanley Hornbeck, supported the loan. Communists and other sympathizers, euphemistically known as "pro-Chinese liberals," were against it. The latter argued that Chiang Kai-shek might use the money in the civil war against Mao Tse-tung and the communists rather than the invading Japanese.

Wallace, always susceptible to extreme left-wing propaganda, wrote in his diary about the Chinese communists being "agrarian reformers."[28] He visited Mao at his headquarters in Yenan Province and naively volunteered to negotiate a settlement between rival Chinese leaders. Mao was quick off the mark and began mouthing platitudes about democracy and how much he admired it. He even cheekily alluded to the need for "foreign capital and free enterprise in China," which in fact he studiously avoided for the rest of his life. But to paraphrase Lenin, which he often did in his *Little Red Book*, why let the truth get in the way of deceiving gullible, greedy capitalists? The ploy worked marvels in the ill-informed popular U.S. press. Even the *Saturday Evening Post* fell for the deception.

"For the foreign reader it is somewhat confusing that this Chinese agrarian reform movement is called 'Communism,'" the paper's Edgar Snow noted.[29] "Communism in China is a watered-down thing today." A chorus of procommunist writers jumped on the popular bandwagon just as Mao began preparing for the last leg of the "long march" that he predicted would take his communists to power. U.S. propaganda, headed by the vice-president, was helping to smooth the path.

———————

Meanwhile, life seemed quite bearable for Straight, based in sleepy Alabama, especially when he could have breaks with Bin and David, who flew to him. The meetings were frequent enough for Bin to become pregnant late in the year, and she gave birth to a second son, Mike, in August 1944. It was a busy period for her as she embarked on a degree in psychiatry in New York.

Straight managed time off in New York and Westbury to see his family. Did he also meet his KGB control on these trips? Straight claimed to the FBI that he finished meeting Green late in 1942. But the KGB still regarded him as an important operative. They did not have a "decommissioning" policy beyond assassination.[30]

———————

By November 1944, when the wars in Europe and the Pacific were turning in favor of the Allies, Straight wanted a change from the uninspiring routine of instructing three classes of more than four hundred French cadets over fifteen months.

A call to Tom Corcoran took him out of the rear cockpit in forty-eight hours and on his way to Lincoln, Nebraska, to be assigned to B-17— "Flying Fortress"—bombers. Just when he was being prepared for combat, Straight learned that his close friend from Cambridge, John Simonds, had been killed flying a glider into battle at Arnhem, Holland.

Corcoran had attended to Straight's minor problem while in the middle of one of the biggest cover-ups by an American administration to that point. It began soon after the night of March 11, 1945, when a five-man CIA forerunner OSS burglar team broke into the offices of the magazine *Amerasia* at 225 Fifth Avenue, New York, which was an "unofficial" organ of IPR. *Amerasia* had been subtly positioned to intellectually guide a "popular front against fascism" as directed by the seventh Comintern congress in 1935. It was a quaint way of not alarming the United States while influencing the State Department, already riddled with KGB agents, and in turn the media and public opinion. According to growing IPR/*Amerasia* propaganda, Chinese communists were not real communists but—in the language taken up by Henry Wallace and a vocal faction of the U.S. government—liberals wanting "agrarian reform, civil rights and the establishment of democratic institutions." This was in contrast to Chiang Kai-shek's Nationalists, who were being portrayed as corrupt and intractable.

All this caused concern and grumbling but not alarm in the noncommunist sections of the administration, until the OSS break-in discovered *Amerasia* was publishing some of its top secret reports almost verbatim. The squad found the suite of offices strewn with classified documents. There was a darkroom for developing microfilmed material, which was smuggled from government offices, photographed, and then returned. The OSS turned the case over to the FBI, which obtained a warrant, raided *Amerasia*, and seized about a thousand classified documents, including papers from the State Department, naval intelligence, OSS, and British intelligence. The FBI arrested six suspects—including the aforementioned Mark Gayn, for whom Straight had obtained accreditation papers; the magazine's editor Philip Jaffe; and Andrew Roth, a naval intelligence officer. The group was charged with conspiracy to violate the Espionage Act.

The fast-talking Corcoran entered the fray and manipulated a brilliant cover-up for the administration.[31] A well-orchestrated response was directed at the FBI, which the liberal and even the popular media accused of curtailing freedom of the press. Consequently a grand jury refused to indict three of the defendants. The government dropped espionage charges against the others, who faced lesser charges of "conspiracy to embezzle, steal and purloin" government property. Despite this brushing under the carpet, the affair highlighted the depth of infiltration in the Roosevelt administration.

———— • ————

Straight observed all these political developments from a useful distance while being given intensive training on B-17s. He expected to be transferred to England early in 1945, although the European conflict was clearly in its last throes. With the *Amerasia* case making headlines, his thoughts were always attuned to communism, politics, and the shape of a world he would inherit once hostilities ceased. He saw the war as propitious for a revolution in property holdings, but he bemoaned the fact that there had been a worldwide counterrevolution. The United States was returning all the empires of European states (such as England, France, Spain, Portugal, and Belgium) to their former owners. Straight saw it as a poor base for a lasting peace. He gave the example of France taking back its colonies such as Vietnam in Asia. His revolutionary soul was offended by this.[32]

———— • ————

On April 12, 1945, President Franklin D. Roosevelt died at age 63, a little way into his record fourth term as president. He had used the federal government's powers to pull the nation out of the Great Depression in what became known as the New Deal. He had been the great white hope for the development of left-wing America, but his passing would shut the door on the chance for liberalism, and anything politically to the left of it, to flourish courtesy of the White House. Roosevelt had played a leading role in creating an alliance with Great Britain and the Soviet Union. He met with Allied leaders Churchill and Stalin in Tehran, Iran, in 1943. Despite his ailing condition, Roosevelt made it to Yalta in the Crimea in early February 1945 for another meeting with Churchill and Stalin. At that meeting, the big three decided how Germany and the rest of Europe should be carved up after Germany was defeated. It was felt by some British and American observers at the time that Roosevelt had been too much influenced in negotiations by pro-Soviet groups in the State Department. Stalin, it was said, had been conceded too much in the desire to get him to support the Allied war in the Pacific against Japan. More precisely, Stalin was better informed than the other two leaders. He had key spies (including Alger Hiss) in the entourages of both Roosevelt and Churchill.

Roosevelt was succeeded by Harry S. Truman, 60, a failed haberdasher but good political manager and decision-maker. Truman was no ideologue, and if anything, anti-intellectual. Liberals left him cold, and he was not open to left-wing influence. (The Cold War would see him take a strong stance against the Soviet Union under Stalin, whom he didn't trust.)

———————

In April 1945 Hitler committed suicide in his bunker, and Germany capitulated. The United States' total focus was now on the war against Japan in the Pacific. Straight's once-somnolent outpost was alive with change. The B-17 he had trained on was usurped by the more sophisticated B-29—"Superfortress Bomber"—the biggest plane built by the United States. It was the single most complicated and expensive weapon produced during the war. Nearly 4,000 B-29s were built for combat in the Pacific Theater. The plane had been assembled in a rush by a vast manufacturing program employing about 300,000 workers from Seattle, Washington, to Marietta, Georgia, and from Wichita, Kansas, to Woodridge, New Jersey. The B-29 was more evidence for Straight that the system in the United States could produce something special under pressure, despite capitalist imperfections. The point would be driven home to him when he was transferred to San Antonio, Texas, to train in the product itself.

In July 1945 it seemed as if he were to see active duty after all when he and his crew were ordered to Colorado Springs to prepare for a mission to fly Four-Star General James Doolittle to the U.S. base on Guam in the mid-Pacific. The colonel who had sent for them discovered they had little experience flying over water. That led to a grilling of Straight and his crew by the Standardization Board about their knowledge of the B-17, which was to be Doolittle's carrier. Their exacting examination found him wanting. The combined lack of experience within the crew also influenced the board interrogators. It was a case of from "Doolittle to do nothing." They were dismissed and sent back to their base by rail.

Straight had mixed emotions about the end of hostilities in the Pacific brought about by two atomic bombs dropped by B-29s on Hiroshima and Nagasaki. Yet he expressed no concern at all about these new weapons of mass destruction. He saw them as important for the Allied victory and the 500,000 American lives that were spared because of Truman's momentous decision to use atomic weapons. In his autobiography he bemoaned the lost opportunities to see combat in not joining the marines, in having the capacity to speak French, and in not going as a copilot to fly B-17s. Straight regretted three wasted years that had interrupted his career as a writer and a member of the progressive movement in the United States. Yet, as he mentally worked through those lost years, he was thankful for the passion he had developed for flying.

He was beginning to consider his future. Sitting on a bunk in his quarters in San Antonio in between flying B-29s in eight-hour shifts, he reflected more and more on the lost chances to serve in combat. A stronger service record would have given him the momentum for a political career, first as a congressman, and later even a shot at the presidency, which was a family expectation for one of its sons going back to his great-grandfather Henry B. Payne. Yet when Straight returned to civilian life, he would not be so concerned with a lack of combat. Politics was still very much on his agenda.

———•———

At the Potsdam Conference in Berlin on July 24, 1945, President Truman turned to Stalin and said through an interpreter, "Our scientists have developed a new weapon. We tested it fully. It has a terrific destructive force."

The president searched Stalin's face for a flicker, some hint of concern from the Soviet Union's leader. His expression remained implacable, even benign.

"I'm glad to hear of it," Stalin responded. "I hope you can make good use of it against the Japanese."

It was Truman who received the surprise. Stalin's reaction meant only one thing. He already knew. In fact, the biggest espionage operation in history had been running for nearly eighteen months in an attempt by the Soviet Union to catch up to the U.S.-controlled development of the atomic bomb, known as the Manhattan Project.

Days later the Japanese cities of Hiroshima and Nagasaki were all but obliterated. The atomic age of destruction was not merely a complex diagram on a blackboard; it was reality. Despite the stolen and home-produced knowledge the Russians already had, the shock was palpable in the Kremlin. There was a not-unwarranted fear that the United States could now turn its attention to Moscow and finish the job left incomplete by Hitler. Some hawks in the Pentagon were advocating a move on the citadel of communism while the United States and its allies in Western Europe were on a roll.

Stalin responded by increasing the huge espionage effort to gain the capacity to produce his own bomb. Yet the United States, it was learned, was moving on to even bigger and more powerful weapons, a hundred, perhaps a thousand times the force of the one dropped on Hiroshima. The KGB was ordered to hold back that progress as much as possible. A "peace movement" was mobilized to retard U.S. development of new weapons. The aim was to put pressure on the vulnerable key scientists involved in the Manhattan Project, who were concerned about one country—the United States—having a monopoly over the use of atomic weapons. The aim was to contact them through "friends" to obtain vital documentation on the technology. In effect, the KGB wanted to make de facto espionage agents out of them, and to also gain their support in the Soviet-inspired peace movement.

The three top targets were physicists: J. Robert Oppenheimer, an American at the University of California, a communist sympathizer with a strong conscience about his part in the bomb's creation; Hungarian-born Leo Szilard, who petitioned Roosevelt to develop weapons using atomic energy, and when the bomb was made, tried to stop it being used against Japan; and Italian-born Enrico Fermi, who had won the Nobel prize in 1938 for his work on radioactivity.

These three and several other scientists, such as the amenable Danish physicist Niels Bohr, were assigned code names by the KGB without their knowledge, such as STAR, EDITOR, and PERSEUS, which covered one or sometimes all of them at one time. The KGB's best agent recruiters were told to focus their skills on gaining the confidence of the scientists and their wives. Elizabeth Zarubin, the wife of the Washington KGB resident, was used to cultivate Oppenheimer's wife, Katherine, a communist supporter. The attractive, sociable Elizabeth established her own illegal network of Jewish refugees from Poland and recruited one of Szilard's secretaries, who provided technical data.[33]

The KGB's resident in San Francisco, Gregory Kheifetz, met the susceptible Oppenheimer himself at a 1938 party to raise money for the Spanish Civil War and worked on the relationship for the next seven years. In 1943, Kheifetz and Zarubin managed a major coup by influencing Manhattan Project leader Oppenheimer to allow Klaus Fuchs, a KGB agent and German refugee from Nazi Germany, to join the team of British scientists at the project research center in Los Alamos, New Mexico. He misrepresented himself to Oppenheimer as having "escaped from a German prison camp," which gained the project leader's respect and confidence. Fuchs proved to be one of the best Soviet intelligence plants of the mission to steal the bomb secrets.[34]

During 1945, the KGB's special task force on atomic espionage (Department S), led by Pavel Sudoplatov, presented Lavrenty Beria, the head of the Soviet Security Service, with updated summaries on the U.S. progress in atomic testing, the results of the bombs dropped, and research into new nuclear weapons. The data came from agents at Los Alamos and the main plants servicing it, especially Oak Ridge, Tennessee. Information also came from companies doing the actual manufacturing work, such as Kellex Corp. (a subsidiary of M. W. Kellog), E. I. Du Pont de Nemours, and Union Carbide.[35]

With successful detonation and then use of the bomb in Japan, Sudoplatov ordered all his agents to push the idea that technology should be shared worldwide and that atomic energy should only be harnessed for peaceful means. Pressure was put on developing a peace campaign for nuclear disarmament.

"Disarmament and the inability to impose nuclear blackmail would deprive the U.S. of its advantage," Sudoplatov said. "We began a worldwide campaign against U.S. nuclear superiority."[36]

Straight would be useful. However, he would have a much wider role as one of the key agents seconded to garner as much intelligence as possible for the Russians about nuclear weapons and the huge industry that was developing around them.

PART THREE

COLD WAR CONFLICT

11

BLUNT'S ROYAL MISSION

England's King George VI called a secret meeting in the library of Windsor Castle in late July 1945. The others present were Sir Owen Morshead, the royal librarian, and Major Anthony Blunt, who apart from his MI5 work acted as an art historian and adviser to the king. George VI wanted the trusted courtiers to travel to Kronberg, where the king's relatives lived. They had correspondence—"hundreds of letters and photographs"—between the British and German royals dating back to Queen Victoria that the king wanted retrieved.[1]

At least that would be the cover story, should the mission be noticed by anyone. The real assignment was to find letters and memoranda of conversations by the monarch's brother, the Duke of Windsor, with Hitler and top Nazis. Blunt and Morshead were to search for transcripts of telephone calls made by the Duke of Windsor (the former King Edward VIII) during his visit to Germany in October 1937. Of particular concern was the October 22, 1937, meeting by the duke and his wife (the American Wallis Simpson) with Hitler in his mountain retreat at Berchtesgaden.

They were sensitive communications, the king informed them. Better that they did not end up in American hands, especially the press. Neither courtier asked questions about the contents of the letters and transcripts.

Suffice to know that their monarch wished them to undertake a mission to secure them all. They realized he was most concerned that they succeed.

In early August 1945, the 38-year-old Blunt, who was in charge of the mission; Morshead, in his mid-50s; and four handpicked British soldiers flew to Frankfurt and then drove an army truck to Kronberg. They found the United States occupying forces using the nineteenth-century palace of Kronberg as a GI rest camp. The British party drove past it two miles to the dark tower of Schloss Friedrichshof, which seemed to hang over the wooded slopes of Taunus Mountains. Blunt left the truck and entered the large entrance hall that featured a wooden-beamed, Scottish baronial-style roof. The walls were adorned with English royal coats of arms and portraits of English kings and queens. He was greeted by a U.S. captain, Kathleen Nash, of the U.S. Women's Army Corps.[2] She was in command of the rest camp. Blunt asked where he could find the Hesse family, the king's German relatives. Captain Nash redirected Blunt to the town-house, where the family had been shunted in the grounds of the old Kronberg castle.

The Hesse family was a bit taken aback when Blunt produced a letter with the royal seal and signed by George VI. It requested permission to remove the royal letters and "other communications" to England for "safekeeping."[3] The problem for the Hesses was that they were technically headless. The titular head, Prince Philip, was a Nazi leader. He had fallen from favor with Hitler and was in Dachau concentration camp, Philip's twin brother, Wolfgang, explained.

"Are you not the head of the family in your brother's absence?" Blunt asked. "We need permission to take the documents."

The family asked Blunt to wait while they conferred. They emerged after an hour with a letter from the mother of Wolfgang and Philip, the 72-year-old Princess Margaret. It gave her permission for the removal of the papers in question.[4] There were about a thousand documents, Wolfgang informed Blunt and Morshead, clearly marked in packing cases. "They're stored in the attic of Schloss Friedrichshof," he said.

In the evening, the party drove back up the winding road through the Hesse estate to the Schloss. The six-man party entered and were again greeted by Captain Nash. Blunt accompanied her down a passage to an office. He produced the two letters from George VI and Princess Margaret.

Nash showed Blunt a chair, sat behind her desk and read them, frowning. "What papers are you wanting?"

"They are private correspondence between the Windsors and the Hesse family."

"Windsors?"

"Yes, the royal family. The British royal family."

Nash shook her head. "I don't have the authority to relinquish control over papers."

Blunt nodded at the letters. "That is all the authority you need," he said.

"What?"

"The king—the head of the U.K., Commonwealth, and the Dominions—has signed that letter."

"Major, everything here is now the property of the U.S. army."

"Not royal correspondence."

"Everything. I have orders."

Blunt could see that Nash was intractable.[5] "I would appreciate you calling U.S. army headquarters in Frankfurt," he said, remaining his glacial self.

"Why?"

"So that I can speak to your superior."

"Look, Major, I'm in charge of this camp. I have my orders."

There was a stalemate. Blunt stood up, excused himself, and moved to the door. "I must consult my colleague," he said. He hurried along to the entrance hall where the others were waiting.

"She's refusing to let us take them," he told Morshead. He glanced at the stairs. "Take the men to the attic, find the papers, and load them on the truck. I'll stall her."

Blunt returned to the office. Nash had lit herself a cigarette.

"You're wasting your time, Major," she said.

"I really do think it would be in your interest to phone HQ," Blunt persisted. "Churchill himself supports our mission."

Nash stared at him. She didn't know if he were bluffing. She had seen some of the imprisoned Nazi paratrooper commandos at close quarters. She had met the toughest of the American leaders, including George Patton. But this languid, ice-cool British officer with the long face and cutaway mouth was a different animal altogether. He was polite yet remote. He behaved as if he had real, if obscure, authority. She remained firm, yet inside she was a fraction insecure. What if Churchill was behind it? Would she be reprimanded by her commanding officer? The argument continued. Nash relented and phoned Frankfurt, asking Blunt to leave the office. He hastened to the entrance just as Morshead and the soldiers came down the stairs with two packing cases. The party hurried to the truck, loaded it, and climbed in.

Nash could not get through to her commanding officer in Frankfurt. She stepped out of the office and walked to the Schloss's front door to see the truck disappearing down the winding road and into the night.[6]

Two days later, the Hesse family entertained Blunt and Morshead at a small castle at nearby Wolfsgarten. The twenty present dined in style with a sumptuous six-course meal served by liveried footmen behind every chair. A different wine accompanied every course.[7] Just before midnight, Blunt retired to a room in the castle's guest quarters. He had placed the cases of documents and letters in the room with a guard outside, on the off chance that the Americans should dare to steal them back. Blunt (according to two of his KGB controls) removed the lids and began to sift through the letters, most of which were unsealed.[8] He was thrilled to find one from Karl Marx, who had been called upon by a German court official in 1847.[9] The correspondence that interested him most concerned messages between Edward (when prince); his youngest brother, the Duke of Kent; and their German cousins, Philip of Hesse and Karl Eduard, Duke of Saxe-Coburg-Gotha. The letters showed that Edward and the Duke of Kent were keen to ingratiate themselves with Hitler when he became German chancellor and with the Nazi regime. Philip had been the link with Edward before, during and after he was king (1936–1937). More damning was strong evidence that Edward had passed secret information to the Nazis during the war.

In effect, the documents and letters demonstrated that the former king of England and Wallis Simpson had passed information secretly to Hitler from at least 1934 to 1943. This meant, whether they perceived their intentions as good or not, they were technically traitors to England from 1939 to 1943.[10]

Blunt now fully realized King George's anxiety about the material. The KGB double agent was astonished at the extent of Edward's links. There was clear evidence that he was preparing to be placed back on the throne as prince regent once the Nazis took power as a pay-off for his support. It would be a reward from Hitler for heading the so-called international peace movement on behalf of the Nazis, which assisted Hitler's plan for taking Europe, piece by piece.[11]

Blunt surmised that if these letters were revealed publicly, it would mean the end of the House of Windsor. The British, not to mention the Commonwealth and Dominions, had just been through a horrific war against fascism, which had taken an enormous toll on people and lives. If the king's tens of millions of subjects were now informed that his brother—the former king—and his wife had been Nazi collaborators, it would never be tolerated.

Over the next few nights and on the return trip to London, Blunt sorted the most important letters. Then he microfilmed them.[12]

The king was delighted and relieved at the success of the mission. It meant that Blunt would maintain his job as Keeper of the King's Pictures, if he wished, as long as the king was alive. Blunt had spent the war at MI5, since Rothschild recommended him to Liddell in 1940. His job as a double agent for MI5 and his ultimate masters at the KGB had exhausted him. He had worked long hours, keeping up the deception without faltering. But now with the Nazis defeated, he wanted to leave MI5.[13] He considered himself a burnt out case even if the Russians had yet to label him as such. He consulted his KGB control, Ivan Milovzorov, at the Soviet embassy in London. Blunt had been a loyal agent since 1934, recruiting some of the best prospects for the cause, such as Straight, Leo Long, and Alister Watson. He had taken risks daily for his Soviet masters and had proved to be one of the best half-dozen or so British agents the KGB ever had. Now he wanted out. The job at the palace was a ticket to a quieter life, if the KGB agreed to it. Blunt told himself, they had to agree, didn't they?

He and Milovzorov met at an East End pub at night. They were an odd couple. Tall, uniformed Major Blunt seemed out of place. His upper-class mien was better suited to the St. James clubs near MI5's offices. Yet he dared not be seen anywhere near the area with this portly foreigner, whose brow often sweated.

They drank and chatted. Milovzorov tended to be heavy-handed and brusque. He had fallen out from time to time with a few of his agents.

Blunt told him he was leaving MI5 and going to work at the palace. Milovzorov was confused. He was a slack spy-master whose reputation had been maintained by the quality agents such as Blunt who fed him valuable information.

"It will be useful for you to have me at the palace," Blunt told him.[14] The Russian asked why. Blunt explained that he would be close to the king, whom he claimed was a "very good friend." He exaggerated the importance of his role. The Russian was not clear how this would help him. If he agreed to let Blunt move, he would have to justify it to the Moscow Center. Blunt explained how much the royal courtiers learned about government, the cabinet, and the leaders of British society. Milovzorov couldn't understand how this would be better than being at the hub of intelligence at MI5, whose charter was the defense of the realm. Blunt went on to mention that he would be on continuous assignment for the king—which was true—to find as much as possible of the communications between his brother and Hitler. The connections and communications were "very extensive," he informed Milovzorov.

Blunt gambled on his mission being of great interest to the Moscow Center. But it would be loathe to lose such a great spy from inside British intelligence. Blunt had acted as a conduit for several of the finest subagents—men and women in positions of power and influence with access to the realm's secrets that Moscow coveted. These subagents, such as Victor Rothschild, would not risk meeting controls themselves but were happy to pass data to a trusted middleman. Blunt was the best.

Milovzorov asked if he would be prepared to carry on in the middleman role, considering so many others depended on him. Blunt feared this request. He felt then, in his weary state, that this demand would place him more or less where he had been for the past four years.

"In certain circumstances," Blunt replied carefully, "I would be available."

Milovzorov, with a report now to file to the center, wanted to know exactly what circumstances. Blunt explained that he would be "terribly busy" in his new position. The Russian extracted an assurance that he would be available in "emergencies" without specifying what that meant.

Milovzorov got up to leave, taking with him the rolled up copy of *The Times* that Blunt had left on the table. Inside the paper was the microfilm containing photos of all the key letters at Kronberg.

The two parted. Blunt was relieved to think that he had engineered a reprieve from the secret world he had been prisoner to for more than a decade. Yet he wondered if it were really the end. He would be haunted by the thought of being contacted again and of more demands. In his heart Blunt knew he would never really be free of his masters. It could be a life sentence, if the KGB wished. They had incriminating details on Blunt's private and clandestine life.

He took solace from the luck of the king's assignment. If he were ever cornered and caught by British intelligence, that microfilm, which would be on its way to Moscow by the next diplomatic bag, was his last-resort insurance policy against unmasking and prosecution. No one, he felt sure, would take action against him and risk bringing down the House of Windsor. In effect, the microfilm was also an insurance policy for Straight and every major agent with whom Blunt was ever linked. Not one of them could ever be charged, for it would expose Blunt, which in turn would expose the reigning monarch because of his brother's links to Hitler and the Nazis. The thought that this was inconceivable allowed the overstressed spy to sleep better at night.

When Blunt was reactivated by his new Russian control Yuri Modin in 1947, MI5 became suspicious of the royal courtier. He was followed. MI5 alerted the palace late in 1947, but predictably, nothing was done about Blunt's traitorous activity. His insurance policy was working well. He simply knew too much and had to be protected by the royal family. The queen also appointed him as Surveyor of the Queen's Pictures when she succeeded to the throne in 1952.

12

POLITICAL PATH TO NOWHERE

Straight spent his last weeks in the military celebrating "peace at last," carousing in San Antonio, making pleasure forays into Mexico, and lounging about in border towns such as Del Rio, where he celebrated his 29th birthday. Early in October 1945 those fun-filled but frustrating last days were over, and he was discharged. Straight drove 1800 miles northeast to Old Westbury.

He was unsure of where his career was headed. His priority, as it had been since Stalin placed him in the United States in 1937, was politics. He had no desire to return to *The New Republic*, although it was always there as a job of last resort. While thrashing around exploring options in the first week out of the military, he joined the board of a new war veterans organization, the American Veterans Committee (AVC). It had been founded by a sergeant named Gil Harrison, who was still in the South Pacific. The AVC had some communist members from the beginning. It soon would be seen as ripe for infiltration as the new body's membership grew rapidly.[1]

Straight presented himself, in his well-practiced, convincing way, as he was—a liberal. He realized after the war he would have to be far more cautious than before about resuming contacts with any of his former communist affiliations. The political climate had changed. The four-decade Cold War had begun. The Soviet Union, a war ally, was now the enemy that Nazi Germany had been.

With this in mind he drove with a veteran companion and fellow AVC member, Charles Bolte, to Dublin, New Hampshire, where there was a conference to discuss the problems the atomic bomb had caused. It had been called by Grenville Clarke, a senior New York lawyer. It was replete with substantial figures, such as Owen Roberts, a Supreme Court justice; a prominent banker, Frank Altschul; Thomas K. Finletter, a lawyer and later secretary of the air force; and atomic physicist Henry Smyth.

Straight became involved with the hot issue of the moment—atomic weapons. His unique position as a B-29 pilot could have seen him flying the atomic bombs destined to be dropped on Japan, but for his inexperience and minor doubts about his competency as a pilot. Straight expressed no moral dilemmas over the bomb. Yet days after he left the armed services, he was in the thick of a conference of experts with definite positions and interests in the issue of the bomb.

Straight met the 55-year-old Leo Szilard at the conference. The rotund physicist, his face pixieish behind horn-rimmed spectacles, used the gathering as a forum for warning about the danger of multiplying atomic weapons. While heartfelt on his part, this approach was what the KGB wanted in its strategy to retard U.S. bomb developments while the Soviet Union played catch-up. Not only was Szilard, unwittingly or otherwise, passing the Russians an abundance of vital technical data via a KGB agent, who had been recruited by Elizabeth Zarubin; he and the other key scientists were now at the forefront of KGB-inspired and aided propaganda.

The meeting led to the formation of the Emergency Committee of Atomic Scientists. Straight became its secretary, working with Beth Olds, Szilard's "girl Friday" in his successive schemes for resolving the atomic crisis.[2] Straight would also have been cooperating with Zarubin's KGB plant in the office.

Szilard managed to secure his friend Albert Einstein as the committee's chairman, which gave it weight as a fund-raiser—its main role on behalf of concerned scientists wanting to spread their views and influence government.

At the New Hampshire conference, the forty-seven conferees agreed initially on one point: only a world authority could prevent a nuclear arms race. There was also some agreement on the rather woolly idea of a

"World Federal Organization," which would take the place of the just-born (October 24, 1945) United Nations.

A declaration was drafted, and thirty of the conferees, including Straight and AVC founding member Cord Meyer, a combat marine war hero injured while fighting on Guam in the Pacific, put their signatures to it. *The New York Times* carried the declaration on its front page. For a moment in history the concept of a world government with a representative legislature had credibility. Soon, its impractical nature surfaced.

As enthusiastic as they were, Straight and Meyer didn't believe it could work. The Soviet government, for one, would not give up sovereignty over its armed forces to an organization it couldn't control. An idea that rose without trace sank quickly, yet it focused Straight's mind on political issues.

The Straight family was based in New York City to accommodate Bin's psychiatry course. They had rented out Weynoke for the war and would not return until at least the end of Bin's studies. Straight disliked the tensions he found in New York. It deepened his worry about a career. He hurried to Washington to see Tom Corcoran, but he was no help this time and had no suggestions about employment in the Truman administration. Straight's in-out record from late 1937 to early 1941 at the State Department (twice), the White House, and the Department of the Interior was not one which would engender confidence in an administration chief. Straight then thought of the United Nations, which he had weeks earlier denounced as impotent in the Dublin conference declaration. He went and saw his old friend from the Department of State, KGB agent Alger Hiss, who reiterated that the fledgling UN had no power and talked Straight out of joining it.[3]

That left him with few options. One was a long-held fantasy about going into politics. This dream had been thwarted in the United Kingdom, but Straight dreamed now about how he might run in the United States. The ultimate reverie was him as president, given the expectation that the United States would continue the New Deal–engendered move to more left-wing acceptance or domination of politics.

His age, 29, was not against him. Many young ex-servicemen of that vintage (including Jack Kennedy and Richard Nixon two years later in

1947) would enter politics soon after the war. But Straight had wanted a better track record and a little distance to hide his noncombat military duties, which he regarded as a drawback. One aspect, however, of his military experience was a help. He had been forced to mix with "ordinary" Americans, not intellectuals or the rich and privileged. He would never be accused of having the "common touch," but his service had been useful if he wished to address the average citizen's concerns.

He could boast about his experience in government and journalism, as long as the press did not uncover the paucity and unsteadiness of those years from 1937 to 1942. The Cambridge academic record looked good, but not nearly as impressive as it would have appeared in the United Kingdom. A U.S. degree would have carried more weight with most electorates. Then again, they would be skeptical of an academic background anyway. Voters in pragmatic, postwar, mainstream America could well ask how it would help them with taxes, services, and grievances in congress.

Straight canvassed a few close family members, friends, and contacts. The consensus was that he should take the chance if he really wanted it. His original sponsors to the United States, the KGB and Stalin, also would have been pleased to see him in congress. This would give them a chance to keep him in active service. Straight's drive, charm, and capacity for the quick study of an issue and manipulative skills would have seen him attempt to sit on the most powerful congressional committees in everything from budget appropriations to foreign affairs. He had the intellect to roam across the political spectrum, which would have suited the KGB. It had been fed a steady diet of data in the United Kingdom by spies such as Cairncross at Treasury and Burgess and Maclean in the foreign office. In the United States, it had done even better with two hundred agents, many in government departments. Another experienced and well-equipped espionage agent would not go astray, provided the KGB could persuade him to stay involved postwar and to deliver what they wanted.

Running for office as a Democrat would be the start of Straight's dream to be something important and fulfill his fierce drive to achieve in politics—held since his days in the Cambridge Union. The move, too, would mark a distinct break from the other members of the Cambridge ring, who had mostly settled in the other direction—of gray bureaucrats for the cause. Philby had his day of minor fame and public recognition as an intrepid war correspondent for *The Times*. Blunt had once been a minor art critic, and Burgess was once at the respectable BBC, despite his outrageous manner, which was a quaint cover in itself.

Yet they had subjugated any personal ambitions for the glory of Stalin and beyond him an even more glorious communist future for the world. Philby was in a back room in Whitehall running Soviet counterintelligence, the most private job of all. Blunt had left MI5, which officially had never existed, and was now (1945 to 1947) on that ultra-secret espionage mission for the king of England. Burgess was in the foreign office trying to make it less dull and bureaucratic, but all the while writing "brilliant" reports for the KGB. By contrast, Straight was about to choose the most audacious career path yet for one of the ring, although there were precedents of high-flying Western politicians working for the KGB. He need not look further than his comrade, Pierre Cot, who had been minister of air and minister of commerce in the short-lived cabinets of the interwar Third French Republic. Cot had presented himself as a radical outside the Communist Party while advocating a strong military alliance with the Soviet Union.

Straight chose to run for office in the Seventeenth Congressional District, in which he was living in New York. The incumbent was a Republican, Joseph Clark Baldwin III, known to his Italian constituents, according to Straight, as "Joe Baldwin de Turd." The challenger thought he had the sitting member's measure.

Straight met Bert Stand and Clarence Laughlin, the bosses of the Democratic Party machine, at its headquarters, Tammany Hall, where money talked. They knew Straight would have an open checkbook and could finance a hefty campaign. They were aware of his generous $10,000 support for Maury Maverick in San Antonio in 1938 and the liberal handouts of the Whitney Foundation. Stand and Laughlin didn't mind his Ivy League appearance and patrician demeanor. Straight's looks could be beneficial in photo opportunities. His more extreme liberal views could be useful here and there, especially with the Jewish vote. His antifascist views had been presented presciently at times in *The New Republic* and could be used now. Straight's other stands on issues could be modified to make them acceptable to the diverse New York voting public. They noted his enthusiastic willingness to stump and door knock. He told them of his skills as a speaker, which were important. He had some experience in election campaigns in the United Kingdom and New York. All in all, the bosses were impressed and welcomed him with open arms.

Straight thought about mentioning his undergraduate communist days in England in a self-deprecating, offhand way, but he didn't want to sow any seeds of doubt in the minds of the bosses with the chubby-faced smiles of welcome. A communist student past, if presented as a vague juvenile aberration, would have been acceptable up until the beginning of 1945. But by the end of the year it would have caused frowns. The Cold War was at its frosty beginning. The glacial shifts of world geopolitics had changed allegiances. Former enemies were now friends, and vice versa. "Reds" were now the target in the popular press. The Pentagon, not wanting its postwar budgets diminished more than necessary, was making the communist threat more menacing than fascism had ever appeared. The FBI and J. Edgar Hoover, although not yet acknowledging foreign infiltration of Russian espionage agents and killer squads, were concentrating on "the enemy within"—the domestic spread of communism. It had become entangled in the director's mind with true liberal values that had little or nothing to do with Marxist doctrines.

Unfortunately for the bright new prospective candidate, others sowed those seeds of distrust and uncertainty. Laughlin called Straight back to Tammany Hall[4] and told him he had a call from the vice-chairman of the Democratic National Committee, Oscar Ewing. He had been told that Straight had been a communist in England.

Straight felt a knot in his stomach, but he showed no outward reaction. His training with Burgess, Blunt, and Green had prepared him for such an eventuality. Instead, he tried to dismiss the statement as irrelevant and went into the well-rehearsed lines that he would use well into old age: it was in his youth. He was just a raw, impressionable kid. Communism was all the rage then. So many at the London School of Economics and Cambridge were "reds." There was good reason. Europe was different. The fascist threat was real. . . .

Laughlin sympathized but said Straight couldn't be supported without Ewing's agreement, especially on a matter so important. An indignant Straight said he would see Ewing and straighten out the matter. Ewing was less sympathetic. Imagine, he suggested, what "Joe Baldwin de Turd" would do with that kind of information, no matter how distant and irrelevant it was. How would the reporters at the *Daily News* handle it if it were ever leaked to them?

Straight protested that he had long forgotten and buried his undergraduate, youthful views. Ewing was not swayed. The matter had to be cleared up before the party would endorse him. Straight wanted to know who said he was a communist. Ewing told him it was the financial columnist, Eliot Janeway. Straight was stunned. He knew Janeway and regarded him as a friend. Later, when alone, he rang Janeway, who had joined the British Communist Party in the early 1930s and was expelled for reasons unknown. He knew Straight had joined the U.K. Party. Straight asked him if he had been spreading stories about his communist youth. Janeway replied that the question was not who spread the story, but how Straight would respond to it. Straight asked how he should respond to it. Janeway said that was for him to decide.

The phone discussion ended. Straight had some thinking to do. He worried about just how much could be uncovered by probing reporters and jackal-like opposition politicians eager for a "red kill." Better to back out now and perhaps wait for a more propitious moment to enter politics. With this reaction, and from the more liberal side of the spectrum at that, his known record was against him. Even a hint of the secret past now would extinguish any hope he had ever had of a political career.

After pumping himself up for the decision to run, this was a bitter, depressing realization, which at his age could mark a major turning point in his life. It was the shocking moment when his hopes and dreams about moving into big politics in the United States evaporated. The undermining by Janeway and Mike Ross—an English adviser to the CIO—as well as others was responsible. Straight rang Laughlin to tell him he would not be running against Baldwin.[5] The KGB had pinned him to the past like a butterfly in an entomologist's lab. There was no thought of his fighting on and admitting his communist background. He had his family to think about: Bin had her career. Her sister was married to Gustavo Duran, who was under pressure. Joe McCarthy had named him as one of his top six enemies. Straight also used his sister Beatrice as an excuse for not coming clean. She was married to another KGB agent, Louis Dolivet. If he stepped forward, all his relatives and associates would suffer. The links to Blunt and Burgess would have been uncovered. Overriding all this was Straight's continued agency for the KGB. He would be committing suicide figuratively and probably literally had he crossed his Kremlin masters this way and at this critical time. They were uneasy about his moves and motivations as it was, and there would have been some relief among the KGB hierarchy that his ambition to be a politician had been crushed. It was not the time for a confession, which he might use as a last resort if he felt confident it could be part of a KGB disinformation campaign.

This was yet another occasion, if he needed a stimulus, to "admit," even in a nondamaging partial sense, that he was somehow mixed up with the KGB. But once more the impulse, or need, was not there, as it had not been during the war.

Despite the serious problems associated with admitting he was a spy, there was also a little matter of pride. A major fear was what his ideological enemies would do with the juicy revelation that such an upmarket figure, and a member of the family that ran *The New Republic*, was a KGB agent. During 1945, the commencement of the Cold War, his confessional, the FBI, was a sieve. People such as McCarthy, for whom he had been gunning via *The New Republic*, would have received a leak. He would have loved it. Straight would have been the highest profile catch yet.

———————

While the disqualification from running for high office sobered and deflated him, his next move demonstrated he had not lost his drive. It was one of the few options left. He rang Bruce Bliven at *The New Republic* and told him he was coming back to the magazine. Bliven's feelings about this are not recorded. Straight felt that the magazine had reverted to its old ways in his absence. In an understatement that would seem arrogant but for the intent in his comment, Straight said he wanted to liven it up.

———————

The FBI completed its debriefing of former communist network runner Elizabeth Bentley's Silvermaster and other spy networks on November 30, 1945. In December, the KGB was informed about the extent of her revelations, which caused a crisis for some of its key personnel. These included Straight's control, the "illegal" Michael Green, who was not protected by any diplomatic status. He had been unmasked by Bentley and would have to leave the United States. The KGB contacted its agents in the United States in January 1946 and warned them of the danger. It advised them "of what action to take to avoid being implicated."[6]

At about the same time, early in 1946, Straight began working on a special issue of *The New Republic* to mark the first anniversary of Roosevelt's
death. If he had to make his career at the magazine for the time being, he
was not content to be just another editor anymore. Straight wished to
take full control of an institution he considered was part of his birthright.

He could only hint at his plans to his family. He was aware that it
would be a major step for Dorothy to allow him, a relative neophyte in
the business of journalism, to take over from the professionals that had
run the little liberal flagship since 1914. He knew she would be concerned
about the reaction to the bumptious son of the owner directing the old
hands, some of whom had been around the magazine for three decades.
But his plans had ramifications for the family and its financial structures
created in 1936 to run Dorothy's fortune, which then stood at $45 mil-
lion. Dorothy had set up several trusts to avoid heavy tax burdens and to
settle equitably on her five children. One trust was the William C. Whitney Foundation, which was to be directed by her American children—
Whitney, Michael, and Beatrice—to make charitable gifts out of its U.S.
base in New York. This donated to several communist front groups,
among others. A second trust was the Elm Grant Trust, which was to be
under the direction of her English children, Ruth and William. It too was
to make charitable gifts from its U.K. base at Dartington. A third trust,
known as the Royal Trust Company of Canada, was the biggest of all. It
covered money "given" to her children as a principal lump sum, which
could not be touched by any of them. They received annual incomes from
investments of that principal sum, which they could spend as they saw fit.
However, it also covered the running of the family's American publications, *The New Republic, Antiques* magazine and other assets. *The New Republic* had bumbled along for thirty years, and the small losses it made, if
any, were covered by the success of *Antiques*. If Straight became too ambitious and led the magazine to running up bigger losses, it could affect the
incomes of each of the children. A complication was found in the relationship between Straight and the 41-year-old American lawyer, Milton
Rose, a trustee who oversaw how that principal sum was invested and how
the interest generated was distributed. If Straight were to influence Rose,
and it were to the detriment of the others, then their relationship could be
seen by Straight's siblings as a conflict of interest.

Rose and Straight, now 29, landed at Southampton on May 3, 1946, and drove through the New Forest to Dartington. It was Straight's first trip to England and his old home in nearly a decade—a third of his life—and it was an exciting if not nostalgic time for him. A war-battered United Kingdom had thrown out its wartime heroic leader Winston Churchill in an election in mid-1945 and had turned to Labour, led by Clement Atlee, for the immediate postwar recovery. It had implemented socialist measures, such as nationalization of the Bank of England, coal, electrical power, railroads, road transport, inland waterways, docks, and harbors. Labour continued war legislation for agriculture, guaranteeing prices and markets, and implemented the "welfare state" with a dramatic extension of the state's services. Such unprecedented socialist measures quickened the heartbeat of communists, who now felt that the step toward a Marxist government was closer than ever.

Straight enjoyed the atmosphere in a country where ideological demarcation between political parties was clear and where Marxist-approved concepts such as nationalization were acceptable, as compared to the United States, where they were not. In the United Kingdom, nearly half the workforce was state employed, which made dependence on government much more the norm. In the United States, much less of a "nanny state" mentality prevailed. Only one-fifth of workers had some form of government employment.

Straight found that even in the microcosm of Dartington, communism seemed to have a foothold. Cells had grown up in the school and were tolerated by the staff.[7] The network of communists he had grown up with were still in some way connected with the place. His friend Michael Young, who had been in charge of the Labour Party's research during the war, had been a frequent visitor.

Straight could talk freely to a wider circle and not be afraid of being branded a red. Rather than being restricted to a small clique in the United States, he could communicate with everyone from sympathizers at Dartington Hall and his old Cambridge companions to Prime Minister Atlee and his government ministers, such as Herbert Morrison, the leader of the Commons. Morrison visited Dartington to see Dorothy and Leonard and met Straight, who impressed him with his grip on world and domestic affairs. After a lengthy chat, Morrison turned to an aide and commented in his vigorous way: "The man's brilliant. Why can't I find people like him to work for me?"[8]

Straight's main task, however, was not to win over the government, but rather his mother. He had, with support from his sister Beatrice, persuaded Dorothy to sanction the $250,000 investment in KGB agent Louis Dolivet's magazine, *United Nations World*. Then Straight had appealed to his mother's desire for international peace in a war-free world. The magazine had been going only a few years and was shaky financially. Other investors were threatening to pull out (they did, later in 1946), which would leave the Straight family investment vulnerable. Rose, well-prepared by Straight beforehand, forwarded the pitch for big changes at *The New Republic*. Straight supposed he knew how to boost circulation from 20,000 to 100,000 and how to make the magazine pay. He envisioned its being far more adventurous, thrusting, and influential.

There was no one to state the case against the proposition. Ruth (just 19 years old) and William (17 years old)—happy with their finances—were too young and inexperienced to have any considered input. Beatrice, in the United States, was in no position to block Straight's plans, even if she wished to, given that he had backed the large investment for her husband.

That left Whitney, who had been occupied during the war. While Straight and Beatrice were helping Dolivet start the magazine, ostensibly to assist in creating a voice for a more peaceful world (in reality a KGB propaganda sheet), Whitney, the air ace, was busy actually fighting for it. He was shot down twice over enemy territory in France and each time escaped. By the end of the war Whitney was weighed down with medals (MC, DFC and bar, Norwegian War Cross, Legion d'Honneur, and Croix de Guerre). He became an air commodore and the youngest acting air vice marshall in the air force. His nice income kept coming into his London bank account for play when he wasn't locked in battle with the Luftwaffe. This was all that mattered during his most distinguished service.

It meant that Straight was unopposed in his ambitions to fulfill his aims for power and influence, made more urgent by his rejection for political backing a few months earlier. Dorothy agreed to his becoming the magazine's publisher later in the year, and also to his plans for its expansion bid to gain another 80,000 readers.

House Tensions: Michael Straight, showing the strain under intense questioning by the Select Committee of the House of Representatives investigating tax-exempt foundations that supported communist-front organizations. *Wide World Photo*

Family Trust Showdown: Dorothy Elmhirst, husband Leonard (center) and Michael Straight at Dartington in early 1950 before the legal battle with Whitney Straight over misuse of family Trust funds. *Courtesy of William Elmhirst.*

Air-ace with the Aces: Whitney Straight, businessman, highly decorated war-time fighter pilot and part-time British spy, in uniform during World War II. Whitney had the upper hand in the battle over the family Trust. He wanted "out" in early 1950 when he learned his brother Michael was a KGB spy. *Courtesy of William Elmhirst.*

The First Man: British agent Donald Maclean. Evidence from KGB-defector Walter Krivitsky eventually led to Maclean being the first of the core Cambridge University spy ring to defect to Russia in 1951. Burgess went with him. *Hulton Archive/Getty Images*

Second Man in Exile: British KGB spy Guy Burgess in Russia in 1957, six years after his defection, with *London Daily Express* photographer, Terry Lancaster. Burgess master-minded Straight's recruitment to Soviet Intelligence in early 1937. *Hulton Archive/Getty Images*

Third Man in Denial: Kim Philby at his London flat in 1955 denying he was the so-called Third Man. He defected to Russia in 1963. *Hulton Archive/Getty Images*

The Fourth Man: Anthony Blunt, the keeper of espionage secrets and the Queen's pictures. Blunt carried out Burgess's plan to recruit Straight to the Cambridge spy ring in early 1937. *Hulton Archive/Getty Images*

The Fifth Man: Victor Rothschild, who used his close friend Blunt as the middle-man to pass on intelligence, especially on weapons development, to the KGB. (John Cairncross, who never met any other members of the ring, but was another major spy, is also nominated by some observers as The Fifth Man.) *Corbis*

Modin, KGB's Cambridge Control: The author (left) with KGB masterspy, Yuri Ivanovitch Modin in Moscow. He took up his decade-long role as Control of the key Cambridge Ring in London in 1947, making a mockery of claims by ring members, including Straight, that they did not spy in the Cold War (1946–1990). *Author photo.*

Meyer, CIA Masterspy: The author (left) with CIA man Cord Meyer, in Washington, D.C. Meyer claimed Straight spied for the KGB in the Cold War years. *Author photo.*

Buoyed by his appointment as publisher-elect, Straight traveled to London to speak with left-wing Labour members of parliament and communists to see, he claimed, if he could gain support for Oppenheimer's concept of international control and development of atomic energy which had been approved by President Truman.

He met Margot Heinemann, now well up in the Communist Party, and had a long chat to his old KGB confidant, Harry Pollitt. The British party's secretary general, to no one's surprise, including Straight's, was as hard-line a Soviet mouthpiece as ever. Straight faithfully reported Pollitt's unilluminating views and filed an article for *The New Republic*.

Pollitt, doing the bidding of his Kremlin masters, was putting out the imaginative and improbable line that the United States should share its knowledge so that the Soviet Union could produce a bomb of its own. This was in the interest of restoring the balances of forces in the world. It was where the arms race would head, but both sides were going all out to gain the ascendancy. This was in contrast to the Oppenheimer proposal (supported by Atomic Energy Commission chairman David E. Lilienthal and Dean Acheson, the Truman administration's secretary of state) for international control of nuclear weapons that had currency during the heady first months after the war.

Straight had a cover, or alibi, for public consumption after he learned that MI6 and the CIA had been monitoring his numerous meetings with key KGB figure Pollitt in the United Kingdom. He claimed that all he wanted to do was to use Pollitt to reach the Kremlin and the KGB and point out the insanity in opposing the Acheson/Lilienthal/Oppenheimer plan.

This was an instance of Straight's attempt decades later to justify to the FBI and others why he kept in contact with yet another KGB operative. His main job was to help retard U.S. bomb manufacturing while the Russians developed their own.

They were closer now to creating their own nuclear weapon than even Pollitt or Straight could have realized. By May 1946 they had built a nuclear reactor but had trouble with plutonium accidents and could not get the reactor to work. KGB Department S head, Pavel Sudoplatov, was desperate. His first plan was to send a scientist, Yakov Terletsky, direct to the United States under the cover of a peace delegation to ask Oppenheimer, Szilard, and Fermi to inform them on how to fire up the dormant reactor.[9] The KGB foresaw FBI surveillance problems. Terletsky was instead sent to see Niels Bohr in Denmark. Bohr was nervous, realizing that the help he and his three U.S. companions had given had finally come to fruition. The Soviets all but had the means to produce the fuel for the bomb.

Bohr insisted that only Terletsky, with a translator, was present, but not his KGB bodyguard, before he explained where the Soviet reactor's problem lay. While poring over diagrams, the Nobel prize-winner pointed to a place on a drawing and declared, "That's the trouble spot." His direct help led to the Soviet reactor working by the end of 1946.[10]

Straight used the London trip also to make contact with some of his former Cambridge friends. He learned that Victor Rothschild was about to marry Tess Mayor. Straight may have realized for the first time why Blunt a decade ago had used him to split Rothschild from his first wife Barbara. This created the chance for Rothschild to have a relationship with Tess. As Straight later suspected (and probably knew), the couple proved a most successful team for the KGB at MI5, at Cambridge during the war years, and in the Cold War.

Straight returned to Washington and began reshaping *The New Republic*. He upped the magazine's political tempo in support of hard-left positions and even took ads for "Soviet Records—originals Made in the USSR, and books such as Behind Soviet Power—Stalin and the Russians."[11] The magazine's layout was improved and made more lively, and front pages became more daring. Yet sales didn't budge much above 20,000 each issue. Straight and his staff knew that they had to put the "new" into the magazine to attract readers.

Straight saw his opportunity when President Truman forced his secretary of agriculture, Henry Wallace, the former vice-president, to resign on September 12, 1946. Wallace had delivered an anti-Republican speech on foreign policy at Madison Square Garden, which he went through "sentence by sentence" with Truman beforehand.[12] Wallace's remarks were heckled and hissed. He later characterized the speech as "neither pro-British or anti-British, neither pro- nor anti-Russian." He had endorsed the administration's stated objective of seeking peace through UN cooperation. Yet the speech had three points of departure which Truman let slip through the net. First, Wallace warned against allowing U.S. foreign policy to be dominated by the British. Second, he warned that "the tougher we get with Russia, the tougher they will get with us." Third, he spoke of a tacit acceptance of a Russian sphere of influence in Eastern Europe, much as the Monroe Doctrine had implied an American sphere of influence in Latin America.

This appeared to be a definite softening of the line being put out by Secretary of State James Byrnes. There were protests from senior people at State and others. Truman backtracked. Wallace was forced out of government.

Straight had never met Wallace, even though he had visited Dartington Hall as early as 1929 for a World Agricultural Economics Conference. He knew Dorothy and Leonard and had written articles for *The New Republic*. Straight persuaded the current long-suffering editor, Bruce Bliven, and the rest of the staff that Wallace should be editor of the magazine. It would be a radical move. But Wallace's politics as unofficial leader of the progressive movement were not a departure for the magazine. He would fit well and widen its appeal to blue-collar groups and a greater variety of liberals.

Straight also saw him as a Trojan horse to reinstall a left-wing Democrat of the New Deal school back in the White House. He regarded him as Roosevelt's heir apparent, behind himself, if he had been given the chance. More than that, Wallace needed no manipulation to accommodate the Soviet view on all foreign policy and a liberal view on domestic issues. Stalin and the KGB viewed him as the best candidate in the United States for their purposes, besides Straight himself.

And right beside him was where Straight planned to be.

13

TRY OF THE TROJAN

Henry Wallace in 1946 seemed far from a long shot for the U.S. presidency given the political climate and the disenchantment with Harry Truman, who was looked upon with derision by unfortunate comparisons with his predecessor. At the July 1944 Democratic Party Convention Wallace had beaten Truman in the first ballot for the vice-presidency by a solid 429.5 votes to 319.5, with the other 428 votes divided up between fourteen favorite sons and local choices. But a second ballot saw the party bosses start a bandwagon rolling for the middle-of-the-road Truman. He won the second and decisive ballot fought out between the two front-runners.

Wallace had fallen short by just 160 votes on regaining the vice-presidency, which he held through Roosevelt's second term from 1940 to 1944. If it had been a best-vote-wins ballot, Wallace would have become president in April 1945 when Roosevelt died. That closeness to winning the highest office touched Wallace, the ideas man, who desperately wanted the opportunity to be president at a key strategic time in postwar history. He was genuine about his fears for further war and nuclear confrontation. Wallace was certain that his politics would mean peace on earth and goodwill to all peoples. He wanted that second chance.

Straight, now 30, bore this in mind in a rehearsed speech when he knocked on the door to Wallace's apartment in the Wardman Hotel, Washington, one week after Truman had pushed him out of government. Mrs. Wallace answered the door and ushered him through to her husband on the terrace, sorting out telegrams with a beefy Texan adviser. Some were offers from publishers.[1] Straight delivered his speech. Wallace looked down at his shoes, stony-faced. The terms that were put to him were alluring. The salary was attractive. Straight was prepared to put an enormous amount into supporting him and the magazine, whose circulation would go up with marketing plans the management had already begun implementing. It would be a strong forum for Wallace, especially with his presidential ambitions, and also for Straight and his political ambitions.

Straight was sure that Wallace dreamt of himself as a peacemaking president, and admitted that he himself dreamt of becoming a political leader, especially in the years 1946 to 1948 when the two were closely linked.[2]

Straight then would be a strategist, if not the key planner, behind a Wallace run for the presidency. His strategy was daring, precarious, and on paper impressive. The best way for those dreams to become a reality was to broaden Wallace's appeal among liberals and a wide range of Democrats, who were disillusioned with Truman and who wanted someone in Roosevelt's mould. If the communists wished to tag along and add their votes for Wallace, that was fine, Straight reckoned. But his expertise and experience told him that they should not be allowed to hijack support for Wallace and fulfill their impractical hopes for a third party with him as its candidate.

Straight had always been kept independent of U.S. communists while a secret agent for Stalin, and he wished to remain that way. If their methods of achieving an end coincided with his work for the Kremlin, then it would give him the ultimate satisfaction. A problem lay in the communist movement in the United States. It was unruly and disunited. There were no guarantees that Straight could keep them out of the way while he ran Wallace's campaign. Straight's aim was to get Wallace elected by putting an acceptable spin on his liberal positions that would widen his appeal to Democrats. U.S. communists hovering too close would ruin the image-building and limit the candidate's attractiveness.

The political view from September 1946 looked smooth enough. If it remained that way, the communists could be kept out of the headlines and away from the candidate.

Straight's first task was to use *The New Republic* to give Wallace a suitable platform and to build his support base throughout 1947. This would be the springboard for a run to the Democratic Convention in mid-1948. Once Wallace was elected, Straight was confident he would beat any Republican candidate for the presidency.

In the last months of 1946, *The New Republic* would build expectations for Wallace's editorship. The December 2 edition had a tantalizing sketch of his eyes and forehead without mentioning who it was. A fortnight later Straight introduced him and his weekly editorial with great fanfare: "This week *The New Republic* is published under a new editor. *The New Republic* was founded to express the promise of American life. No American can express that promise as well as Henry Wallace . . ."[3]

Then followed a glossy short biography showing Wallace's farm-belt background as a corn-growing son of an editor of a farm paper. *The New Republic* stepped up its campaign for new readership with advertisements to "JOIN HENRY WALLACE" and generous starting subscription rates of $6 for the year and a "Special 10-weeks' offer for $1." Straight was nearly giving the paper away to build the readership and so become more attractive to advertisers. The Amalgamated Clothing Workers of America, "on behalf of its 350,000 members," greeted the appointment with a page ad. Century High Speed Drills followed with another page, as did Harcourt, Brace & Company, the book publisher. But apart from this and other sporadic support, the magazine seemed to be struggling at the beginning of its hoped-for renaissance.[4]

Straight, with Milton Rose behind him and his mother's green light, was now on the masthead as publisher and spending fast and big. Straight got hold of every mailing list he could and lured some of the best writers from Henry Luce's publishing empire.[5] He hired experienced editors and brought in the sophisticated, academic-like James Newman to work with Wallace. The new editor advocated innovative programs, but Straight wrote most of the editorials himself. He, Newman, and Wallace would meet Tuesday morning each week in the editor's office to discuss the next editorial. Wallace would sit between the others on a sofa, jingling keys in his pants pocket. Newman would read aloud a couple of paragraphs of a draft he had prepared. Wallace would appear to drift off to sleep. Then he would snap out of his reverie and agree with what had been said.[6]

Wallace did not attend conferences at the magazine, nor did he read it. According to his publisher, he often failed to recognize the prized staff

Straight had spent a small fortune hiring. Wallace managed to escape from the office for an hour's walk with a friend through the streets on New York's East Side. Most of the time he would stay shut away at his desk, enveloped in his own thoughts.

In effect, Straight was the unofficial campaign manager and strategist. He provided the money for the mission, which was a campaign all but in name; his magazine was the forum for Wallace's programs, and he wrote most of his editorials and speeches. As the candidate's image grew Straight struggled to keep him away from the communist-created and -run Progressive Citizens of America (PCA), which was making claim to liberal support across the country.[7]

The first few months of the new year 1947 were promising enough, but then in March two unforeseen bombshells were dropped, which threatened Straight's grand plan. Early in the month, the so-called Truman Doctrine to "contain" Russia was clarified. Truman asked Congress to appropriate $40 million for military and economic aid to Greece and Turkey. He wished to be able to send military personnel to those countries. It was seen by communists in the United States and some liberals as an open-ended commitment to intervene in any nation where communism posed a threat. The Americans for Democratic Action (ADA)—led by Eleanor Roosevelt—which was the other main group vying for liberal support, welcomed the development. The PCA opposed it.

Straight went to his typewriter and belted out a speech for Wallace, which denounced the escalation of the Cold War. It was a chance for "good copy" and to sell Wallace and the magazine. It also happened to be Stalin's position on the issue. Six days later, the unannounced presidential candidate delivered the speech on national radio. The doctrine meant that the United States would "eventually . . . bleed from every pore." The move into Greece meant that the Soviets had been provoked into "possible dangerous retaliation."

Straight expanded on the speech in *The New Republic* a few days later and forecast: "Once American loans are given to undemocratic governments of Greece and Turkey, every reactionary government and every strutting dictator will be able to hoist the anticommunist skull and (cross) bones, and demand that the American people rush to his aid. Today we are asking to support Greece and Turkey. Tomorrow Peron and Chiang Kai-shek may take their turn at the head of the line. American dollars will be the first demand, then American army officers and technicians, then American GIs."[8]

The speech and article were enough to rouse the sleepiest communist and frighten the most wavering liberal. According to Straight, Wallace received 5,000 letters from people thanking him for speaking out and begging him to lead them. Those at the PCA loved the speech. They began to mumble about seconding Wallace as their figurehead. Just to compound the upheaval, a few weeks later on March 23 Truman delivered his Executive Order 9835, instituting a loyalty investigation of federal employees. Its aim was to keep those with allegiances to a foreign power—mainly communists—out of government. Anyone could anonymously report another's "disloyalty" and not be held accountable. Wallace again bounced from his apparent lethargy at a Madison Square Garden meeting arranged by the First Lady's favored ADA.

"The president's executive order creates a master index of public servants," he said in a speech (written and edited by Straight) marked for its verve and passion. "From the janitor in the village post office to the cabinet member, they are to be sifted and tested and watched and appraised. Their past and present, the tattle and prattle of their neighbors, are all to be recorded."

Two weeks later in *The New Republic*, another Straight editorial struck again at the loyalty program, this time swiping at the magazine's archenemy, the FBI. It scathingly dismissed J. Edgar Hoover's recent estimate that one person in every 1,184 in the United States was a communist.

The PCA became vocal in denouncing the loyalty program, whereas the ADA supported it. Straight's words proved more inflammatory than he anticipated. Yet he still felt he could keep Wallace out of the grasp of local communists. They were now reaching for him.

A group from the PCA led by Beanie Baldwin, the director of the Farm Security Administration when Wallace was secretary of agriculture; sculptor Jo Davidson; and PCA's "undercover organizer" Hannah Dorner invited Straight to dinner at Davidson's New York studio. With Wallace present, the group put a request to Straight to allow the candidate loose from *The New Republic* offices for a while.[9] The PCA needed money to keep running, and Wallace on the stump was a sure way to raise funds. It also wanted him to work the Democratic Party precincts in an effort to wrest the 1948 nomination from Truman.

Straight had gambled hundreds of thousands of dollars of family trust funds in an effort to drive up the circulation of *The New Republic*. He knew at that point in March 1947 that if he didn't attract advertising, the gambling loss of his family trust money would run into the millions. He realized also that if Wallace left the magazine to become embroiled in political battles, *The New Republic* might have to be sold.

Straight saved the situation for the moment by insisting that Wallace go ahead with a planned tour of Europe to build his image as a statesman. Straight set up and funded the trip after engineering a "request" for Wallace to visit England by his contacts, including editor Kingsley Martin, at the left-wing *New Statesman* magazine.

It was a critical time. Truman was pressuring the senate to ratify his plans to fight communism abroad and contain Russia, but many of its members needed persuading. In England the Labour Party was in power and divided over the Truman Doctrine. Its vocal communist faction was creating a fuss over the issue. Several members of the British cabinet were against it and siding with Wallace's stance. Following the Stalinist line, Straight was ambitious to drive a wedge between the United Kingdom and the United States, and Wallace presented what appeared to be a very good opportunity for doing it. Straight was not fearful of communist support in the United Kingdom, where liberal views often were indistinguishable from hard-left positions. He arranged for more than fifty communist and other left-wing members of parliament to sign a telegram welcoming Wallace. Yet Straight could not cajole Ernest Bevin, Britain's foreign secretary, into signing his name. Labour, despite its left-wing tilt, could not break with Truman, especially with the Conservative opposition, led by Churchill, unanimously in favor of the president's policy. There was a fear in the United Kingdom as much as the United States of Stalin's expansionist aims.

Straight arrived in England on April 7, 1947, and was driven to Dartington, where the family, unaware of the amount of money being lost on *The New Republic*, welcomed him warmly.[10] He had portrayed his support for Wallace to his parents as a gallant fight for peace. And from what they could see on the surface, this was well worth supporting. Dorothy didn't like Truman or any of his policies and was a strong Wallace supporter. She agreed with Straight's earnest positions on the United States staying out of foreign lands. Dorothy deplored the concept of the loyalty program and was fearful of how the FBI would use it. The heat of these issues had ensured her support for Straight's actions with *The New Republic*, although a proper assessment of the expenditure then may have caused her concern.

The British papers were editorializing on the Truman Doctrine, and Wallace decided he would say something precipitate on the issue when he arrived in England the next day, April 8. It was a contentious approach.[11] It was one thing for an ex–vice-president and potential presidential candidate to make remarks at home, but it was another to make them on foreign soil, especially if they related to sensitive policy issues. It would focus further attention on the candidate, which was what a tour like this was all about.

Wallace went from the airport to the Savoy Hotel where Straight had organized a press conference for fifty reporters. The politician had little choice but to respond to demands to know where he stood on the Truman Doctrine. Yet this was what he wanted.

"The administration has embarked on a course of ruthless imperialism," Wallace began in a tirade against U.S. policy abroad. The reporters scribbled, and he expounded on his thoughts.[12] Straight was pleased to have the spotlight on his candidate. However, he had not quite anticipated the reaction in Washington, where the politician's words caused a furor. Wallace was denounced on the floors of the senate and the house. Republicans and Democrats lined up to berate him. Many who were ambivalent about the Truman Doctrine now wrapped themselves in the American flag. Wallace and Straight had blundered in not accounting for the fervent nationalism still strong among ex-servicemen who had just stopped fighting a major war. The responses had united them behind their president once more. This was reflected in remarks in congress and in the press.

Straight was startled by the intensity of U.S. reaction, which was followed by a critical response in the United Kingdom.[13] "When U.S. Senators, Congressmen and the press began to storm against Wallace," the

Chicago Sun's Frederick Kuh reported, "this was the signal for British conservative papers to start criticizing him too."

Churchill thought he could see a sinister underlying influence in Wallace's pronouncements. Speaking to a Conservative Party rally in the Albert Hall, he called Wallace a "crypto-Communist," which, given his record and sympathies, was not far off the mark. Churchill then went on to link Wallace with his long-term enemy and short-term military ally, Stalin. Wallace, he said, was trying to "separate Great Britain from the United States and to weave her into a vast system of Communist intrigue."[14]

The undeclared candidate seemed to thrive on the abuse. He went on BBC radio, reaching about a quarter of the British population, and spoke of his vision for raising the living standards of all peoples. But the press was not interested in his doctrine for a world utopia. It wanted more on the Truman Doctrine. Wallace gratified them by becoming even more outspoken and pointed in a speech at the Central Hall, Westminster, on April 11. He attacked U.S. withdrawal of financial support for a UN body (UNRRA) giving relief and aid "efficiently in the Ukraine, White Russia, Poland, Yugoslavia, and Czechoslovakia." He saw the Truman Doctrine as a campaign of attrition against the Soviet Union and a policy of "unconditional aid to anti-Soviet governments."[15]

Again, Stalin's speechwriters could not have done better than these lines. Reaction at home built. Representative John Rankin, chairman of the House Committee on Un-American Activities, urged that the Logan Act of 1799 be invoked to prosecute the former vice-president for "dealing with foreign nations to defeat American measures." Rankin was supported by many congressmen. Representative Herbert A. Meyer of Kansas paraphrased Churchill and called Wallace a "red stooge" and a "type of quisling."[16] Next, the Veterans of Foreign Wars urged that Wallace's passport be revoked. The ADA opposed his views but supported his right to state them.

Wallace, who seemed to lack humor, may not have seen the irony in his expounding the rights of the common man while he stayed in luxury at the Savoy. Meanwhile Straight, also enjoying the top hotel's trappings, was beginning to wonder about the axiom "any publicity is good publicity." His candidate was in the headlines, but would it hinder or help his chances of a Democratic nomination in a little more than a year?

Wallace attracted an assortment of guests, both invited and spontaneous, to the Savoy. Straight acted as his strategist and minder, screening those who wished to see him. One uninvited visitor was a counselor from the Soviet embassy, whom Straight thought was part of a practical joke. Straight hurried him to the elevator before reporters, who were sitting and drinking in their suite, saw him.[17] Straight had no reason to raise the temperature on the "Wallace-as-Soviet-puppet" issue, now simmering on both sides of the Atlantic, by parading a Soviet official before the press with the candidate.

Guy Burgess was another unwelcome guest at the suite. Straight rushed him down to the Savoy bar and bought him a double whisky.[18] Yet there was no need to fear Burgess being spotted by journalists. He would have been known to many of them and was not then unmasked as a KGB agent. In fact he had a respectable cover working for Hector McNeil, Britain's foreign secretary.

Straight told his FBI interrogators that he had "bumped into" Burgess in the Houses of Parliament—a common coincidence in London and Washington according to the FBI files and his memoirs.[19] This led to lunch at the Savoy. They had much to discuss. It had been six years since they had been face to face. Burgess would have been fascinated by Straight's grip on Wallace and his chances of gaining the Democratic Party nomination, and ultimately, the presidency. It would have been pleasing to Burgess to see how Straight had developed as a political force in the United States, given his investment in him and his influence over Straight's return to his home country to work for the cause. Especially satisfying would have been Straight's commitment of considerable resources to Wallace's campaign.

According to his interviews with the FBI, Straight claimed that he informed Burgess of the Truman administration's feeling of "complete frustration with the Soviets," who he believed were inviting a "terrible clash." Burgess asked if he (Burgess) could impart this and other information told him to his "friends." Straight agreed he could. According to Straight, he took this to mean that Burgess would be passing on information from him to his "Soviet principals."[20] At the time, Burgess's control was Ivan Milovzorov, but he was about to be replaced by Yuri Modin as the master spy for the Cambridge ring, which he was being sent to London to reactivate as Cold War tensions mounted.

Straight also claimed he mentioned a meeting he had with Harry Pollitt and that Burgess had warned him that British intelligence would know everything discussed. Pollitt had a mistress whom he told everything. She reported weekly to Scotland Yard.[21]

The validity of Straight's comments is doubtful as he, twenty years after the event, would have been trying to justify his actions to his FBI interrogators. In 1947, he was still acting as a fully fledged KGB man meeting agents such as Burgess, Cot, and Pollitt, who he was fully aware were espionage operatives like him.

———— • ————

After London, Wallace toured major cities in England, drawing crowds and headlines and causing the division which matched Stalin's aims in the United Kingdom. He appeared the moderate voice of reason imploring the British not to be tied to U.S. foreign policy, primarily concerning its hostility to the Soviet Union. "Communism is an idea for ending poverty and exploitation," Wallace told his audiences. "It cannot be destroyed by tanks and guns. It can only be made superfluous by a better idea; it can only be ended when poverty and exploitation are no longer a part of democracy . . . communism can never satisfy all the needs of mankind; democracy can, if we give it our full devotion."[22]

In Manchester, as the British tour neared its end after eight days, Wallace gave a broad hint of his future candidacy when he said: "Twenty-five million former Roosevelt voters still exist, and although many may have fallen away from the Democratic Party, they have not yet joined the Republicans. These people are waiting for leadership today."[23]

The little party flew on to Sweden and Denmark where they were greeted by more communist supporters. With the pressures in the United Kingdom behind him, Straight enjoyed himself and got drunk at a reception. The next stop, on April 21, was Paris, where KGB agent Pierre Cot and two other U.S. Soviet spies, Alfred and Martha Stern (who later fled to Czechoslovakia after being indicted by a grand jury for espionage), had been enlisted to organize the visit.[24] A big crowd of communists turned up at the airport, led by two leaders of the French Communist Party. Straight claimed he looked in vain for a sprinkling of political moderates, but Cot had failed to deliver.

Wallace addressed the Sorbonne, and his speech there was judged by left-wing observers as moderate. The party returned to the United States amid controversy but satisfied that Wallace had stamped his claim to being a world statesman. More important, the tour had lifted Wallace's profile, for better or for worse.

———— • ————

Straight returned to New York in late April 1947, spent two days at Old Westbury with his family, and then joined Wallace and his PCA supporters on a grand tour of the United States. He had misgivings. After more than six months of effort, he had failed to bring in advertisers to *The New Republic*. The losses were big. Straight had bound the magazine to Wallace, and now he was drifting toward the communist-controlled PCA. Straight wondered if the progressives' narrow policies would hem the candidate in and possibly restrict his electability as the Democratic Party's nominee. He could only wait and see. Straight had to stay close to the candidate in order to keep some control and influence.

Wallace's political "bodyguard" of PCA communists included the black singer Paul Robeson, whose appearance with songs such as his political version of "Ol' Man River" lifted audiences and helped raise money. Straight, along with the key progressive leaders, was encouraged as Wallace picked up delegates here and there in his efforts to separate the Democrats from their president. The atmosphere at gatherings was heady, but was it representative of a movement across the country? With each city visited, Straight realized that the PCA was preparing the candidate for the possibility of a third party. He would support it if Wallace had a chance of winning a presidential race from such a base. But there would be hurdles such as the legal difficulties of getting a third-party slate onto the electoral rolls, not to mention the short time left to build the necessary street-level organization. Straight knew that the U.S. communist movement was divided on the concept of a third party, which would be another factor inhibiting a thrust for the presidency. The older officials of the communist party opposed a third party because they feared they could not control it. By contrast the young undercover leaders were confident of their ability to manipulate mass movements—mainly in the key U.S. unions—with an aggressive political strategy.

The most prominent were Lee Pressman, general counsel of the CIO; John Abt, general of the Amalgamated Clothing Workers; and Harry Bridges, of the Longshoremen Union. They were confident that they could get strong support for Wallace among American workers.

Wallace continued to urge economic aid to Europe and to oppose "war preparations." In his own words (or Straight's), the purpose of the U.S. tour was to "liberalize the Democratic Party." Wallace told the press that he did not know whether he would back Truman in 1948, but he often urged Truman to meet Stalin to settle American-Russian differences. The *New York Times* of June 1, 1947, was wise to the PCA plans. It noted that Wallace was "leaving in his wake . . . political rebellion that seeks its ends through the formation of a third party."

At the end of the tour, Straight was more confident still about Wallace being tied to the Democratic Party, rather than outside it, in his presidential bid. He claimed that he discussed with Wallace how the communists had organized his support city by city across the country. Wallace was not concerned, and if Straight was worried, he did not express it to Wallace or in any *New Republic* editorial. His warnings were limited then to keeping "progressives"—the communists and the liberals—united.

Straight wrote with hindsight in his autobiography more than thirty years after the event that he and Wallace were like two ships passing in the night. Wallace, he felt, was heading for the land of illusions, from whence Straight had come. His own experience of communist collaboration, he said, suggested that they would destroy Wallace. But Straight could not share his experiences with him. Wallace looked upon collaboration with communists in and out of Russia as an appealing idea but was naive, Straight thought. Unlike Straight, the candidate knew nothing of the back alleys of the political world.[25]

In June 1947 Straight attended the second annual convention of the American Veterans Committee in Milwaukee, which had been infiltrated by communists in the spring of the previous year. The communists had previously directed their veteran members to infiltrate the more established American Legion group but with limited success. Moscow switched tactics, and the Communist Party directed 5,000 members into the AVC, boosting its membership from 10,000 to 15,000. The communists then attempted to take over the leadership of the new group in its formative stage. Cord Meyer prepared for a new form of battle at the 1946 Des Moines convention.

"In spite of our lack of experience in this type of infighting," he noted in his autobiography, *Facing Reality*, "we [were] determined to meet the threat . . . most of the time was devoted to the political struggle."

The "we" was a solid "caucus" of anticommunists, including Oren Root (who had run Wendell Willkie's campaign for the presidency), G. Mennen Williams (later governor of Michigan), Franklin D. Roosevelt Jr., Robert Taylor, and Gus Tyler (of the International Ladies' Garment Workers Union).[26]

This group had the ruling majority on the AVC National Planning Committee, which meant it controlled the national office and the raising of funds. In the following year, the slippery communist element, which Meyer said was difficult at times to pinpoint, attempted to build a record of militant activity.

"We were prepared for the fight [at Milwaukee in 1947]," he said. But the balance of political power at this convention was complicated by the emergence of a third group. It called itself "Build AVC Caucus," and it was separate from the communist element.[27] The new group was composed of "those who felt it was time to call a truce in the bitter factional fighting" and to concentrate on the AVC's objectives.

"I had some friends in this third caucus," Meyer said, "and tried to convince them that their compromise position could only work to the advantage of the communists by splitting the anticommunist vote."[28]

Later, when Meyer was at the CIA, he learned that "a vocal member of this third force had been a controlled secret agent of the KGB, at that time, and that his strategy of splitting our ranks had been devised in Moscow."[29]

In October 1996, Cord Meyer confirmed his accusation about Straight's links in a Washington interview. Meyer told me: "His aim was to play the neutral objective role [between left and right factions], while all the time attempting to split the anticommunist vote. I dealt with him on enough occasions to understand his actions and motives."[30]

The Wallace campaign lapsed during the summer months but came back to life in September 1947. Straight hired Lew Frank, a left-wing member of the AVC, to be Wallace's minder. But he apparently couldn't stop Wallace from Wallace as he addressed a full house at Madison Square Garden on September 11, a year after the speech that forced his resignation from government. He attacked Truman's bipartisan foreign policy and the "war-with-Russia" hysteria. He appeared to be having a two-way bet by saying he would like to continue to work with liberals within the Democratic Party. But if it became a war party and attacked civil liberties, "then the people must have a new party of liberty and peace."[31]

In October 1947, Straight was reading the signals concerning the formation of this third political party organized by the undercover leaders in the U.S. Communist Party, including Pressman, Abt, and Bridges. In the meantime, the KGB wanted to weaken the United States by attacking the Marshall Plan.

Straight followed—through the press and his contacts—the meeting of the leaders of the Communist International controlled tightly by Stalin's henchmen that was going on in Warsaw. The manifesto issued from this meeting denounced the United States for trying to "subjugate the world." The Soviet spokesman, Andrei Zhdanov, maintained as he released the manifesto that "the greatest danger to the international working class is the underestimation of its own power."

Straight took this to indicate that the Kremlin was directing a third party to fight the 1948 election. Stalin and company judged that the mood was right for a serious political push in the United States. Subsequent meetings with the coterie of advisers closest to Wallace showed that a third party announcement was imminent.[32]

In mid-December 1947, Straight suggested to Wallace that he should write an open letter to Stalin with ideas for terminating the Cold War. With the third party announcement pending, this could only serve to elevate the probable new presidential candidate. It was an effort to show that Wallace was a statesmen who could start peace negotiations, in contrast to the Truman administration. He and Straight drafted six key points, which covered disarmament; prevention of weapons exports;

resumption of unrestricted trade; the free movement of citizens "between and within" the two nations; the resumption of free exchange of scientific information; and establishment of a UN relief agency, such as UNRRA, which previously helped members of the Soviet bloc. Straight thought the letter was worth sending to Stalin immediately. There was always the possibility that he would reply. Wallace dithered and put the idea aside.

Late in December 1947 the PCA created that "new" third party, and Wallace agreed to be its candidate for the presidency. Straight saw this formation as compelling "all the undercover leaders of the Communist Party to emerge into the open, to challenge the leaders of the CIO, other union leaders, the liberals [Mrs. Roosevelt and many others], the Democrats in Congress whose seats were threatened, and the press."

Wallace could not play this new official role and be editor of *The New Republic*. Straight forced him to resign and become a "contributing editor" and then took over as editor himself, appointing long-term staffer Daniel Mebane to the hot seat as publisher.

On January 5, 1948, Straight warned his family of the beginning of the break from Wallace and what it would mean for the struggling *New Republic*. Straight felt that he was damned by the communists if he didn't support Wallace, and damned by the Democratic Party liberals if he did. In the end the downgrade of Wallace was a way of letting readers down gently so that the magazine might not lose them. Straight thought there would be a break between him and Wallace at some point on the issues. The watered-down Marshall Plan for aid to Western Europe, which Wallace opposed, would be one.

Straight later gave up on Wallace, who had surrounded himself with communists. The drifting candidate defended the Soviet Union on all issues, including the communist takeover of Czechoslovakia, and its attack on the Marshall Plan. Instead of a new movement within the conventional Democratic Party system, Wallace was creating a bigger version of the Communist Party.

In the end, Wallace had chosen a path that would not allow him to take power, which was the crucial point. Communism could not take hold through conventional democratic means in the United States, which was not like Italy or France, or even the United Kingdom. The only way of getting someone like Wallace in power was to broaden his appeal. The communists' overt capture of Wallace meant that Straight's dream of being a king-maker behind President Henry A. Wallace was over. And

Stalin's hopes of having someone pliable in the White House, and amenable to the Soviet Union on all issues, were similarly dead. The issue of Wallace joining the third party, Straight believed, also led to the beginning of the end of the Communist Party in the United States.

The ambition of undercover Communist Party leaders such as Pressman and his colleagues to influence the election had drawn communists into the open and exposed them. It weakened their position to a point where they would have insignificant influence. The blunder of forming the third party allowed CIO leaders, with the backing of the Association of Catholic Trade Unionists, to destroy the U.S. Communist Party in its only strong base, the CIO. The party was soon after banned in the United States, thus driving the remnants of the movement underground. The heady reaction that Straight had about communism and workers when he first returned to the United States in 1937 had a decade later come to a sudden end.

14

SIDESHOW SUFFERINGS

Henry Wallace's slow political death as presidential candidate of the doomed Progressive Party through 1948, and the near collapse of *The New Republic*, meant Straight had little time to dwell on his disappointment. While Roosevelt had been in the White House and Wallace had a chance to be there, he had been close to the political action with a heady sense of his own potency and the ambition that some day, somehow he could force his way to the White House too. But now with those two links gone, the dream evaporated. Instead of a sensational ride to taking up a probable appointment in a new administration in November, Straight was left with a squeaky-voiced magazine with sales plummeting to less than 20,000 a week and massive debts that could only be met by milking the family trust. His enterprise had been a failure. The paper's market of disenchanted liberal democrats and fellow thinkers had been too tiny to sustain an expanded business.

Straight had not set out to make *The New Republic*'s success his career aim. It became an expensive platform for his aspirations in politics. Previous experiences would indicate that he would jump ship, but this time he could not. He had to shrink the magazine and see if he could at least keep it alive enough to sell off in the short term. While these significant adjustments were being planned in front of a disgruntled staff, the show had to

200

go on through the year. The readers had to be handled delicately to maintain some credibility and sales.

Straight accordingly wrote a fence-sitting editorial on January 19, 1948, about the third party, which finished with a pessimistic note about its chances of providing a winning contender on November 2.[1] In February, the new Progressive Party headed by Wallace took a severe blow with a coup in Czechoslovakia. Before the upheaval and communist takeover, that country had been held up by U.S. liberals as an example of communist and noncommunist forces working harmoniously. Such peaceful models were now viewed as fanciful. Russia, it seemed, had resumed its prewar long-range plans for world conquest. Wallace responded at a press conference by saying that the communists had acted in "self-defense to prevent a rightist coup."[2] He and his advisers had miscalculated. Not even the leftist, or even more gullible, reporters accepted his explanation. His support base for the presidency dropped from 11 percent in January to 6 percent after his pronouncement. Half of his supporters found him lacking credibility.

In the middle of this disillusioning time for Straight, or perhaps because of it, his private life was unsettled. Bin, pregnant with their third child, contracted tuberculosis and had to leave medical school to recuperate and wait for the birth. Straight seemed to be taking out some of his personal and professional frustrations on the president when on April 5 he wrote an editorial, which started on the magazine's cover. It was headed "TRUMAN SHOULD QUIT."[3] The editorial said that the president had neither the "vision nor the strength that leadership demands." A month later, Wallace decided he needed to take a drastic measure to reconstruct his melting credibility. In a speech to another full house at Madison Square Garden, and now against advice, he delivered, belatedly, that forgotten "open letter" to Stalin. Only *The New York Times* took it seriously. It would have been consigned to the waste-paper basket of gimmicky campaign rhetoric had it not been for the surprise response by Stalin himself. He broadcast his reply, declaring that the letter constituted a "good and fruitful" basis for discussion between the two nations. Wallace was elated; Truman wasn't, so he didn't respond and left criticism to congressional members. Congress again called for Wallace to be charged under the Logan Act for unofficially dealing with a foreign power.

The president didn't trust the two new pen-pals in about equal measure. Stalin was stalling for time as his scientists worked untold hours constructing a bomb they could detonate and while his spies stole another mountain of data about the development of the next generation of nuclear weapons. His timing, however, was odd. Had Stalin received the letter when Wallace was editor at *The New Republic* and Straight was still his key strategist, it would have made some sense. But to reply to Wallace when he had cut himself adrift from a meaningful power base in the election perhaps indicated that the Soviet leader was simply attempting to stir the political pot in the United States. There was always the off chance that U.S. Communist Party leaders had convinced their bosses in the Kremlin that Wallace actually had some chance of victory. Whatever the reason, the correspondence had little or no impact as the nation began to focus midyear on the main parties' candidates.

The election year heightened key issues in the nation, and congressmen with ambitions began to ride some of them hard. The House Un-American Activities Committee (HUAC) increased the pressure in its investigation into espionage, which was always sure to gain headlines as the Cold War set in. Prominent witnesses called were Elizabeth Bentley and Whittaker Chambers, former communists who were now prepared to name names. Bentley had been connected to the Silvermaster ring, and she listed thirty American agents. This led to eleven State Department officials being dismissed or allowed to resign as a result of her revelations. Two well-known New Dealers, Harry Dexter White and Laughlin Currie, were said to have cooperated in her work. The officials had been exposed in secret to a grand jury in New York, but HUAC made Bentley go through the testimony again. The officials she named refused to discuss the allegations in front of HUAC. Then Chambers provided more public exposure when he claimed seventy-five U.S. government officials were agents. He named eight. Alger Hiss was the only one who disputed the claim.

Straight claimed he was baffled by the accusation against Hiss, who appeared so cautious, proper, and self-seeking. Hiss had left the State Department and was then president of the Carnegie Endowment for

International Peace. Straight phoned him on the morning Chambers's allegations were made and asked him what the story was all about.[4]

According to Straight, Hiss claimed to be confused about his being named. Straight claimed that he was "suspicious" about Hiss's being calm and assured, as if he had prepared himself for being unmasked, much the way Straight himself would. Apparently hysteria and nervousness were clues to innocence. But this was humbug on Straight's part. He knew of Hiss's Soviet intelligence links. Straight also alleged he sensed that Chambers was telling the truth.[5] But again, in reality he knew all too well.

His own distress centered on a worry that he would be dragged into the public arena with HUAC. Straight feared his name would appear somewhere—in a committee report or from the mouth of a caught spy in the know about him. From 1948 to 1950 he braced himself for a reporter's call. He claimed to be haunted by a sense of guilt that was exacerbated by photographs of those named as spies in the papers—people with whom he shared some of the agony.[6]

His fears may have been unfounded. He kept himself clear of the major communist rings in Washington and reported directly to Russian controls. Unless one of them was caught and confessed, which was unlikely, he would never be exposed. He had become an expert in tradecraft and had not been spotted by FBI agents meeting any Russians. Straight's ring was based in England, not the United States, and he was a member of the U.K. Communist Party. His card was tucked away in a desk drawer at Dartington Hall. If ever asked if he "was now or ever had been a member of the Communist Party," he could easily say "no" with the U.S. party in mind. As a last resort, he could invoke the Fifth Amendment and refuse to testify, as others had. Straight could protect himself also by buying the best legal defense available.

In addition, his convoluted writing style allowed him to avoid incriminating himself with direct stances on issues. *The New Republic* was read by all the HUAC members looking for clues to communist activity. Straight characterized those members in his autobiography as an unsavory bunch. Martin Dies was given to casual cruelties, John Rankin was a fanatical racist, and J. Parnell Thomas was a small-time crook.[7] Only Richard M. Nixon escaped malevolent description in Straight's memoirs (perhaps because he owed him his employment during the Nixon administration). Straight had unfavorable things to say about Nixon in private and to the family. But for public consumption and with Nixon able to read his words, all Straight would say was that Nixon was just another Republican candidate who clawed his way into congress by accusing his opponents of following the communist party line.

Straight's articles shifted just enough to give him an intellectual alibi should he receive the dreaded call and have to front the committee. His signed editorials still attempted to resonate with the rational sounds of an unbiased liberal, who always managed to support at least part of the communist position. But he now recognized a few facts that in the past would have been ignored. In one article about the 1948 coup in Prague, "There Are Great Fears," Straight wrote that the communist seizure of power "has been followed by the creation of a police state."[8] In another piece, "Trial by Congress," he attacked HUAC for being unconstitutional and for its infringement of civil rights. He defended Laughlin Currie and minimized the evidence against the Silvermaster ring. Showing a wobbly if not staggering logic, he noted: "The Bentley Testimony, if true, indicates that the Russians may have got by espionage what the British and our other allies got by sitting at a table in meetings of the Combined Chiefs of Staff and other inter-allied boards." This may have been a debatable point during the war in 1944 when the Russians were allies. But it was now 1948.

He added: "The testimony of Chambers, if true, demonstrates that certain government officials in the early thirties exercised their constitutional right to be simultaneously members of the government and members of the communist party." Again, this was misleading. Chambers named many agents who were active until exposed in 1948. The dual membership argument was irrelevant. Regardless of their affiliations, no officials had the right to be espionage agents. The article tripped on in this tacit deflection from his own secret past. Then incongruously, Straight did an about-face with a solitary begrudging line: "In general we believe that the outline of Elizabeth Bentley's story is largely accurate. . . ."[9]

These little out clauses would be useful, along with his claim to being a middle-of-the-roader in his work with the AVC, should he appear before a congressional hearing. He could claim too that he had fired Wallace as publisher at *The New Republic* because he had been taken over by communists in his bid for the presidency. Straight had even convinced his parents that he was above entanglement with the extreme left in the Progressive Party campaign. But despite his fears and perpetual "guilt," Straight did not hear from anyone from HUAC, and 1948 rolled on.

Through the year, Straight reduced *The New Republic* to a shell compared with the solid weeks of 1947. He had fired six more of the magazine's staff because of the drop in circulation. The magazine had gone full circle since seven years ago when he and Helen Fuller were the only staff in Washington, D.C.

In October 1948, not too long after giving birth to a daughter, Susan, Bin Straight went on with her psychotherapy studies. Part of her training as a psychotherapist was to undergo analysis herself with Dr. Jennie Welderhall. Everything discussed in such treatment was confidential between doctor and patient, so this allowed Bin to vent her fears and feelings about Straight's relationship with Guy Burgess. It had upset her since first learning about the espionage activity of Burgess and her husband in mid-1940. Despite her demanding that Straight finish his underground activity, he had gone on seeing his control, Michael Green. He had not given up contact with Burgess, Pierre Cot, Harry Pollitt, and many other KGB agents either. Bin told Welderhall that Straight's relationship with Burgess had caused him to live in terror.[10]

Straight later told the FBI that Bin "had furnished the names of Anthony Blunt and Guy Burgess to her analyst . . . as two individuals engaged in underground Communist activity in order that the information could be passed on to Mr. Hall [Welderhall's husband, an Australian at the British Embassy in Washington] and the British Government."[11]

This was not accurate. According to both Welderhall and Bin, only Burgess was mentioned in the therapy sessions. In addition, Welderhall could not later recall Bin giving her permission to share this confidential information with her husband. Even if Bin had asked her to give the story to Hall, Welderhall said she would not have done it. Her professional work, she said, could not be shared with anyone.[12]

The information Bin shared had been passed on in analysis and was therefore privileged. In any case, this would not have been an appropriate way of informing the chief of security or the head of chancellery about Burgess. If it had, no embassy official would act on such secondhand material without thorough interrogation of the primary source. It would have been useless to go via such a circuitous and tenuous route.

The FBI certainly was not convinced by this alleged attempt to inform on fellow spies and "come clean." Fifteen years later when interrogating him, its officers wanted to know why he had not contacted them in 1948.

Straight claimed he thought many times about owning up and betraying his Cambridge companions and others in the United States. The thing that stopped him, he said, was that he feared the publicity and the very public hearings, especially when they would be conducted by his direct ideological opponents. He knew that they would have uncontained delight in exposing him. There was also a thought for his family, and no doubt the ever-present fear that Stalin would take action to silence him if he turned against Stalin's great sources of intelligence. But these claims of attempting to confess were simply not true. They appear hollow compared to his continued actions on behalf of the KGB.

By November 1948 the presidential election polling showed that half the electorate believed the Progressive Party to be communist-dominated, which happened to be correct. Accordingly, in a skeptical, wary, and ideologically unbound United States, Wallace scored a mere 1,157,140 votes or just 2.37 percent of the electorate. The much-maligned Truman, whom Straight told to quit in April and then endorsed as the Democratic candidate in July, surprised everyone and won the election against the more favored Thomas Dewey. Dreamtime was over for Stalin and his advisers. Truman's victory ensured the Kremlin faced a hard-liner for another four years. The Cold War seemed permanent.

Straight flew his own plane, a Navion, to the third AVC convention in Cleveland in late November 1948. Meetings of its national planning committee had been split in the past year by disputes over the Marshall Plan and the Soviet coup in Czechoslovakia.

"With our [right-wing] majority," Cord Meyer noted, "we committed the organization to full support of the Marshall Plan against the last-ditch opposition of the left-wing."[13] Straight and his center ("Build AVC") faction opposed the Truman Doctrine and therefore stood with the left-wing "progressive" faction, but they were defeated.[14]

"When one of the leftist leaders attempted to argue that what had happened in Czechoslovakia was merely a routine change of cabinet," Meyer noted, "he was greeted with derisive laughter."

Cleveland was to be the showdown between the communists and the right-wingers. Meyer and the right-wing group had out-maneuvered the left. Those supporting Soviet positions began to reveal their true identity. The long struggle boiled down to whether a member could sign the AVC pledge to the U.S. Bill of Rights and also be a member of the communist party, which meant putting a signature to another, contradictory pledge. The right's numbers led to an amendment of the AVC's bylaws denying communists membership.[15]

The AVC battle provided Meyer with a firsthand look at the "strength and weaknesses of communist organizational strategy." Even in the microcosm of the AVC he found it "formidable."

"My role in this small skirmish," Meyer concluded, "made me realize how much was at stake on the larger stage. . . ."[16] (A few years later, Meyer joined the CIA. The pinnacle of his career was as station chief of the agency based in London in the early 1970s.) Meyer's larger stage included Western Europe and China.

Late in 1948, the communists in China under Mao looked certain to take power. It caused mixed reaction in Washington. Most key administrators were stunned. Their policy of containment had failed to keep the biggest country in the world outside the Soviet orbit. Some, in the State Department particularly, were pleased and vindicated. They had won, with a lot of help from the liberal media, which castigated Chiang Kai-shek's regime for its "arrogance, incompetence and corruption."[17]

The expected communist takeover would mean a victory for the KGB. It had insinuated agents into key administrative posts for fifteen years in order to sway the propaganda war through bodies, such as the Institute for Pacific Affairs, and to limit U.S. financial support for Chiang and his Nationalists.

There was much recrimination in U.S. government circles. The thinking was very much that China had been lost, as if the West owned it. Now in the minds of Washington's leaders it was controlled by the Soviets.

Attitudes hardened; many felt besieged. Others, like Richard Nixon, saw opportunities. He would "fight" communism to make sure what was happening in China did not happen in the United States. He was the only member of the HUAC to doubt Hiss when he publicly rebutted Chambers's accusations. Nixon's public profile blossomed as he squeezed more out of Chambers about his relationship with Hiss. Chambers came up with sixty-five pages of State Department documents copied by Hiss on a Woodstock typewriter, including four pages in Hiss's handwriting. Then came the photo opportunity of the decade for Nixon. Chambers "found" five rolls of microfilm, some containing confidential government dispatches, in a hollowed-out pumpkin in his Maryland garden. Nixon, with a very concentrated, concerned look, was pictured in U.S. papers and across the world holding a magnifying glass while poring over a strip of microfilm.

Days later, on December 15, 1948, Hiss was indicted for perjury. A few weeks later, worry, bordering on hysteria, increased about the communist menace, real and imagined.

Mao's victory over Chiang Kai-shek's retreating forces was confirmed.

15

BARKOVSKY AND THE BOMB SPIES

Vladimir Barkovsky was easy to pick out in the foyer of the Belgrade Hotel, Moscow. He walked with a forward slope, his hands thrust into the pockets of an off-white, knee-length trench coat to keep the early autumn winds of October at bay. Another telltale sign of the spy's garb was his dark glasses. He seemed a little startled when I greeted him and took him up in an elevator to a room on the eleventh floor where British film director Jack Grossman was waiting to do a video interview. From that moment the 83-year-old, elfin Barkovsky never missed a beat. With a deadpan manner, punctuated by spots of dry humor, he delivered the minimum of information in response to questions. Although practiced at handling Western media, there was none of the easy style and joviality of Yuri Modin, or the machine-gun directness of Oleg Kalugan. Yet Barkovsky's long record was impressive. Like Yuri Modin who followed him, Barkovsky was young when he took over the demanding task of running the leading British spies in England after Stalin's purges had liquidated the older brigade of KGB intelligence officers. Among scores of others, Barkovsky had handled espionage agents Donald Maclean and Klaus Fuchs in England and had "known" Victor Rothschild, who, he said, was always popping into the Soviet embassy during the war. Barkovsky was a mechanical engineer who had to get himself up to speed on all matters nuclear as early as 1941 when he became the KGB's case officer for technical intelligence, a job he held until 1947.

When I asked him about his main role there, he replied with a twinkle in his eye: "I was the resident photographer."[1] This was correct but a great understatement. He remembered microfilming Mark Oliphant's magnetron—the basis of his war-winning radar invention—which Barkovsky had received from Anthony Blunt. Rothschild had "stolen" it from Oliphant's Birmingham laboratory while on a visit in late 1942 as MI5's security inspector and had given it to Blunt. Once Barkovsky had photographed the three-inch-diameter device, it was given back to Rothschild, who returned it to Oliphant with a note that told him to tighten up his security.[2]

Barkovsky was part of the team that collected the Maud report (the initial British report on the feasibility of creating an atomic weapon) in the summer of 1941. His first big role was as Maclean's case officer from 1941 to 1944, under Gorsky, the KGB operations control. In 1941 Maclean gave Barkovsky an analysis showing that the uranium bomb might be constructed within two years by Imperial Chemical Industries with U.K. government support.[3] Early in 1943, Barkovsky also microfilmed information and technical drawings about the plutonium route to the bomb, which had been stolen by Rothschild (and articulated with words and sketches by him and Blunt) from Professor G. P. Thompson's laboratory at London's Imperial College.

Rothschild was close to the agent codenamed ERIC—who was exposed in early 2003 as Sir Eric Rideal, a leading Cambridge chemist and a senior figure in the British team working on the A-bomb Manhattan Project. Barkovsky became his contact in 1942. After that, Rideal supplied 10,000 pages of spy material, much of it from the atomic research facilities in the United Kingdom. So prolific was ERIC that the code name may have referred to Rideal plus several other agents.

Barkovsky would not confirm this agent's identity (because, he said, he was forbidden to do so under Article 19 of the Russian Secret Service Act). Yet he did admit that when he first met ERIC, he was intimidated by his knowledge of all the atomic physics that was needed to keep up with the information. Barkovsky wanted to be replaced with another KGB agent who had a background in physics. But the dictatorial ERIC would have none of it. He had begun with Barkovsky and wanted to stay with him.

"Get a copy of *Applied Nuclear Physics* by Pollard and Davidson and study it," ERIC commanded. Barkovsky obeyed. The textbook was still in his library a half a century later.

Given Rothschild's history of close contact with Russian spies, and his strong link to Rideal as a fellow scientist at Cambridge, it is likely that he fed him with as much as he could for passing on to Barkovsky. Another British scientist operating as a spy for the Russians, Allan Nunn May, made a deathbed confession in January 2003, which exposed Rideal as ERIC.

Barkovsky also came into contact with Melitta Norwood—code named HOLA and TINA. Living at Bexleyheath, London, she worked for the British Non-Ferrous Metals Research. There she had access to vital technical data on atomic weapon construction.

Another coup for Barkovsky in the atomic espionage field was the successful running of Fuchs from 1944 to 1947.[4] By the time Barkovsky had finished with him and returned to Moscow, Fuchs was set up to supply vital information on the so-called superbomb that would supersede the atomic bomb and be a thousand times more powerful. Barkovsky's understudy, KGB agent Aleksandr S. Feklisov, met Fuchs in London on February 28, 1947, and asked him questions.[5] Fuchs told him about the theoretical superbomb studies being directed by Hungarian-born Edward Teller and Enrico Fermi at the University of Chicago. Fuchs described certain structural characteristics of the superbomb and its operating principles and maintained that Fermi and Teller had proved the "workability" of this new nuclear weapon. However, Feklisov was not a physicist or even an engineer like his boss Barkovsky. His report back to Moscow "could only very roughly reproduce" the structural details of the superbomb and its operations.[6] According to German A. Goncharov, a Russian physicist who worked on the eventual Soviet thermonuclear (or superbomb) project, "Fuchs did not know if practical efforts had begun in the US on construction of a superbomb or what their results were."[7]

Consequently, the Soviets redoubled their efforts in the United States in the two-pronged strategy of delaying any future developments in new weaponry while stealing as much as they could and forging ahead with their own new bombs. The Fuchs material was a useful start but not enough. He was helpful in "planting the idea" that Fermi, Leo Szilard, and J. Robert Oppenheimer opposed the development of any hydrogen superbomb. The KGB, led by Department S Director Pavel Sudoplatov, still regarded them as de facto agents and "political advocates of the Soviet Union."[8]

Barkovsky and his fellow KGB scientists in Moscow were contacted by an excited Moscow Center in mid-March 1948 to be told about the results of a recent second meeting between Fuchs and Feklisov in London. Fuchs handed over material he had been sent from the United States. It included pertinent information about the theory of a superbomb that had advanced rapidly. The documents described the operating principle of the "initiator"—the technology to trigger the weapon—and several graphs about its performance. The data substantiated that the superbomb could be made.

A month later, a digestible analysis of the material was sent to Stalin, Vyacheslav Molotov, and Lavrenty Beria, who were still skeptical about the chances of the Soviet Union detonating their first atomic bomb—an event at least a year away. Yet Stalin appreciated this new intelligence was direct evidence that the United States was going ahead with superbomb developments. He demanded drastic measures to speed through feasibility studies and imparted official status to the Soviet's own attempts to make a new, much more powerful nuclear weapon.

It was the beginning of the race for the superbomb. The Russians were confident they had the scientists to develop their own this time rather than make a carbon copy of a U.S. design, which they had done with the atomic bomb dropped on Nagasaki—Fat Man. But they still needed to keep abreast of U.S. developments to give themselves the option of copying or incorporating any requirement. This meant a full-scale spying operation to keep the data flowing back to the Soviet version of Los Alamos at Dubna near Moscow.

Barkovsky became KGB station chief in New York early in 1949 in order to coordinate the flow of information. The FBI was intensifying its efforts to find communist agents inside and outside the administration, making it the toughest period ever for espionage. He had to reactivate some agents, give new directives to others, and always encourage division within the U.S. scientific ranks in efforts to stall progress. Officially the United States had not yet decided to produce a superbomb, although its theoretical physicists had already produced several alternative routes to this most terrible weapon. Teller remained the most enthusiastic; whereas Fermi, Szilard, and Oppenheimer were against further developments, he was obsessed with producing a thermonuclear explosive based on hydrogen fusion.

———— • ————

Barkovsky remarked in our interview that he was an avid reader of *The New Republic*. He said he knew Straight and that he believed he "met him at some embassy functions."[9]

Barkovsky's subscription to *The New Republic* was understandable. Straight had focused the magazine in the late 1940s on everything to do with nuclear weapons and atomic energy, the key issue of the day. Straight hired specialist writers and ex-scientists. He tackled editorials on everything from disarmament to the Atomic Energy Commission (AEC), the civilian body that had taken over and resuscitated the remnants of the Manhattan Project after the war. Straight used his great skill at making and charming contacts to glean everything he could. The magazine, despite being a pale imitation of former years, was still a useful vehicle for meeting everyone from David Lillienthal and other AEC directors to the best-placed scientists at key research centers. Straight maintained his links to the key players such as Szilard and Oppenheimer, offering them adequate space in *The New Republic* to air their views, which they took up. Szilard submitted his pacifist, disarmament views, while Oppenheimer used the magazine as a forum for arguing against the FBI screening of AEC employees to weed out communists.[10]

———— • ————

The early months of 1949 saw Straight helping his sister Beatrice extricate herself from a failed marriage to KGB agent Louis Dolivet, alias Ludovic Brecher. He had moved to a hotel in New York. Straight, with his attorney Milton Rose doing most of the negotiating, made him a divorce offer based on a separation agreement that he found impossible to refuse. He and Beatrice would share custody of their young son, Willard. The divorce was granted in May, about the time his paper, *United Nations World*, went bankrupt. It lost the family interests at least $250,000, which was the amount Dorothy agreed to put into it. Dolivet failed to obtain $1 million from a new backer, Richard Mellon, then he left for

France. (Three years later, young Willard drowned in a boating accident. Dolivet had been exposed as a KGB agent and had difficulty securing a short-term visa to return to the United States for his son's funeral. He went back to France and became a successful film producer.)

———— • ————

In June 1949 Straight and Bin flew to the United Kingdom for a visit to Dartington Hall and a reunion with the family and such friends as Michael Young, a frequent visitor to his old alma mater.[11] Young had re-nounced his links to the communists but still held radical views, which he inculcated into his work in the Labour Party's research department and in the occasional article in left-wing magazines, such as *The New Re-public*. Straight managed to slip away to London on his own for a few days where he again met Burgess and Blunt without Bin's knowledge.[12] They and other Apostles, including Rothschild, gathered at an annual re-union dinner. It was arranged by Burgess, who chaired the event in pri-vate rooms at his RAC Club in Pall Mall close to Carlton Gardens.

Thirty Apostles sat down to dine at two tables. Burgess was next to the speaker, drama critic Desmond MacCarthy, at the head table. Straight said he became embroiled in an argument over "Soviet occupation of Czechoslovakia" with a young Marxist historian, Eric Hobsbawn—a most unlikely claim, which was a further attempt to portray himself as at odds with his fellow Apostles.

The trio of Burgess, Blunt, and Straight decided to meet again the next morning at the RAC Club to talk about what each had been doing. Straight claimed in his autobiography that Burgess had arranged the meeting to determine if he had double-crossed him and turned him in to the authorities.

Straight admitted that the discussions reflected his continuing inability to break completely with his past. The old Apostles were hanging on. Yet he was not unfriendly to his old comrades and Marxist mentors, which was the reassurance Burgess (according to Straight) needed. He would not be double-crossing them; his apostolic oath not to betray his com-rades would see him remain silent about their continuing espionage work for the KGB.

Straight alleged that Burgess asked him if he still had allegiance to the Cambridge ring. Straight further claimed that he asked him in return if he (Straight) would be here if he did not have that allegiance. This was meant to give the impression to his FBI interrogators that he was prevaricating and not strong enough to inform on Burgess.

This spin on events was to appease the FBI twenty years later. In reality, Straight was still a fully fledged agent. He had turned up at the Apostles meeting to be with his fellow spies in an environment he would have considered a perfect cover—a reunion with his old university friends. His feeble explanation under the circumstances was not credible. Had he been trying to avoid KGB agents, he would have stayed well clear of such a meeting.

Back at Dartington, the family was preoccupied with Beatrice's problems, and Straight was under no pressure to explain the situation at *The New Republic* to Dorothy. He was the family favorite, worshipped for his gallant fight for liberal positions in the United States, which she feared was turning hard right. Whitney, based in the United Kingdom and moving into business with the skill and dynamism he showed as an air ace, had ignored developments in the family Trust set-up and the Whitney Foundation in the United States.

Whitney visited Straight at Weynoke in 1948 and saw him again at Whitney's club on this trip in London. They had grown a long way from each other and had little in common except for flying and photography. Whitney was a confirmed conservative, bent on making his way in the business world. His natural attraction was to planes. After the war, he had joined the board of British European Airways. Then he formed Alitalia. Whitney was married but kept a rich playboy image with a mistress and his interests in sports. If he wasn't on the ski slopes of Switzerland, he was scuba diving in the Caribbean or indulging his love for photography, good food, and wine. His adventurous lifestyle and endeavors were not appreciated by Dorothy as much as those of Michael, who appeared to have sacrificed much for liberal causes she held dear. Straight could talk her language. She read *The New Republic* editorials and features and loved discussing them with him. Whitney was disdainful of the magazine. He was not ashamed of his privileged life or guilty about being rich; he enjoyed the trappings of wealth but was not idle or a dilettante. Whitney was able to apply himself to a business he knew and be comfortable with it. By contrast, Straight had lived a double life and had not been capable so far of sustaining a lasting interest in a profession or job.

Whitney's easy nature, pragmatic intellect, and good humor had endeared him to the English elite in which he circulated—so much so that he too had a secret. Whitney had been approached by MI6 to "make observations of interest whenever he traveled abroad on business," a not uncommon practice by British executives.[13]

In effect, he too had become a spy.

———— ◆ ————

Straight stayed in the United Kingdom until August 1949, then spent a short time in Rome from where he filed a report to *The New Republic* that appeared on August 22. It was here that the FBI pressured the magazine's Rome correspondent to spy on him. Yet he expected the bureau to use some of his staff in this way. The magazine had been critical of the United States' ECA program in Italy to aid postwar reconstruction.

Straight spent the next ten weeks back in the United States before returning to Dartington Hall with Rose on November 8. Dorothy was considering the reorganization of the family trust setup. That would see her "trustee," the Royal Trust Company of Canada (managed by Rose), succeeded by Trust 11, with Rose and a family member, either Whitney or Straight, as "successor" trustees. This arrangement would give the selected family member control over the considerable funds and a big say in how they were used. Rose was urging Dorothy to select Straight. The suggestion may well have been planted in her mind at this moment, for she would have been more influenced by Rose than any other trustee. He had worked on the creation of the split-up of the estate into the several trusts in 1936. The details had taken him a year, and in that time he and his wife Emily had become "very close friends" with Dorothy. He was the one most responsible for investment of the working capital and its dividends for each of the five children.

However, Rose's recommendation of her son as a fellow successor trustee presented her with a problem. There was something to be said for the trust being run by two friends who had now had a close working relationship over a decade. And Dorothy would have been pleased to know that Rose, then a decade older than Straight, had such confidence in him. Yet Whitney was the elder brother, and he had proven himself a more natural businessman than Michael. He was also a better decision-maker through wider experience.

Once again the words—relayed to her via a medium—from her first husband would have been prominent in her thoughts: "Whitney . . . will mix in the world—stand out but more as a good businessman and good fellow . . . "

The decision gave Dorothy much to ponder over the next year. In Straight's favor was his seeming effort to make *The New Republic* a liberal standard bearer once more. He was clearly far more interested than his brother in the trust's main activities.

Dorothy had started the "old role" of the magazine, with its liberal, intellectual approach. Straight had turned it into a radical political pamphlet and had brought it close to ruin. By returning *The New Republic* back to what it once was, Straight was trying to show his mother that he had matured.

But had these pushes and pulls within him been resolved? They had originally been caused by his hidden espionage work clashing with his desire to be a public figure. Now his public role would be limited to *The New Republic*. At 34 years of age, had he—as he maintained—changed enough to be content with such a minor voice?

———— • ◄ ————

President Truman announced on September 23, 1949, the explosion of Joe 1, the first Soviet atomic bomb. An excited Teller, who was working at Los Alamos, phoned Oppenheimer to tell him.[14] In October he told fellow scientists that the United States should go ahead with a superbomb. Teller was certain that the Russians would decide to create their version. Better, he thought, to make the weapon first in the United States as an insurance policy. Yet with key scientists such as Oppenheimer, Szilard and Fermi cautioning against this huge escalation of the arms race, Teller would have to lobby hard to achieve his wish. Communism had made him, like Nixon, a man on a mission determined to make his name in history. A secret debate began in Washington with less than a hundred people over whether the United States should build the superbomb. There were advocates for and against the concept at the AEC and in the congressional committee on atomic energy. Some at the Defense Department joined in, as did a handful of the most accomplished scientists.

Truman was lobbied from different directions. He was more inclined to take advice from Dean Acheson, his secretary of state; Louis Johnson, his secretary of defense; and the Joint Chiefs of Staff than he was the scientists. The military were adamant that they could not let the Soviets push ahead. Acheson was more troubled but thought it would be intolerable for the United States to fall behind. The scientists, led by Oppenheimer and Fermi, recommended a program to expand the production of uranium and plutonium. They were categorical in not wanting to make the superbomb a priority, although it was to be considered. It was not enough for Teller, who by-passed committees. His argument was compelling. How could the United States afford to let the Soviet Union develop such a weapon that would give it world military superiority? The fear factor was at its feverish best as the military fought for increased funding.

That fear influenced the president. On January 31, 1950, he directed the United States to develop the superbomb. Teller had won his long-held dream. The KGB would now once more have to step up its vigilance and espionage with U.S. scientists involved in this new, more vital program.

Alger Hiss, the erudite diplomat and Harvard-trained government lawyer, was convicted of perjury in January 1950 and sentenced to five years in prison. The courts had not found him guilty of espionage, but as the perjury conviction was involved in the claim and counterclaim of Hiss and Chambers, Hiss was perceived by the majority of the media and the public as a Soviet agent. It heightened the concern over communism and laid the groundwork for Senator Joseph McCarthy to use the issue in his drive for national political recognition.

On February 9, McCarthy began the biggest witch-hunt in U.S. history, which was counterproductive to combating real subversives. In addressing the Republican Women's Club at the McClure Hotel in Wheeling, West Virginia, he claimed he had the names of 205 communists in the State Department. There were no penetrating questions from the women, only collective breath-sucking. The next day he made a speech in Salt Lake City, Utah, where the number dropped to fifty-seven "card-holding" communists at State. Again, the audience in the conservative Mormon city only shook their heads in dismay or nodded approvingly. Ten days later McCarthy made a wild six-hour speech on the floor of the U.S. Senate, saying he now had the names of eighty-one communists, including "one of our foreign ministers." For those who stayed awake through the throaty monologue, there was intermittent uproar but little protest.

In two weeks he had accentuated the Great Fear throughout the nation. A chain reaction of events followed that turned a frightened mood to an atmosphere of hysteria. The Tydings Committee was formed in the Senate on February 23 to investigate McCarthy's accusations. Then on March 1, Klaus Fuchs and Allan Nunn May were arrested in the United Kingdom. March 7 marked the beginning of the second trial of Judith Coplon, a Justice Department employee who became the first U.S. citizen convicted of being a spy. (The conviction was later reversed because the FBI had gained evidence by illegal wiretaps.)

Straight became enmeshed in the furious claim and counterclaim. He wrote in his autobiography that his secret espionage work caused him to have a continuing fear and sense of guilt. Yet as a journalist he still had to cover the week to week allegations about espionage.

Because no one in the United States, except for his wife, knew of his Soviet connection, he could maneuver himself into any position he wished without worrying that anyone such as Eliot Janeway could stand up and accuse him of being a communist in the United States, let alone a spy. Janeway knew he had been a card-carrying member of the U.K. Party, not of the U.S. one. And even if an accuser spoke, Straight could brush aside that period as an adolescent aberration, which he often did. This allowed him to put on his true liberal façade to attack McCarthy editorially on both the substance of his allegations and their effect on civil liberties; this way, he was not seen to be defending communism. But in order to keep inquisitors at bay, he had to create a new image—that of the subtle anticommunist.

16

THE ANTI-COMMUNIST

Straight's fabricated new image as an anticommunist had already been presaged in his formation of the "neutral" faction of the AVC. It received a chance for a more definitive airing when he received a call early in 1950 from a HUAC committee member accepting his offer to appear before a hearing on legislation to outlaw certain un-American and subversive activities.

It centered around debate over the Mundt-Nixon Bill (proposed by HUAC members Karl Mundt and Richard Nixon), which directed that the government act against "communist political organizations by, among other things, forcing them to register with the government." It was viewed by liberals, communists, and conservatives alike as a prelude to a complete banning of Communist Party membership in the United States.

Confident in the knowledge that no one knew his deep secret, and secure because of the legal protection he could afford, Straight seemed to relish the opportunity to appear in front of the HUAC, which he had requested on behalf of the AVC, an organization known to have problems with communists. Straight was by then its chairman.

Straight entered the hearing on March 22, 1950, well armed and prepared with left-wing lawyer Leonard A. Nikoloric, whom he had hired to "advise" the AVC on the Mundt-Nixon Bill. Nikoloric was with one of

Washington's most powerful law firms, Arnold, Fortas & Porter. He was also an AVC member.

Straight looked serious as he sat in front of the eleven HUAC committeemen, lawyers, and investigators. A clerk tapped away as HUAC counsel Frank S. Tavenner asked Straight the infamous query that became synonymous with the feverish hunt for communists that would become known as McCarthyism: "Are you now or have you ever been a member of the Communist Party?"

Straight must have blanked from his mind his membership in the Communist Party of Great Britain. He replied that he wasn't, and never had been, a member of the (U.S.) Communist Party. He may have justified in his own mind that he had not lied, for he had belonged to a foreign party. If Straight were nervous, it did not at first show as he launched into a diversionary attack on the Mundt-Nixon Bill. He and Nikoloric had prepared a legal brief, which explained that the bill was unconstitutional. It attempted to legislate by fiat and punish people "for association and opinion without the safeguard of common law." This would "open up not only the Communist Party but other organizations . . . to a threat of prosecution for holding adverse opinions to the normal trend of the time."[1] This view was held by many fair-minded, noncommunist intellectuals, and Straight felt confident he would be supported in this approach that diverted from the main thrust of the bill.

He gave an example: "The Veterans of Foreign Wars, as a principal opponent of this Bill, had declared, as had the Marine Corps League, that the 'world-government movement' is treasonable . . . " HUAC member Bernard Kearney interrupted and challenged him on the claim. Straight seemed caught, but he skipped away from the congressman by stating: "Advocates of world government are placed in jeopardy if this bill were considered constitutional."

He then launched into his new position as an anticommunist:

We share much of the opinion of many witnesses who have appeared before this committee that the Communist Party is partly directed from abroad by a foreign power. We believe it does advocate the overthrow of the Government by force and violence. We believe . . . the Communist Party is used as a reception center and training ground for espionage agents on behalf of a foreign power.

Straight added: "However, we do not believe that the Communist Party is a clear and present danger."

This seemed to be a contradiction; the Communist Party was wanting to overthrow the government by force, and it was secretly bringing in many espionage agents. But Straight was also saying it was not a danger to the government. Perhaps he was saying that the party's advocacy of violent revolution was waffle, just words, a bluff from a paper tiger too insignificant to cause any serious problem. This debate would be picked up by the committee later in the hearing. For now, he forged on:

> We do not believe it can be isolated, and that it can be found to be concentrated in a very few front organizations such as this bill supposes. On the contrary, we believe the Communist Party can be found to be working in a very broad field of political organizations, perhaps in some organizations that have testified against this bill.

He was going too fast for the committee. Some winced, others scribbled, and most stared. Bubbling down in the deep crevasses of some of their minds was the question of how this articulate, ivy-league-type witness with the rounded vowels and intense, patrician demeanor knew so much about this outpost of the Evil Empire. But the question never quite surfaced. Straight kept his response, now a lecture, coming in a torrent:

> We recognize the Communist Party will be affected by legislation passed by the Congress, but we think nonetheless the advances and retreats made by the Communist Party in American life are made at the fighting fronts of organizations in which the Communist Party is attempting to carry its policy.

His argument was convoluted as he attempted to bamboozle the HUAC members with a lather of words. He seemed to suggest that it was better to take the communists on in battles in organizations they had infiltrated rather than to take action against the party. In the one breath, he was telling them that there was a problem, bigger and more furtive and insidious than they had imagined. And yet it was better to play by the Marquis of Queensberry rules and fight the good fight. It was almost as if he were saying that it was more sporting this way and good for the democratic system to have angst, disagreement, and subversion in every kind of organization.

His thoughts were tumbling too quickly for the committee's consumption. A problem was that the smart communists, Straight informed them further, were brilliant at fudging who was a red and who was not. He hardly drew breath as the HUAC members sat listening to their bemusing expert in communist subversion. Kearney's forehead creased most. He wanted to challenge him again, but Straight was too quick and clever. He brought the hearing back to Kearney himself:

> Mr. Kearney, you know that in your home town of Schenectady a fight has been waging for a long time between communist leaders and the electrical workers. From a superficial knowledge of that fight, I can't believe it will be resolved by what is done in Washington. I think it will be resolved by what is done is Schenectady.

It was almost an argument for getting rid of the legislature and returning to a political wild west. But he had sidetracked Kearney, who could only comment: "[It will be resolved] by the union."[2]

"That is right," Straight said, figuratively patting his questioner on the head. Mouths opened to speak, but the verbal hare was away again, this time telling the attentive audience how the AVC had been "infiltrated."

"As far as we know they [the communists] assigned some of their top veteran leaders to capture our organization," Straight said. "That fight went on for four years. The noncommunists, such as Mr. Nikoloric and myself, counterorganized. We had for a time two caucuses working with considerable secrecy."[3] (This remark was in direct contradiction to Cord Meyer's assessment. Straight never worked against communists. All the evidence and Meyer's testimony point to him being the key organizer for the communists.)

Just to befuddle the listeners even more, he added: "We had to adopt some of the communist tactics to combat them." Straight then made a comment with which Cord Meyer would have agreed: "In the course of that fight the noncommunists demonstrated their ability to out-think and out-work the communist minority."

The committee's chairman, Francis E. Walter, butted in: "Wasn't that due entirely to the fact you were able to spot the communists?"

"No," Straight corrected him like a college professor. "That is a very important point. We could not today name a single communist in our organization who was active." He couldn't even name a single communist sympathizer, he told them, "which is precisely why we have come here today to explain our views."[4]

There were many tough reds under the bed (5,000 at least at one time inside the AVC), Straight was warning, but they were invisible. Yet the noncommunists could still beat them almost every time. He went on to explain that "they" had driven all the communists out of the AVC. Then to complete the scenario, he concluded: "We set a pattern for all responsible organizations to follow."

Committeeman Harold H. Velde got in a question about labor union membership, but Straight had virtually taken over the chair. He started answering his own queries: "I would like to raise this question: would it help in this kind of struggle we have been through to have the kind of legislation [the Mundt-Nixon Bill] now before you? I would think it would not."

He then explained that it would drive the Communist Party underground. That would mean no *Daily Worker*, where the invisible communists put out the "signals" for their next move. Therefore an observer wouldn't know what insidious members were doing.

Straight pointed out that the noncommunists drove a wedge between them and the communists by fighting them on certain issues such as the Marshall Plan, which "appealed to a great majority of noncommunists. We made the fight on the Atlantic pact and military assistance."[5]

This again was untrue. Straight's "third way" inside the AVC was meant to split the noncommunist vote and so defeat it. Straight now conveyed an image of the anticommunist who was nevertheless concerned with the attack on civil liberties if people were prevented from joining the party.[6]

Kearney asked if the AVC had suffered from introducing an anticommunist resolution. Straight was adamant that it had, which was not the experience of Meyer, his anticommunist faction, and Kearney himself. He asked why was it that other veteran organizations "who always introduce such a resolution annually have not suffered?"

A small chink in Straight's verbal armor appeared as he replied, unconvincingly, that it was because "we are smaller," meaning it had been reduced in size. Velde wanted to know how small.

"Approximately 8,000."

"What was your top membership?" Kearney asked.

"20,000."

Straight failed to inform the committee of the organized history of the communist infiltration, which he knew well. There was no mention of the 5,000 directed in 1946, and others afterward, into the AVC. He described the influx of communists in *After Long Silence*—three decades after the event—in a way that would have excited the HUAC and made headlines at the time. Communist applications from all over the country filled up sacks of mail early in the year. Straight said the committee approved them without thinking why there had been such a sudden burst of people wanting to join the smallish veterans group or where they might be coming from. The revelation of what might be afoot, Straight claimed, came two months before the AVC's first convention when its two largest area councils in Los Angeles and New York were "suddenly" controlled by communists.[7]

Straight, of course, knew all along what was happening. He was the mastermind behind the influx of communists.

The information about the 5,000 and other information would have given the HUAC a broader perspective. But Straight wasn't about to give them further data to make their own case and expose him as a KGB agent. Under the guise of the helpful volunteer informant, he was confusing the issue, which was becoming his specialty.

Kearney wanted to know if the recent drop off in numbers was due to the Merchant Marines leaving. They contained the communist element.

"We lost very few of them," Straight said. He evaded that line of probing by adding, "The fact that we had to make this fight cut down our membership." Then he slid into another extraordinary (and revealing) monologue:

We think the Communist Party might be a threat in the event of a depression, as it was in the last depression, and we don't want to see another depression. We think the Communist Party might be a threat in the event of another war, and we don't want to see another war. We think the Communist Party is on the run, and we think it can be kept on the run by continuing prosperity.[8]

Straight would attempt to articulate this "avoid-war-and-keep-prosperous" argument better in *The New Republic*. His next claim was more startling: "We believe if it becomes a clear and present danger, then by that time communism will have triumphed in the rest of the world before it becomes a threat in this country. We think the critical front is in Berlin, Southeast Asia, India, and Rome."9 Straight had named some of the battlegrounds, both political and military, on which Stalinists would fight before tackling the United States.

"We think," he said, sloughing on as if at a lectern, "it is an illusion to believe Americans can gain security by attempting to drive underground or destroy a little band of shabby men on Fourteenth Street, whom we think we can lick by normal constitutional measures within existing laws. We think to that extent we create that illusion, that illusion is a point in favor of Joseph Stalin."

Tavenner chipped in and asked Straight to submit his written legal brief, which he did. Then a discussion centered on the finding of the great liberal, Justice Oliver Wendell Holmes, regarding the First Amendment, which protected beliefs, speech, assembly, and advocacy. Holmes argued (in *Schenk v United States*, 1919) that words spoken or written had to be assessed in the context of whether there existed a "clear and present danger" that they would bring about evils which the congress wished to prevent (such as overthrowing the government).

Morgan M. Moulder noticed Straight had said communism "did not constitute a menace or danger in this country." He wanted to know if Straight confined that to the Communist Party in the United States, or was he referring to "communism being a danger in the worldwide movement?"

Straight replied that he thought communism was "a very grave danger on a worldwide front." This international communism was also "a danger" to the United States. But he added he did not consider the Communist Party in the United States "at the present time" was "a clear and present danger as defined by Justice Holmes."10

This statement again implied that the local party was too small to worry about, yet. Better to fight it everywhere and monitor its growth and activity rather than crush its free speech and opinions.

Velde wanted to know how many of the AVC opposed the Mundt-Nixon Bill. Straight claimed members were unanimously against it. The New England chapters of the AVC, he said, wanted him to testify to this unanimity in front of the HUAC.

Velde wasn't too happy about this response. "I suppose you would say no legislation of any kind is necessary?" he asked pointedly.

"Mr. Nikoloric feels the legislation presently on the statute books is sufficient," Straight responded. "We don't see how it is possible to legislate . . . on matters of opinion."

Velde wouldn't let it go. "I think you realize that the Communist Party of the United States took the lead during the last war in attempting to obtain our military secrets," he said with some indignation. "Do you think we have been successful in convicting members of that espionage ring?"

"No, sir," Straight replied with true authority, "but I think the remedy is to tighten the espionage laws. I think the Communist Party is used as a recruiting ground for espionage agents."[11]

It was safe territory known to anyone who had read the papers over the past half decade, but it was close to a delicate area for him. He neglected to inform the committee that he was aware of even more fertile recruiting arenas outside the party.

Velde, the tortoise, seemed to be catching the hare. He wanted to know how Straight would go about tightening espionage laws. "I understood you to say a while ago the present laws were sufficient . . . "

Straight deferred to Nikoloric, who said he hadn't studied the Espionage Act "with any thoroughness." But he did count twenty-seven laws "specifically designed to take care of the communist problem." Then he said what no government committee ever wanted to hear: "There isn't anything that you are accomplishing here that is not adequately taken care of in those acts [to deal with espionage]."

Hearing members shifted in their seats. Several wanted to press the witnesses. Velde, now more terrier than tortoise, was in first: "Do you agree with Mr. Straight that the laws are not sufficient to handle the espionage problems?"

Nikoloric replied: "I haven't read any hearings [transcripts] on whether you believed the espionage agents were getting by [not caught] under the present laws. . . . You should be able to take care of that under the Espionage Act rather than legislating on opinion."

Chairman Walter was agitated: "This bill does not do legislating as to opinion, and you have addressed all your remarks to that issue."

"That is right," Straight said.

Nikoloric took over the response by giving an example of a "Father Parker" who testified to the hearing the day before: "I don't agree with him, but I respect his constitutional right to do whatever he chooses as long as he doesn't commit any dangerous acts. He is entitled to his beliefs, whether you agree with him or not."

Kearney then had Nikoloric agreeing that the Communist Party leaders in the United States had a "policy" and an "intent" to overthrow the government. Straight interrupted and pushed the hearing back on the track he wanted: "Up to this time there has been no legislation on opinion. You have no precedent for punishing people by reason of association."

Walter tried another tack by asking if Straight had any objection to that portion of the bill that would require "communist political organizations to publish their financial statements"?

Nikoloric stepped in again and said the discrimination against communist "political and front organizations was unconstitutional."

Walter disagreed, saying, "Those statutes have been tested [in the courts] and held to be constitutional." The two of them debated sections of the bill. Kearney asked, "If the committee saw fit to revise the bill to meet your objection, would you then be in favor of the legislation?"

Nikoloric said he would still be against it and once more maintained that the present laws were adequate. He didn't think the government was "riddled with spies." He cited just one example of a spy—Judith Coplon—being caught, pointing out that even that case was questionable.

Velde piped in, asking if Nikoloric thought there had been an espionage ring in the United States during the war. The advocate replied that he would be "very disappointed in Joseph Stalin's ability if there weren't Russian agents here during the war."

It was almost as if Nikoloric knew the situation about the man beside him. Velde didn't like the apparent flippancy in the reply. He pushed his point for the record, saying that the new bill was a means of assisting the government in "combating this espionage ring. If we had this bill, which would require the registration . . . "12

Nikoloric interrupted him. Both he and Straight were scornful of the government's power to force anyone, from spies to most communists, to register. Nikoloric said espionage agents would avoid registering and "just go underground." Velde disagreed, and the argument ran in circles. Walter called a halt by asking if there were any further questions. There was a stalemate. No one had any more to ask. The hearing was over.

Soon afterward, the Mundt-Nixon Bill passed the House, supported by many liberals and Democrats. The measure became law and was widely supported. (In 1954, Hubert Humphrey, the leader of the Senate liberals in the Democratic Party, introduced a bill in the Senate that made it a crime to belong to the Communist Party. It passed with one dissenting voice.)

Hardly anyone in or out of politics—apart from Communists—agreed with Straight's argument that it was better to keep the party alive and defeat them with endless political in-fighting across the United States. He was in a minority in not seeing them as a clear and present danger, despite agreeing with the concept of communists outside the United States being a threat to the nation and its interests.

———

The New Republic was a useful platform for Straight to consolidate his image as a liberal anticommunist. There were constant reminders in the magazine's advertising in 1950, which told its readers that "Michael Straight is not a Starry-eyed Liberal," and such slogans as "Recognize the one in the middle?" that referred to the "independent (of the left and right) reporting you need to maintain your liberal point of view."

Opposed to this, there was an unprecedented advertisement for a new magazine, the *New Leader*, which asked if *New Republic* readers were "one of the snowballing number of American liberals who is done with the self-deception about the communists—whether in Russia or here?" And "are you . . . tired of the way most of America's so-called 'liberal' magazines still pussyfoot about communism?"

Running this would have hurt Straight, especially as the ad listed an impressive group of "recent contributors," some of whom were known to him, including Stewart Alsop, Roger Baldwin, John Dos Passos, David Dubinsky, Hubert Humphrey, Arthur Koestler and Bertrand Russell. But he needed all the revenue he could get. Besides, *The New Republic* was for free speech, even if it didn't agree with the speaker or the sentiment.

Straight was doing his best to put aside any "pussyfooting" image as he tried to lengthen the distance between the liberalism he wanted to be seen

espousing and communism. Articles he wrote seemed to advocate bury-
ing the subject, not praising it. Yet he appeared to be achieving neither.

In the May 1, 1950, edition, in a disjointed article entitled "The Right
Way to Beat Communism," Straight began by stating that "Soviet Communism is today the greatest organized evil in the world." It seemed for a
moment that he may have been Ronald Reagan's original scriptwriter, but
soon he was attacking conservatives who viewed Russia as a police state,
which was backed by its agents and armies. A few lines later, he softened
the message further by quoting his undergraduate hero, John Maynard
Keynes, on the subject: "Communism . . . represents a gigantic enterprise. Its men have resolutely embraced a purpose of reform and live
tensely under the discipline that faith instills in them. . . ."13

Then there was a reminder of the jargon of his undergraduate days:
"The communist appeal was maintained in the thirties by the contrasts of
capitalist depression and the need for a common front against fascist ag-
gression . . ." Near the end Straight added a dash more Keynes, who
noted that the "appeal of communism was not primarily economic and
could not be counted by economic action alone; it consisted not of the
substance but of the fervor of communist faith."

This "faith," readers were informed, could not be suppressed or defeated militarily. In fact, in the end he had made a case for nothing except
communism's invincibility, with some meaningless asides such as advocating "a shift in concentration from the Cold War to the strengthening
of the non-communist world."

Straight, it appeared, was fighting to suppress the clichés of his intellectual development in the 1930s, which had shaped his mind. The remnants of the once inspirational phraseology were not always easy to
suppress. This piece, which Straight held up as meaningful in his autobiography, exemplified similar articles through the year. He presented them
as proof of his anti-communism.

——— ———

The New Republic was noticeably thin in 1950, but the editor did not
hesitate to run up further debts by organizing a team of researchers and
writers to compile four substantial "editorials" in the early months of the
year on atomic energy. They drew on a wide range of source documents
on such topics as politics, supply, use of raw material, and bomb produc-

tion in the most comprehensive press publication on the issue to that point.[14]

It was a return to the frenetic days of 1937–1942, when Straight compiled impressive papers on major military and defense topics, some of which were passed to his Russian control. But this time he didn't need to pass anything on. All the KGB had to do was to keep up its subscription to the magazine to glean useful information—all accessible in free, democratic America—about the state of the nation's atomic energy programs. The four-part study needed interviews with experts, who assisted the journalists in finding useful material. This was a difficult assignment without the vehicle of public interest, which the press provided.[15]

In England, the Elmhirst family prepared for Straight's annual return to Dartington. Only Whitney did not look on it as a joyous occasion. He had recently been informed, by connections at his part-time work for MI6, about his brother's other life.

Diana Barnato-Walker, Whitney's mistress of thirty-five years and mother of his only son, recalled his coming to her home and slumping in a chair. "I knew something was troubling him that evening [in early 1950]," she said, "when he asked me for a second Scotch."

Diana asked him what was on his mind. He took a deep breath and told her that "Michael is a Russian spy." It was a distressing time for Whitney, for the discovery could affect the whole family. He poured out as much as he knew to Diana and swore her to secrecy. Whitney had yet to investigate the ramifications of what he had learned.

The emotion of the time caused Diana to pen a poem dated Spring 1950 and titled: "Suspicions, Circs (and Spies?)":

> *Straight, Rose and Green are all in one office,*
> *A nastier threesome lean far to the left . . .*
> *Are Powers that be completely bereft*
> *To allow* New Republic *to tie up with Moscow?*
> *(If I could get closer I'd shut up their orifice)*
> *But, People, their people, who come from afar*
> *Leaving squeaky doors open or always ajar*
> *For jobs from the Kremlin to dear Uncle Sam.*

> *Or "Marry my sister, she's not what I am"*
> *Now Rose does the finance, and Green fixes speeches,*
> *Of something all tinged with a blood-letting red.*
> *Straight is the cover & Rose does the paying,*
> *And agents I know become horribly dead.*
> *It's more than suspicion, Why can't it be seen*
> *A colorsome trio are Straight, Rose and Green?*[16]

She took poetic license with remarks about Rose, who was not a Soviet spy and had no idea of Straight's secret connections. Yet she was correct on Green, who would have been Michael Greenberg, Straight's fellow Cambridge KGB recruit, not his control, Michael Green. (Michael Greenberg complicated matters by later changing his name to Green.) Diana's line, "Marry my sister, she's not what I am," was a reference to the fact that Straight introduced his sister Beatrice to Louis Dolivet (who Whitney knew was also a KGB agent). It demonstrated the extent of MI6's knowledge of several threads in the KGB networks operating in the United Kingdom and the United States at that time.

Whitney did not wish to confront his brother just yet, if at all. He would not have been able to divulge the source of his information, and he did not wish to upset his mother. He decided to remain quiet and to learn what he could before taking action. Foremost in his mind was Straight's handling of *The New Republic* and the Whitney Foundation in the United States.

His first act was to greet Straight and his son, David, now 7 years old, in London in mid-June as if nothing had happened. Straight was unaware of his brother's feelings and his position with MI6. Whitney met him at the airport and drove them to the four-bedroom family apartment at 42 Upper Brook Street in London's West End, near the American embassy. Dorothy and Straight's 20-year-old half-brother William met them there. Whitney's demeanor appeared normal. There was no hostility or a warning about what might be brewing.

In July, Straight and his son visited Dartington. William Elmhirst recalled the visit and remarked that "the family [except for Whitney] looked on him as heroic for his pursuit of liberal causes in the American sense. In the UK we backed the Labour Party, and were influenced by Michael Young."

During Straight's stay, Leonard was going through a desk drawer when he found Straight's British Communist Party card. Straight made light of the discovery, especially after his sworn statement to the HUAC hearing.

"Can't have just anyone finding that, can we?" Straight said, taking the card from his stepfather. "Better get rid of it."[17]

Dorothy did not pressure her son over *The New Republic*, despite the fact that it continued to accumulate losses, putting the magazine in jeopardy of folding unless it could somehow be made more attractive to advertisers. She knew it had been a problem since inception. Dorothy was also aware that union demands, higher wages, and increased overheads had escalated costs in the postwar era. Coupled with massive blowout from the Wallace "campaign," the magazine was left floundering. Yet she did not intervene. She had full confidence in Rose's judgment and what she knew of her son's endeavors, despite the drain on the finances of Trust 11.

By coincidence Gil Harrison, Straight's friend at the AVC, visited Dartington Hall in the summer. He would later be interested in buying the magazine.

17

THE KOREAN WAR SPIES

While Straight was relaxing at Dartington, his contention that South-east Asia would be a battleground for the capitalist-communist struggle was tested on June 25, 1950, when communist North Korean troops crossed the 38th Parallel—the boundary line established by the allies when the Japanese surrendered in 1945—and invaded South Korea. The United Nations—minus the Soviet Union, which had absented itself—put together an armed force of several nations dominated by the United States to defend South Korea and to "restore international peace and security in the area."

The assembled UN force was under the command of General Douglas MacArthur, a man driven by his sense of destiny. He sent four American divisions to support the South Koreans, but they were forced south. They were reinforced with other divisions and fought back hard. On September 15, MacArthur led U.S. troops on a daring amphibious landing at Inchon, one hundred miles south of the 38th Parallel, which was far north of the main battlefront. This brilliant move cut off the North Korean forces' lines. MacArthur's forces north and south of the invading enemy then converged and shattered them.

The allied forces now advanced northward to the 38th Parallel. The Chinese warned them not to cross it; however, MacArthur was keen to unify Korea. In late September, the U.S. embassy in New Delhi reported to Washington that the Indian ambassador to Beijing, Sardar Panikkar, advised that China would enter the Korean War if the UN forces crossed the 38th Parallel. This confirmed previous intelligence reports that China was committed by a secret treaty with Russia to protect the hydroelectric power system based on the giant Suiho Dam in North Korea. This power was sent as far north as Port Arthur and supplied the strategic, Soviet-run munitions industry in Manchuria. It turned out the latest heavy model Russian tank, among many other products. Other reports from Chiang Kai-shek's Nationalist Chinese intelligence service warned that two Chinese divisions, the 164th and 166th, were in Korea. Communist Chinese General Lin Piao's Fourth Army was moving up the coast to the Korean-Manchurian border, the northeast part of China.

MacArthur scorned the Panikkar report as propaganda, saying that the Indian ambassador was a Beijing stooge. He cabled Truman, telling him that Chinese troops would not enter the war. He asked for authority to cross the 38th Parallel and put an early end to the conflict.

Their vital communications were being picked up in Washington by the KGB's two top-line British agents, Kim Philby and Guy Burgess, who were working overtime sending information on the Korean conflict to Moscow. They used two channels, through their Washington control and through Blunt in London, who passed information to Yuri Modin. Burgess had obtained a posting from the foreign office to be first secretary at the British Embassy in Washington, D.C. He arrived on August 4, 1950. The Russians had a daily monitoring of the conflict from him and Donald Maclean (now on the American desk at the British Foreign Office) in London since the June 25 invasion.

Burgess had built an expertise on events even before that. In April, he had sent Modin a long, hand-written account taken from a report by British intelligence detailing the extent of Soviet aid to the Chinese and Korean forces. This way the Russians knew exactly what the West knew about Russian cooperation with the Chinese and Koreans. This intelligence gave Moscow an idea of how much or how little the United States was prepared for a surprise attack by Moscow's "proxy," the North Koreans.[1] Burgess's KGB assignment was to assist Philby in gathering espionage material on every level—diplomatic and military—of the conflict.

Now the Russians wanted to know just how far the United States was prepared to go "down the road to world-war."[2] Every detail on the intentions of MacArthur and Truman would be valuable, as well as any intelligence on the advance of the UN troops.

The plan to cross the 38th Parallel and "lock up" the whole Korean peninsula was worked out by the U.S. Joint Chiefs of Staff and passed on for acceptance to its allies. Philby and Burgess at the British embassy were privy to the details, which were dispatched to their controls. By October 15, when MacArthur met Truman at Wake Island, the stated plan was to send only South Korean soldiers north of the 38th Parallel. The Chinese said that the presence of UN troops north of the line would cause them to intervene. However, MacArthur had no intention of parking victorious U.S. troops on the boundary line and sending the less proficient South Korean divisions north into battles and probable defeat. Stalin's intelligence sources informed him of this. It was no surprise to the Russians when MacArthur sent all the troops under his command pushing into North Korea.

By mid-November, the allied forces were nearing the North Korean/Manchurian border marked by the Yalu River. Truman ordered MacArthur not to cross the Chinese border and not to contemplate the use of atomic weapons.

Stalin had been pressuring Mao Tse-tung to intervene, but Mao was reluctant. He didn't want the war to spread to China, especially as he was unaware of U.S. intentions. Would MacArthur use the bomb? It was a very real possibility in the minds of Mao and his high command. They, like all world leaders, had been stunned, although not unhappy, by how Truman had ended the Japanese war with the destruction of Hiroshima and Nagasaki. Mao saw MacArthur as a leader with dangerous ambitions. After the Japanese precedents had been set, there was always the potential now that atomic weapons would be used again. There was enough pressure from the hawks in the Pentagon and the far-right wing in the United States for Truman to feel compelled to make it perfectly clear to his general that he must not use nuclear weapons.

As Straight was composing *New Republic* stories while on tour in Asia, China's leader was waiting for the intelligence on the firm intentions and orders from Truman to MacArthur. Stalin was receiving almost daily assessments from fellow members of the Cambridge ring, Philby, Burgess, and Donald Maclean (via Modin and other controls). Vital intelligence received at the Kremlin was passed on to the nervous Chinese leader.

The Russian dictator had put the highest authority on the ring's judgment. He had psychological appraisals of Truman and MacArthur, which showed that the general, despite his bellicosity and desire to go down in history as a decisive winner of major battles, would not disobey firm imperatives. The assessment of Truman was that he was a tough leader who would take action if crossed by an army commander. Coupled with this analysis was the categorical conclusion from Stalin's three agents that the bomb would not be dropped. There would be no invasion of China. This was reconfirmed by Maclean, who accompanied Clement Atlee to the United States. The British prime minister wanted to know Truman's real intentions, and the president told him, in private, that under no circumstances would the bomb be used.[3]

Stalin now had his three best espionage sources and Modin telling him without qualification that whatever MacArthur's ambitions, he would be restricted at the Manchurian border. In sixteen years of espionage through three major wars—in Spain, World War II, and now Korea— and through countless other incidents, Stalin had never had other than first-rate intelligence from the Cambridge ring. He informed Mao with full confidence that he could attack U.S. troops and invade North Korea without the threat of the bomb.

At this critical moment, Straight was close to the action. He filed stories from India and then moved on to Hong Kong. From there, on about November 20 (for the November 27 edition of *The New Republic*), he wrote an article titled, "Will Communism Win in Asia?"

"Thirty miles inland," he wrote, "Communist soldiers guard the frontier [to China] with loaded rifles. The traveler, staring across the bare mountains, must remember that Hong Kong is not China, and that it offers no clues to China . . . refugees flood back and forth across the frontier, journalists pass in and out, seamen bring back stories . . . traders keep open lines of communication. From these people the traveler can gather the scattered pieces of a missing picture. . . ."

According to KGB sources, at this time Mao was not quite convinced about Stalin's intelligence resources. He needed to hear the information, not via the Russians, but straight from the mouth of one of Stalin's Western agents. Was Straight the man? Was he one of those journalists who passed "in and out"? Once more, he was close to the action and could easily have slipped across the border for a meeting with the Chinese party chairman.

———•———

Straight or someone else at this time did convince Mao to act. Unlike Stalin, he was yet to think of tens of millions of lives as expendable in the name of communism. But because of information he had received face to face, Mao was now prepared to take a big risk. The Chinese amassed 400,000 troops on the other side of the Yalu, and waited in ambush.[4]

MacArthur sent light American columns—the First and Twenty-fourth Cavalries—to the Manchurian border to see if there would be any resistance. On November 24, he announced that U.S. troops would be home by Christmas. The next day, the Chinese struck. Waves of massed troops bore down on the surprised Americans. Guerrillas sprung from behind them and destroyed their communication lines along the west coast. After heavy fighting, thousands of U.S. soldiers were left dead. Many were wounded, captured, and tortured. Over the next month, the United States and its allies were pushed back to the 38th Parallel. The communists began a second invasion of 500,000 troops, but their attack faltered in the face of incessant allied bombing. The U.S. troops held their positions, and the front lines stabilized along the Parallel. Mao's gamble on Stalin's advice had paid off thanks in large part to the accurate intelligence from Philby, Burgess, and Maclean. Instead of Mao's worst fear of atomic bombs dropped on major Chinese cities, there had been a "conventional" conflict against the might of the allies with "acceptable" losses. The end was a bloody stalemate, without communism losing ground in Southeast Asia. If Stalin, and Mao in turn, had not had such precise intelligence, it's highly probable that the Chinese would not have invaded. Many American and allied soldiers would not have been killed or injured.

———— • ————

In his book, Straight wrote of another chance meeting with Burgess, in March 1951, a few months after the height of the Korean crisis. Earlier he claimed he had bumped into Burgess in Pall Mall and that on another occasion Burgess had turned up uninvited at the Savoy. All these instances were concoctions for his (later) FBI interrogations. Straight was still a fully fledged agent in the business of dealing with other fellow agents of whom Burgess was just one of many. Yet Straight persisted with his fabrications. In this "story" he was driving along when he happened to come across Burgess trying to hail a taxi near the British embassy in Washington, where he was working. Burgess hitched a ride. In their brief conversation in Washington, Straight ascertained that Burgess had been in the city during the Korean conflict.

Straight claimed he thought that if Burgess was in Washington, he would have known of U.S. plans to advance into North Korea. In turn, Straight suggested, Burgess would have sent the information to Moscow. The Kremlin then would have handed it to Beijing. Straight said that in this way, Burgess could have caused the deaths of many American soldiers.[5]

Straight's claims to chance meetings with Burgess are at odds with the testimony of Alan Baker, one of Blunt's lovers who visited Washington at this time. Blunt was keen for Baker to get in touch with Burgess and give him Blunt's latest book, *The Nation's Pictures*. There is little doubt, according to Yuri Modin, that there would have been a message in the book for Burgess, warning him to get out of the United States. The intelligence services were closing in on him.

Baker, unaware he was a middleman for key Soviet spies, felt uncomfortable with his mission of delivering a book. Burgess knew which hotel he was staying at, but Baker wasn't given his address. On his third day in the American capital he had a phone call from Burgess. Burgess claimed he didn't have time to meet Baker. Instead, according to Baker, he told him that a Mr. Straight would come to his hotel at a specified time, take him to dinner, and collect the book. Baker always assumed that this was

Michael Straight. Straight, however, sticking to his version of events at this critical time, could not recall meeting Baker.

———•———

Straight has never denied that he was fully aware of the value of his comrades in the Cambridge ring in the Korean conflict. The ring collectively would have judged its outcome as another vital victory for them and the cause. Straight's critics construed that if he was taken at his word as being anticommunist at this point, his failure to inform the United States and the United Kingdom about the spying of his Cambridge comrades made him a tacit accomplice.

Writer Sidney Hook, in a review of *After Long Silence* in *Encounter* magazine of December 1983, commented:

> To this day he seems unaware that his prolonged and stubborn silence about his involvement in the Soviet espionage apparatus, long after he claimed to have shed any trace of faith or loyalty in the Communist cause, in effect made him complicit in the hundreds of deaths that were contrived by his erstwhile comrades.[6]

William Safire, in a *New York Times* review, thought Straight's "greatest contribution to the Soviet spy system" came in this Korean War episode. "Did he turn in his old friends?" Safire asked. "Hardly. . . . "[7]

Raymond A. Scroth's assessment in the magazine *America* was that this encounter with Burgess was "the high point of the story."[8]

Straight alleged that on learning of Burgess's probable involvement in traitorous activity over the Korean War, he became angry and said to Burgess that in 1949 he (Burgess) had told him he was going to leave the U.K. Foreign Office. Straight wrote that he accused Burgess of breaking his word.

Straight then maintained that he threatened to turn him in if he wasn't out of the British government inside a month. Sidney Hook, William Safire, and other critics charged that in a decade of opportunity, Straight never got near turning in his comrade and mentor. The apostolic oath, and Straight's fears of Stalin and the KGB, they felt, seemed stronger than any concern for his country and the people of it.

If Straight had informed on Burgess in the decade before 1951, it would have had enormous ramifications for many agents on both sides in the Cold War. A big section of the Cambridge ring would have been finished. Blunt, the key postwar "middleman agent," whom many subagents used as a conduit to KGB controls, would have been in strife, as would Philby, the head of Soviet counterintelligence.

Other KGB agents such as Leo Long, brought into the Apostles by Straight and then recruited for the Russians by Blunt, would also have been caught. Long worked in intelligence for the British Control Commission in Germany until 1952, where he was meant to be infiltrating Western agents behind the iron curtain. Instead, according to John Costello, "Long was a link in a major Cold War plot to infiltrate Soviet agents in the U.S. intelligence services with the connivance of their other [KGB] moles in MI5 and MI6." In his position Long may also have been responsible for the "disappearance" of hundreds of agents in East Germany who were sending information to the West.[9] Apart from the rolling up of the Cambridge ring, any confession by Straight up until 1951 would have meant momentous arrests in the United States of such people as his control Michael Green and his wife, Helen Lowry. Straight remained outside the major U.S. rings, but he knew the key people involved.

Yet on all counts, Straight alleged at this time that he was still bound by loyalty to his oath to the Apostles, fear of exposure once he "confessed" his past, or even concern about reprisals from the KGB. For these reasons, he said, he remained mute. But again, none of these claims were true. He had never stopped plotting and consorting with KGB agents.

Straight was still very much one of them.

18

FAMILY FEUD

Whitney forced a showdown during the family meeting at Darting-ton in April 1951, a year after he learned of his brother's KGB links. He had done his homework as far as he could and consulted lawyers on where he stood with the family trust. The problems had been compounded by Dorothy's decision to appoint Straight along with Rose as the trustees in Trust 11, succeeding the Royal Trust Company of Canada.

Straight could not quite grasp Whitney's sudden attempt to get out of the trust. He thought it had to be because he was upset, as the oldest child and the only successful businessperson, that he wasn't given control of Trust 11. But it was deeper than this. Whitney was not going to stand by and watch what he saw as certain destruction of the family fortune, all in the name of communism.

The technical argument against Whitney taking control was that he was now a British citizen, not American, and therefore was somehow less eligible than Straight for the position. But Whitney's lawyers did not believe this. He and they were concerned about far too much money being used to prop up *The New Republic*, which looked to Whitney as nothing more than a Soviet propaganda sheet.

Straight suggested that money given to the magazine was from an independent corporation, Editorial Publications, which had been set up to administer Dorothy's holdings (the magazines *Asia, Antiques, Theater Arts,* and *The New Republic*). But this was misleading. Editorial Publications was owned by Trust 11, and Straight and Rose were in charge of it. They had total say on what money went to propping up the hemorrhaging *New Republic.* Before the Henry Wallace episode, *Antiques* earned enough to keep *The New Republic* alive. After the Wallace fiasco, not even the profitable *Antiques* was enough to save the other publication; it needed a big transfusion of money from Trust 11 via Editorial Publications.

Straight, not his better-equipped brother, was now in control of the family fortune. It was a bitter blow to Whitney, especially coming on top of his secret knowledge of Straight and the way *The New Republic* had been used and, Whitney thought, financially abused. Whitney had tried to get hold of the magazine's accounts, but strict trust rules stated that only trustees and not beneficiaries (unless they were one and the same) could peruse them. He had his lawyers send letters full of queries about the running of the trusts, all to no avail as Rose filibustered.

Whitney knew from snippets of family discussions that *The New Republic* was in a financial mess and that *United Nations World* had cost plenty. It was enough for him to make demands and even threats, if need be. His prime bargaining position would be a request for Milton Rose's head. Whitney's ultimate "weapon," which he would use as a very last resort, would be to expose his brother to his mother as a Soviet agent.[1]

It heightened the sense of a showdown as Straight, Rose, and Beatrice flew in from the United States to confront Whitney. In essence, Leonard, Ruth, and William were nonparticipants, as was to a lesser extent Beatrice. The real fight was between the other four, with Dorothy in support of Rose and Straight.

The Dartington Hall meeting started peacefully but degenerated into a shouting match. Whitney, very much on his own in the argument, accused Rose of being criminally negligent in the way he was running the trusts in the United States and especially over the near-collapse of *The New Republic.* This caused Dorothy much consternation. Whitney went on to threaten he would pull out of the trust. "I will not allow my share to support that magazine," he told them. "It's losses are a scandal."[2]

Whitney wanted to say more about Dolivet being a KGB agent but because of Beatrice restrained himself to complaining about the disaster of

United Nations World and its $250,000 loss. "I want [Rose's] resignation," Whitney said, "otherwise I'll put him in jail."[3]

With that, he left for London early the next morning before anyone else was awake. He arranged meetings between the family members and their respective lawyers. Dorothy tried once more to heal the breach before the family feud developed into a costly legal wrangle. She, Rose, Straight, and Beatrice took the train to London and the family house there—the Aviary. Whitney came home from a cocktail party to an acrimonious confrontation with his mother. He was most angry about the way *The New Republic* had been managed and its huge losses. Yet he appeared to hold the whip hand over his threat to sue Rose on the allegation that the trust had been mishandled. Whitney repeated his desire to leave the family trust structure, telling Dorothy that he had no confidence in Straight and Rose.

Dorothy told him that if he forced Rose to resign, a corporate trustee would have to be appointed. She might have to close down *The New Republic*. Whitney thought that was a good thing.[4]

The family met again the next day in London. Whitney had made it clear he was not bluffing about a lawsuit. Straight conceded that it was acceptable for Whitney to say he did not want his share of the trust supporting *The New Republic*, but he didn't find it acceptable that Whitney sell his share of the trust to the rest of the trust beneficiaries for cash. Straight claimed that they didn't have the cash and that there was no way of measuring what the share was worth.

There would, it seemed, be an impasse unless the magazine and some other losing assets were sold off. The money from such divestments after costs would be plowed back into the trust's principal amount to in part make up for the losses incurred on the magazines.[5]

A day later Dorothy turned up at a meeting with her solicitor, Ian Wilson, as did Whitney with his advocate, Tom Overy. Straight had Rose beside him. (Beatrice had flown back to New York the day before.) Dorothy gave a speech at the beginning, stating why she had created *The New Republic* and the Whitney Foundation and why she had made outright settlements on her children. She claimed that she had set up Trust 11 for her grandchildren; the income from the trust was for her children to spend. But she had seen to it that none could get his or her hands on the principal.

This put the onus on Whitney, who wanted to bust the trust and take a share of the principal. He deferred to his lawyer, who said much the same thing as Whitney had at the two previous meetings: the trust had been run in the interest of Beatrice (bearing in mind the Dolivet fiasco) and Straight (the *New Republic* financial farce); the interests of Whitney and his family had been ignored and hurt. Nothing would be left for Whitney's children under the administration of Straight and Rose. That was the pressing issue, Overy informed the others.

Ian Wilson tried to deflect the argument, but Overy brought it back to his client's main point of grievance: because Whitney's heirs could only obtain 20 percent of the income, all "deficient operations" (such as *The New Republic* and *United Nations World*) were "intolerable."

Rose had been "delinquent," Overy noted. Whitney had been kept in the dark; information had been withheld from him. Dorothy protested at the attack on Rose. Overy continued, ever so politely. He said his client, "he felt certain," was entitled to sue for breach of trust because of losses incurred by the two magazines. He hinted that Whitney would use his power as a "life beneficiary" to block the reorganization of the trust and the appointment of Rose and Straight as new trustees. Whitney would go to court, object to the trust accounts, and force a sale of *The New Republic*.[6]

Wilson, Rose, and Straight retorted that he could not block anything. Straight began a little speech of his own urging Whitney to state that in fairness he had no interest in *The New Republic*. Whitney listened and again turned his case over to his lawyer, who repeated the complaints about Rose and Straight as trustees. "How can I agree to a trust management that sanctioned $250,000 in expenditure on *United Nations World*?" Whitney asked plaintively.

Straight once more conceded that Whitney should be allowed to segregate his interests in the principal money in the trust, but he added that Rose and the reorganization, that is, Straight's own appointment as a trustee, should go ahead. After that, the meeting broke up, the main problems unresolved.

Whitney, however, had made up his mind. He was not going to stand for the loss-making operations any more. Further legal threats were made, this time on paper. Whitney was determined to sue if he could not get out of the trust with his share. He would see *The New Republic* sold, along with *Antiques* and the Old Westbury property, which was another "deficit operation."[7]

In return, Rose and Straight could run the whole show. Whitney didn't care; he would be out.

Finally, Dorothy and Straight were forced to agree. William Elmhirst, now in his mid-70s, remembers supporting Straight against Whitney. "We were all left and liberal-minded, and Mike was the family standard-bearer," Elmhirst remembers. "We thought he was doing all those wonderful things in America. Whitney on the other hand mixed with an entirely different set in London. All conservatives. I could not understand his motives for splitting the family and the trust. None of us could. He was painted as the villain of the piece."

However, in April 1951 Whitney, it seems, held all the aces. Elmhirst believes that "Whitney used his threat [over Straight's KGB links] of exposure to force my mother to agree to his breaking out from Trust 11. But as far as I know she never confronted Mike and asked for the truth. This would suggest that Whitney threatened to expose Mike without declaring in what way. He may have been constrained out of brotherly feeling."[8]

Whitney's win meant he then had to face a costly legal maneuver to extricate himself and his share from the family trust.

———

A month later, in May 1951, Burgess and Maclean defected from England to Russia after Venona messages from Maclean's control to Moscow had been deciphered. His code name, HOMER, had been uncovered. The information Maclean was sending, coupled with evidence from Walter Krivitsky a decade earlier, allowed British intelligence to narrow down the suspects to him and another foreign office operative. Modin arranged their departure. Blunt and Rothschild had learned from Dick White and Guy Liddell at MI5 that Maclean was under surveillance, so Blunt alerted him. Burgess, initially his chaperone for the trip, went all the way to Moscow with him.

If Maclean alone had defected, the ramifications for the rest of the Cambridge ring would have been minimal. But Burgess's departure pushed the crisis for the KGB into a new dimension. Instead of one lead to links, MI5 had two, and Burgess's connections were greater. It didn't take long to learn that Burgess and Blunt had been lovers. Burgess had spent his recent months in Washington living with Philby and his wife. Rothschild and his wife Tess had been close to Burgess and Blunt, and so it went. Many in the ring fell under suspicion and were questioned. Philby was interrogated, MI5 had discreet chats with Blunt, and Rothschild was interrogated eleven times. Cairncross was followed, and Modin narrowly avoided being caught with him in a public toilet near Ealing Common underground in London.

The disappearances of Burgess and Maclean shocked Straight. His mentor may have finally revealed his true allegiances. What if Blunt were arrested? Would he name names? Once the dust settled, Straight felt secure. Only a full confession could endanger him, and while Blunt's lover Burgess was alive, this would be unlikely. He was expected, perhaps, to return to London. Blunt's devotion to Burgess and affection for Philby would see him carry on the deception, it seemed, indefinitely.

Now two members of the Cambridge ring had shown they were willing to declare their allegiance to another country, something to which Straight had said he was vulnerable because of his claimed lack of roots. Philby, perhaps the most dedicated to the cause of all, would sooner or later be under pressure to follow.

19

A TAXING TIME

Rose and Straight did not waste any time in obeying Whitney's dictums following his threats. They put Old Westbury up for sale in May as soon as they returned from the United Kingdom. Straight went on a search for a buyer for *The New Republic*. He wished to secure a sale to a "wealthy liberal" and had plans to carry on in some way with the magazine. Without the magazine, he was just another wealthy dilettante with creative aspirations as a writer or painter. With it, even if he were sneered at by right-wing politicians, there was still an air of respectability and importance about the owner or editor of a magazine such as *The New Republic*. It also gave him entrée anywhere he wished. Now he had to get rid of it. He flew around the country seeing prospective buyers, including Averell Harriman in New York, without luck.[1]

Then in mid-1951, Gil Harrison and Straight went as delegates of the AVC to Rome for a conference of the World Veterans Association. Harrison's fiancée, the wealthy heiress Nancy Blaine, accompanied them. Harrison had no real background in journalism apart from editing a student newspaper, the *Daily Bruin*, at the University of California. Yet he was keen to take over *The New Republic*.

It depended on his marrying Blaine, a dedicated liberal. She was the granddaughter of the rich Anita McCormick Blaine, a communist who set up the New World Foundation and financed Henry Wallace's campaign for the presidency in 1948. It was a near-perfect pedigree for Straight's purposes.

Whitney kept the pressure on Rose and Straight through 1951 as they attempted to appease him by their efforts to sell the properties. In December, Rose rang Straight to tell him that the magazine "was in worse shape than we had supposed." He wanted it closed down and thought at best they could keep it going until the spring of 1952. Without being able to draw on the funds of Trust 11, Straight had to take drastic action at the magazine.[2] He fired staff, including the long-serving Helen Fuller. The magazine appeared poverty-stricken now compared to its halcyon, high-spending days in 1947.

Meanwhile Straight continued to be active, using *The New Republic* and the AVC as vehicles for his views. He was having minor political influence. In early 1952, he (again) called for Truman to withdraw from the campaign for the presidency. Straight preferred Adlai Stevenson, the governor of Illinois, whom he regarded as a man of rare distinction. He greeted Straight like a long-lost relation. His grandfather was vice-president under Grover Cleveland and was close to Straight's grandfather.

Straight demonstrated he was learning the value of attacking Joseph McCarthy as opposed to his attempts to appear as if he were against communism. It was proving popular and safe, from his point of view.

Straight called McCarthy "a beast of the political underworld." The line was picked up by the newspapers. Straight seemed to enjoy the thrust and parry with the extreme right in the United States, especially with Rose sending threatening letters if encounters became too rough or close to sensitive areas. A far-right-wing journal called *The Cross and the Flag* quoted a small section of an article by Straight in *The New Republic* that praised Dwight Eisenhower. The journal's piece was headed "Even Red Mike Likes Ike." Rose wrote a letter saying the use of the term "Red" had been held to be libelous per se in a New York court. Straight's positioning in the AVC and *The New Republic* were then used to show he had a record opposing the Communist Party. The journal published a retraction as demanded by Rose, but its editor noted he was delighted to oblige. It was well established, the journal remarked, that the most dangerous reds were the anticommunist reds. Straight claimed that this upset Rose but that he found it hilarious.[3]

Whitney was kept at bay by the sale of Westbury in April 1952, then Harrison married Nancy. Later in the year, Straight had secured a commitment from him that he would buy the magazine as soon as Anita Mc-Cormick Blaine died and Nancy came into her inheritance from the estate. In July, Rose visited London and Dartington to inform Whitney, Dorothy, and their lawyers of their progress in selling assets.

———— • ————

A package sent by registered mail arrived at the office of the William C. Whitney Foundation in October 1952. It contained a disconcerting twenty-four page questionnaire from the Select Committee of the House of Representatives created to "investigate tax-exempt foundations." This was a euphemism for challenging the right of organizations to avoid tax while funding communist fronts. Straight found most questions "tiresome rather than threatening." But a few worried him and Rose. Question 9 wanted to know if they had investigated the organizations they were funding to see if they were "subversive" or if they had been "cited" (that is, named by the HUAC or the Senate's Subcommittee on Internal Security as subversive or potentially so). Question 14 asked if the Whitney Foundation had made any "grants, gift, loan, contribution or expenditure" to anyone or a group that had been cited.

Rose and Straight, secretary and president of the Whitney Foundation respectively, were summoned to appear before the Select Committee on December 5, 1952. Straight characterized it as controlled by southerners with chips on their shoulders concerning wealthy foundations whose board members lived in the North and East. Nevertheless some of committeemen were genuinely concerned with uncovering and preventing subversion.

At 9:30 A.M. they were ushered into the office of Harold M. Keele, counsel to the committee. Keele motioned for them to sit in chairs opposite his desk while he perused their responses to the questionnaire. Then he looked at them like a schoolmaster about to chastise a couple of schoolboys. Keele told them that his purpose was to bring about corrective action rather than to punish those who were guilty of past errors. If they would cooperate, there would no public humiliation at the hands of certain committee members. Rose and Straight thanked him. Keele turned to page nine. The answer from them to a certain question, he said, saddened him. Who was the board member who had joined so many fronts that had been cited?[4]

Straight told him it was the well-known columnist Max Lerner, who had willingly submitted a list of his past political affiliations. Straight described how Lerner had been reviled by the Communist Party and its allies. Keele cut him short. The Whitney Foundation, he said, had supported the Highlander Folk School, the Southern Conference for Human Welfare, and a number of other organizations to which the Select Committee took strong objection. Keele had the impression from Straight's written responses that Lerner had advocated making the grants to these cited groups. If Straight and Rose conceded that much, and if corrective measures were taken (that is, if Lerner were fired from the Whitney Foundation), then no public examination of their grants would be called for.

That gave the witnesses pause. Whatever the impression they had given in the responses, Straight was forced to admit that Lerner had not been responsible for the money grants by the foundation to the cited organizations that were either communist fronts or controlled by communists. For that reason, he should not be fired. Straight was quick to add that they could not concede that the cited groups were improper. Whitney grants were made to organizations certified as educational or philanthropic (and therefore tax-exempt) by the treasury board.

Keele shook his head. There was nothing more to be said.

At 10:35 A.M. the Select Committee was called to order in a hearing room, with the Honorable Aime J. Forand presiding. Next to him were Keele and two other representatives, Messrs. Simpson and O'Toole.

Straight was pleased that the chairman of the committee, Eugene Cox of Georgia, was not present. He had promised the press he would give the witness a good working-over. That was before Thanksgiving, Straight noted callously, when Cox had eaten too much turkey. He had died of a stroke.[5]

There were several journalists and photographers present as Straight and Rose took their seats at a table facing the committee. A teletypist sat beside the witnesses, tapping out shorthand.

Keele asked Straight the amount of his foundation's assets: it was about $1.5 million. He was then asked his average annual income over the past five years. Straight thought it was $60,000, but Rose corrected him and said it was $75,000. Keele wanted to know about the directors at the foundation. Straight explained that his mother put her philanthropy work on a more institutional basis in 1927 when she set up an advisory committee concerning gifts. It consisted of Ruth Morgan, "well known in various international peace organizations"; the writer Herbert Croly; and Dr. Eduard Lindeman of the New York School of Social Work. The committee became a foundation in 1936 when Dorothy set up all the family trusts. The five directors were Rose; Thomas J. Regan, a New York banker; Max Lerner; Straight; and his sister Beatrice.

The foundation had $60,000 a year—from investments of the capital—to give away, mainly to tax-exempt organizations. The average grant was about $1,500. Straight pointed out that they liked to give money to "labor organizations, particularly in the field of labor education." This included propaganda material about Russia. Typical was the Labor Education Service. Others were the National Planning Association and the AVC, which had received "substantial" contributions.

The questions and answers wallowed in inconsequential areas for some time before Keele brought up the fact that the foundation had given twenty grants to six groups that had been cited. He mentioned a few of them—the Southern Conference, the League of Mutual Aid, and Frontier Films. He then asked about grants to cited groups that Straight and Rose had left off the list. Straight replied: "I think you are referring, sir, to the American Council of the Institute of Pacific Relations, and that is a fact. That was an inadvertence on our part due to, I think, a careless reading of your questionnaire."[6]

> Keele: And that was as late as 1948, wasn't it?
> Straight: Yes, sir . . .

The reporters present began to sit up and scribble. Rose and Straight were beginning to look uncomfortable. A photographer positioned himself near their table.

> Keele: Why was it that as late as 1948 you were still making grants to the American Council?

Straight gave a long answer extolling the virtues of the IPR and saying it was "very much more than the American Council." He then concluded that whether or not the foundation would give it further grants was "an open matter."

> Keele: You also failed to list in your answers—did you not?—a grant to the IPR in 1943?
>
> Straight: That is correct. That 1943 grant, I think, was related to the Mount Tremulant Conference [of the IPR], which I described.
>
> Keele: You did not include—did you?—the American-Russian Institute Grants. In 1937 you gave $500; in 1938, $1000; in 1939, $500; in 1944, $500; in 1945, $500; in 1947, $500.
>
> Straight: Yes, sir.[7]

Straight and Rose now looked concerned. A photographer knelt on one knee in front of them, set off flash bulbs in their faces, and captured their nervousness. Keele and the other members of the committee added further pressure. Straight was forced to defend some of the propaganda for the Soviet Union.

> Straight: I think that we sincerely felt [in the war years] that this was an effort to spread further information concerning an ally of the United States.
>
> Keele: What about the grants to Commonwealth College in 1937 and 1938? You have not listed them either, have you?
>
> Straight: That was three years before I came onto this foundation. I frankly don't know about it.
>
> Keele: I am not asking you now about the grants. I am asking you why they were not listed here in your answer as grants made to organizations which had appeared on the Attorney General's list or on the House Un-American . . .
>
> Straight: I assume we have no record at all of its being cited. I take your word that it has been.
>
> Keele: Well, Commonwealth College was cited as Communist by the Attorney General in the letter to the Loyalty Review Board released 27 April 1949. It is on page 40 of the *Guide to Subversive Organizations and Publications* . . .

Straight's technique in the interrogation was to distance himself from the decisions to give grants, where possible. He conceded errors but always had an answer that sounded plausible and rational. He would drop into his responses that he and his board were "anticommunist."

When Keele began to probe about grants going to "fields where the greatest possibility of danger [from communist groups] occurs," Straight's response emphasized the coincidence concerning money going to them.

> Straight: As you can see from our grants, we are particularly interested in these fields of labor organizations and education, and there is no question at all that in those fields the Communist Party was a very active underground force during the life of this foundation. I think it would have been remarkable—it would probably have been more a matter of luck than intuition—had we had a perfect record during that period from your point of view.

He reiterated his old argument that congress and government should not interfere in organizations infiltrated by subversives. It was better, he maintained, that they be purged from within. Keele pounced on this. He had read the transcript of Straight's March 1950 testimony before a HUAC hearing.

> Keele: You are quoted here as saying, "We don't believe that the Communist Party today is a clear and present danger."
> Straight: It certainly is a danger, but I question—I am not sure it is one in the sense that Justice Holmes used the phrase in denying that a Communist Party member at the time could be prosecuted with such a . . .
> Keele: I take it from what you have said that speaking now within the framework of Justice Holmes' remarks, you would say the Communist Party is a clear and present danger today; is that right?
> Straight: I certainly would; yes.
> Keele: I wanted to give you that opportunity because I thought you meant it in an entirely different light than you stated here.
> Straight: Thank you. I certainly would.

Straight disliked being cornered into this admission on the "clear and present danger" point.[8] Nevertheless, he felt that he and Rose had come through unscathed, despite the mistakes and nervousness exhibited at the hearing. The press reports on their submissions were not damaging.

Straight assumed that the worst was over, but three weeks later, in December, he received a shock at breakfast while reading the *Washington Post*. A former Communist Party functionary, Maurice Malkin, had mentioned Straight in testimony before Keele's Select Committee.

> Keele: I think you told us at one time about Michael Straight, at the Whitney Foundation. Am I correct about that?

Malkin had then claimed that Straight was used in Communist Party in-fighting to defend Stalinists against Trotskyites over the Moscow show trials in 1937–1938. Malkin didn't think Straight was the type to be a card-carrying member.

Straight complained and made the appropriate threats. Malkin checked his papers and wrote to Keele saying he had confused Straight with a Michael Strong, who was a close and trusted party follower from 1931 to 1939.[9]

Fourteen months after facing the Select Committee, congress again investigated foundations. Straight and Rose were summoned on February 5, 1954, to the New York offices of an attorney named Rene Wormser, who was counsel to a house subcommittee. He and his partner wanted to know about the Whitney Foundation's past mistakes. Why had it given grants to subversive groups? Who had made the decisions? Which board members voted for them or against them?

Rose and Straight stuck to the answers given to the Select Committee. They admitted to making "mistakes," but Straight argued that giving money to the Institute for Pacific Affairs was not an error. Straight asked Wormser how he would define "mistakes" and was told about a large foundation financing a study on cybernetics, which contained criticisms of capitalism. Straight responded that every year he had an application for funding from the League for Industrial Democracy that openly criticized capitalism, and yet it had a Treasury Department ruling for tax-exemption. He asked if that meant he could not support the league.

Wormser didn't respond, but instead put the investigators' argument concerning the probes into the activities of private foundations:

The money you are spending under today's very high tax rates belongs to the people of the United States in the sense that they would otherwise collect it in taxes. I question very much whether the people have not the right to ask whether their money should be spent on behalf of ideas that the majority strongly approve of.

This sort of soft, circular argument, coupled with the "very genial" atmosphere generated by the two congressmen, gave Straight confidence that he had weathered the worst that investigators could throw at him.[10]

———————

Despite his background and the various interrogations that he faced from hearings, Straight never felt threatened by McCarthyism. The senator, his staff, and supporters made haphazard, indiscriminate attacks. Even if they had stumbled on something, Straight was building a great deal of experience with his lawyers in handling onslaughts, probes, and slurs. His wealth protected him. But others suffered, such as his sister Beatrice, an accomplished actress, who was prevented for a long time from working in Hollywood. Also according to Straight, Gustavo Duran, who married his wife's sister, was persecuted by McCarthy.[11]

Clearly, no one in government, including the FBI or congress, had anything substantial on Straight, and certainly no one had an inkling of his secret affiliations. Straight reported for *The New Republic* in April 1954 on a house subcommittee into allegations and counterallegations between the army and Senator Joseph McCarthy. McCarthy's charges against the army were to discover who was responsible for obtaining the promotion of a Captain Irving Peress, an army dentist, to the rank of major. McCarthy was attempting to show that army officials were protecting communists, but he couldn't demonstrate any credible collusion. (Later, it was found that minor bureaucrats had requested throughout the army that there be appointment of officers who had been brought in as captains, but who should have been majors from the beginning.)

The army's counterclaim was that McCarthy (chairman of the Permanent Subcommittee on Investigations); the committee's counsel, Roy Cohn; and its executive director, Francis Carr, "had sought by improper means to obtain preferential treatment for one Private G. David Schine." There were forty-six counterclaims by the army "to force discontinuance of further attempts by that committee to expose communist affiliation in the Army."

To many observers, McCarthy, a senator from Wisconsin, had set himself up as almost a second president, using his fervent anticommunism as a vehicle for pronouncing on domestic and foreign policy. He and his staff of fourteen had taken it upon themselves to enforce the nation's security, for which, Straight was relieved to relate, they were underequipped.

Straight conceded in his book, *Trial by Television* (which covered the Army/McCarthy hearing), that McCarthy was able to expose security procedures that were weak or ill-defined. But McCarthy's primary concern was publicity. He wished to take public credit for the measures the executive branch had taken or was preparing to take.[12]

With this knowledge, Straight felt buoyed enough to tackle McCarthy more vigorously in print. He had summed up the scattered and underresourced nature of McCarthy's political forays and accusations. Straight felt comfortable about reporting on him, especially as the army hearing marked the beginning of the decline of McCarthy's power and influence. Even the Republican president, Dwight Eisenhower, would have applauded the analysis in *The New Republic*.

Senator McCarthy's attacks (1949–1954) became the standard by which all false political accusations were judged from that time on. By 1954, the word "McCarthyism" became an official term in the English language.

When McCarthy began his anticommunist crusade, Republican Dwight D. Eisenhower feared it could sway the election for the Democrats. But McCarthy's support actually aided the Republicans. Their share of the vote increased in traditionally democratic, ethnic, Catholic (and therefore anticommunist), working-class areas, particularly in the Northeast. Long before Ronald Reagan wooed this powerful sector in his successful 1980 bid for the presidency, McCarthy had shown the way.

The senator was correct in his belief about the broad sweep of communist infiltration in U.S. government, but in his fervent drive for publicity and popularity, he attacked some innocent yet powerful victims within government. Over time this caused a natural revolt in influential places in Washington and the liberal media against McCarthy and his bullying tactics.

His biggest target was China scholar Owen Lattimore, director of the School of International Relations at John Hopkins University. Franklin Roosevelt chose him to advise on Chinese Nationalist leader Chiang Kai-shek. Lattimore spent the war years as head of Pacific relations in the U.S. Office of War Information. He advised that the United States should stop subsidizing Chiang Kai-shek. American conservatives therefore viewed Lattimore as supporting Chiang's nemesis, Mao Tse-tung, and his communists.

McCarthy told the U.S. Senate that Lattimore was Moscow's "top espionage agent" in the United States and the boss of Alger Hiss. This was an over-the-top, unsubstantiated claim that caused McCarthy's credibility to slip. Lattimore hit back publicly and was soon seen as a hero among genuine American liberals desperate for someone to stand up to McCarthy. Lattimore said that the Chinese communists (who came to power in 1949) were more nationalist than pro-Soviet and that they would eventually break with Stalin and his successors, which they did by the late 1950s. Lattimore thought that the communist victory in China would be a "magnificent" opportunity for American foreign policy. This proved a truism that slowly gained wide acceptance. It led to another Republican president, Richard Nixon, taking the opportunity to better relations with China, two decades later.

Lattimore's pro-Chinese communist positions saw him in close proximity to real Soviet and Chinese agents, whether at the State Department or at the Institute of Pacific Relations. Yet attempts to label him as a spy in his own right or by association did not work.

Another formidable target for McCarthy was General George C. Marshall, a hero of World War II and a mentor to Eisenhower. In a long speech on June 14, 1951, McCarthy alleged that Marshall had helped sell out China to Mao and had thus aided the drive to communist world domination. McCarthy charged that Marshall had stood by Roosevelt's side (with Alger Hiss) during the February 1945 Yalta Conference of the Allied leaders—Roosevelt, Churchill, and Stalin. They met in the Crimea to plan the final defeat and occupation of Nazi Germany and to decide the political makeup of "liberated" countries, particularly Germany and Poland. Agreements were also reached on China and Japan. All the agreements, McCarthy charged, were treacherous and served "the world policy of the Kremlin." Even conservative Republicans judged this assault on Marshall as unfair. It drew negative publicity for McCarthy. Undaunted, he charged on, claiming that Marshall's charity toward Mao and the communists, and his contempt for Chiang, were part of a "conspiracy on a scale so immense as to dwarf any previous such venture in the history of man."

There was nowhere to go but down after reaching such a summit of hyperbole. By the time of the televised hearings on the counterclaims of McCarthy and the army in 1954, the cumulative effect was a swaying of public opinion against the Wisconsin senator. He was giving anticommunism a bad name. The hard left in the United States was able to dismiss any concern about American communism as a McCarthyite smear. It was the moment for Straight to attack with impunity.

By going after McCarthy, Straight, perhaps for the first time in his career, found himself in league with majority opinion, at least among the media opinion-makers. He relished the opportunity to demonize (literally) McCarthy with high-mileage writing. "A roll of flesh beneath his black eyebrows came down over his upper eyelids," he wrote in *Trial by Television*, "making slits of his eyes, and giving to his face an almost Satanic look."[13]

With such a gift of a target, Straight didn't need to position himself as an anticommunist. He simply had to keep McCarthy in his sights while discussing constitutional crises or the weaknesses of Eisenhower.

Straight made much of McCarthy needing the great evil of communism on which to ride to political prominence. But equally, Straight used the great evil of McCarthyism to fulfill part of his agenda.

20

MORE MOSCOW CONNECTIONS

While Straight castigated McCarthy for looking for reds under every bed, he was having no trouble finding his own and maintaining his espionage work. In May 1954, just after the army hearings, he met Sergei Romanovich Striganov, whose job was political counselor at the Soviet embassy in Washington, D.C. The relationship began, according to Straight, when Adam Watson, a Soviet specialist at the British embassy, arranged a meeting between them. The link and the middleman caused concern at the FBI and in MI5, who may have been concerned about Watson.

Straight told in his memoirs (and to the FBI) how Watson took him across the lawn at the home of the British cultural attaché to the bar where Striganov, a KGB operative, was waiting for a drink.[1] Straight claimed to be meeting him as part of his work as editor of *The New Republic*, which he and Gil Harrison were struggling to keep alive by borrowing money where they could. (Anita McCormick Blaine had died in February 1954, but funding from the inherited estate would not be forthcoming for at least a year.) Straight felt he was obligated to communicate with the KGB to help prevent a major conflict. As with all such explanations, this sounded implausible against his protestations that he was anxious to avoid all contact with KGB agents such as Burgess. His assertion that his communications with the KGB could in any way ease pressure in the Cold War has no substance.[2]

Straight and Striganov agreed to meet for lunch once a month, which was about the regularity of his former meetings with Michael Green. Yet this was in the open. Straight alleged he wasn't passing his lunch companion any documents, just opinion. Straight said they followed a strict protocol. Striganov would take Straight to lunch at the Hotel Mayflower Grill; Straight in turn would take him to the University Club. Both places were within a block of the Soviet embassy. Their protocol broke down when Striganov would ring and ask if he could have lunch on that day or the next. Straight spoke of a pattern emerging in their conversations. Striganov's bosses in Moscow would send him a telegram with a query that needed a quick reply. Straight characterized the queries as innocent, nothing more potent than a question about a domestic development in U.S. politics.[3] He wanted his answers to make sense to Striganov's bosses in Moscow. He claimed also to be conscious of the possibility of the CIA monitoring and intercepting all Striganov's cables, which was a cheeky assertion given that this was the reason he was later interrogated.

The response from Straight, he said, would have to seem sound to the CIA too. Straight's explanation to the FBI was that he interpreted current political events to his KGB friend, such as the meaning of a hard-line, anti-Soviet speech by Vice-President Richard Nixon. But was Striganov that feeble an agent that he had to be spoon-fed interpretations by Straight when he could have made such simple analyses himself by reading the American papers?

In *After Long Silence*, Straight demonstrated impressive recall—nearly thirty years after the event—by repeating the verbal intercourse on paper as if in a novel. The Russian kept reporting back Straight's information. It must have pleased his superiors. They met for the next two years.

———— •• ————

Straight monitored senate attacks on the Institute of Pacific Relations, which he continued to defend as a worthwhile group of the liberal left. Yet it was a classic communist front. An international secretariat made up of prominent Asian scholars, politicians, and businessmen acted for branches that contained communists and their sympathizers. There was a section in Moscow. "One of the representatives of the British branch was Gunther Stein," author John Costello wrote, "the Shanghai journalist with NVKD [KGB] connections and links to Mao Tse-tung's American eulogist, Agnes Smedley."[4]

The U.S. Senate investigating committee summed it up when it said: "The IPR itself was like a specialized political flypaper in its attractive power for communists. . . . A remarkably large number of communists and pro-communists showed up in the publications, conferences, offices, institutions of the IPR, or in letters and homes of the IPR family. . . . The 'effective leadership' of the institute had diverted that organization's prestige to promote the interests of the Soviet Union in the United States."[5]

The IPR was run by an executive committee that included Owen Lattimore, Edward C. Carter, and Frederick Vanderbilt Field. All were alleged to have communist affiliations. Congressional testimony linked Lattimore, a John Hopkins University academic, to the same communist cell as Field. Lattimore denied these accusations (see Chapter 19). However, Luis Budenz testified that he was present when the U.S. Communist Party chairman in 1937 instructed Lattimore to influence American journalists into playing down Chinese communists as harmless agrarian reformers.[6]

Straight, aware from the attacks that there was no substantial evidence of Lattimore's KGB links, defended him, and so defended his own position and the Whitney Foundation's investment in IPR. *The New Republic* became a vehicle for the defense, running articles critical of committees investigating Lattimore.

———————— • ————————

One of McCarthy's many targets was Straight's close friend, Gustavo Duran, the husband of Bin's sister, Bronte. He had been attacked since 1951, and matters were brought to a head when he faced the U.S. Civil Service Commission's "Loyalty Board" hearings. They began in May 1954 and went on intermittently until January 1955. The main point of contention in Duran's mercurial career centered on a vital three weeks in 1938, when he ran the Spanish Republicans' Servicio de Investigacion Militar (SIM) in Madrid. It was created in 1937 as a counterespionage service but soon became an all-powerful political police force, able to make arrests without trial or investigation. SIM was immune to the authority of the minister of war. It had more than 6,000 agents and was in control of prisons and concentration camps. Duran appointed militant communists to all the important posts.

The Loyalty Board accused him of a link to Soviet intelligence and also that he had been removed from his post in charge of SIM for making "numerous unauthorized appointments of Communists." Duran denied the charge for four years, but now one further detail about his duties emerged. He had reported to the Spanish government's National Intelligence Service. It had informed him on which experts' advice to follow in making SIM appointments. Duran attempted to downplay this by saying they were "temporary." But when pressed on who these "experts" were, Duran became evasive. He later gave a clue that they were probably linked to Soviet intelligence when he was asked to comment on his knowledge of twenty-five named persons. They included Alexander Orlov, a key Soviet intelligence officer directing the purge of communists who were not following the Stalinist line in Spain.

Duran answered: "I was introduced to a member of the Russian Embassy whose name was Orlov by the then head of SIM, Mr. Sayagues. I never knew what Orlov's first name was. I spoke with Orlov once or twice. I remember that he told me how necessary it was to organize an effective counter-espionage system in the Republican Army."[7] Orlov, then, was one of the "experts" instructing him on appointments in SIM.

After his fifth and final hearing in January 1955, Duran was cleared of all charges and allowed to continue his career at the UN. Once more the grapeshot approach to investigation had missed Duran's most important KGB intelligence link—his brother-in-law, Straight.

———————

Striganov asked Straight in October 1955 to receive at his home a delegation of Soviet writers, led by Boris Kampov-Polevoy, who was secretary of the Union of Soviet Writers, which was also under KGB control. Far from steering clear of Russian contacts, Straight now seemed to be encouraging them.

An FBI agent reviewing his FBI file (accumulated from 1963 to 1975), probably in the early 1970s, raised the possibility that Straight was dissimulating. The agent also accused him of being naive for even questioning whether Striganov, Fried (a possible agent he met in Moscow in

1969), and others were connected with the KGB. Straight countered by clinging to his argument that if he could reach (KGB) intelligence experts with sound reasoning, that was enough for him.[8] Straight made the well-worn, spurious claim that he was not passing on espionage but rather informing the Moscow Center in the interests of world peace.

In general there was FBI and CIA concern about any contacts with Russians in the United States by American citizens. The FBI vaults were full of files on everyone from journalists to atomic scientists who had or might still have links. At this time American intelligence services were aware that the Soviets were—as ever—very keen to learn how the U.S. nuclear weapons program was progressing. Any information to do with policy, new programs, and developments was of vital interest. By 1955 the Russians were on a par with the United States in the nuclear arms race as both countries developed horrific thermonuclear weapons.

Nancy Harriman had not yet obtained access to the money from her grandmother's estate in 1955, and *The New Republic* did not quite belong to her husband. Straight's name was still on the masthead as editor, but he had written a "farewell" editorial. It marked the fortieth anniversary issue in 1954. While doing research for this editorial, he fell out with Felix Frankfurter over the issue of freedom of speech. Straight had been for unconditional freedoms, whereas the Supreme Court judge had supported some restrictions in the 1950s.

While in Europe for the summer of 1955 for his annual visit to Dartington, Straight took time off for a trip to Geneva for an East-West summit, which was meant to "identify sources of tension" between the Soviets and the West. Straight was there using *The New Republic* as his usual cover for his KGB work. His job was to report anything that would be useful to the Soviet side. He passed on analysis of the in-fighting in the U.S. camp just prior to the summit between John Foster Dulles, the secretary of state, and Nelson Rockefeller, Eisenhower's special assistant for Cold War strategy. Straight attended meetings of the cabinet, the National Security Council, and the Council on Foreign Economic Policy.

The Geneva summit's aim was to consider the problems that lay between the two superpowers. After that, the disagreements would be referred to the foreign ministers of participating nations for detailed discussions to see if any agreements could be worked out. Dulles was happy for this arrangement; Rockefeller saw problems. He had summed up the Russians and thought that Nikita Khrushchev, who had taken over as general secretary of the Communist Party after Stalin died in 1953, would bring a number of solid proposals for arms reductions to the summit table. The Soviet leader, always on the lookout for ways to outshine the United States in world opinion, would, Rockefeller believed, make his proposals public. Straight learned that Rockefeller feared the United States would be put on the defensive. If the United States was perceived to hesitate, much esteem might be lost. Straight observed that "he [Rockefeller] saw the meeting as theater and proposed to pre-empt the stage by a bold gesture that would capture the imagination of the world."[9]

It was Straight's job to find what that gesture would be. But all he learned was that Rockefeller's argument won over the Dulles plan. Rockefeller and his staff of six (including Nancy Hanks, whose biography Straight would later write) moved into a hotel in Lausanne, thirty miles from Geneva. Security was extra tight, but there was no safe in the rooms. The staff carried classified information in a metal satchel. Classified data that they wished to dispose of had to be flushed down the toilet.[10] This meant that Straight had to be content with tidbits rather than documents to pass on to the Russians.

After three days of preliminaries, Eisenhower told Soviet leaders that "the time had come to end the Cold War." He handed them Rockefeller's Open Skies Plan. Straight and his fellow Soviet spies had failed their leaders. Straight said that the Soviet side was stunned by the plan. Western diplomats and correspondents called it "fantastic" and "unprecedented"; Soviet journalists disappeared for several days.[11]

But it mattered little. Although Rockefeller had won a public relations coup for Eisenhower, the plan later fizzled. One of its main concepts was a detailed plan for on-site inspection after agreed arms reductions or cessation of an arms buildup. This was fine for the United States. It had long-range, high-altitude aircraft to check on developments; the Soviets did not. There would be no "Open Skies" agreement for a long time yet.

Vladimir Barkovsky was sent to Washington as the KGB's chief-of-station at the beginning of the summer of 1956 in an effort to speed up its acquisition through espionage of U.S. developments in everything from military aircraft to biological weapons. Money was no object as the Soviet Union turned over 50 percent of its national income to defense, and espionage was allocated a sizable chunk of it. Barkovsky, who had served in the London embassy during the war, and in New York until the early 1950s, was one of the most experienced, hardworking, and demanding controls ever placed in the United States. His specialty had been nuclear weaponry, and he had done as much as possible in stealing U.S. atomic and hydrogen bomb secrets, which went some way to the Soviet Union's creating their own major weapons of destruction. Now, as station-chief in the most important embassy outpost in the world, his responsibilities had increased.

Barkovsky set out to cast a wide espionage net in the United States with hundreds of agents in Washington and dotted around the country in "strategic" cities and remote locations such as the Midwest—those close to major U.S. military centers. He admitted in our interviews that he recruited people everywhere, even attempting to reactivate agents long considered burnt-out cases. It was now more than a decade since the United States and Soviet Union had been allies, and the Cold War had become worse with no thaw in sight. Now the GRU—the Soviet military's espionage arm—and the KGB wanted to know about every single U.S. development that indicated a threat or a turning point in policy, strategy, or tactics. Main highways, designed for quick military maneuvers, were being constructed throughout the United States. The KGB wanted to know everything about them, from the contractors commissioned to build them to the routes they would take. A military command and control bunker was planned for construction in Colorado. Barkovsky, who jokingly underplayed his role during WWII at the London embassy by describing his role as a "photographer," now was in charge of a massive picture-gathering operation of his own. Within months, the new KGB chief-of-station had created the largest foreign espionage operation in peacetime. Barkovsky sent hundreds of agents into remote areas of the United States to create maps and take photographs.

One of his more experienced agents called up for one such assignment was Straight.

PART FOUR

SPIES FROM THE PAST

21

CAREER CHANGE

Straight turned forty in 1956, and the year proved to be one of change, at least in his professional life.

He claimed to have assessed his options. He was modestly famous as an orator. Organizations such as the Americans for Democratic Action sought him as its chairman. But his connections to the Cambridge ring—particularly Burgess and Blunt—had ruined any chances of his ever entertaining a political career. Straight could not now go on with his easy life at *The New Republic*, which his brother Whitney had seen to by forcing him to stop financing the magazine from Trust 11 money. That left Straight no option but to sell it off and therefore end his own association with it as owner, editor and even eventually a sometime journalist.

This was an accurate summary as far as it went without being the full story. Whitney argued that Straight's handling of the magazine had to be stopped. Gil Harrison had finally paid for *The New Republic*, and Straight turned over full responsibility for the magazine to him. It was not difficult. Ever since the Henry Wallace campaign debacle, Straight faced the reality of the magazine's leaving his family's control, but he had stayed on through necessity. Now it was time to move on. But to what? He didn't need money. That would always roll in from the trust. But it was nice to be occupied. And his only long-term true "employer," the KGB, always had intriguing projects for him. It wanted him and made him feel useful. He was also locked in and obligated to carry out espionage.

For the latest directive from Barkovsky, Straight needed a better cover than being a political journalist. If he snooped around the West in his allotted states—Wyoming and Nebraska—taking pictures and notes of every military establishment for research, troops, and training, he would invite suspicion. He could have claimed he was doing "local color" stories. But this would have looked strange after one or two articles from a man known for mixing in hot political circles around the power portals of Washington, D.C.

Straight needed something more layered and creative as a cover. He hit on the idea of being a novelist. But what sort of novel would he write? First he surveyed the area.

During the summer, he and the family vacationed at a ranch at Saddlestring, Wyoming. Straight became familiar with the region, first on horseback and by car, and then in the air in his Navion, which he flew over the Big Horn Mountains. He took a keen interest in the area's history. He noted in his diary that the so-called Fetterman Massacre took place on the road to Sheridan in northern Wyoming, not far from the Montana border. Then it came to him: he would write a Western.

Over time he had to justify this writing move, and his choice of genre, from his past inclinations. He decided to become an author.

But not just any author. Straight was bound to tackle deeper subjects and needed a certain amount of solid background before he wrote. This meant, even with fiction, accessing locations and archives that the layperson might find difficult to get into. As long as authors or writers had the right story to explain why they needed to visit a certain location or to access an archive, they usually succeeded in obtaining the material they wanted. Straight, as a journalist, had useful experience in gaining information. Now as a would-be novelist, he would have similar access. It was a clever, even ingenious new screen as an excuse for wandering around his two target states. As ever, he felt compelled to deceive the family and justify his move into Western fiction writing. He told his parents that he was making a break from his past. Straight said he needed a new challenge and that it was coming in the form of a novel, which was beginning to take shape in his mind.

But he was unconvincing. He had never dreamed of being a novelist as a teenager or youth. He had claimed that books and writers did not move his generation (except for the British economist John Maynard Keynes). There was no unpublished manuscript of his tucked away in a desk drawer at Dartington or a vault at Cambridge. In fact, creative writing had never challenged him. His horizons had been limited to considering a biography of English economist David Ricardo (1772–1823). Yet suddenly at 40, he had contrived to be a fiction author when until this point he had been consumed by hard-nosed, very political nonfiction journalism.

The first reassertion of this alleged long-dormant urge came in the form of a Western novel—not quite Wyatt Earp or Billy the Kid, but nevertheless a Western. It was a most unlikely genre for Straight to tackle. The story would be set in a ruined fort near Sheridan, the site of the Fetterman Massacre. The theme would be human responsibility. Straight had a further fascinating explanation for setting his first fiction effort in the remote West. The location came first, then the story; the characters and the themes were settled on the geography. The story emerged from true history with the characters who had actually lived out the action around the fort. Once the key people were discovered, Straight set them down on the landscape around which he wished to do his espionage work for Barkovsky.

Straight was working part-time at *The New Republic* on the outside chance that liberal Adlai Stevenson should be elected U.S. president in the 1956 elections. In that eventuality, Straight planned to go back full time to make sure the magazine supported him. In the meantime he was researching his novel in the national archive. His claimed aim was to produce something that lasted as opposed to editorials he had written weekly for a decade.

The book would recapitulate his experience on *The New Republic*. This meant that a lot of pent-up energy would flow into the novel, which he called *Carrington*. It was one of the more inventive espionage covers yet attempted.

While this first novel was brewing, his deeper attitudes to the communist movement were being tested just after the Hungarian Uprising in

Budapest in October 1956. An attempted overthrow of the ruling communist party was put down by an invasion of Russian tanks ordered by Soviet leader Nikita Khrushchev. It demonstrated the brutal nature of the Kremlin regime in the true Stalinist tradition. Straight's attitude was exposed the night after the election won by the incumbent, President Eisenhower, when he spent time with Cord Meyer and an acquaintance, Leo Cherne, who had just delivered supplies to Cardinal Mindzenty. Josef Mindzenty was the Catholic clergyman who personified uncompromising opposition to fascism and communism in Hungary. He had been arrested by the communist government in 1948 for refusing to let Catholic schools be secularized. He was convicted of treason in 1949. Sentenced to life imprisonment, he was set free during the uprising. When the communist government regained control after the tanks rolled in, he sought asylum at the U.S. embassy in Budapest. Meyer said that Straight believed the U.S. government was covertly supporting Mindzenty and that this support seemed to have led to the uprising.[1]

The Soviet line, as espoused by such agents of influence as Australian communist journalist Wilfred Burchett, was that Mindzenty was a CIA stooge and a traitor who should be surrendered by the Americans to the authorities. Straight had spent time with Meyer and his wife Mary on the last night of the uprising. Meyer had been listening to the last, desperate broadcasts from underground radio stations in Budapest. He was responsible for the CIA's relationship with Radio Free Europe (RFE), hence his interest in the final broadcasts. A KGB disinformation program was created that charged RFE with inciting and provoking the uprising. The KGB used the Romanian Communist Party newspaper on November 3 to make the accusation, followed by Vasily Kuznetsov, the chief Soviet delegate at the UN, during a security council debate. It became official communist history in the Hungarian regime's publication, *The Counter-Revolutionary Forces in the October Events in Hungary.*

Meyer did a careful review of the taped broadcasts that had been made in the weeks before the revolution. "We could not find evidence that in this period RFE had violated the standard instructions against inciting to violence or promising external assistance," Meyer wrote in his autobiography, *Facing Reality.*[2] "Far from having planned or directed the Uprising, both RFE and officials in Washington were taken very much by surprise when the fighting broke out."

Since the collapse of communism in Hungary, the evidence is that the CIA had nothing to do with the uprising. Yet Straight's accusation came just three days after the first piece of propaganda came out of a Romanian paper. At the time Meyer had been cultivated as a friend by Straight, and he had no idea of his KGB links. (Meyer wondered later how much confidential information passed on in conversation between friends was reported to Moscow, especially in the light of Straight's regular lunches with Sergei Striganov.)[3]

A contributor to *The New Republic* in 1957 was H. A. R. ("Kim") Philby from Beirut. He had been eased out of British intelligence after Maclean and Burgess defected. He was suspected of being the so-called Third Man in the Cambridge ring, but Philby had enough supporters in the establishment to prevent his being charged. MI6 thought he might be useful as their man in the Middle East. It arranged for him to work as a journalist for *The Observer* and *The Economist*. With these credentials and his acute understanding of the Middle East problems, it was not surprising he would write for the left-leaning magazine.

Straight was asked about the connection by British intelligence when interrogated by it in 1964, but he maintained he knew nothing of Philby's link to the magazine, saying he had left it when the Englishman began writing. But this was not accurate. Straight had relinquished his role of editor, yet he was still associated with it. His name was on the masthead as Editor-at-Large and his by-line appeared early in February 1957 on a light article about mules titled, "Are the Joint Chiefs Erring Again?"[4] Straight had written the light piece after ten days in Wyoming and Colorado as part of his research into *Carrington*.

There is no doubt Philby would have known of Straight after he was recruited by his close friend Burgess. Straight would have realized Philby's position at the very least after he denied publicly in 1955 that he was the Third Man.

For a short while, *The New Republic* was the outlet for two Cambridge ring members, one of whom was living in the West on borrowed time.

The wedding of 1957 in the United States was between businessman-professor Newton Steers, 40, and the beautiful 19-year-old Nina Gore Auchincloss, in the tiny St. John's Church, Washington, D.C., famous as a place of Sunday prayer for presidents. Among the groomsmen were three sometime brilliant aspirants for the White House. All had fine intellects, a capacity for public speaking, and the mandatory massive egos. One was Straight, who could aspire no more; another was writer Gore Vidal, the half-brother of the bride, who may have been a fine Oval Office occupant in the nineteenth century or the twenty-first; the third was Jack Kennedy, who would make it, along with his sensational wife, Jackie, the bride's stepsister and matron of honor.

A black-and-white photograph featured in Vidal's "memoir," *Palimpsest*, captured the three hopefuls at the wedding. Vidal, self-assured and superior, stood at the front, looking every inch the front-runner in the race for highest office. Behind him, Straight was just in the picture but not the race. At the far right was Kennedy, the only one of ten faces not looking directly at the camera. In half-profile, he seemed to be looking at Straight, as if he were an interloper. But he was far from that. Straight had cultivated Steers, the former Atomic Energy Commissioner (1951–1953), as a friend and tennis partner and had admired the string of attractive women he brought to play on Virginia summer weekends. One of them was Nina.

The wedding was a setting in which Straight, with his endless charm, reveled. He engaged the guests with his sharp mind and broad knowledge of major issues. Those on the political right, on rarefied occasions such as this, would listen to the torrent of carefully placed and articulated words coming from the acceptable face of liberalism. To those of the left, he seemed to have a position of wisdom on every issue from McCarthy to missiles. Straight's social fluidity allowed him to develop relationships with whomever he pleased. There were useful pickings at this wedding, from senators to CIA men, business tycoons to academics. After such events, he could write a voluminous report on what he picked up that would be useful for the KGB. He was also in his element with a feast of stunning young women, some experienced and elegant like Jackie, others virgins such as her stepsister about to step down the aisle. He fancied them both, and they were attracted to him too. Straight, in fact, was just the type that these upmarket women gravitated to. He was rich, good-looking, and urbane, and he knew his art. What more could a socially conscious girl want?[5]

After the wedding service, Kennedy and Vidal drove across the Potomac river for the reception at the Auchincloss family home, Merrywood, on the Potomac palisades. They spoke of politics, then the event at hand. Kennedy, in his usual analytic style, reckoned that Nina should have married his brother Teddy.[6] But she had chosen Steers. (Seventeen years later, when marrying a second time, she would again avoid the Kennedy clan and elect Straight.)

Soon after the wedding, Straight prepared to take off with Rose for England for the less pleasant task of sorting out the legal tangles into which his family had stumbled. Whitney was engaged in the costly withdrawal from the family trust now that all its "operational losses" had been sold. The problems had multiplied since their half-sister, Ruth, had—with her husband Maurice Ash—complained about the failure of the trust to generate more income for them.

Aware that a wedge had been driven between Whitney and matriarch Dorothy since the confrontation at Dartington in 1951, Straight had written to Whitney in an attempt to clear up misconceptions. Dorothy had remained distant and cool to Whitney, who had advanced his already successful business career by becoming a director of the prestigious Rolls Royce company. Yet Whitney held firm in his quest to rid himself of financial links to a family he no longer trusted.

Ruth and Maurice proved less tricky when Rose and Straight learned that Maurice was behind the fresh attempt to leave the trust. He wanted Ruth's "share" of the Trust 11 capital to invest in a vineyard in France. Rose told him it was not suitable for the trust to indulge in because it was a foreign investment. He and Ruth were easily dissuaded. Rose was able to head off their implied threat to follow Whitney out of the trust.[7]

Straight spent the next eighteen months researching *Carrington* in and around Wyoming and Nebraska in extraordinary detail, all the time gathering the sort of material that would please Barkovsky.

The cover story was set mainly at Fort Phil Kearney. He traversed the country, sometimes on foot, notating and photographing the area with the diligence of a map surveyor. Straight described his approach in a 1970 television interview with John Milton, the then-professor of English at the University of South Dakota, an expert on the American West:

> I kept going back [to the fort], at all seasons, so that I could see and feel just how it had been when Carrington and his garrison were there. So I stayed there when it was very hot, in thunderstorms, and by moonlight. I made a great many notes, and I took many colored slides, and studied them later on, as I described each scene.[8]

Straight later related how he visited Kearney, Nebraska:

> [It] was the settlement where the Battalion wintered before it set off for Laramie. And, from Kearney, I tried to retrace its journey, mile by mile. It meant leaving the road at times, and driving along dirt trails. Later on, it meant riding up to Cloud Peak . . . and rolling down ravines where the troops had fun, under Indian fire. I spent one day scrambling around the sage bush and gullies near the Crazy Woman's Crossing of the Powder River . . .[9]

The timing of this 1970 interview with Milton is relevant. By then, Straight had already been interrogated for six years by British and American intelligence services. The CIA was particularly fascinated by his 1956–1962 roaming in the West. They were far from convinced by his novel researching explanation. The 1970 interview was opportune. He could use it to air his impressive literary mien and lay out the elaborate background to his very literary Western.

Milton seemed puzzled by this excessive research. If "mile by mile" is taken literally, Straight covered up to 350 miles from Kearney, in the middle of the southern region of Nebraska, to Laramie, inside Wyoming's southeast border. Each step of the way, he took notes and photographs, in what may have been the best backgrounded Western ever written. The professor was further perplexed by why an Eastern liberal would bother to write a novel about the Wild West. Straight skipped over that, saying that the ruins of the frontier fort near where he had vacationed in 1956 took hold of him. Milton was further furrow-browed about his approach. *Carrington* was a novel, but Straight approached it more like an historian. The historical novel was a hybrid, Straight explained. The writer started off as an historian "and then pushes on, by himself, while the historian stands watching him and shaking his head."

Milton began to pursue Straight on his approach to factual material. He responded by explaining how he covered everything from an ancient manuscript written by Colonel Carrington's first wife to the Old War Records Branch of the National Archives in Washington. He studied photographs at his former workplace, the Department of the Interior, where he had once pilfered files for his KGB control. In the end, he amassed "more material about the fort than anyone else had put together."[10] Once he had the detail, he took off his historian's hat. Straight said:

> For me, the important truths lay beyond verification, in the realms of human motivation. . . . Aristotle said that the historians tend to the particular, and poets to the universal. I was after the universal, seeking to reach it through some grasp of the minds and feelings of the men who played the leading roles in the story. For I sensed . . . the story was contemporary and relevant. I did not want to reconstruct the past. I wanted to interpret the present.[11]

This further confused Milton. By all means, research, but instead of behaving like an historian, why not perform like a novelist from the beginning?

Straight went on with his sophisticated explanation. It would be a useful public outpouring that he hoped would explain satisfactorily his heavy leg work day and night. But this daring attempt to scramble his tracks backfired. The CIA didn't buy it. Yet unless they could prove that he passed on the data to the KGB, they couldn't charge him with anything. And as Straight was very careful about what, when, and where he conveyed things to the KGB, it was unlikely that anything would be uncovered.

———

While Straight was wandering remote areas of the West with his trusty Leica, occasionally ducking bullets from hunters, Michael Young was publishing his book, *The Rise of the Meritocracy*, a satirical, sociological appraisal of a futuristic British society run by an IQ-justified hierarchy.

Young's tongue-in-cheek account made use of his pent-up communist sympathies, nurtured in the 1930s at Dartington and the London School of Economics. Those sympathies had been released through his membership in the Communist Party and endeavors to develop progressive institutions in consumerism and education. The final, almost science-fiction, section predicted a 2034 revolution against the new elite by the "poor, bloody-minded and unintellectual."[12]

Young wrote:

> The movement of protest had deep roots in our history . . . opposition even to the greatest institutions of modern society is inevitable. The hostility [in 2034] has long been latent. For more than half a century [since, not coincidentally, 1984], the lower classes have been harboring resentments which they could not articulate, until the present day. . . .
>
> May 2034 will be at best an 1848 [the revolution in Germany, which Marx observed was a precursor to bigger things in industrialized societies], on the English model at that. There will be stir enough. The universities may shake. There will be other disturbances later on as long as the Populists survive. But on this occasion anything more serious than a few days' strike and week's disturbance, which it will be well within the capacity of the police [with their new weapons] to quell, I do not for one moment envisage.[13]

The cataclysmic upheaval in Britain that Young had hoped for fervently as a student had been reduced twenty years later to creative yet unconvincing science-fiction. This last part of the book was taken less seriously than the rest by all critics, while the treatise as a whole made Young's reputation as a sociological thinker.

————————

While *The Rise of Meritocracy* was being received by a wide range of criticism (mainly positive) that created much discussion in the United Kingdom, Straight, in early 1959, was finishing a draft of *Carrington* with the help of editors at Alfred A. Knopf. The publisher had decided to publish the book despite the inconsistent standard of the writing. Knopf disliked Straight's philosophizing.[14]

Carrington's reviews in early 1960 were generally good and seemed to endorse Knopf's assessment of Straight's potential to become a successful novelist. The *Chicago Star* and *Newsweek* called it "an American Classic." The *Chicago Daily News* said it was "a virtuoso performance, vivid, brilliant, overwhelming and profoundly moving," while *The New York Times* saw it as "a deeply moving tale . . . spare, poetic, and thrillingly timed."

Such praise would normally have been a motivation to go on. But Straight would have no reason, beyond a curiosity or perhaps a vanity, to proceed. His excuse for not capitalizing on this impressive start was that he didn't see himself as a novelist, charting a course over a lifetime. *Carrington* had been a metaphor for his *New Republic* years when he wished he had been doing something else. His book writing interlude was similar and transient. Again, the two demons that had torn him when he wanted to run for politics in 1946 were still there. One part of him craved the public fame and the glory of the successful writer, while his main occupation of spying restricted him as before.

Straight decided to go on with a second book, but without the true creative writer's desire, and without strong support from his publisher. The project would again be a cover for spying, the most dangerous and daring assignment he had yet undertaken.

Early in President Kennedy's administration, the United States decided that there could not be any sanctuary from the hydrogen bomb that the Russians had now developed. Kennedy sanctioned the building of a massive blast- and shock-protected military headquarters well below Cheyenne Mountain in Colorado. It was to be the biggest such installation ever built. It would house the US-Canadian North American Air Defense Command (NORAD). Part of its operation would be to warn (later by satellite) allies, particularly the United Kingdom, of a nuclear missile attack by the Russians.

When Vladimir Barkovsky was informed by his Pentagon agents of this development, he wasted no time in dispatching Straight to map and photograph the entire area where the military site was to be located. It would now have to be top priority for disabling and destroying in the event of a nuclear encounter.

22

THREATS FROM THE PAST

Straight's new assignment meant he had to find some historical base for a second novel so that he could repeat his cover. It had to be set in Colorado's mountains somewhere in the vicinity of the proposed mighty military bunker. It took him no time at all to settle on another massacre story that occurred in 1864 at Sand Creek, some 15 miles south of Cheyenne Mountain. Sand Creek was about 10 miles north of the town of Chivington on State Highway 90.

While his mission was more specific, the story was much harder to create. He decided to base it not on Chivington, a fanatical army colonel who massacred the American Indians, but a friendlier, warmer character discovered by Agnes Wright Spring, the head of the Colorado State Historical Society. She researched the files surrounding the massacre and came up with a manuscript written by Ned Wynkoop, a young follower of Chivington's who once fought, then sided with the Indians. Wynkoop felt betrayed by Chivington when the Indians were slaughtered. This was more like the image Straight wished to explore.

Wynkoop then was the good guy Straight could build something around. He had his manuscript, which would be more than useful. He rented a car and drove south to Colorado Springs to see another author who was writing a book about Wynkoop's wife and her two sisters. Then it was on to Sand Creek, where Chivington had led the massacre of defenseless Indians. Straight took out his camera and notebook. He had his route to book two, titled *A Very Small Remnant*. This title was in reference, Straight claimed, to the minority who have been willing to die for their beliefs. They had saved what was "best" in their society by resisting the abuse of authority. Straight no doubt had in mind liberals like himself and, for instance, fighters for civil rights.

Thus he began his second big mission for Barkovsky in gathering detail about the area in which the military bunker would be built. It meant that when it was constructed in the early 1960s, the KGB had all the intelligence it wanted concerning the area. Should there be a nuclear encounter, the Soviet military had plans to destroy the bunker and its surrounds.

Soon after finding his way to make the cover story work, he had a flirtation with *Carrington*'s being made into a film. An agent from Famous Artists Incorporated met Straight and in the time-honored tradition of Hollywood told him how to make it more marketable for the movies. Straight wasn't impressed. Then his publisher urged him to write a contemporary fiction.

Knopf was mystified by Straight's need to set another book in a particular, remote point on the map in the West and then make it viable by finding a historical story to work around it. The publisher saw the author's capacity at handling characterization as something that could be worked up into a real skill. Knopf felt it was squandered by a writer with no real background in the West, who did not have a natural feel for its rhythms. Straight had huge sensitivity to the major issues of the day and the hub of world political power in Washington. Why wouldn't he focus on the contemporary, the publishers wished to know. It would be more salable to a big reading public, rather than competing in a saturated market dominated by Western writers since the war.

Straight didn't think he could attempt to do it. What he didn't say was that he wouldn't ever bother. In effect, his front for espionage operations had worked too well. But that was better than not being convincing at all.

A perfect opportunity for a great novel of the time may have been presented by the 1960 election battle between Richard Nixon and Jack

Kennedy. Straight knew the characters well from his socializing and connections in the capital, particularly Kennedy and his wife Jackie. Straight was a year older than Kennedy and three years younger than Nixon. These other two had run for the Eightieth Congress in January 1947, at the time Straight's bid was thwarted. In effect, the two candidates were where Straight would love to have been in 1960, and where he may have been but for being educated in England and not the United States in the 1930s. If passion counted in creating characters, he had plenty of it for these two. He had an intense dislike for them both. Nixon represented all that a concerned liberal would be expected to detest. His political opportunism, right-wing views, not to mention his five-o'clock shadow, made him a target nearly as superb as Joseph McCarthy.

Kennedy was different. He was a liberal Democrat from a rich, privileged, and educated background similar to that of Straight. Perhaps this was the source of antagonism. He would have been envious of Kennedy, having measured himself against him on the occasions they met, such as at the Steers/Auchincloss wedding. Yet in 1960, they were worlds apart. Straight, by ignoring his publisher, was doing everything to ensure that he would become at best a minor novelist, and in a field unrelated to his career expertise in big-time politics. Kennedy, at the same time, was wearing the liberal banner and leading the faithful in the actual thrust of political battle.

Straight kept his antipathy to Kennedy to himself while happily sniping at Nixon.

The new year, 1961, began with a renewed hope for world peace with a young, handsome couple in the White House. Yet Kennedy's pronouncements during the election, and his actions in the Oval Office, were at least as precipitate in the Cold War as those of his predecessor.

———— ◼ ◼ ————

Straight kept abreast of major issues despite his seclusion from Washington, D.C., while he labored over his second novel. For instance, he kept in contact with Leo Szilard, who informed him on developments in nuclear weapons. This way he could keep his reports to the KGB up-to-date.

———— ◼ ◼ ————

Contacts like Szilard were a minor distraction—perhaps a dip into the hard, practical issues that he no doubt missed tackling at *The New Republic*. Yet they did not take him far from the new novel. It was his priority as he spent a 1961 summer break at a holiday home at Chilmark on the island of Martha's Vineyard, Massachusetts, across Nantucket Sound from the Kennedy compound at Hyannisport. He was there with some of his five children, including 3-year-old Dorothy, who had been born in 1958. It seemed he couldn't hide from the public fascination with the new president and his glamorous wife Jackie, as rumors circulated at Martha's Vineyard suggested that they were going to use the hill on Straight's property for a heliport.[1]

Straight completed *A Very Small Remnant* in the summer of 1962 and felt drained by it, despite it being a novella at just 158 pages. It was such a struggle to fabricate the book around the area near Cheyenne Mountain that he was exhausted. In the autumn he began a short, chaste relationship with "Rachel" while his marriage to Bin deteriorated.[2] If he had been serious about writing, and using his personal experiences, he could have really tested himself with reflections on this episode. But the inclination and need for a cover of book-size dimensions was not there anymore. His third novel, aptly named *Happy and Hopeless*, could also have been called *Woeful and Empty*.

In the story, the main male character explains that he has been faithful to his wife, which was always going to limit the dramatic possibilities. He did not want to hurt her as he had hurt a previous partner, who was "dark like a gypsy," which was Straight's description of Margaret Barr, the dancer at Dartington.

The story drew much from Straight's own life, but didn't have the force, drive, or shape of his first two novels. There was none of the previous verve or desire for writing it. Hence its lackluster feel, despite the usual accomplished dialogue. His only apparent motivation was to record, even in veiled fictional terms, something hidden within him, or a turning point in his life.

Happy and Hopeless was described on the book cover as "the joyous encounter of a failed playwright and an army officer's wife, both needing to love and be loved, both bound by forces they only dimly understand."

The setting was Washington in the Kennedy years. The subject was what Freud called "the concurrent or opposing action of the two primal instincts—Eros and the death-instinct."

The main character, the playwright Julian, turns up at a parents' night at his children's school to deliver a clever address—"In Praise of Defeat." He meets another parent, Catherine Carter, wife of an army colonel. They become friends; they carry on like a couple destined to become lovers. But love is unrequited. Julian is torn by a tragic secret that he can't relate to Catherine or anyone—and certainly not to the reader. No doubt Straight here was dwelling on his agency for the KGB.

Was "Catherine" inspired by Jackie Kennedy? There were some clear similarities between them. Their children were at the same school and were friends. Julian and Catherine bumped into each other picking them up, as did Straight and Jackie. "Catherine" was an art buff living in the capital and married to a colonel, who was not unlike the president, who was the commander-in-chief of the armed forces. The Straight-Jackie relationship (similar to the Julian-Catherine nonaffair) was platonic, according to her stepsister Nina, although there was a strong mutual attraction. The two couples—the real and the fictional—vacationed in the same place.

Just as Julian was seeing Catherine in and around Washington, D.C., Straight was seeing a lot of Jackie in and out of the White House. Most likely, the fictional "Catherine" was an amalgam of Jackie and "Rachel"— the recent nonsexual dalliance in his life.[3]

Straight arranged for a portrait of President James Monroe to be "loaned" to the White House, which Jackie redecorated. Both the Kennedys liked it and appreciated the gesture. Jackie had it reframed and placed it with six other presidential portraits in the Blue Room of the White House.

Straight was after a job in the Kennedy administration, almost with the same intensity he showed when he rushed to get back into the Roosevelt administration to monitor Krivitsky. This "gift" would have helped his new quest enormously. His mother-in-law had engineered the efforts of a close friend of hers, Senator Paul Douglas, to seek a job for Straight in the arts in government. Jackie also would have been most helpful. She liked Straight, knew of his aesthetic interests, and would have had a great deal of influence over the president concerning the appointment.[4]

This close proximity to the U.S. president at a critical juncture in history must have been a tantalizing prospect for the Kremlin. Straight had the First Lady's ear. He mixed in the right circles. It didn't matter that he was not quite on the president's A-list of friends, acquaintances, and advisers. He knew a lot and had endless contacts. His secret KGB links also made him, at the very least, a contentious figure with such easy access to the center of power in the United States.

And at this point he wanted to get closer, in a very similar way to his rush to rejoin the State Department to help the KGB track and liquidate Walter Krivitsky. Senator Douglas, unaware of Straight's espionage activity, went to the White House three times on Straight's behalf in 1963. This was a most persistent effort on behalf of someone who alleged he didn't know was interceding for him. While waiting to see if he would get in, Straight drifted into 1963.

———— • ————

Kim Philby had had enough of British intelligence interrogations by early 1963. His latest inquisitor, MI6's Nicholas Elliott, had returned to London from Beirut, where Philby was working as a journalist, on January 17 with Philby's "confession." This was nothing more than a false declaration about when he finished working for the KGB (he said 1945 when he was still an operative) and names of fellow spies and double agents, who were later found to be innocent. Yet it was the end of a long road of questioning by MI5, MI6, and even his masters in Moscow, who early in his career had been uncertain if he were a British intelligence plant. Philby was drained from it all and in the throes of a breakdown. It was time to run, so on January 23, he fled to Moscow. The news was greeted with some relief at MI5 and MI6 headquarters.

The damage control from the huge publicity to follow would be easier to handle than if he had decided to return to London to confess and face more questioning. Yet it still left other members of the ring, such as Blunt, the Rothschilds, Cairncross, Long, Straight, and others, extremely vulnerable.

23

FIRST IN . . .

The defector, Anatoli Golitsyn, had led U.S. intelligence a merry dance in the fifteen months since he had left the KGB and fled west in late December 1961. Some believed his tale that Soviet intelligence was on a vast mission of disinformation with agents and other defectors. Others did not. By March 1963, it was time for him to be debriefed by British intelligence, which was in turmoil after Kim Philby's defection to Russia two months earlier. Some MI5 officers were in a vengeful mood after nearly two decades of failed operations against the KGB, which they attributed to moles inside their organization. Golitsyn played to their fears and helped precipitate a witch-hunt. He did, however, provide some leads, which in view of Philby's departure, seemed to MI5 investigators to be credible.

Golitsyn spoke of a Cambridge ring of five KGB agents. Three—Philby, Burgess, and Maclean—were known. Anthony Blunt was, to MI5 agents Peter Wright and Arthur Martin, "almost certainly" the Fourth Man.[1] He had been suspected since 1951, when Burgess and Maclean defected. But due to his connections inside intelligence, government, and most important Buckingham Palace, Blunt had not been interrogated with any intent or ferocity. His proximity to the reigning monarch, it was understood inside intelligence, afforded him special consideration. He had been questioned, and had managed to field queries with ease, even at times disdain. Yet the combination of the Philby defection and Golitsyn's information had put the focus on Blunt. He was feeling the pressure.

Another relevant factor was the condition of Burgess in Moscow. A recent visitor to his hospital bedside was his old Cambridge friend, Whitney Straight, in Russia on business for Rolls Royce. Whitney had reported back to MI6 and people who knew Burgess that he was very ill and did not have long to live. This put Blunt's long-term resistance to British intelligence probes in a different perspective. He had held off admitting any connection to the KGB in the hope that Burgess, his close friend and former lover, would one day return to the United Kingdom. Now that that was an impossibility, Blunt felt no further urge to be loyal. In the hope of ending the pressure on him, he was prepared to give a "selective" confession. This, in effect, would be misleading and send British intelligence on false trails for more than twenty years.

Always implicit in dealing with Blunt was his protection because of his links to the royal family. Blunt had been a trouble-shooter for Queen Elizabeth when the Duke of Edinburgh almost became embroiled in the Profumo Affair, a sex and spy scandal. This involved society osteopath Stephen Ward, who introduced an 18-year-old showgirl, Christine Keeler, to both British minister for war John Profumo and Soviet GRU officer Eugene Ivanov. Ward was an artist who sketched prominent society figures and the aristocracy. The Duke of Edinburgh had sat for him. The resultant drawings were put on show in a Mayfair gallery. Michael Adeane, the queen's private secretary, asked Blunt to purchase all the portraits. Blunt did the job on the first day of the exhibition, thus saving the royals great embarrassment.

The Queen was further beholden to him because of his judicious purchase for her and other members of the family fine artworks by classic and modern artists. His guidance had increased the wealth of individual royals and the institution. Blunt had made the royal collection more accessible to the public in the 1950s, thus helping in a small way to increase the popularity of the monarchy. He was also one of the queen mother's favorites, especially as he was always available for parlor games, such as charades, after dinner at Buckingham Palace. Blunt, it was said, played a superb elephant.

Intertwined with these special factors was the most important reason for Blunt's protection: his special assignments for George VI, during

1945 to 1947, when he stole and recovered documents showing the Duke of Windsor (the former King Edward VIII) and his wife Wallis Simpson had collaborated with Hitler and the Nazis. This mission saved the House of Windsor from ignominy and possible dissolution. In 1963, revelations of the traitorous activity of Edward and Mrs. Simpson would still be a threat to the Windsors.

Straight visited Dartington in April 1963—his third trip inside a year—in which he met up with Michael Young and others. While in London, he stayed at 42 Upper Brook Street. It was a short walk from Blunt's flat in Portman Square.

The odds are that these two now mature intriguers would have met, using their long-time skills at avoiding the watchers from MI5. The topic of Golitsyn, which was presently hot within British intelligence circles, would have been discussed. Perhaps this was the time when they decided—at the next propitious moment—to make a deceptive confession.

Straight believed that Golitsyn had something on him and Blunt. It was highly likely that this caused both spies to consider jumping in first before any Golitsyn revelations were put in front of them. If so, Straight and Blunt would be in damage control and able to manage any accusations.

Regardless of how they reacted to Golitsyn, the game was almost up for several members of the Cambridge ring in this momentous, watershed year. It was a matter of who jumped into the open first and why. Members of the ring, even before exposure within intelligence, would already be thinking about disinformation.

The family in the United Kingdom was fearful about Richard Nixon having joined Milton Rose's New York law firm, which had looked after the family business and trusts for thirty years. For more than a decade, Nixon had been billed by liberals and communists as a dangerous right-winger.

But Straight shocked the family. He did not express anger or disappointment. He was not worried about Nixon. Straight expected Nixon to go back to politics and that his foray into law—his original profession—

would be short-lived, especially with the 1964 presidential elections a little more than a year away.[2]

———

Arthur Schlesinger Jr., President Kennedy's special assistant, and August Hecksher, his consultant to the arts, asked Straight if he would like to be chairman of the Fine Arts commission. He made some unconvincing noises about starting his third novel. His second, *A Very Small Remnant*, which was published at this time (May 1963), had received good reviews, he told Hecksher, which was true. The *London Times Literary Supplement* said it "recalls [Herman] Melville, and Mr. Straight can stand the comparison." *Time* wrote that the story "has the ring of truth, both artistic and actual." Straight claimed that he was encouraged to try again, so he rejected the White House offer.

However, he had no intention of going on with a career as a novelist (apart from a future work, which he saw as therapeutic), despite publisher Knopf's encouraging words. The writing cover had served its purpose. The espionage activity had given him a chance to explore if he had any real skills as an author. The challenge and the cover were over—for the moment.

———

Early in June 1963, Kennedy created the Advisory Council on the Arts, which consisted of a chairman, the heads of several federal agencies, and thirty private citizens. Straight was one of the thirty whom Kennedy had himself selected after consulting Jackie. Next to his name in red pencil was the word "Collector" and a presidential tick. Straight was happy with this appointment;[3] it required little time and effort. Then came the next creation, the body that would actually administer the new agency, the National Endowment for the Arts. Straight was offered the chairmanship of this and the advisory council by Bill Walton, the new chairman of the Arts Commission. He had once worked as head of the Washington office of *The New Republic* and knew Straight well.

Walton told him he was the right person for the job. He was a "damned good" novelist, respected in the arts community and with many friends in congress. He predicted that he and Kennedy would get along well because of their similar backgrounds. Straight asked Walton what Kennedy thought about the appointment. He was all for it.

Straight was attracted to the position. The chairman would have the final say on who would get what in the way of federal government arts funding. There would be some power associated with it. He would have influence with a wide range of groups, from the trustees of the Metropolitan Opera to black militants, and, as Straight characterized it, from egomaniac conductors to unintelligible poets.[4] The chairman would have to know how to handle congress and the press to slip through his choices for funding. Straight was tempted by the opportunities that such a position would afford. He could hand money to anyone he wished, including groups that fitted his own philosophy and ideology.

Straight was given a night to think it over. He met Walton the next day and went through the job specification in more detail. Straight asked how long he had to finally consider the offer. Walton said no longer than a few days.

Walton told him that the president was ready to commence the position right away. There were only two provisos. He had to be cleared through congress, then the FBI had to run a check on him.[5]

Straight showed no reaction. Then he went home and thought about those FBI checks. He was confident they had nothing on him, but he could not be sure what Golitsyn had on him. He guessed he would be exposed in some way, and there was no point now in trying to get another job in government for whatever new assignment the KGB may have had for him. He could now use the handy excuse that he could not face the media coverage if his appointment led to someone like Eliot Janeway in 1946 again stepping forward and accusing him of communist connections.[6]

The sudden rush to join the government—twenty-two years after his hasty rejoining of State in 1940 for the Krivitsky assignment—had to be aborted. Straight now had to cut his losses and back off. The prospect of FBI checks offered a useful, if not risky, excuse to withdraw with limited damage in the face of possibly problematic revelations from Golitsyn.

Straight rang Walton and told him he couldn't accept the chairmanship, using the excuse that there was too much explaining to do about Louis Dolivet and Gustavo Duran, all the family ghosts, and his own past as a radical. Walton remarked that Kennedy knew they had all been radicals. Straight replied that he was from another age. It was difficult to explain one age to another.[7]

Walton informed the president that Straight had turned down the chairmanship. Kennedy was skeptical.

"Why?" the president asked.

"I don't know," Walton replied. "There's something in his background. . . ."

"What?" Kennedy said. "Is he a queer?"[8]

The matter could have ended there. Straight had every right to reject the offer and walk away without explanation. But he stunned intelligence agencies by insisting on making a statement to the FBI. Newton "Scotty" Miler, a CIA agent involved in debriefing Golitsyn, said: "We were all taken by surprise and totally unprepared. The FBI had nothing on him."

Straight first went to see presidential assistant Arthur M. Schlesinger Jr. in the East Wing of the White House and alleged that he told him his complete story. (This was not accurate. Schlesinger did not ask any questions. It took the FBI and MI5 the next twelve years to extract information from him. Neither organization considered that it had the complete, accurate narrative.) Schlesinger phoned the attorney general, Robert Kennedy, and he directed Straight to the deputy director of the FBI, William Sullivan, on Connecticut Avenue.

Sullivan was polite. He told him that there was a young agent on his staff who knew him. Sullivan thought Straight might prefer to give his statement to him. A lean man came into the room and shook hands with him.[9] It was Jimmy Lee, the second son of his mother's head gardener at Old Westbury.

Straight said that any pride left in him was stripped away because Sullivan had acted out of kindness. Straight noted that his humiliation was complete. Yet despite being so humbled, it was an easy introduction to the FBI and its methods of interrogation. During his statement to Lee and a stenographer, they chatted about their families. Later, feeling relieved of a burden, he went to a movie at the MacArthur Theater. He was shocked to be greeted by the stenographer in the kiosk, who had a second job issuing tickets.

Straight spent many hours in the next few days with Sullivan. It led to nothing more than a number of searching questions about the appeal of communism for the intellectuals of Europe. Sullivan told him stories about his early days in the FBI hunting killers like John Dillinger.

Through June, over fifty or so hours, the FBI began its methodical, efficient, and nonthreatening interrogation with pairs of agents—"impersonal and interchangeable"—who would ask "unexpected" questions. It caused Straight no anxious moments. His inquisitors, with their trim haircuts, well-shined shoes, and drip-dry shirts, were out of their depth. They were intent on checking the addresses in which he lived and were reassured when his information could be verified.

Straight found them easy to deal with. Much of his "confession" was incomprehensible to the FBI agents, who had Dickensian views of old England, if anything at all. The only Cambridge they knew was in Massachusetts.

Straight's training for such occasions would make sure that any vaguely tangible clues were few and far between (as he would later do in his memoirs, which were devoid of chronology or form). The agents showed him pages of photos of heavy-set, scowling, Slavic faces. One he did admit to knowing was Michael Green, his control.[10] Yet this too was a safe revelation. Green would have been gone from the United States nearly two decades.

Straight described Green's wife then innocently asked about her and what had become of them. The FBI agents didn't know who she was at that point, and Straight was told they had returned to Moscow.

He began to use his charm. He could measure how much they knew and how he could respond without giving anything of substance away. The FBI agents were suspicious, partly because of their ignorance, and partly because they were suspicious by nature. There had to be something more than the loose threads that Straight was presenting to them. The agents continued to phone him over the next four years (until 1968). But the connection was not threatening. In time, the debriefing was controlled by one man, whom Straight knew as Agent Taylor. It was easy, even cozy, and pressure free. He was an "old-timer" who wanted his weekends free for golf. He was preparing for retirement. Straight claimed that they trusted each other and even became friends.[11]

The decision to take the initiative and "confess" was fortuitous. He had the upper hand. If he had waited until any Golitsyn evidence had borne fruit or for a confession from Blunt, and the FBI had knocked on his door first, Straight would have had a lot tougher time.

He spent the summer of 1963 at Chilmark attempting to settle into his third novel after his FBI statement and questioning. The writing had no motivating force. He had to show something in the first two. If he had not, they might have been seen for what they were, just fronts for his espionage work. But now his authorship was purely indulgent. He didn't need to put his heart into it, and it was going nowhere special. It certainly wasn't substantial enough to ever be published other than by himself.

Straight was also preoccupied with the intelligence probes, which led to some anxiety. Yet he had learned to live with this emotion.[12] A major concern was Golitsyn's return to the United States in August for continued debriefing under the control of James Angleton, the CIA's head of counterintelligence. The Russian had been successful in gaining a look at British files from March to July 1963 in order to make judgments on moles and double agents. Now he was demanding the same treatment in the United States.

Despite the terrors that haunted him in the summer of 1963, Straight managed to enjoy the good life at Chilmark with sailing, the occasional party, time with the children, and plenty of visitors. His spirits seemed lifted by the visit of his half-brother, William, from Dartington, who idolized him. There also would have been a measure of relief to learn at this time from his brother Whitney that Guy Burgess was dying in Moscow.[13]

Whitney also reported to MI6. It was leaked in Fleet Street in the summer that Burgess would soon be dead. On August 30, 1963, Burgess finally succumbed to the ravages of alcoholic poisoning—virtually a slow act of suicide over the twelve years since his defection. The man who had devised the emotional blackmail to help ensnare Straight in the KGB web was no more.

Milton Rose arranged a meeting between Straight and Nixon when he was appointed head of Rose's firm, Mudge, Stern, Baldwin and Todd, which became Nixon, Mudge, Rose, Guthrie, and Alexander. Nixon's move from California to New York meant he was leaving his political power base and moving into Nelson Rockefeller's Republican stronghold, thus ruling himself out of a bid for the 1964 presidential election. But as Straight predicted, Nixon was never going to be as interested in the law as he was in politics.

Rose took Straight and Nixon to lunch for that first meeting at the India House restaurant. They walked down Broad Street in New York's banking and financial district. Straight told William Elmhirst, who, like Dorothy, was still distressed about Nixon, that bankers who passed them acknowledged him (Nixon) and welcomed him to Wall Street. Waiters in the restaurant were also most deferential. It set the scene for an uncomfortable meal.[14]

Nixon, awkward on social occasions at the best of times, was ill at ease. But he was a pragmatist; he could play the accomplished diplomat and turn on his own brand of charm when necessary. Now, as head of the law firm, he had to be diplomatic. Straight was one of the firm's most important clients, having represented his family since 1926.

That constraining factor apart, Nixon enjoyed, perhaps in a challenging way with someone like Straight, engaging and pinning down "the enemy." Nixon was proud of his native intellect. If he felt inferior about his social status or background, he fell back on his sharp, well-read political mind. His knowledge of the grand art of international relations on one level, and parochial gutter politics on another, was unmatched in American history. Straight, too, had few peers in the United States in both his comprehension of international events and his experience in the back-alleys of political intrigue.

Straight was nervous because of all the harsh attacks he had made on him, but he felt Nixon was even more on edge. Nixon babbled on for a while. After a short silence, Nixon took the opportunity to shift the conversation to politics by asking Straight what he thought of the political situation in England. It was a useful opening and loosened up Straight. He spoke about the Labour Party's historic contradictions and conflicts. Nixon nodded his agreement. He said that a Labour victory in the next general election would indicate a trend toward "neutralism" in England. This meant it would give up its development of nuclear weapons and its own deterrent to any attack by the Soviet Union.

Straight disagreed, putting another view on the issue by saying that if British Prime Minister Harold Wilson surrendered England's independent nuclear deterrent, it would lead to a greater dependence on the United States. England would need the United States to defend it from attacks. Nixon would have been more aware than most that the United States wished to use the United Kingdom as a huge floating aircraft carrier off the coast of continental Europe—a massive forward base for its nuclear arsenal. The concept of going neutral would mean that the United States would not be allowed to place its nuclear weapons on U.K. soil because England would not be a Soviet nuclear target.[15]

Straight's views were right in line with the Kremlin's. It wanted to stop the concentrated arming of Great Britain by the United States. Its scores of military bases the length and breadth of the tiny country was an attempt to confine any future conflict between the superpowers to Europe and away from the U.S. mainland.

Nixon was adamant. He wanted the British to have their own deterrent. He had always believed in showing as much strength as possible in dealing with the Russians. Great Britain's closer proximity to Russia meant more pressure on it.

Both knew that no matter what the international political rhetoric, Britain would always be militarily dependent on the United States. The conversation ended with Nixon surprising Straight by saying he wanted to see Dartington, a desire that stunned the family.

After all the railing against Nixon since he first emerged as an ambitious senator in the late 1940s, Straight contrived to get along well with him. He even proposed him as a member of India House, the lunch club founded by Willard.[16]

Soon after this encounter, Straight and Rose flew to London and visited Dartington from October 11–14, 1963. According to files at Dartington, it was Straight's second visit there since seeing the FBI, the other being a short trip in late June. In late October he and Rose took a plane to Greece for an unspecified meeting, which possibly concerned business for Rose with the shipping magnate, Stavros Niarchos.[17]

A melancholic Straight returned to Weynoke in early November 1963 with nothing to keep him occupied. He returned reluctantly to his uninspired and aimless novel writing as steady rain in Virginia drew a gray, dark autumn to a close.

While Straight was laboring with his story in his study on November 22, 1963, Lorraine, the laundress, came in sobbing. It was being reported on television that President Kennedy had been shot. Straight switched on the TV to see the reports from Dallas. Dorothy, his five-year-old daughter, who was home sick from school, began to cry. She was a school friend of Kennedy's daughter Caroline. Dorothy asked why it couldn't have been someone else. Straight, who said in his memoirs that he remained unemotional over the shocking incident, asked Dorothy whom she had in mind. Between sobs, she nominated Rockefeller and Khrushchev.[18]

In the days after the assassination, Straight was on the phone to the family in England, talking about the incident and how he felt about Kennedy. He told them of a party he had been to on November 17 in honor of the poised, vivacious Mary Meyer, who was a long-term friend of Straight's and had formerly been married to Cord Meyer.

Mary's family, the Pinchots, were wealthy and prominent. Mary's father, Amos Pinchot, was a lawyer and a close friend of President Teddy Roosevelt. Her uncle, Gifford, was a two-term governor of Pennsylvania. Mary, an accomplished painter, went to Vassar, the elite all-women college, where she first met Kennedy. Straight told the Elmhirsts that Mrs. Pinchot informed him that the president had come to the Pinchot home to declare it a national monument so that he could bed Mary and another woman.[19]

Mary's affair with Kennedy over the duration of his presidency has since been well documented. It is claimed that he found her more attractive than Jackie, both mentally and physically. Despite Kennedy's serial philandering, this was said to be the one relationship that upset Jackie. Straight told the Elmhirsts he was reminded of Kennedy's womanizing when he watched his funeral cortege. Straight viewed Jackie's sadness as the work of a very good actress getting on with a polished performance, the implication being that she had no love, only hate, for her philandering husband.[20]

Despite his antipathy toward Kennedy, Straight seemed unsettled when he reflected on the horrific events of November 22 in his memoirs. Straight noted that the assassination ended the year for him.[21]

24

BLUNT REVELATIONS

Arthur Martin of MI5 flew to Washington in January 1964 to interview John Cairncross about the Philby, Burgess, and Maclean defections. He was surprised to be introduced to Straight by the FBI's Sullivan at the Mayflower Hotel. The three chatted for twenty minutes and then Sullivan left.

Martin, regarded in the United Kingdom as self-made and earthy, was found by Straight to be "sophisticated and urbane" compared with the FBI agents with whom he had dealt. Straight told him the story he had given to the FBI. He considered Burgess to be Blunt's recruiter and controller at Cambridge. The plot to send him to J. P. Morgan (the New York banking/investment group) reflected Burgess's smart yet callous style.[1]

Martin asked for names of others recruited by Burgess and Blunt. Straight mentioned a deceased comrade. He also said he believed Leo Long, whom he had brought into the Apostles, may have joined the Cambridge network of spies. Martin was grateful, pointing out that this was the first "hard evidence" that MI5 had been able to obtain on Burgess and Blunt.

Martin had been one of MI5's interrogators who interviewed Blunt in the 1950s. He was convinced that he would deny everything, even when told about his talking to Straight.[2]

Martin asked Straight if he would be prepared to confront Blunt. Straight claimed he said he was prepared to do anything required—even go to court to tell his side of events.[3]

These brave words were a long way from Straight's refrain since 1948 that he was frightened to go public because of the humiliation to himself and his family. He had found the courage to step forward. For its part, MI5 would not dare bring prosecutions against Blunt thanks to his special protection. There would be no public airing of horrific sagas about KGB penetration of Cambridge, Oxford, the military, the foreign office, and the intelligence services. The Philby defection and Profumo scandal were enough for any government for at least a decade.

Yet at that moment, Martin and MI5 were excited. They seemed to have concrete leads at last. Martin hurried back to England, thrilled by his "coup." Three months later, on April 23, 1964, he visited Blunt at his apartment at the Courtauld Institute in Portman Square. Martin told him he had evidence he was a Soviet recruiter at Cambridge and a KGB spy until the end of the war. Blunt denied it. Martin then mentioned that Straight had told them about him. Blunt remained ice-cool. His behavior indicated he had foreknowledge of Straight's "evidence." He would have learned of the "confession" from his close friends Victor and Tess Rothschild. They would have heard it from Dick White and/or the garrulous Peter Wright.

Blunt stared at Martin and didn't respond.

Martin then hurried into offering him protection: "I've been authorized by the Attorney-General to give you a formal immunity from prosecution."[4]

Blunt got up from his living room chair, poured himself a large Scotch, and turned to Martin. "It is true," he said, without emotion.

The two men talked for a few minutes. Martin added a condition. The immunity deal stood if he had not been a spy recently. He would not be prosecuted if, as Straight had indicated, he had only been a spy until 1945, the end of World War II.

This was the standard line that all those accused would claim. They had worked for the Russians only during the war to ensure victory over the Nazis. How could anyone call them traitors for such activity? They had not spied against Great Britain and the United States, but rather for the Russians to help them overcome Hitler. Blunt, Cairncross, Long, Burgess, Maclean, and Straight had all maintained the same argument.

Rather than criminals and traitors, they considered themselves great patriots, worthy of acclaim.

Martin, relieved to have what he saw as a confession, accepted Blunt's assurance that he had not spied since 1945. At subsequent meetings, he was also pleased to see that responses and statements by Blunt and Straight were the same except for a few anomalies.

Blunt, the more "senior" KGB man, went further. He admitted recruiting Leo Long, which Straight claimed he suspected. Blunt also named John Cairncross. Straight had mentioned Alister Watson, without indicating directly that he was a spy. Blunt had added to suspicions about Watson. This tallied with Philby's "confession" in Beirut to British intelligence's Nicholas Elliott.

Thus three men pointed the finger at Watson. All research by others, and my own investigation, found Watson was innocent. He had been recruited and was at points in his career as a scientist in place in government employment deemed highly secret. But when the pressure was on, Watson could not deliver. He refused to pass on intelligence, much to the anger of his KGB controls and the contempt of fellow members of the ring—hence their willingness to cause him more angst by suggesting that he was a KGB spy.

Philby had also claimed that Blunt was not a spy. In the excitement of the early apparent breakthrough, Martin and his partner in the investigation, Peter Wright, grabbed at the correlations and ignored the anomalies.

The first seed of doubt came from Wright's initial encounter with Blunt. His tape-recorder broke down during a question-and-answer session. Wright knelt to thread a loose tape spool, which had jammed the recorder. Blunt remarked to Martin: "Isn't it fascinating to watch a technical expert do his stuff?"[5]

Wright looked up and glared. He had never met Blunt before. The comment showed Wright that Blunt knew who he was. Rothschild, according to KGB and British intelligence sources, was most likely the one who informed Blunt that he would be interrogated by Wright, a scientist from MI5's technical section. Rothschild had befriended Wright since 1958, going out of his way to make contact with him and—along with Tess—assist his work at MI5. Wright had divulged every secret he knew at MI5 to the Rothschilds.[6]

The ring members, from Blunt and the Rothschilds in the United Kingdom; to Cairncross in Italy; to Philby and their controller, Modin, in Moscow, were combining in a major deception to avoid detection of their widespread activities. They had all continued well into the Cold War.

When the months slipped by, MI5 began to wonder if Blunt was divulging all. They suspected he was covering up. Martin questioned Long and suggested he would not be prosecuted if he cooperated. With this virtual offer of immunity, he did admit to passing Blunt information during the war, but nothing more. He too denied spying for the Russians in the Cold War. Cairncross, who had been suspected and accused by British intelligence of being a KGB agent in 1951, made similar admissions when Martin visited him in Rome. Once more it was suggested he would not face prosecution if he confessed.

Further doubts began to seep into the investigators' minds. They had dead agents named by Blunt and Straight. The only new, living names were Long and Cairncross. The latter had been known, for all practical purposes, for thirteen years. Like Long, he admitted to little. The only person to verify how little was Blunt. It was a small haul after such promise was offered when Straight spoke up. The other concern that began to dawn on MI5's tenacious sleuths was the fact that even if they uncovered something sensational, the traitors could never be prosecuted. Wright was first to express the thought that no one could be charged because, for example, Long would call Blunt as a witness. This would lead to questions about why the Keeper of the Queen's Pictures had not been himself charged. Wright and Martin realized prosecution of any member of the Cambridge ring was an impossibility.

This frustrated them. They tried ways around the roadblock of immunity. First, they began a good cop, bad cop routine in interviews with Blunt. This was done in the hope of squeezing out more that could lead to disclosures of such significance that they could not be ignored. Martin appeared friendly and reasonable, while Wright became "nasty."[7] Yet MI5's director-general, Roger Hollis, warned against pressuring Blunt too much. He said he feared he might defect. This would be more embarrassment for British intelligence and the government. But Hollis, a true Whitehall bureaucrat, knew that Blunt had to be protected.

The point was driven home when Wright was summoned to attend a briefing at Buckingham Palace by Michael Adeane, the queen's private secretary. "He assured me that the Palace was willing to cooperate in any enquires the [intelligence] Service thought fit," Wright wrote in his book,

Spycatcher. "The Queen," he said, "has been fully informed about Sir Anthony, and is quite content for him to be dealt with in any way which gets at the truth." There was only one caveat. "From time to time," said Adeane, "you may find Blunt referring to an assignment he undertook on behalf of the Palace—a visit to Germany at the end of the war. Please do not pursue this matter. Strictly speaking, it is not relevant to considerations of national security."[8]

Restricted by this information and by directions from their superiors, Wright and Martin battled on. Blunt's flat was bugged. Recorded conversation made it clear he was aware of the bugging. They followed the leads provided by Blunt and Cairncross, which led to other "suspects." All were found to be inconsequential; some were investigated and cleared. Frustration and doubts grew about the veracity of what MI5 had been told from the beginning. They began to consider ways of putting more pressure on Blunt.

———— • ————

Straight tried selling *Happy and Hopeless*, his thinly veiled personal short novel about a sexless love affair. Publishers rejected it. Straight was not surprised.

It must have been a disappointment to Knopf. He would have been puzzled by Straight's lack of will to write after the considerable research and construction efforts by Straight and his editors put into the first two novels.

Straight tinkered with the structure but came to see it as a failure. Distractions such as a trip with Rose to London and Dartington in mid-May 1964, and thoughts of leaving Weynoke, his Virginia farm, took him away from his writing.

Straight returned to Virginia mid-year and thought about leaving, but not selling, Weynoke and moving to Georgetown. The Straights liked the look of Jackie Kennedy's N Street house, where she had lived since the assassination. She had purchased it for $175,000. The agents, J. F. Begg Inc. Realty Co., were responding to journalists' queries when they said it was worth "in the vicinity of $265,000" because of "improvements." The owner before Jackie (Jimmy Gibson) had originally asked $325,000 for the place. He had sold it to her for the much lower price of $175,000, perhaps, as suggested at the time, out of compassion. She could hardly have put it back on the market six months after moving in for twice the purchase figure. Hence the impression from the agent of the compromise price and the excuse of the modification costs.

It had been built in 1825 by Thomas Beall, son of Ninian Beall, and was of historic importance. At $265,000, and anything less, it was considered a bargain. Straight was well aware of Jackie's intention to leave Washington and avoid the stares of endless tourists wandering N Street with their cameras. No other buyers, it seemed, had a chance. Straight's discreet, close, personal relationship with Jackie meant that the home was his for the taking. Bin Straight flew down from Chilmark to Washington in early August to view the house, which she liked. Straight wondered if the Kennedy presence might haunt it and make it a somber place. He was uncertain about moving in. But he was looking at an opportunity he would find difficult to refuse.

In early September 1964, he received a request for a further meeting with Martin, this time in London. Straight, wishing to appear as the ever-willing informer, obliged by flying to London mid-September. Martin met him at the Elmhirst family apartment in Upper Brook Street. They walked the short distance to an MI5-owned house on South Audley Street. Martin offered him a drink and then told him how Blunt had "given up and confessed." He made it sound as if MI5 were satisfied with what had been divulged. But, Martin told him, there were just a few divergences in their two stories. He was almost apologetic about asking Straight if he would meet with Blunt. Would it be too painful for him, Martin inquired. Straight replied he would do whatever he was asked. That pleased Martin. He had already prepared Blunt for a meeting at his Portman Square flat. Martin asked Straight to get there fifteen minutes early so they could have a few words in private.[9]

Straight walked to his appointment on time, pressed the button to Blunt's flat, and then walked up the stairs. Blunt was at the entrance to his flat and Straight found him, as ever, thin and pale. But to Straight's surprise, he said, Blunt wasn't hostile.[10]

They were aware that the flat was bugged. Whatever they said to each other would be staged with that in mind. Blunt took him into the living room.

First, there was Straight's version, in which he claimed Blunt said to him: "I just wanted to tell you: thank God you did what you did!" He added: "I was sure that it all would become known sooner or later. I couldn't muster up the strength to go to the authorities myself. When they said that you had told them your story, it lifted a heavy burden from my shoulders. I was immensely relieved."

"I'm glad that you told me that," Straight claimed he replied. "I assumed that you would be bitter."

"I am curious about one thing," Straight claimed Blunt said. "Why did you act when you did?"

"Because of the arts," Straight allegedly replied. "Because our government finally decided to support the arts. Kennedy was going to make me head of his new arts agency. That forced me to face up to it at last."[11]

The MI5 technicians listening to this tape would have been baffled by Straight's version of events. Straight was suggesting that he had not been driven by loyalty or his oft-professed anticommunism. No sense of patriotism or an attempt to limit the huge damage done by the Cambridge ring during World War II, the Cold War, or Korea had driven him to confess. Not even late recognition of the iniquities of Stalin and Stalinism moved him. No, it was . . . the arts.

"The real question that has to be answered," Straight claimed that he said, "is, Why didn't I act long ago?"

"I see," Blunt was alleged to have said. "We always wondered how long it would be before you turned us in."

Straight's version fitted the line in his autobiography that portrayed him as a victim caught in a web of intrigue. He was forever the insect struggling to slip away from his past.

With the mysteries of how and why allegedly cleared up, Straight claimed the discussion drifted to art.

"We were talking about Dughet and Cezanne," Straight recalled, "when the doorbell rang and Arthur Martin walked in."[12]

The three men then talked for an hour. Straight said in his memoirs, published nineteen years later, in 1983, that he could recall little of the discussion. This seemed odd when recall of his version of the private chat with Blunt before Martin arrived was perfect. Nevertheless, he did claim to remember one thing. Blunt was concerned the story would become public. It would completely destroy him. By contrast Straight said he was prepared for it. In other words the reader of this account was meant to be left with the impression that Straight was the open character of the two. He was the strong one willing to face his past no matter what the consequences.

Straight's version of events seemed a contrivance too far. It suggests that he was the near-innocent party who never actually spied for the KGB. The line he attributed to Blunt—*We always wondered how long it would be before you turned us in*—makes it seem as if there is a big difference between Straight and the others—Blunt and Burgess. In other words, they were the espionage agents, when he wasn't, when in reality Straight's spying and agent of influence activity had been just as strong and over a longer period than the others.

What started as a collusion and an attempt to cover up Straight's work had backfired on Blunt. He had been painted more as the major spy than he wished, while Straight was portraying himself as an innocent.

In 1980, after being exposed as a spy, Blunt had a different version of the meeting. Yes, they did discuss art, but that was it. Straight avoided speaking of his FBI confession.

In 1983, Straight sent Blunt a copy of his autobiography inscribed, "Anthony from Michael 1983. Too bad—that we don't have more than one life to live." Blunt put a large "No!" in the margin next to the account of the 1964 meeting with a string of question marks and disclaimers concerning Straight's account. At the bottom of the page Blunt wrote: "We actually talked about a painting by Bellaye that he'd bought."

Arthur Martin thought that Blunt's account was more credible but judged the meeting a failure from MI5's point of view. "They must have had something in common when they were undergraduates," he said, "but that had gone by 1964."

A second meeting arranged by Peter Wright later took place at the MI5 safe house on South Audley Street. The FBI and MI5 doubted Straight's testimony concerning the last time he saw Michael Greenberg. Blunt was there to assist his attempt to recall "facts." Martin was absent; Wright or another MI5 agent was present.

Straight claimed that he last saw Greenberg accidentally (similar to the coincidences of him "bumping into" Burgess and Blunt in the postwar years) outside the White House in 1942. But the FBI had kept a surveillance on Greenberg. He visited Straight early in 1946 at the New York offices of *The New Republic*. Straight said he couldn't remember the visit but maintained Greenberg was probably looking for a job. The FBI version was that Greenberg was running around New York and Washington warning members of communist networks that they should destroy evidence, look out for wire taps, and watch for tails since Elizabeth Bentley had confessed. After this, the FBI (accurately) put Straight in the category of still active, or as an agent of influence. This meant that he was seen as a spy—a sleeper always ready to be reactivated.[13] After the safe house meetings in 1964, Straight said that Blunt was pleased that the matter had been resolved. Blunt disagreed with Straight's neat resolution. It ended like a traffic accident, with witnesses giving different versions of events. However, the result was the same for Blunt, who was injured in reputation beyond repair. Not long after this meeting, his twenty-year era as Keeper of the Queen's Pictures was terminated. According to former members of the royal household staff, the queen had been uncomfortable about Blunt for some time, even though she knighted him in 1957. Apart from his investiture, contact with her was avoided. Yet she had been obliged by her governments and intelligence services, and perhaps loyalty to her father's memory, to keep him on. The queen mother had been better disposed toward Blunt because of his secret missions for her husband, King George VI. Royal courtiers from 1948 to 1965 had whispered about Blunt and called him "our Russian spy."[14]

The interrogation of Straight didn't end in 1964. For the next eleven years he was summoned for more discussions. As the willing informer, he was obligated to attend. The MI5 investigators came in pairs and met him in his room at the Connaught, where he stayed in preference to the family flat. He kept his "confession" and questioning secret from all his family. Whitney would have been aware of it, but he too kept the secret.

MI5 reviewed his years with Blunt and his control Michael Green and delved back into the communist cells at Cambridge. British intelligence gave him photos to look at and lists of names of public servants, fellow students, and others. Straight assisted by dividing them into nonmembers of the party, student activists like him, hard-core members of the party, and so-called moles. Straight was asked to group moles into those who would take up "non-sensitive" professions, such as law, and those who would move into jobs in, for instance, government weapons research. From there, they would gain access to "sensitive" material.

MI5 followed up Straight's tidbits thrown out every so often over the years. Like the cumulative clues given by Philby, the Rothschilds, Blunt, Cairncross, Long, and others, they led nowhere. The ring's long and broad disinformation campaign was working well.

Straight was stunned in October 1964 to learn that his friend Mary Meyer, formerly President Kennedy's lover, had been murdered while on her daily stroll along the Canal towpath not far from her Georgetown studio. The allegation was that she had been raped by a black and then shot after she resisted. These were the bare facts, although the black charged with her murder, Raymond Crump, was later acquitted. According to witnesses, a black was seen in the area, but there were doubts over whether it was Crump. Mary Meyer was shot in a way reminiscent of a professional killing, with one bullet to the brain and another to the aorta. There were signs of a struggle. Over the years, conspiracy theories developed around the slaying. Stories circulated about her diaries. They were held by the CIA's James Angleton before Tony, Mary's sister, burnt them. The conspiracy theorists wondered if the diaries contained any clues to Kennedy's assassination. This, it was thought, would be a possible reason for Mary being on the long list of strange deaths that it was claimed were linked to the president's demise. But because Angleton had read the diaries, and Mary's brother-in-law Ben Bradlee, the *Washington Post* editor, had at least learned of their main contents from Tony, this seemed unlikely. Apart from that, there appeared no motive for her death other than rape. It was common in random attacks in the U.S. capital. Yet doubts lingered over the decades.

By early in 1965, Straight had decided to move into Jackie Kennedy's town house in Georgetown, despite his reservations about ghosts of the recent past. An article in the *Washington Evening Star* on February 18 quoted Pamela Turnure, Jackie's press secretary in New York, as saying that "the papers have not been signed as yet but that the Straights have indicated strong interest in buying it." Another source said the house was "considered sold" by real estate agent J. F. Begg Realty Co., who had handled the sale for the former First Lady since the summer of 1964. The "principals"—Jackie and Straight—had agreed verbally. The contracts were being drawn in New York. When pressed, the agents admitted that the settlement price was expected to be less than the $265,000 asking figure. The *Star* reporter, Daisy Cleland, claimed that Straight's intended purchase baffled many friends when they heard about the move from rural Virginia to the hubbub of Georgetown. Yet Straight, with his ascetic appreciation of history and architecture, did not have to be told of the value and prestige of such a move. The final settlement price was rumored to be $200,000 or less. Considering the original figure of $325,000 before Jackie moved in, Straight had secured an amazing deal, which was confirmation in itself of his claim of a strong relationship with the former First Lady. He planned to restore the house with new wiring and roof, knowing that even if he spent $100,000—a huge sum for renovations in the mid-1960s—he would still be well ahead financially.[15]

—•—

After the election of President Lyndon Johnson, Straight considered his work options. Again, as was the case with his decision to leave *The New Republic* in 1956, they were few. Now approaching a decade later, at age 48, he had no career to follow outside KGB espionage and his subtle anti–federal government activity, often using his own money to achieve goals.

Straight had found the novelist cover hard work. When the KGB called on him again, he would need something simpler and easier to use as a front for his spying. He let friends and contacts know he was toying with being a painter, but that could cause problems. He could hardly set up his easel at a hot trouble spot and pretend he was an artist while spying. Straight began talking up a yearning to write a play or an opera. He was waiting for the muse to strike, he told anyone who would listen. These two areas—especially the playwright angle—were clever covers and less difficult to pull off than being a novelist, with the need to follow through with published books.

—•—

The year 1965 rolled by with time taken up by overseas trips, including two to London and Dartington in April and October, where he responded to more MI5 queries. These meetings, which Straight did not attempt to avoid or discourage, allowed him to monitor where Wright and company were in their investigations.

In the United States Straight chaired the board of the American Dance Theatre and had his commitments at the Whitney Foundation. It swallowed more of his time as he presided over donations to a wide variety of groups. The Whitney Museum in 1965 received a three-year grant, about which Straight expressed ambivalence. He didn't like its art collection, which had concentrated on unappealing mainstream impressionism.

Straight maintained his usefulness to the KGB cause by putting an anti-American, pro-Soviet spin on major issues. Amnesty International, which was often anti–federal government, was an obvious vehicle for this. The Whitney Foundation kept the organization solvent and paid its debts. Straight organized the U.S. section of the group, which sought to inform public opinion about violations of human rights.

Amnesty International publicized government wrong-doing in newsletters, annual reports, and background papers. With its genuine altruistic and humanitarian aims, the organization provided a vehicle for Straight consistent with the strategies of political protest that he had involved himself in for more than thirty years. He noted that by the mid-1960s Amnesty International had taken over the role of American liberals after the failure of disarmament and other protest groups. Like Straight and the KGB, Western intelligence groups, such as the CIA and MI5, attempted to influence Amnesty International.

Straight did not find any fulfilling occupation in 1965 or 1966. This left him open to again taking up a KGB mission in 1967. Now 50 years of age, he was on his way to Malta. Three years earlier the withdrawal of British military and naval personnel from its famous Dockland created economic and political problems. Malta was governed by the Nationalist Party, which was aligned to the West. But the developing strength of the opposition Malta Labor Party, backed by the Chinese, was causing concern in the Kremlin. At a time of growing tension between the Soviets and the Chinese, the Soviets did not want the Labor Party, even though it was communist-leaning, in power if it meant the Chinese filling the political vacuum left by the British withdrawal. The Soviets were keen to replace the British in terms of influence. Straight was sent to assess the political and economic climate.

He needed a new cover. Straight knew that the tempestuous homosexual sixteenth-century painter Caravaggio had exiled himself in Malta after escaping prison. Straight contrived to write a play on him. He was a student of Caravaggio's revolutionary technique of tenebrism (the dramatic setting of brightly-lit figures against a dark background) that created a resurgence of art in the seventeenth century. It influenced Rubens, Velazquez, and Rembrandt. Straight also fancied Caravaggio as a subject because, in his terms, he was politically correct. His approach overthrew a hundred years of idealism in art representing human and religious experience while keeping an eye on the ordinary man. Straight was attracted to his story of rebellion against Catholic doctrine and authority that dictated style in art at the time. The church wanted ethereal works, such as when Caravaggio was commissioned by the Spanish Order of the Discalced Carmelites to paint the death of the Virgin Mary. They expected a work that would express the doctrinal belief that she passed through death without dying. Caravaggio's brilliant *Death of a Virgin* portrayed a corpse. It was not quite what the commissioners had in mind.

Straight would also have been drawn to the complexities of the painter's sexuality. Though heterosexual himself, Straight had been caught in the underground homosexual web at Cambridge, which was inextricably bound to the other secret demimonde of espionage.

The subject had many threads of interest that he would have to pull together while gathering information for his report to the KGB.

After a trip to London and Dartington in mid-1967, he toured Malta, where Caravaggio had escaped after being imprisoned. Straight wanted to search archives, including those at the Royal Maltese Library. Once more, he was suspected of being an intelligence agent, but this time for the CIA.

He wrote in a foreword to the script of the play that some were intrigued by his plan to write about Caravaggio, while others accepted it as "an amusing cover story." The British were moving out of Malta, Straight recorded, and the Russians were ready to move in. According to him, there were also plenty of CIA agents with their cover stories.[16]

The research done and his KGB report filed, Straight wanted to follow through with a script. He planned to begin the search for a producer. He needed to make the Malta exercise convincing, given that he was now in an ongoing process of being interrogated by Western intelligence, particularly MI5. It was hardly demanding. In a perverse way he enjoyed the game with the British agency and the thrill of always keeping several steps ahead of them. By being in such close contact, Straight could assess how much British intelligence knew. He had let them know his plans for writing the play, and they had been only mildly interested. He now had to follow through on production, if possible, just to keep his cover credible.

Straight ran into all the usual problems that faced producers of plays. Possible backers took their time assessing it before sending him rejections. He spoke to Jackie Kennedy about the play and then enlisted her stepsister, Nina Steers, and her half-brother, Gore Vidal, to help. Despite the hard work put in, it did not take off. It was only performed a few times in obscure theaters from 1968 to 1971, including the Vineyard Players of Ithaca College; the H. B. Studio; the Gallery Circle Theatre in New Orleans; and the Playhouse-in-the-Park in Cincinnati.

How good a cover was it? Did it measure up to the books that gained some critical acclaim?

John Slavin, an arts critic for the Australian Broadcasting Corporation and a Caravaggio expert, reviewed the play's script, self-published by Straight's Devon Press in 1979:

> *The Boston Herald* critic's response to this play raises the correct avenues: "It would," he writes, "make a striking motion picture." Hollywood's treatment of the artist is heavily biased towards the visual artist, not only because he/she is immensely pictorial but also because it offers the paradigm of the tortured, isolated individual suffering for his art. Who could forget Kirk Douglas's Van Gogh slurring: "I jest want you to be my friend," or Charlton Heston's Michelangelo announcing: "I am answerable to no one but God."
>
> Straight's Caravaggio falls easily into such cinematic typecasting. From the moment he appears in Del Monte's palace as one of the hired boys, he is, improbably, convinced of his greatness. He continues to broadcast this as a forgone conclusion until the close of the play. Contrasted with this hyperbole is the detailed depiction of his scandalous, antisocial behavior. This is drawn without much dramatization from the police records, scrupulously recorded by Baglione, one of his victims and chief detractors.

Baglione was also his earliest and least reliable biographer. This is the Hollywood cliché: "the boy is a genius"—a syndrome combined with the melodrama of the misunderstood, original artist. Straight suggests that Caravaggio is dangerous, difficult and violent because he didn't receive the recognition that he deserved.

Such a line is not supported by the historical record. Caravaggio was certainly a revolutionary artist who shifted the focus of aesthetic values. But . . . he was highly successful in the stream of commissions both public and private that he received from the Roman elite. Straight himself acknowledges that "the whole world was traipsing through the Contarelli Chapel to look at the St. Matthew paintings." It was only the conservative element at the lower end of Church sponsorship (whom Straight trots out as archetypal betrayers of genius at S. Maria della Scala) who complained about his challenge to orthodoxy.

This distortion is in keeping with Straight's principal theme. The reader is left with the impression that the great artist is being exploited by unknown forces. This figure is being used to explore not just the dilemma of the originating artist in society, but also the dilemma of the author in society. The play may be a kind of psychic X-ray of the author himself projected onto the figure of Caravaggio. As violent and unpredictable as he is, Caravaggio is consistently painted as a victim of his circumstances. In the final scenes he confesses that his main resentment is that of class, which lowers his value in the eyes of his peers. He is the innocent transgressor. Concomitant with this idea is the astonishing erasure of the most dramatic event in Caravaggio's life—the murder of the Ranuccio Tomassoni on 26th May 1606. It is simply reported as the trigger that fires him into the stronghold of the Knights of St. John of the Cross on Malta. . . .

An astonishing omission is Caravaggio's homosexuality . . . but for every hint of a relationship there is resistance and rebellion . . .

All this is wrapped up like a Christmas bon-bon in the forlorn gestures of rejected masterpieces.

In short, it was a superficial, unconvincing flop with ideological tendencies. But it didn't matter. Only experts like Slavin would recognize it as such. The fact that Straight had written the play and tried to get it up was all the evidence he needed if someone ever suggested it was other than a bone fide creation by a would-be playwright/producer.[17]

Straight returned to Dartington with Rose in 1967 after another meeting with MI5 in London. British intelligence, under the guidance of the dogged Peter Wright, was causing havoc among former Cambridge graduates and other communist circles. He and his colleagues were frustrated by the lack of success as they followed all the false trails laid down by the Cambridge ring over the four years since Philby's defection. The KGB continued to run circles around their British counterparts as mission after mission against the Russians went wrong thanks mainly to Victor Rothschild's schemes. Alister Watson, the head of the Submarine Detection Research Section of the British Admiralty, had been named by several of the ring and was one of many who were hounded. Some committed suicide. Sir Andrew Cohen, a diplomat and former Apostle, had a heart attack and died just prior to being questioned.[18]

During the hysteria, there was much shredding of documents and burning of files by communists fearful that Wright and his "Gestapo" (as he characterized his team) might stumble on incriminating information. According to two sources connected to Dartington Hall, a former student (not Straight) returned in 1967 and went through the files, removing any data that could be used against fellow students in the prevailing climate.[19]

The year 1968 exploded into a period of revolution that on the surface would seem to excite all communists. After all, the ideology of Marx, Lenin, and Mao preached it. Demonstrations and barricades were evident in many countries as would-be revolutionaries caused unrest and tried to overthrow ruling authorities and regimes. It was enough to keep high the heart rate of any hard-left-winger such as Straight, who had waited three decades for upheaval. Even at a mature rebel age of 51, he would be willing to embrace whatever radical events occurred or any change that resulted.

But there were complications. While it was pleasing for procommunists to see students and other left-wingers attacking the barricades in Paris, Washington, and Chicago, there were disturbing activities bubbling in Poland and Czechoslovakia. The virus of revolution did not seem to recognize the political hue of the ruling elite. In Prague students and intellectuals were equally keen to rid themselves of a stagnant, repressive regime as their counterparts in Paris.

The fever began in the Vietnam War between South Vietnam, supported by the United States, and communist North Vietnam. On January 30, 1968, national liberation front (Vietcong) guerrillas, supported by North Vietnam conventional forces, launched a massive attack on the South to mark Tet, the Vietnamese New Year. In Saigon, the Vietcong penetrated the U.S. embassy. The U.S. media carried pictures of U.S. soldiers lying dead in the compound.

The Tet offensive marked the turning point in the war, in which the communists would gradually gain the ascendancy. For Western communist true believers, this was seen as a major advance in the Cold War armwrestle between the communist superpowers and the United States and its allies. The antiwar movement in the United States intensified. At the same time as the Tet offensive, police in Warsaw arrested fifty students protesting the forced closure of a nineteenth-century play that included anti-Russian references such as "all that Moscow sends us are spies, jackasses and fools." It led to all Polish universities going on strike in March. There were major student protests in Rome and Madrid soon after that led to universities in those countries being shut down. The world of the privileged classes, at least among the budding intelligentsia and future national leaders, was in turmoil.

Upheaval of a different kind occurred a few weeks later on April 4 when the leader of the black civil rights movement in the United States, Martin Luther King Jr., was assassinated in Memphis, Tennessee. Soon afterward, young blacks went on the rampage in Washington. Straight was on Martha's Vineyard. Expecting to perhaps witness some sort of attempted revolutionary action, he flew to Washington but was most disappointed to find there had only been rioting and looting. The blacks had gone after radios, TVs, and clothes. Straight saw this as an attempt, in effect, to join in with the mainstream of the U.S. competitive society.[20]

Less than a month later, unrest in Czechoslovakia's capital Prague reached new heights for a communist country in Eastern Europe when on May 1 a long procession marched through the city's Wenceslas Square. Banners proclaimed: "Of our own free will, for the first time." People from organizations silenced for twenty years since the communist takeover in 1948 were speaking out.

Two days later a sudden crisis in Paris took everyone by surprise. Endemic student disorders, which had been prevalent for some time, accelerated when a rally of student radicals at the main Paris university, the Sorbonne, was broken up by the police. Barricades went up in the Latin Quarter that housed the Sorbonne, street fighting broke out, and the Sorbonne was occupied by student rebels and converted into a huge commune. Unrest spread to other French universities. Workers took up the banners of spontaneous protest, and factories were shut down by strikes that rolled across France. Soon millions of workers were involved, and the nation was paralyzed.

Straight kept one keen eye on events in Europe while following, again from a frustrating distance, the 1968 presidential candidate nominations by the parties. Lyndon Johnson, much to Straight's relief, was not going to run again for the White House after occupying it for nearly five years since Kennedy's assassination. This left the way open for several Democratic potential nominees, including Jack Kennedy's younger brother Robert, Hubert Humphrey, and Eugene McCarthy.

On the other side, Ronald Reagan, a former actor and California's governor, was an outside chance. But Straight was fascinated that the man from his law firm, Richard M. Nixon, the nemesis of both the left and the Eastern Establishment, was running again and the favorite for the Republican bid for the highest office. This was just as Straight had predicted before and after that first meeting in New York in 1962. "Tricky Dick," as his opponents and even his friends called him, had a few cards up his sleeve after just losing the presidency to Kennedy in 1960. He was using a slick advertising campaign to position himself as the "new Nixon." The big difference from the "old Nixon" was his image. He was the same character, but now instead of a five o'clock shadow to give him a shady appearance on TV, there was clean-shaven Richard. Clever "advertorials" were selling the new product, just like soap powder, except Straight and anyone who ever talked to him knew that this politician was no flake. He was particularly well read and knowledgeable on politics and history. He was also more than ambitious to get the job. One more developed characteristic in Nixon was his ruthlessness.

Straight was never going to support Nixon, despite the fascination with his candidature. If anyone was going to get his vote, it would be Eugene McCarthy, he told the Elmhirsts. McCarthy wanted Straight as his campaign finance chairman. Clearly he had not consulted Henry Wallace (who died in 1965) or Whitney Straight. Yet Straight declined his flattering offer. He didn't think McCarthy was a winner. Watching him in political action would have brought back memories of the Wallace campaign twenty years earlier. McCarthy had a habit of throwing away speeches his aides had researched and scripted in favor of some off the cuff remarks. American writer David Halberstam commented that "one sensed that if elected President he might abolish the U.S. Government . . . "

McCarthy mocked Robert Kennedy for his interest in the ethnic vote and his plan to set up twenty-six committees to deal with the main ethnic groupings in the country, saying: "26 varieties of Americans—like 26 varieties of ice cream. Like a jigsaw puzzle." Amusing, perhaps, but vote catching, no. Straight sensed the odds were against this whimsical candidate. Besides, Straight was once bitten, twice shy. Why again waste time on a campaign that was sure to fail? And one too that would eschew real radical policies. Anyway, Straight was sure the candidate, if he reached as far as the party convention, would become institutionalized by the straight-jacket the Democrats would place on him. He was less enamored with Robert Kennedy, but admitted he was a stronger and more durable candidate.

These two fought out the all-important California primary on June 5. Kennedy won. He spoke graciously at the Hotel Ambassador about the vanquished McCarthy and asked his supporters to join him. Moments later Kennedy was shot dead by a lone assassin, Sirhan Sirhan. Robert joined his brother as a victim of violence and conspiracy in America.

It left the way open for McCarthy to battle Hubert Humphrey at the Chicago Convention two months later, where Straight now found McCarthy petulant and self-pitying. He was also lukewarm about Humphrey, who won the party nomination. He told the family back in England that if Nixon, the Republican candidate, were to win the 1968 election, it wouldn't be so bad, in the long run. "That really still surprised us," William Elmhirst said.[21]

——— ——

Meanwhile, the Soviet Union reacted to the "problem" in Prague by leaving its troops in Czechoslovakia after Warsaw Pact military exercises finished. In effect, the country was under military occupation. In July, the Moscow newspaper *Pravda*, the Soviet government's propaganda organ, suggested Czechoslovakia would soon establish "a bourgeois regime." It lead to a suppression of any potential revolution. In Western Europe, unrest abated as 1968 moved toward its final months. The student/worker pseudo-revolution in France fizzled out. The Vietnam War was at a stalemate, leaving America bogged down in a military conflict that only Pentagon hawks wanted.

——— ——

Straight and Rose made their annual pilgrimage to Dartington in late October, where they were able to reassure the family that if Nixon became president, it would not be a disaster. Rose spoke about his positive qualities and his knowledge of foreign policy. He had been a good administrator at the law firm and was well liked. Everyone was in awe of his work habits and his capacity to absorb complex cases.

The visit gave Straight a chance to ease his mother into the idea of his divorcing Bin and his starting a new relationship with Nina Steers, whose marriage was also breaking up.

He also surprised the Elmhirsts by defending Jackie Kennedy's marrying of the Greek shipping magnate, Aristotle Onassis, which had drawn some criticism in the United States. Straight remarked that she had endured endless humiliations from Kennedy in the marriage. He supported U.S. Cardinal Cushing in his defense of Jackie's decision to remarry.

Straight continued to give the Elmhirsts a favorable impression of Nixon when he won the 1968 election, with a subtle indication that he would join the new administration.

——— ——

On December 14, 1968, Straight received a call from Leonard Elmhirst at Dartington to say that Dorothy had died the night before, without warning, and with no undue pain. She was 81. Suddenly, the matriarch whose approval Straight needed all his life was gone.

Dorothy was cremated and her ashes buried in the garden at Dartington. Family and friends gathered for a memorial service held in the Great Hall. The Dartington Quartet added a second violinist and performed the Schubert Quintet. A second service was held at St. James's Church in New York, at which Beatrice read Dorothy's essay, "The Arts of Dartington." Straight and Whitney were forced together on these occasions. Neither wished at that point to reconcile the differences between them.

So ended a remarkable year of revolution, counterrevolution, assassinations, and change. Dorothy's passing allowed Straight's transition to a new life to be facilitated more easily. He didn't have to continue to explain why he planned to divorce his wife (which he did a few months later in 1969) and marry the beautiful and much younger Nina. Nor did he have to attempt to rationalize why he desired to do an employment deal with that former devil to all left-wingers and communists, Richard Nixon.

PART FIVE

ART OF THE PROVOCATEUR

25

ARTS AT LAST

The Nixon era represented change and opportunity for Straight that he would never have dreamed of in the days he ran *New Republic* campaigns against him. His closeness to Rose and association with Nixon through the New York law firm meant there was a chance he could slip into a post in the much-coveted area of the arts that he had denied himself under Kennedy. He was assisted by the fact that a good friend, Leonard Garment, also from the Nixon/Rose law firm, had been appointed Nixon's assistant in the arts. Straight was on the inside of a new regime for the first time since the Roosevelt days. After twenty years of frustration, he was excited by the prospect. Yet still he would have to indulge in one of his finer skills—political manipulation—to secure a job.

He was aware that his FBI record that he had himself beefed up over the past six years would not allow him to get through public senate confirmation hearings. To slide around this, he proposed that the new administration appoint a part-time chairman who would then be approved. The chairman would be supported by a full-time deputy, who would actually control the show. The deputy would not have to run the gauntlet of public hearings, just a check from the administration and an approving tick from the new president. Straight knew before he began that the Nixon team would be happy if he were the deputy.

The political maneuvering commenced when he had Garment charge him with finding the chairman. He approached six prominent Republicans who were arts patrons. They included John D. Rockefeller III, John Hay Whitney, and Douglas Dillon. They all turned down the offer. A seventh, Morton "Buster" May, a department store executive in St. Louis, caused a problem when he didn't want Straight as his deputy. His choice was John MacFadyen, an experienced arts administrator. Such an appointment would allow May to go on with all his other time-consuming activities.[1]

May's name was sent to a senate subcommittee for approval. An "old friend" of Straight's, Senator Claiborne Pell, was the subcommittee's chairman. Pell claimed he objected to May on the grounds that he would not be on call whenever congress wanted him. This was at odds with the White House, represented by Garment and Straight, who had wanted a part-timer. Now it seemed a full-time operative was required. It provided a pretext for wiping May from the list. John Warner was then suggested as chairman, but he was turned down by the White House because he was a Democrat.

The next approach was to Thomas Hoving, director of the Metropolitan Museum; he wasn't interested. Others were considered. No one seemed promising until about choice number twelve on the list—the attractive and energetic Nancy Hanks, 41, staff director of the Rockefeller Panel on the Performing Arts and president of the Associated Councils on the Arts. Straight knew her. She accepted the offer.[2]

There was one proviso, which was later put to her by Garment. She had to choose Straight as her deputy. She agreed to this, and Straight accepted her offer.[3]

———

With the positions secured, Garment and Straight prepared to go off to Moscow to be judges at the 1969 film festival there. Even though Straight had not yet been appointed to the Nixon administration, he would be going to the heart of Russia under the auspices of an expected hard-line, anticommunist regime. It was the best political protection he could ever manage. Given Straight's past and his growing FBI file baggage, such a visit for a Democratic administration would have been impossible. But he was going as a representative of Richard Nixon, the fierce foe of communism, who had grown to world public prominence attacking it.

This was to be Straight's first trip to Russia since 1935, when he accompanied Blunt after being picked out as a likely future KGB agent. He had to gain the approval of Agent Taylor, the FBI man in charge of his case since 1964. This was not an obstacle. Taylor was more interested in his upcoming retirement and golf than anyone's travel plans.

Straight, who had been dealing with other KGB agents since first recruited by Blunt and Burgess in 1937, visited the FBI. He asked Taylor what he should do if he were approached by a Russian intelligence agent. Taylor told him not to worry; they would never approach him again. A no doubt bemused Straight pressed the question. Taylor was adamant no one from the KGB would speak with him again. But, of course, they did. The KGB organized and controlled the film event, and it was inevitable that Straight would make contact, even without his knowledge.

Straight, Garment, and the rest of the U.S. delegation stayed at the Rossiya Hotel. It was a time of acute tension between the United States and Russia. Various government arts officials, academics, film producers, stars, directors, and writers from around the world were watching flickering screens at venues dotted across the city. Others were using the festival as a cover for more clandestine meetings. Soviet leader Leonid Brezhnev was testing the mettle of the new U.S. administration over China. The Chinese were deploying nuclear weapons for the first time since detonating one in 1964. They were being placed on the Sino-Soviet border. This was making the Kremlin's residents as nervous as they had been during the Cuban Missile Crisis of 1962 when Kennedy had nuclear weapons deployed in Turkey and aimed at Moscow.

Brezhnev had used intermediaries during the festival to see what Nixon's reaction would be to a proposed preemptive strike by Russia on China's nuclear bases. Would the U.S. stay out of any possible conflict created by the Kremlin, thus sanctioning it by default? Nixon had responded that the United States disapproved of any military attack on China. The president also implied that the United States could not guarantee it would sit idly by and avoid intervention.

Other KGB and CIA activity carrying on behind the scenes was not tense. In fact, it was friendly. Special assignment groups in the two agencies had combined in an operation against the Chinese during the Cultural Revolution.[4] They had a convivial reunion.

Meanwhile, Straight was concentrating on the festival choosing the U.S. film entry the winner. The panel of three he was on supported Stanley

Kubrick's *2001, A Space Odyssey*. It was considered a politically correct choice that would please the hosts. In the film's story, the offending "intelligent" computer in the spacecraft was called HAL, a snipe at IBM (each letter of HAL being the one before the corresponding letter in IBM). A French critic suggested that HAL's preparedness to shut an astronaut out of the spacecraft in order to complete its programmed mission would be interpreted by the doctrinaire Marxist Russians as the ultimate example of man's alienation from his labor. The fault would be seen as lying with the capitalist producers of computers such as HAL that had pushed mechanization to such a point. There were also antiwar sentiments in the film.

The panelists were surprised to see the cold reaction from the predominantly Russian audience of 7,000 at the film's showing on a giant screen in the Palace of the Soviets. This was despite the dramatic effect being heightened that night by U.S. astronauts taking off for the moon on Apollo 9. Straight wanted to know why *2001* had not been appreciated. He pointed out to one Russian woman that the subordination of the computer to narrow, military objectives led to its breakdown and destruction. He even offered an interpretive talk because he had spent a day with Kubrick. The woman listened and then commented bitterly that he didn't understand. The film was a challenge to the imagination, she told him. Soviet citizens were not permitted to use their imagination. It was a danger to the state.[5]

After this refreshing interlude in the summer, Straight and Garment returned to Washington to find Nancy Hanks's nomination in jeopardy. As a resident of New York, Hanks had been vetoed by Senator Jacob Javits. He thought that by blocking Hanks, Nixon would fall back on Democrat John Walker.

Straight devised a counterplan with Garment. An article under the byline of Howard Taubman appeared in the *New York Times* on August 22, 1969, suggesting that Nixon was expected to nominate Straight as the new chairman of the Arts Endowment. It was a setup. Straight was to be Nancy Hanks's (and his own) stalking horse to force Javits to withdraw his objection to her. The senator reacted by summoning Straight to his New York law office. Javits fumed at the White House tactics. He then asked him several questions to judge if he were a suitable choice. The bluff continued when Straight went to see leading Democrats, who controlled congress. In his book, *Twigs for an Eagle's Nest*, Straight claimed that they assured the White House that he would have no trouble being confirmed. The bluff worked; Javits withdrew his objection to Hanks.

Garment submitted Straight's name to Nixon along with the disclosure (in reality nothing more than Straight's misleading version of his espionage life, supplied to Garment by Straight himself). The creative summary also went to the FBI and the CIA. Straight alleged he was surprised to learn that Nixon accepted Garment's recommendation.

"Well, he's on our side now," Nixon remarked. The relationship of the oddest couple in U.S. politics, from Straight's point of view, was good and helpful to the arts.[6] Hanks was announced by Nixon at San Clemente as his choice for the chair of the National Endowment for the Arts (NEA).[7]

Now the FBI and the CIA couldn't stop Straight, even if they wished to. At last, he was in arts administration.

He proved to be a skilled lobbyist with congress in gaining a big increase in funds for NEA. A major part of his philosophy for handing out money followed a pattern first established by him at the Whitney Foundation. He considered that he presided over turbulent years (from 1969–1977) encompassing three upheavals: the fight by blacks for rights, the feminist movement, and America's involvement in the Vietnam War.

Straight expressed the stark view that the arts could be a vehicle for each of these areas for showing feelings of bitterness, rage, and alienation. Drama and dance performances that attacked government, for instance, could also demonstrate rejection of traditional values and exhibit a new-found sense of freedom.[8] No doubt if Straight had said this while in his job, there may have been some rage and bitterness from Republicans and some Democrats, who would have wondered about this use of taxpayer funds. Yet Straight was enjoying himself. Instead of tightly disciplined fronts controlled by Moscow, which he once helped keep afloat with family trust money, he could now use the public purse to dramatize attacks on the U.S. establishment. It was perfect for his ongoing role as a KGB agent provocateur and agent of influence.

Straight needed all his manipulative capacities to maintain this radical dramatic commitment, while lobbying to keep the confidence of the congress. He had many a battle against objections to taxpayers' money being given to groups for expressing strong protest against mainstream values. When asked for a "please explain" from irate congressional representatives reflecting their constituents, Straight hid behind a clause in the NEA act. This prevented any government employee acting as a censor. First, he would nudge grants toward the fringe, cultural "revolutionaries" who stretched the boundaries. When protests came in from outraged citizens, he would slip in behind the clause, saying, "sorry, I'm prevented by law from intervening in any way."

An example of this was the black dance group the Eleo Pomare Company. It came to Washington to perform at the Kennedy Center and to give demonstrations in city schools. One protest dance, "Embers," was accompanied with shouts that the United States had fought three wars in order to suppress colored peoples and to keep up the price of rice. The *Washington Star* reported that the group would be visiting schools. It asked if public funds should be used to impose "Black Panther" attitudes on impressionable children.

Straight was called to the office of Senator James L. Buckley of New York, whose assistant, William Gavin, met him. He was asked if he would exclude "Embers" from future performances supported by the endowment. Straight, poker-faced, said it was impossible under the terms of the Endowment Act. He couldn't even call the company to find out if the offending dance were scheduled for further performances.[9]

Straight's method of handling the arts in the United States impressed, it seems, even the Presidium of the USSR. It sent its only woman member, the formidable Soviet minister for culture, Yekaterina Furtseva, to the United States in January 1972, with very short notice. Demonstrating the esteem in which he was held at the Kremlin, she went to Straight's home for lunch on her first day.

The hard-line Furtseva had made news in the West for her attacks on writers Boris Pasternak and Aleksandr Solzhenitsyn. She had voiced her displeasure at the Jewish Defense League in the United States. The group had staged persistent protests against touring Soviet artists. It wished to highlight the suppression of Jews and Jewish culture in the Soviet Union and its restriction of movement out of the country, particularly to Israel. Furtseva, it was thought, had turned up without invitation in an attempt to persuade U.S. officials to stop the protests. She had rarely traveled outside her country.

Furtseva made the arrogant, if not ignorant, assumption that the U.S. government could abuse its powers concerning civil rights the way her own regime did. She insisted that the Jewish Defense League be curbed after it caused the cancellation of the Bolshoi's first ballet performance at Carnegie Hall. She was told it could not be done. Furtseva responded with scathing remarks about the United States' lack of resolve to stop violence.

Aware of her attitudes, Straight was thrilled to play host to her, as she was to be received by him. Furtseva was impressed by his home as she eyed the tall columns of the ancient Georgetown house. She seemed confused (Straight alleged) to learn that his boss, Nancy Hanks, lived in a much smaller house.

Furtseva was not impressed by Straight drinking champagne while she plied herself with strong gin and tonic. Real men in Russia wouldn't touch it. She illustrated this with a story about a 1905 Russian revolutionary feeding champagne to his horse after czarist officers offered it to him in a restaurant. Not even the horses would drink it.[10]

The next night Straight took her to the heavily policed premier performance of the Balalaika Orchestra at the John F. Kennedy Center. The two got on so well that she sent him an ironic gift—Soviet Champagne Number 4—at the end of her stay.

Clearly, Furtseva appreciated Straight's work. Intelligence contacts suggested that this was the time when Straight was honored with the high Soviet/KGB award—the Order of Lenin—for his lifelong services to the cause. It would explain Furtseva's singling him out for a private audience and their cozy relationship.

———

While he enjoyed more public status than ever before, Straight's clandestine past continued to nag him as MI5 reviewed his file and compared it with information supplied by Blunt. The frustration caused by not being able to identify the mole inside British intelligence had caused a resurgence in the early 1970s of interest in the responses by the Cambridge ring.

Straight's discussions with MI5 had been going on for about a decade, and he was wondering when they would finish. His case had been taken over first by Cecil Shipp, MI5's top interrogator (later its deputy general). He had a tough reputation after his ruthless inquisition of Alister Watson in the mid-1960s. Yet Straight was handled gently. He was categorized as a voluntary "confessed" informer, not a suspect. His manner and breeding made him someone not to be trifled with, so "chats" were agreeable. Straight used his well-practiced charm to secure the confidence, trust, and in some cases the friendship of his interrogators. The FBI men had been easy. The British, with their mannerly and apologetic approach, were deceptive. They prefaced their requests with "would you mind awfully if . . ." and "it would be most helpful if you could . . ." when in reality he had no choice but to oblige.

On one visit to London he found another MI5 officer, P. A. Osmond, had reviewed Blunt's interviews and had discovered apparent discrepancies. The question arose as to whether Blunt had recruited Brian Simon, a Cambridge man of their era and a staunch Communist Party member. MI5—namely, its boss, Sir Dick White—wanted Straight to find out. The way Straight handled this quaint "mission" exemplified just how much he was in control of the situation. He played along, took Brian Simon out to dinner, and had lots to eat and drink. After a convivial evening with this fellow traveler, he came back and told Osmond (who reported to White) that Simon was in the clear. He never left the party, Straight told his MI5 masters, and he certainly did not go "underground" for the KGB.

The story that Straight reported to MI5 was that Blunt had tried to recruit Simon but that Simon had said any move by him would be too obvious since he (Simon) was close to Blunt (so close, in fact, that they were lovers, Straight alleged). This seemed a feeble bit of intelligence on Straight's part, but it was apparently accepted by MI5, although Peter Wright thought this excuse was too thin, and he remained suspicious of Simon. Straight also reported to MI5 that Simon was in love with Tess Rothschild and that the two had a relationship in 1939. This was after the time (1938) when many sources believe Tess was recruited by the KGB. Any relationship in 1939 would have been directed by the KGB, which points to Tess attempting to seduce Simon into the Russian intelligence network. She may well have failed to have him recruited.

This report by Straight would have paved the way for him to have a future meeting with Tess and/or Simon should he choose to return for the 1987 fifty-year reunion of the Cambridge class of 1937. If they were both accepted as nonagents—as Straight portrayed them to MI5—then they would be free from surveillance. Since Straight had been involved with Blunt in Tess's recruitment, his keeping MI5 off the track a half a century after the event would have given him great satisfaction.[11]

Dorothy Elmhirst's passing left a vacuum at Dartington and a change in the control of the trust running it. Leonard was the chairman of the trust. He was fit enough to continue, but was lost and lonely without Dorothy and ready to retire.

A conflict developed on the board of trustees with William Elmhirst, a trustee since 1957. He had started the Solar Quest, a charitable organization that attempted to bridge the Western esoteric tradition with the Eastern, as practiced by Rabindranath Tagore in India.[12]

This rift lead to a crisis in the trustee body. Maurice Ash, William's brother-in-law, and other trustees objected to the charity being based in the hall. Leonard had often used Tagore's teaching and philosophy in speeches.[13] Dorothy, with her spiritual leanings, had approved also of William's interests and had encouraged him.

Leonard was persuaded to oppose William's work being centered at the hall. The majority of the board was against him. He was forced to leave with his wife, Vera, who was a "visionary," or medium. The rift between William and his father was never healed. He realized later that his half-brother Michael had "pretended to mediate between me and Leonard" when he had other reasons for wanting them out of Dartington.

Leonard retired as chairman. He married Susanna Isaacs, a former pupil at the school, in December 1972. She had been offered a teaching post in California for two years, and they moved there. Leonard could never really settle in the United States. He tried to get a loan from the trustees in 1974 to build a house on the Dartington estate. It was refused. He died in the United States in April that year.[14]

A few weeks later, Straight, 57, married Nina Steers, 37, at the Cathedral of St. John the Divine in Washington. It was a rewarding time for him in his fifth year as deputy chairman of the Arts Endowment. He was enjoying his status and power, first under Nixon before he was forced to resign the presidency over the Watergate Affair in August 1974, then with Gerald Ford's administration.

A small hiccup occurred when *The Washington Monthly* discovered that Garment was renting Straight's Virginia home. Garment's high profile in the final dark days of Nixon's presidency meant he was a target for media attention. Straight complained that the magazine described the rental of his home as a scandal. He threatened a libel suit, and Jay Rockefeller phoned the magazine to support Straight. The *Monthly's* reporter, James Fallows, interviewed Straight for a square-off article.

This incident did not interrupt the enjoyment of his position. There were endless glittering nights, if he desired them, with his attractive new young wife. Ford was beaten by Jimmy Carter in the 1976 presidential election, and it took a year for the new government to decide who would run the Arts Endowment. Hanks thought she might be awarded a third term. Despite personal meetings with the new president, she failed to secure it, so she decided to resign. Joan Mondale, the wife of Vice-President Walter Mondale, was Carter's adviser on the arts, replacing Garment. She asked Straight to stay on as acting chairman until a replacement for Hanks was found. He accepted the appointment, thinking there was a chance he could slip into the senior role by default. There was always the hurdle of FBI checks, but he may have been able to avoid them. After all, he had been the "loyal" deputy chairman for eight years. He felt also that he was the token Democrat in the Republican arts administration of Nixon and Ford. Carter's choice, Livingston L. Biddle Jr., was not popular. *The New Republic* and the *Wall Street Journal* attacked the probable appointment. When Hanks failed to get reappointed, she started a campaign to stop Biddle. It was uncovered by the White House. This caused it to dig in on its choice. Biddle's name was sent to the senate for confirmation.

Straight was more than miffed. "I've never seen Mike so angry," William Elmhirst noted. "He was fuming about being fired—or not reappointed—by Carter. He would lose all his power and status. It hurt."[15]

Straight reacted while still acting chairman. He told *Los Angeles Times* journalist Barbara Isenberg that "President Carter was politicizing our culture by appointing Joe Duffey to the Humanities Endowment, Livingston Biddle to Arts, and George Seybolt and Lee Kimche to the Museum Services Institute."[16]

He repeated it all to Grace Glueck of *The New York Times*. It seemed odd to many observers, who recalled that Straight had said when appointed in 1969 that he was attracted to the job because it was "a way of combining the two things I care about—politics and art." His actions in supporting "revolutions" while in the job had done more than anyone to politicize the endowment.

Joe Duffey rang Straight and accused him of being a "God-damned elitist." "You and your snob friends may not know it," Duffey told him, "but your day is over."[17]

It was, almost. Straight was summoned to meet White House staffer Peter Kyros. He was asked for an assurance that he would not criticize the administration again while acting chairman. He agreed. Kyros then told him why the White House had acted the way it did to Hanks. She had gone behind the backs of White House staff in seeing Carter. She had also started the campaign against Biddle, and then denied it to Kyros's face.[18]

Biddle was sworn in on November 30, 1977. Straight, 61, was out of a job for the first time in eight years. With few prospects in sight for a future career, he set up a publishing group, Devon Press. It produced his books in 1979, except for his paean to communism, *Let This Be the Last War*. He must have judged it as embarrassingly political in its vision of Stalin and the Soviet Union. With time on his hands, he was able to make a second trip to Australia, which was arranged by Jean Battersby of the government cultural body the Australia Council. She had met Straight when he was at the Arts Endowment.

In late 1979, Andrew Boyle published *The Climate of Treason* about the Cambridge ring. It hinted at the identities of the fourth and fifth members. Journalists began speculating, particularly on the fourth man. It became an open secret in late 1979 that it was Anthony Blunt. Until now only intelligence officers from the FBI, CIA, MI5, MI6, and, of course, the KGB knew that Blunt was a spy. Then on November 15, Prime Minister Margaret Thatcher confirmed it in parliament. Blunt "had been recruited as a talent spotter for Russian intelligence before the war, when he was a don at Cambridge, and had passed information to the Russians while he was a member of the Secret Service between 1940 and 1945."

(Modin would have been pleased that the prime minister of England had accepted the propaganda about 1945 being the end of the ring's activity. Modin had been posted by the KGB to England to be its control for ten years starting in 1947.)

The Thatcher statement caused shock waves around the Cambridge ring. Straight realized that his 17-year secret "confession" could come up in relation to Blunt. In order to present an innocent self-portrait to his family, he collated personal diary entries, letters to his mother, and a few to his first wife Bin. He edited them to avoid any remarks that could give clues to his secret life. He placed them in a bound book, *For Noah, His Uncles, His Aunts, and All His Relations* (Noah was a grandson). He distributed copies in 1980 to the family. Whitney had just died, so Straight felt free to show the letters that painted him unfavorably in the family trust dispute. There was no one then to challenge his version of events. Much of the correspondence was about his children; it created an image of the loving father and dedicated husband.

There was a lull until March 1981. Straight was asked by the Washington correspondent of the *London Daily Mail*, Angus Macpherson, to comment on an article appearing in his paper. It was an edited extract from a book by Chapman Pincher, *Their Trade Is Treachery*:

A middle-aged American belonging to a rich and famous family was invited to undertake a political task by the White House. Having a guilt complex about his secret past, he went to FBI headquarters in Washington hoping to clear himself before accepting the White House post. There he confessed that he had been a communist while in England and at Cambridge University, had been recruited to Soviet Intelligence and had served the Russian interests for several years. . . .[19]

The long, private game of confession and cover-up was now public. Straight began giving interviews, attempting to explain himself. He emphasized his alleged confession and the image of being the one who blew the whistle on the Cambridge ring. He objected to the flippancy of a Washington radio interviewer who said in an introduction: "And now we go to Maryland to talk to the spy who came in from the cold."[20]

The word "spy" concerned him. Yet in anyone's language he acted as an espionage agent, or in common parlance, a spy. Seven months later, in October 1981, Straight told Simon Freeman of the London *Sunday Times* he had informed MI5 that Leo Long had been recruited by the KGB. The ensuing article identified Straight as the American "who had himself spied for the Russians." Then the *Times* described him the same way. Straight reacted by writing to the paper saying that to characterize him as a spy was "simply not true."

"I did give my own appraisals of the political situation," he wrote, "to a gentleman who called himself Michael Green." The difference now was that his audience was much wider than a handful of charmed interrogators at the FBI and MI5.

A magazine article in 1981 about his wife Nina's novel, *Ariabella: The First*, painted Straight as an heroic spy-catcher. The piece referred to Straight "as the source of information that helped break the Soviet spy network—fictionalized in *Tinker, Tailor, Soldier, Spy*." He was deceptive in the article when he claimed that he "flatly" turned down attempts to recruit him. In 1963 "he gave evidence that later forced a confession from the man who had tried to recruit him, Sir Anthony Blunt."[21]

Despite this, his image-making was not working. Scores of papers and media outlets in the United Kingdom and the United States were describing him as a spy. He knew that it would be impossible to refute in court. Instead of suing them, he decided to write his own book, *After Long Silence*. He sought his own FBI file under the Freedom of Information Act. This was given to him piecemeal. He also relied on his memory of submissions to the FBI and MI5 from 1963 to 1975. The FBI file had gaps in it in the form of blacked-out passages, which ended in September 1963. After that date there were missing pages. Straight later indicated to U.S. agents, such as the CIA's Newton Miler and the FBI's Sam Papich (the liaison officer with the CIA), that he had misgivings about those omitted passages. He guessed that they dealt with briefings about him and other KGB agents, such as Dolivet and Duran, by Golitsyn and others.

Straight's book, rather than being an autobiography or his memoirs, would attempt to counteract the FBI files. He interwove the tightly edited versions of his family letters (mostly to Dorothy) to provide an image of the innocent, loving family man, much as he had done in the cover-up 1980 publication *For Noah* for his relatives' consumption. He threw in literary diversions as further sweeteners. The end product was as far from his secret life as he could get, given what was already public. *After Long Silence* was devoid of much chronology, with intermittent chapters trying to explain away the FBI dossier. It was perhaps a too clever cover-up. The book opened up far more questions than it answered.

Straight would have been encouraged by the KGB to write it as part of the continuing disinformation campaign directed by Yuri Modin concerning all the members of the Cambridge ring. He began this with Kim Philby in 1968. Modin edited Philby's book, *My Silent War*. Rothschild wrote two semi-autobiographical books, which stayed away from his own story and concentrated on essays to do with his work as a scientist and member of the Edward Heath government's think tank. He mentioned his relationships with Burgess and Blunt in passing, and dismissively. In 1981, Blunt too was drafting his story (which was never completed), as was John Cairncross (who tried to get it published in the United States and United Kingdom for the decade up until his death in 1995. The book, *The Enigma Spy*, was published in 1997).

Straight's book continued his deception. He even sent a courtesy manuscript copy to Blunt. This demonstrated—until this point—their relationship had not diminished after Straight was supposed to have double-crossed him by the exposure in 1963. Blunt marked up the copy where he claimed Straight was not accurate and gave it to journalist John Costello and others.

Had the two lifetime comrades fallen out at this critical moment? Blunt had kept in touch with English authors Nigel West and Robert Cecil. Straight's main defense when they contacted him was that the promotion of *After Long Silence* was out of his control.

Straight was concerned now that he might be double-crossed by Blunt. He wrote to him saying he was coming to London. They agreed to meet.

Straight was also in touch with Michael Young, who was now Lord Young of Dartington, having been appointed a life peer by Prime Minister James Callaghan a few years earlier. Young was horrified by Straight's book. He felt it was a dangerous self-indictment. He told me in a 1996 interview that Straight had been a lifelong Soviet agent. When I asked him what he meant, he suggested I read *After Long Silence*. The answer and explanation were imbedded in it, he said.

Young urged him not to return to Great Britain, suggesting he might be imprisoned, but Young was unaware that Straight had been through lengthy interrogations since 1964.[22] Straight, aware from his MI5 contacts that there would be no attempt to interrogate him further, flew to London to face the crisis. He and Blunt were forced to cancel the rendezvous for fear of being followed by the news-hungry media. Blunt then made a statement to the press. He placed Leo Long and Straight in the same category as espionage agents, the implication being that Straight had spied on well into the Cold War. This was a clear betrayal of their secret positions and sworn oaths of allegiance both as Apostles and Soviet agents.

Blunt felt the severe strain of what he saw as Straight's betrayal and the fact that their disagreements had become public, so exposing and threatening to unravel many secrets of the KGB and its operatives. Blunt and the others had been restrained by fear of reprisals from the KGB all their lives. This sort of media exposure broke all the rules.

Soon after his press statement, on Saturday morning, March 26, 1983, Blunt died of a heart attack in his London flat. The night before, his brother Wilfrid had spoken to him and had found him "in good form." Blunt's death took the pressure off Straight. He was interviewed by Ludovic Kennedy on BBC TV and held to the view that Blunt had been controlled by Burgess. "The unanswered question," Straight remarked, "was why a man of his intellectual stature could have been the willing captive of a gypsy vagabond like Burgess."[23]

Straight's body language during the interview exposed his stress. Yet he also appeared to deliver candid responses. Overall the program may have done Straight a favor. Instead of being at the center of controversy, as he had been in the clash with West, he at times appeared the thoughtful, almost detached expert who had plausible explanations for becoming entrapped at Cambridge.

When published in 1983, *After Long Silence* featured a revealing back cover photograph of Straight. He was 65 when the shot was taken. It was the look of a concerned man. He appeared uncertain of what the camera might portray as he stared at it. Gone was the semiprofile pose of self-assurance of a few years earlier when he was forced out of the Arts Endowment by President Carter. Nearly half a century of acting out, then concealing, a double life had etched itself into his former sharp, aquiline features. It left a drawn, ever-suspicious impression. The defensive stare, which interviewers at times found "ferocious," moved upward from beneath an aggressive ridge of thick eyebrows and heavily lined forehead.

Straight used literary allusions to put his case, but they didn't quite resonate with readers. He drew on British writer Joseph Conrad's story, "Under Western Eyes," published in 1911. Each extract was meant to evoke sympathy for Straight. Kyrilo Sidorovitch Razumov, the main character, betrays Victor Haldin, a mature and admired student, to the secret police. Haldin had assassinated the czarist minister of state. Straight's attempts to show how he turned in Blunt invited judgment that Straight was not a betrayer but rather a courageous individual for doing so.

Straight quoted Conrad's description of Razumov after he has betrayed Haldin, who is sent to his death: "An incredible dullness, a ditch-water stagnation was sensible to his perceptions, as though life had withdrawn itself from all things."

This was meant to parallel Straight's feelings when he informed the FBI about Blunt, although nothing in his private archive, letters, or diary conveyed any apparent concern for Blunt's fate.

Then later in *After Long Silence*, Straight again used Razumov's deception of Haldin. Razumov went out into the wintry, snowy night wondering what to do. If he helped Haldin, he would become an accomplice in a crime. If he went to the police he would betray Haldin and eventually himself. The reader was invited once more to be sympathetic to his "no-win" situation. Straight further quoted Conrad: "Who knows what true loneliness is—not the conventional word, but the naked terror."

In the same passage in *After Long Silence*, Straight turned to an image of himself when he arrived in the United States in 1937, saying that he was on his own. He claimed to have no roots in the United States, no old friends, no accepted tradition to support him, and finally nothing rational to look forward to.

This portrait seems anomalous to his experience. He had roots at Old Westbury. He was young enough to create many new friendships, which he did with gusto. Straight's name opened doors in accessing everyone from the president down. He had a choice of attractive women for a wife. His wealth enabled him to take the chosen one with him. Their home was never short of friends and visitors. Rather than a poor little rich boy locked in a state of terror, his actions and utterances gave an impression of a confident young man bursting with ambition.

Straight lamented that he could not reconcile the position he was in (presumably in 1937 when he arrived in the United States to act as a

KGB agent). He claimed he faced a life of deception if he continued as a KGB man, and that this would make him ingrown, suspicious, and unloving. He wouldn't, he said, ever be able to share his mind and his heart with another human being. It was the dilemma facing all the Cambridge ring, except perhaps for Victor Rothschild, who did share his secret life with his wife Tess.

This was Straight's description of how he perceived his character and life developing, if he acted as an agent. Yet he did go on with a career as a KGB operative. Over the years of his actions as an agent, did he develop inwardly and become suspicious and unloving? Some family members and friends said he did.

Straight's book raised more questions than it answered. This caused the exercise in writing it to backfire on him. Confused journalists and reviewers now had more information—or disinformation—to mull over than the sketchy reports from the Blunt affair of two years earlier. Some accepted him as naive and misguided. They accepted his claimed ignorance of how a communist underground operated.

Many reviewers and commentators sat in judgment of him and found him guilty. William Safire's piece in *The New York Times* asked if he could fairly be called a traitor. "Not really," Safire wrote, "because no purpose or passion guided his double life. Evidently that word [traitor] is not currently applied to White House aides who do political analysis for the Kremlin, or to citizens who fail to report what they know to be espionage until they know the spy is safely gone." Safire compared him unfavorably to Admiral Canaris, the German officer who tried to assassinate Hitler.[24]

Allen Weinstein's review in *The New Republic* was also unfavorable. Straight may have been expecting his old magazine to endorse him. Instead, Weinstein touched on the major questions the memoirs raised concerning Straight's unconvincing portrayal of his control, Michael Green, and his remaining silent when Burgess was doing damage during the Korean War.

Weinstein questioned Straight's reliability "as a witness . . . on the dramatic events" of the memoir. He cited the example of Straight while at State in 1940. Straight claimed he distributed to other government agencies a "strictly confidential" report by the ambassador to England, Joseph Kennedy. The report predicted military defeat for the British. According to Straight, the report appeared on the front page of leading newspapers late in the 1940 presidential campaign. He maintained it led Roosevelt to consider Kennedy's endorsement "worthless." It forced Kennedy, Straight said, to leave his ambassadorial post "in disgrace."

In fact, Kennedy returned to Washington from London late in the campaign, Weinstein pointed out, "to endorse FDR for the third term." The ambassador delivered radio addresses publicized by the Democrats to reinforce FDR's support among isolationist conservatives.

> Only after the election did Kennedy give an interview to *Boston Globe* reporter Louis Lyons. This expressed his belief that "democracy is all but finished in England." The interview damaged his standing sufficiently to force a 1 December, 1940, resignation. The facts are described in Michael R. Beschloss's *Kennedy and Roosevelt: The Uneasy Alliance* (Norton).

This example in Straight's book at once demonstrated to Weinstein the unreliability of his recall and his distaste for the Kennedys. Straight took Weinstein's piece as a declaration of literary warfare with his old magazine. He used the next opportunity of political disagreement (over publisher Martin Peretz's defense of Israel's invasion of the Lebanon) to cancel his subscription.

The *Encounter* review by Sidney Hook said:

> To this day he seems unaware that his prolonged and stubborn silence about his involvement in the Soviet espionage apparatus, long after he had claimed to have shed any trace of faith or loyalty to the Communist cause, in effect made him complicit in the hundreds of deaths (in Korea and elsewhere) that were contrived by his erstwhile comrades.[25]

The impact of this period put strains on Straight's second marriage. Yet in 1983, Straight seemed to have maneuvered his way through the minefield he had in part created himself. Some in the circles he mixed with shunned him. But he was ostracized only to the point of a few people refusing to socialize with him, a small price to pay, and typical of attitudes to his politics he had become used to since the 1940s.

Straight seemed inured to attacks. He once felt certain he was part of a world movement that would overrun petty bourgeois rightists opposed to him and his fellow travelers. It was a toughening experience as he weathered the realities of post-WWII Cold War America and the McCarthy period. This, coupled with his social standing, wealth, and protection afforded by top lawyers, allowed him to sail through the decades insulated from witch-hunts, black bans, the political vicissitudes of various administrations, and those years of probes by Western intelligence.

Straight also had the knack of engaging any opposition with his charm and class. He had the measure of the intelligence operatives and journalists who could uncover evidence dangerous to him. As long as he was up with current revelations, such as new information coming in to the NSA, the CIA, and the FBI, he would stay in a position of power over his adversaries.

A chance to stay on top of events came in April 1983, a few weeks after Blunt's death. Straight was invited to the Conference on World Affairs at Boulder, Colorado, by the organizer Howard Higman, a sociology professor. There were discussions on a wide range of intelligence, political, economic, and cultural issues. The participants and audience included spies, students, academics, fiction writers, and journalists. Straight delivered an essay, "Death of a Butterfly," at a plenary session, which kept his views on a theoretical level and away from his personal history. Newton Miler, the CIA man who had interrogated Anatoli Golitsyn with James Angleton, was in attendance. So was Sam Papich, former FBI liaison officer between the FBI and the CIA. Both implied that Straight had not disclosed the complete story behind his relations with Blunt and Soviet intelligence. "He tried to intimidate by name-dropping," Miler recalled. "'So-and-so believes me, who are you, you little peasant, to say otherwise'—that sort of inference."

Twenty years earlier, Miler had been puzzled by Straight's "confession" to the FBI, maintaining that there was nothing damaging in the file and that he would have been given a clearance to work at the Arts Endowment under Kennedy. Straight was adamant that Golitsyn said he was a continuing Cold War spy and agent provocateur. Miler denied it.

Higman asked Straight to return the next year, 1984, now that he had achieved minor celebrity status with his book *After Long Silence*. Straight realized that he could stay abreast of intelligence attitudes and perhaps make some useful contacts. He turned up and spoke for an hour to students. He was antagonized by what he said was Miler's negative attitude. However, he was given a better reception by Papich and the CIA's Hayden Peake.

Miler attacked him for saying he did not understand what Stalinism really meant. Straight responded by saying that he was the age of the students in the audience when he was seduced by it. He maintained that he was studying all day and had no way of knowing what was happening in Russia. More to the point, at that stage, Straight *did not want to know what was really happening in Russia.* And he certainly was not deep in study at any time apart from during the weeks before exams. Instead he was intriguing with the communist movement and putting himself in a position to be recruited by the KGB.

Miler also thought that his claim about being preoccupied with study was at odds with his other statements about his working on his communist connections at Cambridge when Blunt recruited him. Despite his starry-eyed deification of Stalin, he had visited the Soviet Union in 1935 and was aware of the conditions, even if only on the surface, in one of the world's most brutal police states.[26]

Higman invited Straight back for another two years. He made some lasting friendships, one of which was with Hayden Peake, whom he continued to meet twice a year in Washington. This connection was one of many that kept Straight abreast of issues in intelligence. If anything surfaced that affected him, he would know about it before the media did.

———•—•———

I lunched with the semiretired Peake (a professor at the Center for Counterintelligence and Security Studies, along with Nigel West and others) in October 1996. A soft-spoken and studious man, he brought with him copies of two previous books of mine on intelligence: *The Exile,* a biography of KGB agent of influence Wilfred Burchett, and *The Fifth Man,* about Victor and Tess Rothschild and Yuri Modin. He asked me to sign both books. They were notated with colored strips on scores of pages. Peake told me he had 5,000 books on espionage. He had just returned from a series of meetings in Russia with KGB operatives, including Modin. We discussed the book, *Spies Without Cloaks, the KGB's Successors,* by Amy Knight, the professorial lecturer in Russian history at the Johns Hopkins School of Advanced International Studies, Washington. Her conclusion was that the KGB was renamed when the Soviet Union collapsed but that it was not reformed. Knight maintained that the "new" Russian security services had acquired more power than the old KGB. It was the only organ of government whose power had been increased rather than diminished. I agreed with Knight. Peake was emphatic that the new security forces had been trimmed.

I asked, Why had he kept such a close relationship with Straight?

"He is a very interesting man," Peake replied, which was the same unexpansive response he gave when asked how he found Straight personally. The CIA man was not forthcoming about the nature of the discussions with him. However, he agreed that Straight was keen to learn if any new, potentially damaging material about him ever emerged. And if anyone had his pulse on all things to do with the intelligence community, it was the well-informed and -read Peake.

He confirmed that Straight was particularly interested in Venona—the U.S. National Security Agency program to decipher cables sent to Moscow by Russian control agents via their diplomatic missions. This was understandable. He was featured in them.

———————

The U.S. army had been collecting Soviet encrypted cables since 1939. In 1943, the army learned that Stalin, then an ally, was attempting to negotiate a separate peace treaty with Hitler's Germany. The U.S. army decided to decrypt—decipher—the cables. The military was shocked to learn that only about half the 750,000 cables concerned diplomacy and its foreign ministry or trade. The rest was espionage. Soviet agents had penetrated the U.S. State Department, Treasury Department, Justice Department, Senate committee staffs, the military, the Office of Strategic Services (OSS), the Manhattan Project, all wartime agencies, and the White House itself.

It was a huge shock to the few Americans who were allowed to know. The Soviets had made the biggest penetration of any government in the modern era. The medium-term aim—regardless of the wartime alliance—was to weaken and overthrow the democratically elected federal government from within. It would be replaced by a communist regime under Moscow's control. Venona also found that the Soviets were similarly well ensconced in the United Kingdom, Canada, France, and Australia, with the same intentions.

The Venona decrypts—only about 5 percent of all the cables sent—were declassified in 1995. Straight, code named NIGEL, was confirmed as one of Stalin's agents. Some of the others officially unveiled were:

- Lachlan Currie, a senior White House aide to FDR, who alerted the KGB to FBI investigations of its top agents;
- Martha Dodd, the libidinous daughter of the American ambassador to Berlin, William Dodd, in the 1930s. She had an affair with the first secretary of the Russian embassy and passed on confidential diplomatic information to the KGB;
- Alger Hiss, chief of the State Department's Office of Special Political Affairs. He accompanied FDR to Yalta and helped Stalin run rings around the ailing president. Hiss also chaired the founding conference of the United Nations;
- Harry Dexter White, assistant secretary of the treasury and U.S. director of the International Monetary Fund (IMF). He was also senior adviser to the American delegation of the founding conference of the UN. He made sure Soviet agents were employed in his department;
- Harold Glasser, vice-chairman of the U.S. War Production Board and assistant director of the treasury's Office of International Finance;
- Gregory Silvermaster, a treasury economist. He controlled a sizable spy ring, which, among other things, provided the KGB with huge amounts of information from the War Production Board concerning arms, aircraft, and ships;
- Victor Perlo, chief of the aviation section of the War Production Board. He supplied Soviet intelligence with aircraft production details;
- William Weisband, the NSA linguist who disclosed the Venona project to the Soviets;
- Duncan Lee, a senior aide to the Office of Strategic Services (the CIA forerunner, 1942–1946) chief William J. Donovan, who became one of Soviet intelligence's sources inside American intelligence during and just after World War II;
- Judith Coplon, a Justice Department analyst. She alerted Soviet intelligence to the FBI's counterintelligence operations—that is, exactly what the FBI was doing to counter subversion by Nazis and communists;
- Laurence Duggan, Secretary of State Cordell Hull's personal adviser. Duggan provided Soviet intelligence with confidential diplomatic cables;
- Boris Morros, a Hollywood producer-director. He became an FBI informer;
- Samuel Dickstein, a New York Congressman (code named CROOK because he wanted fat payments for his intelligence services). He provided the Soviets with information on fascist groups and war budget materials.

Ironically, he played the key role in setting up the House Committee on Un-American Activities. It was meant to investigate fascist and Nazi groups. But when the Nazis were defeated, it turned its attention to communist subversion.[27]

Most of these agents had been publicly named, and the Venona program served to titillate by revealing the code names of the spies. Straight's exposure in 1981, and his attempt to justify himself through *After Long Silence*, served to soften the blow of the new surge of interest in the late 1990s in his secret life as an agent of a foreign power.

26

A REUNION OF OLD COMRADES

The pressure was off Straight by 1985. He no longer had to report to MI5 when he visited the United Kingdom, and the embarrassment of his public unmasking, which had been exacerbated by the publication of his autobiography, was subsiding. He even met up with Tess Rothschild at the bar of the Dukes Hotel, around the corner from the Rothschild's townhouse in St. James's Place, overlooking Green Park.

Straight described this meeting to journalists, who were later inquisitive about their relationship after its romantic depiction in his book. He told them that she was grateful for his saving her life. This was in reference to his blocking her move to join the Cambridge communist movement. He vetoed her application. Straight maintained that she was most unhappy about his action at the time. But after 1981, when the Cambridge ring was in part exposed, she allegedly understood why he had stopped her from joining the party. This was true as far as it went. What Straight did not tell journalists was that by bypassing the party, Tess was ripe for recruiting by Blunt and him for underground KGB work.

A further "coming out" was possible for Straight two years later, in 1987, when he attended his class of 1937 reunion at Cambridge. This would have been unthinkable in the 1950s, 1960s, and 1970s. But the years of interrogation by the FBI and MI5 were behind him. Peter Wright was living in far-away Tasmania, and the witch-hunts had wound down. The MI5 old guard who had fought the KGB was being replaced by a new breed with instructions to widen the net beyond communist spies to terrorists.

Despite some worrying—even terrifying—moments, Straight's "management" of the long-running disinformation campaign, with connivance from the KGB and fellow Western agents, allowed him to emerge back where it all began. There would still be surveillance of a sort on all members of the Cambridge ring and suspects. But Straight was now free of any obligations to British Intelligence. The reunion was a time of quiet celebration in cloistered halls and bug-free hotel rooms. Spies like Straight and Tess Rothschild had got away with their espionage. They were soon to be the last of the Cold War spies who had begun their careers after being recruited at the university in the late 1930s.

Old comrades lunched and dined in the days before and after the reunion. Straight found himself frequenting clubs such as the Athenaeum in London. The actual night of the reunion, which took place in the dining hall at New Court, Cambridge, was a glittering affair. Straight's old contemporaries, dressed in dinner jackets, were there sipping aperitifs. Straight mixed with them, especially Hugh Gordon, whom he had first resided with at Trinity College in 1935. Gordon was then working in scientific research for American foundations. Then there was Gerald Croasdell, whom Straight had also drawn into the Apostles in the fresh intake of communists in 1937. Croasdell gave up his work as a barrister to spend his career as secretary-general of International Actors Equity. They, like him, had not changed their fundamental beliefs, which came out in their conversations about world affairs, the fate of communism, and their hopes for a certain kind of future. (Their attitudes would not change with the collapse of the Soviet Union three years later.)

Peter Astbury was one notable absentee from the reunion. His name came up in hushed tones. He had been another of Straight's recruits to the Apostles. Peter Wright had started hounding him after Straight had given Wright Astbury's name as one who *may* have been recruited for the Soviets by Blunt and Burgess.

Astbury worked for years on CERN's European nuclear accelerator project, and this alone would have put him under suspicion. According to MI5 sources, including Wright, Astbury maintained his innocence, and his case had not been "reactivated"—that is, he was not being hounded—in the 1980s. Astbury, like Alister Watson and others, were names submitted by Straight, Philby, Blunt, and the Rothschilds when MI5 interrogated them, leading Peter Wright and his MI5 witch-hunters up blind alleys for decades. It's possible that Astbury had been recruited and trained by the KGB, but when the crunch came and he was under orders to spy, he could not go through with it. The KGB would have put enormous pressure on him. Later MI5 would do the same, which meant that Astbury, like many others, would have been driven to despair over time. (He was to die two months later in December 1987. Some suspected it was suicide.)

As Wright acknowledged in his book *Spycatcher*, and begrudgingly in interviews in Tasmania in the late 1980s, all the names given up by Straight and other key members of the ring were either known to MI5, dead or false leads, or such small fry that following them up deflected from the main aim of uncovering the major spies.

This all meant that the 1987 reunion was special. It signaled a significant victory for the KGB.[1]

Yet Straight was ever vigilant in the late 1980s as writers probed into activities of the Cambridge ring. There had been a lull since the initial rush of analysis and reports from 1981 to 1983. Straight worried about writer John Costello, author of *Mask of Treachery*. But he died in 1996 from complications brought on by AIDS when he was on a plane from London to his home in Miami. His comprehensive files disappeared, perhaps absorbed or destroyed by his strong contacts in Western intelligence.

Straight and Michael Young kept a lifelong interest in Dartington Hall. In the late 1980s it saw a large scaling down and selling of operations. The school, a nursery in the 1930s, 1940s, and 1950s for many future fellow-travelers and communists, closed. However, the newly formed Estate Council at the Hall was soon preparing a successor college to maintain the old philosophies in a more digestible, modern form. Communists had been replaced by ecologists. It manifested from 1990 as Schumacher College.

Straight may well have been pleased with developments. On May 26, 1996, the BBC's Radio 3 broadcast a study of Dartington Hall. Journalist Patrick Wright reported:

> Some of these deep ecologists seem more inclined to dive into . . . inner space. Listening to their more apocalyptic utterances, I find myself strangely reminded of the revolutionary Marxists who bided their time, in whatever fraternal retreats they could muster, waiting for the crisis to worsen so that their great millennial day would finally come.[2]

According to BBC Senior Producer Simon Coates, Wright's analogy followed from what Dartington trustee John Lane had said about the "inevitability of the success of green politics and the intellectual approach underlying it."

"He amplified his belief that current [British government and Western] economic policies would be unsustainable," Coates said, "and that such options [including 'Green' policies] would no longer be marginalized."[3] In other words, Lane, reflecting the "new" agenda at Dartington, was saying that radical, Green policies would take over from the current economic wisdom in the West.

"Neither Patrick Wright nor I thought this approach consistent with Dartington's history of improving experiment and active engagement with the outside world," Coates added, "but rather one reminiscent of a different argument advanced in the past by other critics (particularly communists) of the current 'system.'"[4]

Lane and trust secretary Ivor Stolliday characterized the old Dartington approach as "social engineering." Lane said that by avoiding the previous ways, Dartington would in future influence the mainstream.

———————

Straight's marriage to Nina deteriorated until they divorced in 1993. This was followed by another burst of creativity from 1994 to 1999 when he turned to painting. After this further unsustained effort in the arts, Straight in 1999 married his third wife, Katherine Gould, the daughter of a renowned teacher in Boston, Frank McCarthy. She worked as an art teacher, sculptor, and art critic and later became a child psychotherapist. Katherine, also on her third marriage, had two children with her first husband, Ricardo Levisetti, who was once head of the Fermi Laboratory. She works at a Chicago hospital for disturbed children, Rush Day School.

The Straights' home base was Chicago, while keeping Chilmark for the summer months. Straight was still fit enough to play tennis regularly, but in September 2003, just after his 87th birthday, he went for a medical checkup thinking he had a hernia. In surgery, the doctors discovered Straight had pancreatic cancer. It was diagnosed as terminal. Straight opted not to have chemotherapy. His doctors told him he had just three months to live. On January 4, 2004, the last member of the twentieth century's most important spy ring died.

27

SPLIT IMAGE OF A SPY

One of the most telling comments in Michael Straight's career was the acknowledgment by his publisher and survivors of the exceptional potential in his writing. Straight would have thought about the what-might-have-beens in his life. Had he not been recruited by the KGB, would he have been a successful politician, even U.S. president? If he had gone to an American university and not Dartington, London School of Economics, and Cambridge in the 1930s, would he have taken his place as a respected writer or playwright?

These ambitions welled in him in his stated aim to "gate-crash eternity." They could not be reconciled with a subterranean life as a Russian espionage agent that he chose in 1937 as his main career. His truer career instincts surfaced postwar when in late 1945 he tried and then backed away from endorsement from the Democratic Party. When the reviews for his first two fiction works were favorable, he pondered what it would be like to go on as a creative writer in the early 1960s. But he did not. He had other more lasting and demanding agendas.

After knowledge of his student communist days was leaked to the Democratic Party machine, he had barely recovered from the shock when he was working as an important backer, strategist, and speechwriter in Henry Wallace's bid for the presidency. If Wallace had succeeded, he may have offered Straight a place on the ticket or a position in the cabinet that could have prepared him as a future candidate. His final facing-up to the impossibility of ever having a political career came in the early 1950s when he appeared before congressional committees that were hunting subversives. The hostility toward his views and suspicions about his motivations would have driven home to him that he was not electable to public office in the United States. After that, his disdain for most candidates running for the Oval Office, especially Jack Kennedy, was caused in part by the frustration of not being able to reach for the position himself. He had met them all and considered he was better equipped as a thinker, speaker, idealist, and even administrator. Yet he would never have a chance to prove it.

When his insipid third novel—the only contemporary fiction—failed in the mid-1960s, he didn't need to work hard at it or follow through. But his play on Caravaggio, in contrast, was a more thorough performance. It was another clever cover for a KGB assignment. After that, he dried up. There would be no more smoke screens of that exhausting proportion. And anyway, the CIA and British intelligence would be on to him, if they were not already.

In the beginning at Cambridge, the allure of the cause was understandable, given the time and the company he kept. For all the denigration of "grubby" Guy Burgess, his contemporaries were dazzled by his intellect and dedication. Blunt with his cultured manner and knowledge of the arts represented something superior. Their combined loyalty to the cause was seductive in itself. They romanticized the higher political creed of international Marxism with its emphasis on the right economic interpretation of history. No thoughts were expressed that could lead to penetrating analysis of the Stalinist state, propped up by terror. Within the secluded cloisters of Cambridge, gullible idealists like Straight were fed sugar-coated propaganda that played to their privileged backgrounds and juvenile guilt over them. There were other characters on the scene that reinforced Straight's move, including Victor Rothschild, John Cornford, Tess Mayor, and James Klugman. He could not feel superior in breeding or intellect to these impressive peers and several more like them.

Another important factor was his wealth. He never needed to work. He was therefore open to a movement offering other than monetary remuneration. Straight's covers were as a bureaucrat, political official, administrator, writer, publisher, and journalist. His own money facilitated them. Wealth placed him from birth in an insulated establishment structure. He learned to use his connections, as exemplified by the way he manipulated Franklin and Eleanor Roosevelt, and later Jackie Kennedy, when they were in the White House. His inherited fortune also allowed him to buy the best legal advice to protect him against prosecutors in search of subversives and media probes into his life. But because he didn't sustain a career, there were voids in his life. The KGB manipulated those empty periods by flattery and cajolery. Russian controls played to his ego and made him feel important and wanted.

As Straight was being drawn into the network, he acted himself as a recruiter of others into the Apostles Club. In the 1930s, it was an important breeding ground at Cambridge for the KGB.

It all helped secure him in the Soviet web. The knowledge that Stalin himself connived in his placement in the United States propelled him into a dangerous yet thrilling clandestine world when barely out of his teens. Rebecca West in her book, *The Meaning of Treason*, wrote of the peculiar attraction of the espionage demimonde and the sentiment and adrenaline rush which kept Straight inspired from age 21.

Straight did not quite fit Rebecca West's description of the mid–twentieth-century espionage agent: "The life of the political conspirator offers the man of restricted capacity but imaginative energy excitements and satisfactions which he can never derive from overt activities."

She was writing just postwar based on analysis of Nazi spies and the few insignificant Soviet agents then exposed. She would have revised her thinking had she been aware of the "talents" like Philby, Blunt, Maclean, Cairncross, Burgess, Rothschild, Mayor, Straight, and others. They all had abilities that would have facilitated other brilliant careers. Straight's skills would have allowed him thrills and satisfactions in "overt activities" such as politics. But where he differed from the others was in character. Despite their talents, they were able to sublimate them to a degree where these other aspirations did not interfere with their main occupations as Russian agents. By contrast, Straight thought for some time he could combine a very much more public career with his covert life.

A shocking point of realization that he was captured forever, and that it might restrict his public ambitions, came early in 1941 when Walter Krivitsky was murdered in a Washington hotel room. Straight, whom Burgess directed into the web of complicity in the assassination, was reminded that no agent should ever stray or turn against the cause once recruited. Not that Straight ever deviated. Once presented with an assignment, he did his spying and agenting his way.

Straight spent four decades as a KGB agent and an agent of influence. His most enterprising work was done in the Midwest from 1956 to 1962. Perhaps his most daring espionage effort was his spying on Cheyenne Mountain and its surrounds while pretending to do research for his second novel.

Many people provided evidence of his KGB operations and witnessed his long service. They began with his lifelong friend Michael Young, who in an interview with me went out of his way to emphasize Straight's long KGB service. Others included Blunt, Anatoli Golitsyn, Cord Meyer, Whitney Straight, and some FBI and CIA members.

On top of that, Straight's actions as an agent of influence and agent provocateur for the KGB, as well as his financial donations, were further proof that he was always supportive of the Kremlin's ideology, aims, and views. He backed the U.K. *Daily Worker* with his substantial pocket-money contributions for several years. He poured funds into communist fronts and supported KGB agent Dolivet to the tune of $250,000 in his publication of a propaganda sheet. Straight's first book, *Let This Be the Last War*, published when he was 26, demonstrated his continuing accord with Soviet propaganda. Though submerged, refined, and made more digestible to a wider audience, that hard intellectual base, constructed at his educational institutions in Great Britain, never left him.

Straight was directed to work for "peace" over nuclear weapons with people the KGB had targeted for retarding U.S. weapons development, while the KGB worked overtime to gain the technology for the Russian's own bombs. He was a campaign strategist and main financier for the first part of Vice-President Henry Wallace's bid for the 1948 presidency. Wallace was the only serious U.S. presidential candidate in history who stood for appeasement with Russia and would have been the nearest thing to a Soviet puppet in the White House.

Straight's work at the AVC, particularly from 1945 to 1948, according to Cord Meyer, always had a procommunist agenda directed from the Kremlin. Meyer wondered what information Straight fed back to the Kremlin from his insinuation into the most powerful circles in the United States. He was a master at networking where it counted, even cultivating the wife of a U.S. president (Kennedy) all the time he was in power.

Straight also financially supported the Institute for Pacific Affairs that played its part in helping bring communism to China, a development that made him proud. Buoyed by this sudden surge of hope for communists everywhere in the late 1940s, Straight in early 1950 felt compelled to put the case for maintaining a Communist Party in the United States while attempting to maintain the image of an anticommunist. He put his convoluted arguments with dazzling effect to the HUAC, but nearly tripped up on his own feverish rhetoric:

We [he and his counsel] believe if it [the U.S. Communist Party] becomes a clear and present danger, then by that time communism will have triumphed in the rest of the world before it becomes a threat to this country. We think the critical front is in Berlin, Southeast Asia, India, and Rome.

The HUAC committee left the hearing confused at a higher level by Straight's testimony. Once they were over their bamboozlement, the hearing's transcript was pored over by them and other congressmen. Straight's attempt to appear open and anticommunist backfired. He and the Whitney grants to communist fronts came under closer scrutiny.

In explaining contact with Burgess in Washington in 1950, Straight wrote in *After Long Silence*:

If Guy [Burgess] was in Washington in October [1950], he would have known of our plans to advance into North Korea. He would have sent the information to Moscow. . . . The Kremlin in turn would have handed it to Peking [Beijing]. . . . Guy could have caused the deaths of many American soldiers . . .

Straight's critics saw his failure to denounce Burgess before or at the time of the Korean War as an inaction that made him complicit in causing the deaths of those American soldiers. Furthermore, if he was the Western spy who convinced Mao to attack U.S. forces, his complicity was even greater. But this possibility aside, his critics judged the failure to act over Burgess as his greatest travesty. It demonstrated that at this critical time Straight put his former allegiances to the Apostles and the KGB ahead of his country and countrymen. His loyalties were never in doubt.

His contact in 1954 with Sergei Striganov, the KGB agent at the Soviet embassy, went on for at least two years. It highlighted that he had to make such contacts, even if they were dangerous for him. As mentioned earlier, Cord Meyer wondered what tidbits of information from his connection with Straight may have been passed on to Striganov.

Straight had hope in the mid-1950s that there may still be a revival of mainstream support for far-left agendas in the United States. Yet as the Cold War temperature dropped, mainstream opinions hardened against countenancing in the United States anything remotely like even Communism in Italy or France. There wasn't a moderate liberal candidate in sight who had any real chance of becoming president and thus setting the pace for political change.

In 1956, Straight followed the Soviet line over the crushing of the uprising in Hungary and blamed the attempted revolution on the CIA. In discussing "neutralism"—the proposal that England give up its nuclear weapons program—with Nixon in 1963, Straight's case for it was parallel with Moscow's position and propaganda.

He was always on the lookout for ways to act as an agent of influence and to shore up radical liberalism, lost from American mainstream politics by the mid-1960s with the failure, Straight felt, of disarmament and other protest groups. He directed Whitney Foundation funds into Amnesty International, which kept it afloat. Like the Australian radical communist writer Wilfred Burchett, Straight often responded when the whiff of revolution was in the air. In 1968, he rushed from Martha's Vineyard to Washington when blacks rioted in response to the assassination of Martin Luther King Jr. Yet Straight was disappointed the rioters were more interested in looting than in revolution.

His final act of influence came from his own political use of federal government funds to support protest through drama and dance. Instead of the 1930s youthful, messianic drive to revolution in the streets, he was satisfied, in his late 50s, with dramatized revolution on the stage. In post-1968 language reminiscent of German-born U.S. Marxist/Freudian philosopher Herbert Marcuse, Straight supported artistic vehicles showing feelings of "bitterness, rage and alienation" toward the establishment.

The irony was in the fact that he managed this under the auspices of the Nixon administration.

From his early years, betrayal and deception became part of Straight's life, from passing information to a foreign power to relations with all the family. Straight's only deep loyalties were to the ring and the KGB. Even if he wanted to, he could not afford to be disloyal because he would be implicated in espionage operations. It was the KGB's insurance policy. After all, if agents like Straight could betray and deceive family and country, they could betray anything or anyone at any time. This mutual blackmail worked beyond 1963 when he was compelled to make misleading "confessions" to the FBI about Blunt.

Some of Straight's dearest friends and acquaintances over sixty years were spies and sometime fellow-travelers, including Young, Klugman, Cornford, Burgess, Blunt, Tess Rothschild, Victor Rothschild, Long, Astbury, Dolivet, Duran, Michael Greenberg, Michael Green, Striganov, and many others.

Leonard Garment, in his book *Crazy Rhythm*, noted that Straight had been cursed for "being able to do everything well." This flattering but fair observation would apply to Straight's espionage more than any other activity.

If Straight had written his own epitaph, he most likely would have listed the *New Republic* years, his novel writing, and his role in bringing his radical form of government support to the arts as the efforts he would like to be remembered for. They were his covers for his espionage work and activities as an agent of influence over forty years, from 1937 to 1977.

For the man who began his career under Joseph Stalin and ended it under Richard Nixon, there is a temptation to think he could not have a true sense of loyalty to anything. But he held true to his masters and his convictions even working for the Republicans as he encouraged the arts of protest and dissent. Dartington Hall, some members of his family, his love of the arts, and adherence to radical liberal principals held his commitment from time to time.

Stalin and the Communist cause held him for life.

ACKNOWLEDGMENTS

Many people in the United States, the United Kingdom, Russia, France, and Australia contributed to my research for this book, and I am grateful to them all. It seems unfair to single out anyone from the rest. However, several members of the extended Straight/Elmhirst family on both sides of the Atlantic, and friends of Michael Straight, such as the late Lord Young of Dartington, were particularly helpful in their contributions.

My agent, Andrew Lownie, was loyal and encouraging with this difficult project. His knowledge of his alma mater, Cambridge University, and its principal players from the espionage *demimonde* of the period from 1920 to 1970 was more than useful in his prodding me to carry on.

A special word of thanks is due to Moscow-based Yuri Ivanovitch Modin and the late Vladimir Barkovsky, both of whom were formerly Moscow controls running the Cambridge spies. I visited Moscow several times, and they were unfailing in their courtesy and assistance. They both indicated at the beginning of our conversations that they would provide information that wasn't already known by Western intelligence. I was happy with this assurance; it put me ahead of the investigative game before I began to probe further. The late Cord Meyer was also of great assistance. Other contemporary and retired employees of several spy agencies—notably the Australian Secret Intelligence Service, the Australian Security Intelligence Organisation, the CIA, the U.S. National Security Agency, the KGB (RIS), French intelligence, MI6, and MI5—were all essential sources in establishing solid information and facts, and certain theories.

Several journalists, particularly Verne Newton, Philip Knightley, John Slavin, and the late John Costello, were also helpful with their information and insights. Researcher Ellen MacDougall was of great assistance in raiding Washington, D.C., institutions and files.

Finally thanks also to the chief editor Robert L. Pigeon at Da Capo Press.

Roland Perry
July 2005

NOTES

CHAPTER 1: DESTINY DICTATOR

1. For further information on the background of the Whitney and Elmhirst families, see Swanberg, *Whitney Father, Whitney Heiress.*

2. For Dorothy and Willard diary entries, here and following, see Swanberg, *Whitney Father, Whitney Heiress.*

CHAPTER 2: BIRTH, DEATH, AND CIRCUMSTANCE

1. Swanberg, *Whitney Father, Whitney Heiress,* p. 401.

2. Young, *The Elmhirsts of Dartington,* pp. 57–58.

3. Ibid.

4. Swanberg, *Whitney Father, Whitney Heiress,* p. 331.

5. Young, *The Elmhirsts of Dartington,* pp. 57–58.

CHAPTER 3: MARX AND SPARKS

1. Interview with Lord Young, September 1996.

2. Ibid.

3. Ibid.

4. Ibid.

5. Straight, *After Long Silence*, pp. 46–47.

CHAPTER 4: CAMBRIDGE CONSOLIDATION

1. Interview with Yuri Ivanovitch Modin, October 1996.

2. "KGB" is used in this book to cover all the Soviet and Russian intelligence services from 1930 to 2002. They are essentially the same, no matter what the propaganda to the contrary. Amy Knight in her book *Spies Without Cloaks* makes this point and further argues that today's post–Cold War Russian intelligence activity has expanded, not contracted.

3. Costello, *Mask of Treachery*, p. 247.

4. Michael Straight admitted to giving money to the British Communist Party. His contributions have been confirmed though information gathered from the KGB Archive in Moscow and further corroborated in an interview with the KGB's former "publicity" head, Oleg Tsarev, October 1996.

5. According to Yuri Modin, Arnold Deutsch suggested the people who should be taken on the trip. Interviews with Modin, October 1996.

6. Interview with John Costello, October 1993. Whatever Straight's claims about connected histories between the two men, both believed in the cause and its roots, which they were about to explore in a more concrete way inside the Soviet Union.

7. Comment by Wilfrid Blunt to author John Costello, interview March 1982.

8. Brian Simon interview with Barry Penrose, and Simon Freeman, *Conspiracy of Silence*, p. 162.

9. Interview with Michael Young, September 1996.

10. *Conspiracy of Silence*, p. 162.

11. Mayhew, *Time to Explain*, p. 24.

12. Wilfrid Blunt in interview with MI5 officer, 1981. Story relayed to author.

13. Bukharin was executed March 14, 1938, after being a defendant in the last public Moscow purge trial. He had been falsely accused of counterrevolutionary activities and espionage.

14. Interview with Lord Young, September 1996.

15. Ibid.

16. Interview with Michael Young, September 1996, and subsequent verification in facsimile exchanges, October 1996.

17. *Spectator*, August 6, 1937.

CHAPTER 5: IN THE RING

1. Straight, *After Long Silence*, p. 65.
2. Interviews with family members, August 1996; and interview with John Costello, October 1993.
3. Ibid.
4. Straight, *After Long Silence*, p. 67.
5. Carter, *Anthony Blunt, His Lives*, p. 187.
6. The source for this observation was another Cambridge contemporary of Tess's who was less besotted by her than Michael Straight, Brian Simon, and Victor Rothschild. Interview, 1999.
7. Straight, *After Long Silence*, p. 81.
8. Interview with John Costello, October 1993.
9. Information supplied by an English espionage "expert" and confirmed by a member of the Rothschild family.
10. Perry, *The Fifth Man*, pp. 46–47 and source notes.
11. Although Blunt told Rothschild that the painting would be bequeathed to him and his family, this promise proved to be another piece of deception. Blunt left the Poussin to a British Museum.

CHAPTER 6: GRADUATE IN THE ART OF DECEPTION

1. Vassiliev and Weinstein, *The Haunted Wood,* p. 73, and the KGB Archive, Moscow, file 58380.
2. Costello, *Mask of Treachery,* pp. 267–268.
3. Straight, *After Long Silence*, pp. 101–102.
4. Interviews with Yuri Modin, October 1996. Modin and the author discussed the issue of Michael Straight's sleeper role as a potential U.S. presidential candidate.
5. Costello, *Mask of Treachery,* pp. 267–268, and Straight, *After Long Silence,* pp. 101–103.
6. Rothschild, *Meditations of a Broomstick*, p. 64.
7. John Costello, interviews with Michael Straight, and Costello, *Mask of Treachery,* p. 269.
8. Ibid.
9. Interviews with Yuri Modin, October 1996.
10. The author has seen several letters between Franklin Roosevelt and Leonard Elmhirst, and between Dorothy Elmhirst and Eleanor Roosevelt. Many examples of this close connection in the 1930s and 1940s are on file in the Dart-

ington Hall Trust Archive at High Cross House in Devon, England, and in the Franklin D. Roosevelt Library in Hyde Park, New York.

11. One such photo portrait, taken by Ramsey and Muspratt of Cambridge and dated 1936, appears in Straight's *After Long Silence*. Posed and serious, it is the type of image he wished to project during his staged breakdown in the months of February–May 1937.

12. Straight, *After Long Silence*, p. 106.

13. Costello, *Mask of Treachery*, p. 269.

14. Straight, *After Long Silence*, p. 109.

15. Ibid.

16. Costello, *Mask of Treachery*, p. 270.

17. Young, *The Elmhirsts of Dartington*, p. 236.

18. KGB Archive, Moscow, file 58390; see also Vassiliev and Weinstein, *The Haunted Wood*, chapter 4.

19. KGB Archive, Moscow, file 58390. Italics added.

20. Interviews with family members, September 1996.

21. Interview with John Costello, October, 1993.

22. Ibid.; and also interviews with former MI5 operatives, 2003.

23. Ibid.

24. This conversation was related to author John Costello by Michael Straight. See also Costello, *Mask of Treachery*, p. 273.

25. Ibid.

26. Interviews with family members, September 2002.

27. Costello, *Mask of Treachery*, p. 275.

28. FBI interviews with Michael Straight.

29. Ibid.

30. KGB Archive, Moscow, file 58390; see also Vassiliev and Weinstein, *The Haunted Wood*, chapter 4.

31. Ibid.

32. Ibid.

33. Ibid.

CHAPTER 7: GREEN SPY

1. Straight, *After Long Silence*, p. 120.

2. KGB Archive, Moscow, file 58380; see also Vassiliev and Weinstein, *The Haunted Wood*.

3. The October 1937 date is critically important. Michael Straight claimed in *After Long Silence* that contact was made in April 1938. Later he corrected himself after accessing his own FBI file, where he had stated that he made contact

sometime between October 1937 and March 1938, and probably in December 1937. This is significant. The earlier date demonstrates that Michael Green, his KGB control, was directing him from the beginning of his stay—before Straight began working at the State Department. Straight's FBI statements make it clear that the direct link to Green, when Straight became an agent, began in *October* 1937. Furthermore, all document sources and his own testimony indicate that he was in New York then, not Washington. He admits to meeting Green in New York first. It was later, when Straight was operating from within the State Department, that his control met him in Washington. See FBI file on Michael Straight, p. 5, 6–11, interviews, June 1963.

4. FBI interviews with Michael Straight, report of July 31, 1975.

5. Costello, *Mask of Treachery*, pp. 379–380.

6. From the NSA analysis of Venona traffic, Robert Louis Benson, *The 1944–1945 New York and Washington-Moscow KGB Messages* (Venona Historical Monograph No. 3), published 1995.

7. Straight, *After Long Silence*, p. 128.

8. FBI interviews with Michael Straight, 1963 and 1975.

9. Benson, *The 1944–1945 New York and Washington-Moscow KGB Messages*.

10. Straight, *After Long Silence*, p. 123.

11. Interviews with Yuri Modin, and interviews with Vladimir Barkovsky, October 1996.

12. FBI interviews with Michael Straight, June 25, 1963, and July 31, 1975 (WFO 100-3644).

13. KGB Archive, Moscow, file 58390; see also Vassiliev and Weinstein, *The Haunted Wood*.

14. Ibid.

15. Interviews with Yuri Modin, October 1996.

16. KGB Archive, Moscow, file 58390; see also Vassiliev and Weinstein, *The Haunted Wood*.

17. Ibid.

18. Michael Straight letter to the *New York Review of Books*, December 1997. The author had several interviews with Alger Hiss from 1979 to 1986. Hiss spoke about Michael Straight at the State Department, calling him "bright and ambitious."

19. Straight, *After Long Silence*, pp. 130–133.

20. FBI interviews with Michael Straight, June 25, 1963, and July 31, 1975 (WFO 100-3644).

21. KGB Archive, Moscow, file 58390; see also Vassiliev and Weinstein, *The Haunted Wood*.

22. FBI interviews with Michael Straight, June 25, 1963, and July 31, 1975 (WFO 100-3644).

23. The FBI files on Michael Straight reveal that he identified Franklin from FBI photos.

24. FBI interviews with Michael Straight, who identified Adler from photos as Solomon Aaron Lichinsky, who he then recalled had been linked to the revelations made by Elizabeth Bentley's Soviet espionage in the State Department.

25. FBI interviews with Michael Straight, June 25, 1963, and July 31, 1975 (WFO 100-3644).

26. Straight, *After Long Silence*, p. 135.

CHAPTER 8: THE INFORMANTS

1. Interview with retired French intelligence officer from the General Directorate for External Security, June 1996.

2. Louis Waldham's papers in the Manuscripts and Archives Division of the New York Public Library.

3. Newton, *The Cambridge Spies*.

4. Brooke-Shepherd, *The Storm Petrels*, pp. 152–153.

5. Andrew, *His Majesty's Service*, p. 423.

6. J. Edgar Hoover's reaction to Krivitsky is clear from his own memos and his notes in the margins of memos from FBI agents urging him to take action. See declassified FBI files 1940–1944, especially 100-59589; 100-26044; 100-65-6807; 1001146-17; 100-11146-16; 100-11146-14; 100-11146-13; and 100-11146-5.

7. Straight, *After Long Silence*, especially the chapter "My Lies," pp. 134ff.

8. The author's research led him to believe that Alister Watson may have been recruited but that he did not pass on any intelligence. "He didn't have the stomach for it," was the assessment by one MI5 officer.

9. Straight, *After Long Silence*, pp. 144–145.

10. Ibid.

11. Ibid.

12. Ibid.

13. From NSA analysis of Venona traffic by Robert Louis Benson, *The 1944–1945 New York and Washington-Moscow KGB Messages* (1995). Also CIA sources on Michael Green.

14. Levine, *Eyewitness*.

15. Information supplied by a retired French intelligence operative.

16. Levine, *Eyewitness*, p. 196; see also testimony before the Senate Internal Security Subcommittee Hearings, June 6 and 7, 1956.

17. U.S. National Archives, file 761, 62/09-2239.

18. *New York Times*, October 12, 1939.

19. The Louis Waldham files at the New York Public Library, Folder 2, November 25, 1939, from Immigration Director Houghteling of the Labor Department.

20. Costello, *Mask of Treachery,* p. 348.

21. Philby, *My Silent War,* p. 102.

22. The source for this is Peter Wright, *Spycatcher.* Chapman Pincher also covers this in *Too Secret Too Long.* His source, although unnamed at the time of the book's publication, was Peter Wright.

23. The source for Liddell's reaction is a former MI5 officer, who was informed by Arthur Martin. Martin reviewed the Krivitsky material when Philby was interrogated, and he sat in on the questioning of Philby.

24. Sources for the report by Jane Sissmore, *née* Archer, include Kim Philby, *My Silent War,* and Brooke-Shepherd, *The Storm Petrels.*

25. The source is the former MI5 officer cited above who was informed by Arthur Martin.

26. Ibid.

27. Borovik, *The Philby Files,* pp. 243–244.

28. Ibid., pp. 83, 122, 243–244, 275, 298.

CHAPTER 9: A DEFENSIVE MEASURE

1. Burgess's visa dates taken from the U.S. National Archive, NA\710.4111, Burgess, Guy 7-840.

2. Costello, *Mask of Treachery,* p. 271.

3. FBI interviews with Michael Straight, June 24, 1963.

4. Young, *The Elmhirsts of Dartington,* p. 343.

5. Ibid., p. 344.

6. Both the U.S. National Archives and the Roosevelt Library at Hyde Park, New York, have a record of a letter regarding Michael Straight being sent by Franklin Roosevelt to the State Department (NA\111.24/131 1/2, July 29, FDR to State).

7. Newton, *The Cambridge Spies,* pp. 21–22.

8. Interview with former MI5 officer, December 2002.

9. Newton, *The Cambridge Spies,* pp. 21–22.

10. Interview with Wright, 1988. Rothschild told Wright that he had been chosen by Liddell to go to Washington to debrief Krivitsky again.

11. Interviews with Modin in 1993 and 1996; interviews with Vladimir Barkovsky, October 1996.

12. Flora Lewis, "Who Killed Krivitsky," *Washington Post,* February 13, 1966.

13. Dallin, *Soviet Intelligence,* pp. 409–410.

14. FBI report to J. Edgar Hoover, February 14, 1941, file no. 100-11146-22.

15. Chambers, *Witness*, pp. 485–486.

16. Ibid.

17. Dallin, *Soviet Intelligence*. His desire to purchase a gun seems odd, considering that, according to Chambers, he already carried one. One explanation could be that he was forced to buy a weapon by his killers, who were setting up the "suicide."

18. Newton, *The Cambridge Spies*, p. 24; *Washington Star*, February 11, 1941.

19. Ibid.

20. Dallin, *Soviet Intelligence*.

21. Ibid.

22. This is Waldman's explanation of the lock.

23. FBI reports from file no. 100-11146; serials 13, 14, 16, 17, 19, 22, 28, 28, 29, 34, 43, 53.

24. Brooke-Shepherd, *The Storm Petrels*, pp. 176–177, and Newton, *The Cambridge Spies*, pp. 28ff. Italics added.

25. Ibid.

26. Via Internet—1: Cold War Spies and Espionage; 2: Venona: Soviet Espionage and the American response, and links; 3: Nova On-line, and links.

27. Borovik, *The Philby Files*, p. 122.

28. Newton, *The Cambridge Spies*, p. 30; see also Report no. 15 in the Senate Judiciary Files, U.S. National Archives, dated April 8, 1954, re: The Murder of General Walter Krivitsky in Washington, D.C.

29. Ibid.

30. Straight, *After Long Silence*, p. 140.

31. Ibid., p.143.

32. Interview with Modin, October 1996.

CHAPTER 10: NEW REPUBLIC, OLD WAYS

1. Straight, *After Long Silence*, p. 157.

2. Ibid.

3. Ibid.

4. Young, *The Elmhirsts of Dartington*, p. 236.

5. Straight, *After Long Silence*, p. 159.

6. Ibid.

7. *New Republic*, February 17, 1941.

8. Ibid.

9. Straight, *After Long Silence*, pp. 160–161.

10. Ibid., p. 166.

11. *New Republic*, April 28, 1941.

12. See FBI file no. 100-3476; also Hoover to his special agent in charge of investigating the *New Republic*, September 15, 1942, file no. 100-619296-26; also relevant are the FBI interviews with Michael Straight, June 24, 1963.

13. Ibid.

14. *New Republic*, May 26, 1941.

15. From Michael Straight's FBI file. The article was by Benjamin Stolberg.

16. Straight, *After Long Silence*, p. 268.

17. Leaming, *Orson Welles*, p. 276.

18. Ibid.

19. Straight, *Let This Be the Last War*, p. 162; see especially the chapter titled "The Crisis of the War of Liberation."

20. FBI file no. 100-619296; FBI interview with Michael Straight, June 24, 1963.

21. References to code names from Venona material at the NSA.

22. In 1945 Gayn would be arrested in the so-called *Amerasia* case. The Office of Naval Intelligence found hundreds of secret government documents strewn around the offices of *Amerasia*, a small pro-Maoist journal published by Philip Jaffe and partially funded by the Institute of Pacific Affairs. Gayn was never prosecuted. This led to speculation in intelligence circles that he was turned into a double agent. It would certainly explain Gayn's position. No other journalist, not even Australia's communist-supporting agent of influence Wilfred Burchett, had access to the highest echelons of power in Moscow, Beijing, and Washington during the 1950s. In 1963 the ubiquitous Gayn was said to have foreknowledge of the plot to assassinate President Kennedy. According to Richard Case Nagell, a U.S. military intelligence officer, a Soviet agent ordered him to eliminate Lee Harvey Oswald before he and two Cuban accomplices could carry out a plan to assassinate Kennedy. That Soviet agent, Nagell claimed, was either Gayn or Tracy Barnes, a CIA spy, who was Michael Straight's cousin. These claims are explained in the book by U.S. journalist Dick Russell, *The Man Who Knew Too Much*.

23. Costello, *Mask of Treachery*, p. 477.

24. Ibid.

25. The FBI file on Michael Straight, 100-3644.

26. Harvey et al., *The Secret World of American Communism*, pp. 249–259. In the end, Browder found Josephine Treslow Adams, who started the link to the Roosevelts when she was commissioned to paint Eleanor in 1941. Adams claimed to Browder that she had personally intervened with the president to release Browder from prison, to which he had been sentenced in 1941 for using a false passport on his trips to the Soviet Union. Roosevelt had Browder released in May 1942—three years short of his full term. In mid-1943, messages flowed

from Adams to Browder, which she claimed came originally from her verbal communication with Roosevelt. They were sent to the Moscow Center and Stalin. The communications "coup" of supposedly having the president's ear gained Browder some kudos. Later the "verbal" messages were found to have been concocted by the skillful Adams, who was diagnosed as mentally ill.

27. See Venona at NSA for May 1943.

28. Blum, *The Price of Vision*, pp. 347–358.

29. Edgar Snow, "Must the East Go Red?" *Saturday Evening Post*, May 12, 1945.

30. See Michael Straight's FBI file.

31. See Klehr and Radosh, "Anatomy of a Fix," *New Republic*, April 21, 1986; see also their updated book of 1996, *The Amerasia Spy Case*.

32. Interview with William Elmhirst, August 1997.

33. Sudoplatov, Sudoplatov, and Schecter, *Special Tasks;* see especially the chapter titled "Atomic Spies."

34. Ibid., p. 189.

35. Ibid.

36. Ibid.

CHAPTER 11: BLUNT'S ROYAL MISSION

1. Historian Hugh Trevor Roper recalled Blunt telling him in some detail about the assignment. See *Times Literary Supplement*, October 1945. There is also an account of Moorhead's visit with Blunt in the Royal Archive, Royal Collections Department, Windsor, Berkshire.

2. Report on Nash in *New York Times*, June 10, 1946. She was arrested for gem theft at the Kronberg Castle after Blunt's visit. She was inspired—with her friend Colonel Jack Durant, an army flyer—to act criminally when she realized the value of items and treasures at the castle.

3. *Times Literary Supplement*, October 1945.

4. Costello, *Mask of Treachery*, pp. 446–447.

5. Interview with Peter Wright, June 1988; and another MI5 source, June 1992; also interview with Modin, July 1993.

6. Ibid.

7. Blunt to British historian Hugh Trevor-Roper, *Times Literary Supplement*, October 1945.

8. Information from British intelligence source, February 1997.

9. *Times Literary Supplement*, October 1945. This supports information from Modin, Wright, and two other British intelligence sources that Blunt read the letters and transcripts.

10. Information from John Costello, November 1994, and a British intelligence source, June 1996; see also Costello, *Mask of Treachery,* p. 446.

11. Sources include Modin and Wright. This is the assessment of several journalists, historians, and intelligence operatives in the United Kingdom and Russia.

12. Information from Modin, July 1993.

13. Interviews with Modin, July 1993 and October 1996. A further Russian source added some detail in an interview, August 1993.

14. Interviews with Modin, July 1993 and October 1996.

CHAPTER 12: POLITICAL PATH TO NOWHERE

1. Interview with Cord Meyer, October 1996.

2. Smith, *A Peril and a Hope,* p. 283; interview with Cord Meyer, October 1996.

3. Straight, *After Long Silence,* p. 200.

4. Ibid.

5. Straight, *After Long Silence,* p. 201.

6. FBI interview with Michael Straight, July 18, 1975; file no. 100-61927-10.

7. See Maria Elena de la Iglesia, ed., *Dartington Hall School.*

8. Interview with William Elmhirst, February 1997.

9. Sudoplatov, Sudoplatov, Schecter, *Special Tasks;* see especially the chapter titled "Atomic Spies."

10. Ibid.

11. See *New Republic* editorials throughout 1946.

12. Schmidt, *Henry A. Wallace, Quixotic Campaign 1948,* p. 19.

CHAPTER 13: TRY OF THE TROJAN

1. Straight, *After Long Silence,* p. 204.

2. Ibid., pp. 221–222.

3. *New Republic,* December 16, 1946.

4. See all editions of *New Republic,* December 1946.

5. Ibid.

6. Straight, *After Long Silence,* p. 205.

7. Ibid.

8. *New Republic,* March 1947.

9. Straight, *After Long Silence,* pp. 206–207.

10. Dartington Hall visitor's book signatures show Michael Straight's arrival on April 7, 1947.

11. *London Times,* April 7 and 8, 1947.

12. White and Maze, *Henry Wallace,* pp. 246–247.

13. *Chicago Sun,* April 9, 1947.

14. Conservative Party Archives, London. Winston Churchill's speeches, 1947.

15. *Chicago Sun,* April 12, 1947.

16. Schmidt, *Henry A. Wallace.*

17. Straight, *After Long Silence,* p. 209.

18. Ibid.

19. FBI interviews with Michael Straight, p. 14.

20. Ibid.

21. Straight, *After Long Silence,* p. 209.

22. White and Maze, *Henry A. Wallace,* p. 250.

23. Ibid., p. 251

24. Straight, *After Long Silence,* p. 210.

25. Ibid., p. 214.

26. Meyer, *Facing Reality,* pp. 51–55.

27. Ibid.

28. Ibid., p. 55.

29. Ibid.

30. Interview with Cord Meyer, October 1996. According to Meyer, Miler, and other CIA operatives, Straight believed that KGB defector Anatoli Golitsyn told the FBI (and the CIA) that he (Straight) was active as a KGB agent and that one of his missions was at the AVC.

31. White and Maze, *Henry A. Wallace,* p. 254.

32. Schmidt, *Henry A. Wallace,* p. 73.

CHAPTER 14: SIDESHOW SUFFERINGS

1. *New Republic,* January 21, 1948.

2. Schmidt, *Henry A. Wallace.*

3. *New Republic,* April 5, 1948.

4. Straight, *After Long Silence,* p. 231.

5. Ibid.

6. Ibid., p. 229.

7. Ibid., p. 227.

8. "There Are Great Fears," *New Republic,* March 22, 1948.

9. "Trial by Congress," *New Republic,* August 16, 1948.

10. Information from Verne Newton, who spoke with Bin and Michael Straight and was in correspondence with Dr. Welderhall.

11. FBI interviews with Michael Straight, report of July 31, 1975.

12. Newton, *The Cambridge Spies,* pp. 220–221.

13. Meyer, *Facing Realities,* p. 55, and interview with Cord Meyer, October 1996.

14. Interview with Cord Meyer, October 1996.

15. Ibid.

16. Ibid.

17. *New Republic,* May 2, 1949.

CHAPTER 15: BARKOVSKY AND THE BOMB SPIES

1. Interview with Barkovsky, October 1996.

2. Perry, *The Fifth Man,* pp. 116–117. The Barkovsky information provided the missing link in this revealing espionage scenario involving Oliphant (innocently), Rothschild, Blunt, and Barkovsky.

3. NKVD/KGB file, no. 13676, vol. 1. This reveals Maclean's message.

4. Interview with Barkovsky, October 1996.

5. *Physics Today,* November 1996, p. 51.

6. Ibid.

7. Ibid.

8. Sudoplatov, Sudoplatov, Schecter, *Special Tasks,* p. 207.

9. Interview with Barkovsky, October 1996.

10. Oppenheimer, "A Letter from the Chief of Los Alamos," *New Republic,* June 6, 1949; and Szilard, "America, Russia, and the Bomb," *New Republic,* October 31, 1949.

11. Dartington Hall visitor's book.

12. Michael Straight makes several references to his meeting with Burgess and Blunt in 1949 in *After Long Silence.*

13. Interview with a former senior operative in British intelligence, September 1996.

14. Rhodes, *The Making of the Atomic Bomb,* p. 767.

CHAPTER 16: THE ANTI-COMMUNIST

1. From the HUAC hearing on legislation to outlaw un-American and subversive activities; see the complete transcript, including the written legal brief, pp. 2211–2225, March 21–23 and March 28, 1950.

2. Ibid.

3. Ibid.

4. Ibid.

5. Ibid.
6. Ibid.
7. Ibid.
8. Ibid.
9. Ibid. Italics added.
10. Ibid.
11. Ibid.; and interview with William Elmhirst, March 1998.
12. HUAC hearing on legislation to outlaw un-American and subversive activities.
13. *New Republic*, May 1, 1950.
14. *New Republic*, April 3 and 10, 1950.
15. Interview with Barkovsky, October 1996.
16. Copy of poem given to author by Diana Barnato-Walker during interviews, August 1999.
17. Interview with William Elmhirst, March 1998.

CHAPTER 17: THE KOREAN WAR SPIES

1. Interviews with Modin, October 1993; see also Modin's book, *My Five Cambridge Friends*, pp. 181–184.
2. Ibid.
3. Interviews with Modin and other KGB sources, June 1993 and October 1996; see also the article by Roy Medvedev in the *Washington Post*, June 19, 1983.
4. Interviews with Modin, October 1993.
5. Straight, *After Long Silence*, pp. 249–251.
6. Sidney Hook, "The Incredible Story of Michael Straight," *Encounter*, February 1983.
7. William Safire, "The Michael Straight," *New York Times*, January 10, 1983.
8. Review by Raymond A. Scroth, *America*, May 1983.
9. Costello, *Mask of Treachery*, pp. 470–471.

CHAPTER 18: FAMILY FEUD

1. From interviews with family members, September 1997.
2. Ibid.
3. Ibid.
4. Private diary of Whitney; also interviews with family members, September 1997.
5. Ibid.

6. Ibid.
7. Ibid.
8. Interview with William Elmhirst, March 1997.

CHAPTER 19: A TAXING TIME

1. Straight, *After Long Silence*, p. 297.
2. Ibid., p. 262.
3. Ibid., p. 276.
4. Ibid., p. 277.
5. Ibid., p. 278.
6. Transcripts of hearings before the House Select Committee to investigate tax-exempt foundations and comparable organizations, November and December 1952.
7. Ibid.
8. Ibid.
9. Ibid.
10. Straight, *After Long Silence*, pp. 283–284.
11. Ibid., p. 265.
12. Straight, *Trial by Television*, p. 71.
13. Ibid., p. 88.

CHAPTER 20: MORE MOSCOW CONNECTIONS

1. Straight, *After Long Silence*, p. 290.
2. Ibid.
3. Ibid.
4. Costello, *Mask of Treachery*, p. 476.
5. U.S. Senate, report of the Committee on the Judiciary, *Report on the IPR:* Report no. 2050, 83d Congress, 2nd Section, p. 97.
6. Letters from Edward C. Carter to W. L. Holland, May 6, 1940, reproduced in IPR Hearings, p. 3924; and IPR Hearings, p. 3794.
7. Hearing before the International Organizations Employees Loyalty Board, pp. 6, 19–20.
8. Interview with former CIA agent Newton Miler, July 1977; also FBI file, 1963-75.
9. Straight, *Nancy Hanks*, p. 46.
10. Ibid.
11. Ibid.

CHAPTER 21: CAREER CHANGE

1. Interview with Cord Meyer, October 1996.
2. Meyer, *Facing Realities*, pp. 125–126.
3. Interview with Cord Meyer, October 1996.
4. *New Republic*, February 4, 1957.
5. Interview with Nina Gore Auchincloss Straight, July 1996.
6. Vidal, *Palimpsest*, p. 11.
7. Interview with William Elmhirst, August 1997.
8. Transcript of Michael Straight interview with John Milton, p. 122.
9. Ibid.
10. Ibid.
11. Ibid., p. 124.
12. Dench, Flower, and Gavron, eds., *Young at Eighty*, p. 157.
13. Young, *The Rise of the Meritocracy*, pp. 150–151. Italics added.
14. Interviews with Nina Straight; also interviews with William Elmhirst, August 1997.

CHAPTER 22: THREATS FROM THE PAST

1. Interview with family members, July 1996.
2. Interview with Nina Straight, September 1996.
3. See Straight, *Happy and Hopeless*, especially the first three chapters. Jackie trusted Straight and asked him to sit next to her daughter Caroline's prospective mother-in-law, Mae Schlossberg, at the wedding dinner at Hyannis in July 1968. Straight appreciated the honor. In 1981 Jackie bought a property at Martha's Vineyard just two miles from Straight's home. This maintained their long-term friendship, as did Straight's marriage to Jackie's stepsister Nina.
4. Straight, *After Long Silence*, p. 315.

CHAPTER 23: FIRST IN . . .

1. Wright, *Spycatcher*, pp. 174–180.
2. Interview with William Elmhirst, September 2000.
3. Straight, *After Long Silence*, p. 316.
4. Ibid., pp. 317–318.
5. Ibid., p. 318.
6. Ibid.
7. Ibid.

8. Interview with Verne Newton, who was told of JFK's comments by Walton, July 1996.

9. Straight, *After Long Silence*, p. 320.

10. Ibid.

11. Ibid., p. 322.

12. Ibid.

13. Interview with William Elmhirst, September 2000.

14. Ibid.

15. Interview with Lord Longford, March 1983.

16. Interview with William Elmhirst, September 2000.

17. The source for the possible Rose-Niarchos link is a New York lawyer.

18. Straight, *After Long Silence*, p. 323.

19. Interview with William Elmhirst, September 2000. Mary had left Cord in 1957 and moved into a town house on Georgetown's N Street, the favored district of Washington's political leaders, journalists and lobbyists. She was a painter and regarded as a liberated woman for the time. Now single, she took many lovers, including the abstract painter, Kenneth Noland. She confided to one-time vice-president of the *Washington Post,* James Truitt, that she had an affair with Kennedy. Mary kept a diary and it detailed her time with him. According to one of her closest companions, she had a strong theory about the reasons for Kennedy's assassination, which distressed her.

20. Interview with William Elmhirst, September 2000.

21. Straight, *After Long Silence*, p. 323.

CHAPTER 24: BLUNT REVELATIONS

1. Straight, *After Long Silence*, p. 324.

2. Ibid., pp. 324–325.

3. Ibid., p. 325.

4. Penrose and Freeman, *Conspiracy of Silence,* chapter 18.

5. Wright, *Spycatcher*, p. 222.

6. Peter Wright spoke of his close confidences with Rothschild to the author and to Wright's manager, Peter Murray. Wright wrote of the shared secrets in *Spycatcher.*

7. Wright described himself this way in handling Blunt's interrogation. See Wright, *Spycatcher*, p. 222.

8. Wright, *Spycatcher*, p. 223.

9. Straight, *After Long Silence*, pp. 325–328.

10. Ibid.

11. Ibid.

12. Ibid.

13. Interviews with several MI5 and CIA operatives, 1996 and 1997.

14. Sources include former royal household employees, Sir Allen Lascelles, the former private secretary to King George VI, Peter Wright, and Yuri Modin.

15. Reports from the *Washington Post,* including the July 4, 1973, edition, and the *Evening Star* edition of February 18, 1965.

16. Straight, *Caravaggio,* p. xxiii.

17. Paper written by John Slavin for the author.

18. For more on Alister Watson, see Perry, *The Fifth Man.*

19. Information supplied by family members.

20. Interview with William Elmhirst, August 1996. Straight visited Dartington Hall in late October 1968 and told the family about political events in the United States in 1968.

21. Ibid.

CHAPTER 25: ARTS AT LAST

1. Straight, *Twigs for an Eagle's Nest,* especially the chapter titled "Present at the Creation."

2. Ibid.

3. Straight, *Nancy Hanks,* p. 112.

4. Perry, *The Fifth Man,* pp. 485–487.

5. Straight, *Twigs for an Eagle's Nest,* p. 114.

6. Interview with William Elmhirst, August 1996.

7. Straight, *Twigs for an Eagle's Nest,* especially the chapter titled "Present at the Creation."

8. Ibid., p. 8.

9. Ibid., p. 86.

10. Ibid., pp. 37–42.

11. Interview with Peter Wright, December 1989; interview with an MI5 officer, August 1997; interview with John Costello, November 1993.

12. Interview with William Elmhirst, August 1996.

13. For example, Leonard Elmhirst's essay "About My Father," December 26, 1960.

14. Interview with William Elmhirst, August 1996.

15. Ibid.

16. Straight, *Nancy Hanks,* chapter titled "Working Under Jimmy Carter."

17. Ibid.

18. Ibid.

19. *Daily Mail,* March 24, 1981.

20. Straight, *After Long Silence,* p. 330.

21. *People Magazine,* September 1981.

22. Interview with Lord Young, September 1996.

23. BBC TV interview, Michael Straight with Ludovic Kennedy.

24. William Safire, "The Michael Straight Story," *New York Times,* January 10, 1983.

25. Sidney Hook, "The Incredible Story of Michael Straight," *Encounter,* February 1983.

26. Interview with Newton Miler, October 1996.

27. Via Internet—1: Cold War Spies and Espionage; 2: Venona: Soviet Espionage and the American response, and links; 3: Nova On-line, and links.

CHAPTER 26: A REUNION OF OLD COMRADES

1. Interview with Tess Rothschild, November 1993; interviews with Peter Wright, November 1989; interviews with members of the class of 1937, August and September 1996.

2. BBC Radio 3, "Sunday feature," May 26, 1996.

3. Information in correspondence with family members, October 1996, from Simon Coates.

4. Ibid.

BIBLIOGRAPHY

Andrew, Christopher. *Her Majesty's Secret Service: The Making of the British Intelligence Community.* New York: Viking, 1995.

Andrew, Christopher, and Oleg Gordievsky. *KGB: The Inside Story.* London: Hodder & Stoughton, 1990.

Andrew, Christopher, and Vasili Mitrokhin. *The Mitrokhin Archive.* London: Penguin Books, 2000.

Blum, John Morton. *The Price of Vision: The Diary of Henry A. Wallace, 1942–1946.* Boston: Houghton Mifflin, 1973.

Blunt, Anthony. *Artistic Theory in Italy, 1450–1600.* London: Oxford University Press, 1973.

Bonham-Carter, Victor. *Dartington Hall.* Somerset: Exmoor Press, 1970.

Boyer, Paul. *Bomb's Early Light.* Chapel Hill: University of North Carolina Press, 1985.

Borovik, Genrikh. *The Philby Files.* New York: Little, Brown & Co., 1994.

Brook-Shepherd, Gordon. *The Storm Petrels.* New York: Harcourt, Brace, Jovanovich, 1977.

Cairncross, John. *The Enigma Spy.* London: Century, 1997.

Carter, Miranda. *Anthony Blunt, His Lives.* London: Macmillan, 2001.

Caute, David. *The Great Fear.* London: Secker & Warburg, 1978.

Chambers, Whittaker. *Witness.* New York: Random House, 1952.

Costello, John. *Mask of Treachery.* New York: William Morrow and Company, 1988.

379

Costello, John, and Oleg Tsarev. *Deadly Illusions.* London: Century, 1993.

Cradock, ed. *Recollections of the Cambridge Union, 1815–1939.* Cambridge: Bowes & Bowes Limited, 1952.

Croly, Herbert. *Willard Straight.* New York: Macmillan, 1924.

Culver John C., and John Hyde. *American Dreamer: A Life of Henry Wallace.* New York: W. W. Norton, 2001.

Dallin, David J. *Soviet Foreign Policy After Stalin.* Philadelphia: J. B. Lippincott, 1960.

Dallek, Robert. *Franklin D. Roosevelt and American Foreign Policy, 1932–1945.* New York: Oxford University Press, 1979.

Dan, Jerry. *Ultimate Deception.* Somerset: Rare Books and Berry, 2003.

Deacon, Richard. *The Greatest Treason.* London: Century, 1989.

Dench, Geoff, Tony Flower, and Kate Gavron, eds. *Young at Eighty.* Manchester: Carcenet Press, 1995.

Denner, Frank J. *The Un-Americans.* New York: Ballantine Books, 1961.

de la Iglesia, Maria Elena. *Dartington Hall School: Staff Memories of the Early Years.* Extere, Devon: Folly Island Press, 1996.

Dutta, Krishna, and Andrew Robinson. *Tagore.* London: Bloomsbury Publishing, 1993.

Emery, Anthony. *Dartington Hall.* Oxford: Clarendon Press, 1970.

Fariello, Griffin. *Red Scare: Memories of the American Inquisition.* New York: Avon Books, 1995.

Flynn, John T. *The Roosevelt Myth.* New York: The Devin-Adair Co., 1948.

Garment, Leonard. *Crazy Rhythm.* New York: Random House, 1997.

Halberstam, David. *The Powers That Be.* New York: Alfred A. Knopf, 1979.

Herken, Gregg. *The Winning Weapon.* Princeton, NJ: Princeton University Press, 1988.

Hewlett, Richard G., and Oscar E. Anderson Jr. *The New World.* Berkeley: University of California Press, 1990.

_____. *Atomic Shield.* Berkeley: University of California Press, 1990.

Hoare, Geoffrey. *The Missing Macleans.* London: Cassell & Co., 1955.

Holloway, David. *Stalin and the Bomb.* New Haven, CT: Yale University Press, 1994.

Hyde, Montgomery H. *The Atomic Bomb Spies.* London: Hamish Hamilton, 1980.

Jones, Vincent C. *Manhattan: The Army and the Atomic Bomb.* Carlisle, PA: Center for Military History, U.S. Army, 1985.

Kalugin, Oleg. *Spymaster.* London: Smith Gryphon Publishers, 1994.

Kennett, Lee. *A History of Strategic Bombing.* New York, Charles Scribner's & Sons, 1982.

Kimball Smith, Alice. *A Peril and a Hope.* Boston: Massachusetts Institute of Technology Press, 1965.

Klehr, Harvey, John Earl Haynes, and Friorikh Igorevich Firsov. *The Secret World of American Communism*. New Haven, CT: Yale University Press, 1995.

Klehr, Harvey, and Ronald Radosh. *The Amerasia Spy Case*. Chapel Hill: University of North Carolina Press, 1996.

Knight, Amy. *Spies Without Cloaks: The KGB's Successors*. Princeton, NJ: Princeton University Press, 1996.

Kurzman, Dan. *Day of the Bomb: Countdown to Hiroshima*. New York: McGraw-Hill, 1986.

Leaming, Barbara. *Orson Welles*. London: Penguin, 1987.

Levine, Isaac Don. *Eyewitness*. New York: Hawthorn Books, 1973.

Lewis, John Wilson, and Xue Litai. *China Builds the Bomb*. Stanford: Stanford University Press, 1988.

May, Gary. *Un-American Activities*. New York: Oxford University Press, 1994.

Meyer, Cord. *Facing Reality*. New York: Harper & Row, 1980.

Meyhew, Christopher. *Time to Explain*. London: Hutchinson, 1987.

Modin, Yuri Ivanovitch. *My Five Cambridge Friends*. London: Headline, 1994.

_____. *Mes Camarades de Cambridge*. Paris: Robert Laffont, 1994.

Moorehead, Alan. *The Traitors*. London: Hamish Hamilton, 1952.

Newton, Verne W. *The Cambridge Spies*. Lanham, MD: Madison Books, 1991.

Penrose, Barrie, and Simon Freeman. *Conspiracy of Silence*. New York: Vintage Books, 1988.

Philby, Kim. *My Silent War*. New York: Random House, 2002.

Philby, Rufina, with Haden Peake and Mikhail Lyubimov. *The Private Life of Kim Philby*. New York: International, 2000.

Pincher, Chapman. *Too Secret Too Long*. London: Sidgwick & Jackson, 1984.

Perry, Roland. *The Fifth Man*. London: Sidgwick & Jackson, 1994.

Pincher, Chapman. *The Spycatcher Affair*. New York: St. Martin's Press, 1987.

_____. *Traitors*. London: Sidgwick & Jackson, 1987.

Rhodes, Richard. *The Making of the Atomic Bomb*. New York: Simon & Schuster, 1986.

_____. *Dark Sun: The Making of the Hydrogen Bomb*. New York: Simon & Schuster, 1995.

Riley, Morris. *Philby: The Hidden Years*. London: Janus Publishing Co., 1998.

Rose, Kenneth. *Elusive Rothschild*. London: Weidenfeld & Nicolson, 2003.

Rositzke, Harry. *The KGB: The Eyes of Russia*. London: Sidgwick & Jackson, 1982.

Rothschild, Lord. *Meditations of a Broomstick*. London: Collins, 1977.

Russell, Dick. *The Man Who Knew Too Much*. New York: Carroll & Graf, 1992.

Schmidt, Karl M. *Henry A. Wallace: Quixotic Crusade, 1948*. Syracuse, NY: Syracuse University Press, 1960.

Sheldon, Michael. *Graham Greene: The Enemy Within.* New York: Random House, 1994.

Sinclair, Andrew. *The Red and the Blue.* London: Weidenfeld and Nicolson, 1986.

Stone, I.F. *The Haunted Fifties.* New York: Vintage Books, 1969.

Straight, Michael. *Let This Be the Last War.* New York: Harcourt, Brace, Jovanovich, 1943.

_____. *Trial by Television.* Boston: Beacon Press, 1952.

_____. *Carrington.* New York: Alfred A. Knopf, 1960.

_____. *A Very Small Remnant.* New York: Alfred A. Knopf, 1962.

_____. *Happy and Hopeless.* Berkeley, CA: Devon Press, 1979.

_____. *Twigs for an Eagle's Nest.* Berkeley, CA: Devon Press, 1979.

_____. *Caravaggio: A play of two acts.* Berkeley, CA: Devon Press, 1979.

_____. *After Long Silence.* New York: W. W. Norton, 1983.

_____. *Nancy Hanks: An Intimate Portrait.* Durham, NC: Duke University Press, 1988.

Szasz, Ferenc Morton. *British Scientists and the Manhattan Project.* London: Macmillan, 1992.

Sudoplatov, Pavel, and Anatoli Sudoplatov, with Jerrold L. Schecter and Leona P. Schecter. *Special Tasks.* New York: Little, Brown & Co., 1994.

Swanberg, W. A. *Whitney Father, Whitney Heiress.* New York: Charles Scribner's & Sons, 1980.

Tagore, Rabindranath, and L. K. Elmhirst. *Rabindranath Tagore: Pioneer in Education.* London: John Murray, 1961.

Thomson, David. *Rosebud.* New York: Little, Brown & Co., 1996.

Vassiliev, Alexander, and Allen Weinstein. *The Haunted Wood.* New York: Random House, 1990.

Vidal, Gore. *Palimpsest: A Memoir.* New York: Random House, 1995.

Volkogonov, Dmitri. *Stalin: Triumph and Tragedy.* New York: Grove Weidenfeld, 1991.

Weinstein, Allen. *Perjury: The Hiss-Chambers Case.* New York: Random House, 1997.

West, Nigel, and Oleg Tsarev. *The Crown Jewels.* London: Harper Collins, 1998.

_____. *The Illegals.* London: Hodder & Stoughton, 1993.

West, Rebecca. *The Meaning of Treason.* London: Penguin, 1949.

White, Graham, and John Maze. *Henry A. Wallace: His Search for a New World Order.* New York: Free Press, 1973.

Wolton, Thierry. *Le KGB en France.* Paris: Bernard Grasset, 1986.

Wright, Peter. *Spycatcher.* Sydney: William Heinemann Co., 1988.

Young, Michael. *The Rise of the Meritocracy.* Harmondsworth: Penguin, 1961.

_____. *The Elmhirsts of Dartington.* London: Routledge & Kegan Paul, 1982.

INDEX